Breaking New Ground in Art History

Also by New Academia Publishing

Art History/Theory

THE INNER LANDSCAPE: The Paintings of Gao Xingjian,
by Jason C. Kuo

SIAMO QUEL CHE MANGIAMO? Sostenibilità e arte,
Antonio d'Avossa, ed.

*INVENTION AND UNDERSTANDING: A Pedagogical Guide to Three
Dimensions,* by Steven Careau.

*CONTEMPORARY CHINESE ART AND FILM: Theory Applied and Re-
sisted,* Jason C. Kuo, ed.

ART CRITIQUES: A Guide, by James Elkins

GIORGIO VASARI: Artistic and Emblematic Manifestations,
by Liana De Girolami Cheney

VASARI'S LIFE AND LIVES: The First Art Historian, by Einar Rud

SELF-PORTRAITS BY WOMEN PAINTERS, Liana De Girolami Cheney,
Alicia Craig Faxon, Kathleen Russo, eds.

ARTISTS WITH PHDS: On the New Doctoral Degree in Studio Art,
James Elkins, ed.

VISUAL CULTURE IN SHANGHAI 1850s-1930s, Jason C. Kuo, ed.

*STONES FROM OTHER MOUNTAINS: Chinese Painting Studies in
Postwar America,* Jason C. Kuo, ed.

PERSPECTIVES ON CONNOISSEURSHIP OF CHINESE PAINTING,
Jason C. Kuo, ed

*THE COMMUNITY ARTS COUNCIL MOVEMENT: History, Opinions,
Issues,* by Nina Freedlander Gibans

Breaking New Ground in Art History

A Festschrift in Honor of Alicia Craig Faxon

Margaret A. Hanni, editor

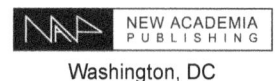
NEW ACADEMIA
PUBLISHING

Washington, DC

Library of Congress Control Number: 201494047
ISBN 978-0-9915047-4-9 paperback (alk. paper)

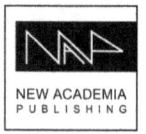

New Academia Publishing
PO Box 27420, Washington, DC 20038-7420
info@newacademia.com - www.newacademia.com

Contents

List of Illustrations

Chapter 3: The Pre-Raphaelization of the Modern Literary Heroine

Chapter 4: Edward Burne-Jones's Love Songs: Art, Music and Magic

Chapter 5: *The Waverly Oaks*: Something Borrowed, Something New

Chapter 6: Maurice Prendergast: Confronting the Culture of Early Twentieth-Century Boston

Chapter 10: Reinventing Silverpoint: An Ancient Technique for the Twenty-First Century

Acknowledgments

In addition to the individuals and institutions whose help is acknowledged separately by the authors of the essays in this volume, I am grateful to all who have contributed to the project and helped to make our festschrift a reality. To each of the authors who offered an essay, my very special thanks, as this volume would not exist without your efforts and your commitment to honor Alicia Faxon. To each of the artists, galleries and museums who have allowed us to publish images, my sincere gratitude for helping us to produce a wonderfully well-illustrated collection of essays.

I'd like to acknowledge key support from Simmons College, including financial support of the project by the former Provost, Charlena Seymour, and the present Provost, Katie Conboy. Dean Renée White of the College of Arts and Sciences has also provided crucial support. I'd also like to thank my colleagues in the Department of Art and Music for their ongoing encouragement, and Marcia Lomedico for her unparalleled and ever-present assistance in all things. My appreciation to Professor of English, Pamela Bromberg, and Professor Emeritus, Bob Oppenheim, for their continued enthusiasm for the project and special thanks to Kimberlee Cloutier-Blazzard, whose help was invaluable in the completion of the manuscript.

Special thanks to Todd, Eben and Nicole for their patient, positive and always good-humored inquiries about progress on the project.

Finally and especially, to Alicia Craig Faxon, thank you for inspiring us all to accomplish this (and so many other things)!

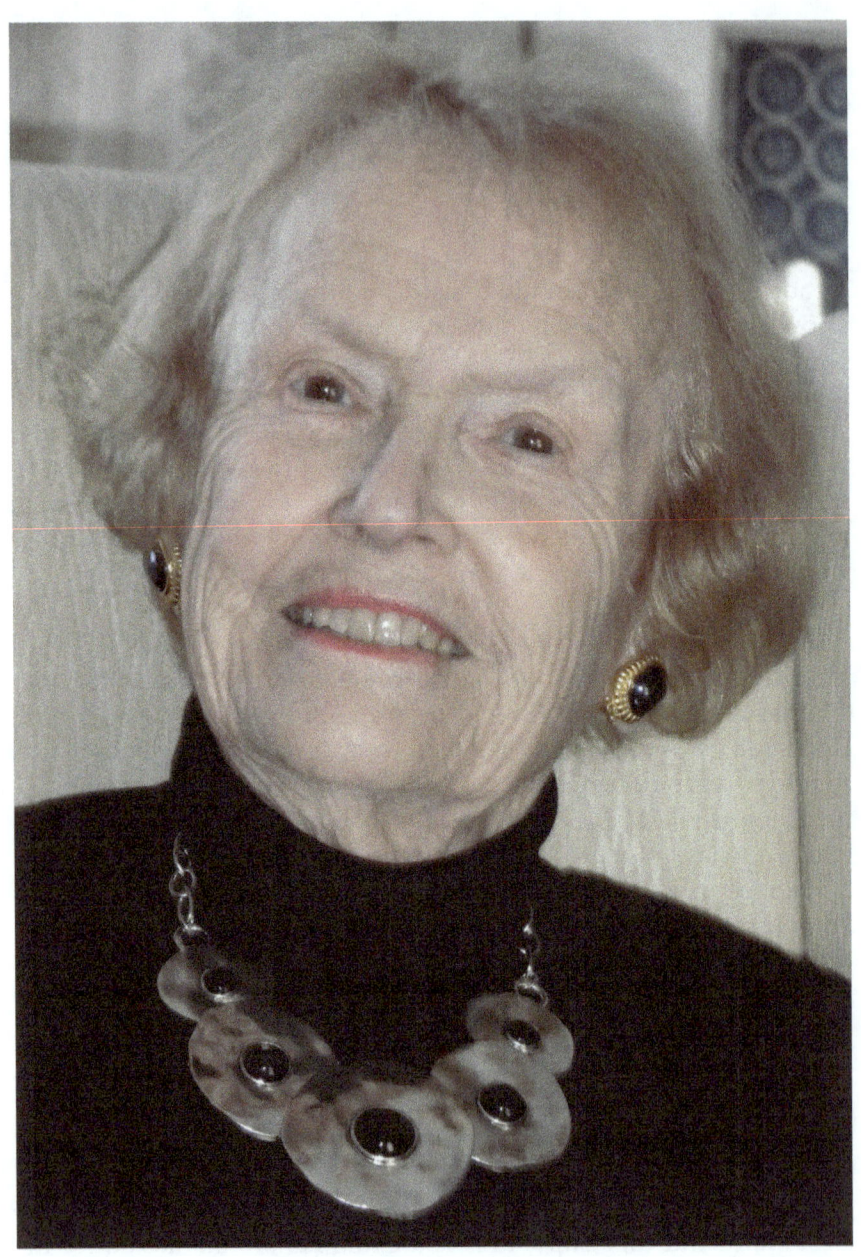

Alicia Craig Faxon, Ph.D., 2013
Photo: Suzanne Volmer

Introduction

This volume honors Alicia Craig Faxon, whose career as a scholar, professor, art critic, editor, curator, collector, and patron of the arts has contributed so much to the fields of art history and art criticism. Moreover, her unflagging support of women in the arts, for over five decades, continues today. The scholars and artists whose essays appear here celebrate Dr. Faxon's diverse scholarly publications, creative collaborations and spirited generosity as a colleague, mentor, and friend.

Alicia Faxon's educational background marks her long-term fascination with history and early commitment to women's equality. She earned her Bachelor's degree (*Summa Cum Laude*, Phi Beta Kappa) in history from Vassar College when the Seven Sister colleges represented women's most rigorous and prestigious alternative to the Ivy League. Her first Master's degree, also in history, was earned from Radcliffe College while Mary Ingraham Bunting was its president. Bunting is remembered, in part, for calling attention to the unacceptable "climate of unexpectation" for educated women and her advocacy for increasing the representation of women scholars in academia, a message that Faxon took to heart. Her subsequent studies at Boston University, where she earned an M.A. and a Ph.D. in art history, led to her prolific writing and successful teaching career, primarily as a Professor of Art History at Simmons College, where she, in turn, has encouraged and supported so many young women.

Dr. Faxon's primary field within art history is nineteenth-century French and English art, but her interests and research extend far beyond that rich territory to include women as artists, models, and patrons as well as twentieth-century and contemporary painting, sculpture, prints, and photography. Her articles have appeared in *The Art Bulletin, Metropolitan Museum of Art Journal, Master Drawings, Journal of Pre-Raphaelite Studies, History of Photography,*

Woman's Art Journal, and *Sculpture Magazine*, to name only a few. Faxon's nineteenth-century studies belie her background in history and the importance of that context to our understanding of cultural production. Her *Jean-Louis Forain: A Catalogue Raisonné of the Prints* (1982) remains the definitive source on this impressionist and social critic's printed *oeuvre*. Faxon's exhibition, *Jean-Louis Forain: Artist, Humanist, Realist* (1982-83) situated Forain's personal attitudes and varied subject matter in relation to academic as well as impressionist artists and writers of the period, and increased our understanding of the artist's significance.[1] More recently Dr. Faxon has co-curated with Nancy M. Work the exhibition *Forain's Pilgrimage* (2011) that examines the heretofore little-studied Christian themes in the artist's prints and paintings.

Faxon's contributions to Pre-Raphaelite studies are legion. Her *Dante Gabriel Rossetti* (1989) made an outstanding contribution to the re-evaluation of Rossetti and his contemporaries that occurred during the 1980s and 1990s. This insightful and beautifully-illustrated volume (now in its third printing) offered fresh interpretations of the relationship between the artist's colorful personal life, his poetry and paintings as well as new information and perceptive analysis about Rossetti's creative employment of diverse visual sources in his work. Typical of Dr. Faxon's support of other art historians, she has consistently encouraged new scholarship, as co-editor with Dr. Susan Casteras of *Pre-Raphaelite Art in its European Context* (1995) and, among others, at sessions she chaired at College Art Association conferences on the Pre-Raphaelites in their historical context (2000) and the mythic image in Pre-Raphaelite art (2005).[2] Dr. Faxon's ongoing research has added new lines of inquiry and interpretation to Pre-Raphaelite studies. She has explored Rossetti's use of the then-new technology of photography, both to obtain images of objects and paintings that influenced his work, and to disseminate his own paintings to a wider European audience without exhibiting them on the continent.[3] So, too, Faxon's feminist perspective has provided many opportunities, in books, conference papers, lectures and articles, to consider the women, divine and earth-bound, who fascinated the Pre-Raphaelites and populated their pictures.[4]

It would be difficult to overstate the contribution that Alicia Faxon's feminist scholarship has made to the study of and support for women in the arts. The Women's Caucus for Art recognized this in 1996, when they presented Dr. Faxon with their award for Outstanding Achievement in the Visual Arts. Over the subsequent years, her work in this area has expanded and continued. Her publications on women artists, models, and patrons (past and present), the exhibitions of work she has curated or reviewed and her investigations of historical and cultural meanings carried by images of women are far too numerous to list. The diversity of her work also demonstrates an open-mindedness and intellectual curiosity that has inspired many colleagues through the years. Books she has written or co-authored consider subjects ranging from how to start an art collection to women and Jesus to pioneering women in the arts of New England and self-portraits by women painters.[5] Articles and catalogue essays elucidate topics as different as American women sculptors in nineteenth-century Rome to post-modern and ethnic female artists.[6] So, too, Dr. Faxon's curatorial projects speak to her broad interests, from German Expressionist influences on contemporary women artists to Neo-Surrealism at the millennium and a Women's Caucus for Art exhibition of member artists.[7] Dr. Faxon's decades of digging for often-scant information about various women artists of the past taught her the importance of creating an historical record in the present. She has regularly published or contributed to catalogues that accompany these exhibitions, providing essential documentation to lesser-known artists and augmenting the critical literature about others.

Through her editorial work and dozens of exhibition reviews, Faxon has consistently brought attention to new scholarship on women artists and by women scholars, and assured that women are well represented in the periodical literature on contemporary art. As editor of the *Woman's Art Journal* since 1990, she has reviewed much important new scholarship by and about women and has supported the publication of important feminist research. As a regular writer for *Art New England* and Rhode Island editor for the journal for several years, Dr. Faxon's commitment to contemporary art in all its forms is enthusiastic, insightful and informed by her art-historical knowledge. The range and quality of this work was recognized in 2008, when she became a member of the International Association of Art Critics.

Dr. Faxon's influence as a scholar and curator is well complemented by her years as Professor of Art History at Simmons College, now *Emerita*, where she held the Alumnae Chair in the Humanities at her retirement in 1993. Her lively and stimulating classes, intellectual generosity and personal encouragement of students has resulted in dozens of women choosing a career in the arts. She recognized early on that in order to compete successfully in this arena, young women needed not only a strong background in art or music but also marketable skills in communications or management. As a result, in 1986, Dr. Faxon started the Arts Administration major at Simmons, one of the very first of its kind in the country. The program has continued to grow, and through it young women successfully pursue a wide variety of careers in museums, galleries, performing arts organizations, auction houses, and corporate art collections, among many others. Simmons College recognized Dr. Faxon's creative scholarship, energetic support of women and outstanding reputation in the cultural community of Boston and beyond when it awarded her the honorary degree Doctor of Humane Letters in 1998.

Although this volume was not planned to reprise Faxon's areas of research and criticism, many of the subjects in *Breaking New Ground in Art History* resonate with her publications and interests. As colleagues, many of us have been fortunate to share research subjects with Alicia Faxon, and to benefit from her feedback and encouragement in many ways. It was this collegiality that inspired Diane Radycki to suggest a festschrift in Faxon's honor and I am grateful to her and to Beth Gersh-Nešić for getting the project started. All of the contributors share with Alicia a commitment to widening the opportunities for women in the arts and contributing new voices to the art historical and contemporary critical literature. In this festschrift we present original scholarship informed by a great variety of approaches by both artists and art historians to honor the creativity, energy and generosity of Alicia Faxon.

Two essays on the Pre-Raphaelites form a fitting tribute to Dr. Faxon's own scholarship and provide evidence of the diverse directions in which scholars are inspired to consider these artists and their influence. Liana De Girolami Cheney explores the magical world created by Edward Burne-Jones in his *Love Songs* paintings, 1865-1894, seen partly through the lens of his complex relationship with Greek sculptress Maria Zambaco, but also through the artist's own romantic concepts of beauty. Susan P. Casteras brings readers into present-day literature with the first study to examine how writers, in the realms of the mystery genre and historical fiction, have incorporated Pre-Raphaelite characteristics, particularly of women, into their novels.

The reception of art by nineteenth-century critics and the public inform two essays on American art. Lucretia Giese considers the context in which Winslow Homer created *The Waverley Oaks*, 1864, and argues that with this work, the artist departed from genre paintings for which he had been known, in favor of using landscape as a signifier of meaning. Sister Ellen Glavin considers differences in the early and later paintings of Maurice Prendergast, especially the influence of Cézanne on his style. She describes the cultural environment in which these changes were received as his popularity shifted away from Boston toward New York critics and audiences.

Three of the essays in *New Perspectives* concern portraiture and suggest the different means by which these images draw on artistic and cultural precedents to inform—or perform—their characterizations of the sitters' status and identity. Amy Golahny demonstrates the ways in which Rembrandt chose to emphasize communication between spouses through speech, gesture and gaze, and discusses his innovative adaptation of an Italian source, thus producing an unusual image of gender roles in a Baroque marriage portrait. Portraits of spouses are the subject of Margaret Hanni's essay as well, in which she argues that English marriage portraits that situate the couple on horses or in carriages rely on cultural conventions to speak of gender roles, family bloodlines, and the social control that eighteenth-century marriage represented to the landed classes. The relationship between artist and sitter is highlighted in Beth Gersh-Nešić's discussion of Kathleen Gilje's contemporary images of art historians and critics whose portrayals are inserted into masterpieces from the history of art chosen together by sitter and artist. These portraits may be seen as performances that reference the sev-

eral layers of relationship –personal, art historical, professional--
that underpin their creation.

Domestic relations and concepts of home are at the center
of innovative approaches to understanding creativity in essays
by Diane Radycki and Joyce Cohen. Friendships and marriages
within the artists' colony at Worpswede, Germany are explored
in the context of their influence on the artistic production of three
couples: poet Rainer Marie Rilke and sculptor Clara Rilke-Westhof;
painters Paula Modersohn-Becker and Otto Becker; and weaver
Martha Schröeder-Vogeler and designer Heinrich Vogeler. Images
of house and home in the work of self-taught artist, Nellie Mae
Rowe, are examined by Joyce Cohen, whose essay places this artist
in a wider historical context. Cohen demonstrates that the subjects
and materials used by Rowe in drawings, dolls, quilts and the ever-
changing installations at her home in Georgia dealt with themes
later advocated by 1970s feminists.

Three contemporary artists contribute unique perspectives on
how techniques and ideas continue to evolve in art of the present
and the changing role of the artist in society. Susan Schwalb provides historical background on the unusual technique of silverpoint
with special attention to its use in the twenty-first century. She considers not only image-based drawings, but also abstract, minimalist and conceptual representations in silverpoint. Suzanne Volmer
argues that twenty-first-century sculpture is about form in relation
to audience engagement. Discussing works by Petah Coyne, Louise
Bourgeois and others, Volmer demonstrates ways in which sculpture now is conceptually driven as sculptors seek physical and spatial means of interpreting cultural experience. The artist's role as
a creative critic of culture is at the center of Bridget Lynch's essay,
which considers the meaning of the Fool in art, past and present.
She argues that both artists and fools may play the part of tricksters, wise characters, or innocents, and therefore reflect confusion
and transgression within an ordered society, a conflict that sharpens our focus on what is proper and what needs to change.

The scholars and artists whose essays make up this festschrift
have collaborated on it as a means of saying "thank you" to Alicia
Faxon for her guidance, kindness, leadership, scholarly influence
and sage advice. We bring to this project the kind of joy and dedi-

cation that Alicia has brought to her work and to her friendships with colleagues. We hope our efforts convey our genuine affection and enormous respect for all that she has given to so many over the years, and our very best wishes for many years to come.

End Notes

[1] Alicia Craig Faxon, *Jean-Louis Forain: A Catalogue Raisonné of the Prints*. (New York: Garland, 1982). *Jean-Louis Forain: Artist, Humanist, Realist*. Washington, D.C.: International Exhibitions Foundation, 1982.

[2] Faxon, *Dante Gabriel Rossetti* (New York: Abbeville, 1989; 2nd printing, 1994; 3rd printing, 2011). Also published by Phaidon, London; Belfond; Paris; Idealibri, Milan and Tokyo. Susan Casteras and Alicia Craig Faxon, eds. *Pre-Raphaelite Art in its European Context* (Cranbury, N.J.: Associated University Presses, 1995). See also Faxon's introduction to *The Letters of Dante Gabriel and William Michael Rossetti* (Lewisburg: Bucknell University Press, 1995).

[3] Faxon, "The Medium Is NOT the Message: Problems in the Reproduction of Rossetti's Art." *Victorian Periodicals Review* 24/2 (1991): 64-70. Faxon, "Rossetti's Reputation: A Study of the Dissemination of His Art through Photographs." *Visual Resources* 8/3 (1992): 219-245. Faxon, "Dante Gabriel Rossetti and photography: some newly-rediscovered correspondence," *Apollo: The International Magazine For Collectors* 140 (1994): 23-27. Faxon, "Rossetti's images of Botticelli," *Visual resources* 12/1 (1996): 53-62.

[4] Faxon, "The Pre-Raphaelites and the Mythic Image: Iconographies of Women," *Visual Resources* 27/1 (2011): 77-89.

[5] Faxon, *Women and Jesus* (Philadelphia: United Church Press, 1973). Alicia Faxon and Sylvia Moore, eds. *Pilgrims and Pioneers: New England Women in the Arts* (New York: Midmarch Art Press, 1987). Liana De Girolami Cheney, Alicia Craig Faxon, and Kathleen Russo, *Self-Portraits by Women Painters* (London: Ashgate, 2000). Paperback: Washington D.C.: New Academia, 2009.

[6] Faxon, "The White Marmorean Flock," in Faxon and Moore, eds. 1987. Faxon, "PostModern and Ethnic Female Artists" in Liana De Girolami Cheney, ed. *Essays On Women Artists*, Book 2 (Lewiston: The Edwin Mellen Press, 2003), 79-93.

[7] *Generations: Christina Lanzl, Erika Marquardt and the German Expressionist Tradition* (Attleboro Museum, 1995). *Dream Worlds: Neo-Surrealism at the Millennium* (Attleboro Museum, 2000). Women's Caucus for Art, Boston, 2nd Annual Entitled/Untitled Members' Exhibition, Brickbottom Gallery, May 5-28, 2000.

1
Rembrandt's Dialogue with Italian Art:
The Shipbuilder and His Wife of 1633

Amy Golahny

Introduction

Rembrandt is most often regarded as a portrayer of figures expressing psychological depth and physical presence, whether they are
his contemporaries or historical characters.[1] Among Rembrandt's
earliest paintings are depictions of figures in animated conversation and with forceful gestures. Typical of these is the 1628 *Two Old
Men Disputing* (Fig. 1). Rembrandt depicted two men discussing
the material in the large books they hold open. Compositionally,
this painting has long been recognized as deriving from an engraving by Lucas van Leyden of *Saints Peter and Paul Seated in a Landscape* of 1527 (Fig. 2). Undoubtedly, Rembrandt was familiar with
and inspired by the print by Lucas van Leyden, his illustrious pre-
decessor in his hometown. But where Lucas clearly identified the
apostles by their attributes of keys and sword, Rembrandt omitted
such identifying signs. Depicting two old men in discussion, the
Rembrandt painting and the Lucas print share a thematic kinship,
even as Rembrandt omitted to identify the figures.[2] This is a typical case in which an example provided a prompt for the concept
and design, in Lucas' paired figures with animated gestures and direct gazes, but Rembrandt's resultant painting achieves a physical
and psychological intensity that is quite far from precedent. Rembrandt's *Two Old Men Disputing* serves here as an exemplar of the
artist's dialogue with others' inventions, with the goal to emulate
and surpass them.

The *Two Old Men Disputing* here serves to emphasize Rembrandt's interest in showing speech and listening. The man seen full face is open-mouthed, as in speech, while the other, seen in lost profile with a prominent ear, appears silently listening. Their contrasting postures and actions indicate a single moment of their relationship. One guiding principle in Rembrandt's approach to portraits and historical subjects is the inclusion of speech and its consequence. That is, one person speaks while the other is quiet, so that both figures do not speak at the same time. However effective this approach may be, it had not been articulated until relatively recently by Julius Held, and this approach is in contrast to many, if not most, portrayals of conversation in illustrations of the Renaissance and baroque.[3] This principle may be followed throughout the artist's work, from an outward, physically manifested display toward an inward, psychologically-implied expressiveness. Furthermore, this principle involves not only the corollaries of speech and hearing, but also the physical manifestations of verbal communication and its consequences.

In all his work, Rembrandt strove for an expressive movement, both physical and mental, that affected the viewer. In so doing, he may be placed firmly within the intellectual developments of Dutch philosophy. The prints and paintings by other artists, both his contemporaries and earlier, that provided his source material have been eagerly traced by art historians during the past century or so. Such sources, including the *Two Old Men Disputing* and its Lucas model, reveal how thoroughly Rembrandt studied the art of others. These models contribute to his wide and deep visual experience. Yet identifying Rembrandt's sources and analyzing how the artist derived inspiration from them still fascinate the viewer; answers to these questions, whether conclusive or tentative, offer fresh insight into the artist's creative process. Rembrandt arrived at his original solutions by emphasizing communication, through speech, gesture, and gaze. We are able to follow Rembrandt's transformations of visual sources, toward wholly original and unprecedented results. The *Two Old Men Disputing* is but one example of Rembrandt's reshaping a conventional theme.

In this essay, I explore a well-known composition by Rembrandt of two figures in dramatic communication, to demonstrate how he adapted a pictorial model from Italian art to achieve an unprecedented dynamic result.

Griet Jans Interrupts Jan Rijcksen at Work, 1633

One of Rembrandt's earliest formal portraits depicts a married couple, traditionally called *The Shipbuilder and his Wife,* signed and dated 1633 (Fig. 3). In this large canvas, the man is seated at a table, located in the corner of a room with a window; a purse and paper hang on the wall, and stacked papers, books and inkwell lie on the table. He holds a drafting compass in one hand and rests the other on a sheet of paper, on which he has drawn the cross-section of a ship's hull. The woman bursts into this space by opening a door, grasping its handle to push it to the wall; she leans forward over the man's chair to give him a letter. The two figures unite over the chair: the man, seated, leans toward his wife, and she steps forward and reaches over the back of the chair. As he has been interrupted, he turns around slowly, and she rushes into the room, her arms stretching between door and desk. Their actions are not only markedly different, but also relate to gender distinctions. The man has been at work, while the woman has presumably been attending to the domestic scene. Yet, as he calmly sits, and she stands and reaches over to him, their conventional gender-based postures are reversed. In two significant ways, Rembrandt is an innovator here: the active/passive gender-based roles are reversed, and the domestic setting is of a daily work routine, rather than a formal pose.

In Dutch portraits generally, a couple pays their attention to the artist, for whom they pose. A man indicates his wife by gesture or embrace, and the man's pose is more forceful than the woman's. Usually, both are seated, and the man gestures toward his wife, who keeps her hands close and her gaze demure. Occasionally the man stands and the woman sits, again a gender-based juxtaposition of active and passive roles. The foremost portraitists who followed the convention of active men and passive women—in double or pair portraits—include: Frans Hals, Nicolas Eliasz Pickenoy, Thomas de Keyser and Bartolomeus van der Helst. These artists shaped the immediate context for Rembrandt's portraits. This tradition has been well examined by David Smith and Eddy de Jongh, who have set forth the social conventions and pictorial requirements of marriage portraiture, and, at the same time, demonstrated how Rembrandt worked both within this tradition and without it, to explore innovative solutions in each case.[4]

All Rembrandt's marriage portraits conform to this type of active man and passive woman, except the *Shipbuilder and his Wife*. (This is even the case in Rembrandt's *Anslo and his Wife* of 1641, Berlin, Gemäldegalerie, another case that is wholly unusual in its narrative of speaker and listener, and in its portrayal of the man in his working role as preacher, wherein the man is active and the woman passive.) The Shipbuilder slowly turns as the woman bursts into the room and leans dramatically over his shoulder. They contradict convention not only in their postures but also in their speaking and listening roles. The woman opens her mouth in speech as the man harks to her noisy entrance. The dramatic communication is comparable to the 1628 *Two Old Men Disputing*, but the identifiable living people in a domestic setting and the active/passive gender-role reversal call for further examination.

Archival research provides some information about the couple portrayed. I. H. van Eeghen identified the couple as Jan Rijcksen (ca. 1561-1637) and Griet Jans (dates unknown).[5] The grand double portrait appears in the 1659 Amsterdam inventory of their son's goods, among a number of artworks.[6] We may surmise that the couple was pleased with Rembrandt's portrait. In the inventory of their son Cornelis Joan Reyxse (d. 1659), the painting is listed as *"een schilderije van des overledens vader ende moeder geschildert by Rembrant van Reen,"* in *"de beste kamer"* ("A painting of the father and mother of the deceased by Rembrandt van Rijn located in the grand room"). The son's inventory lists twenty additional paintings, including a portrait by Rembrandt of a male relative, two heads by Jan Lievens of Saints Peter and Paul, a landscape by Jan van Goyen, and two pieces by the sixteenth-century artists Lambert Lombard and Pieter Aertsen. The family was Roman Catholic, which might account for the few religious paintings in the son's inventory. It is most likely that these paintings, as well as others in this list, were inherited by Cornelis Joan from his parents. Lievens, an associate of Rembrandt, and Jan van Goyen, also a Leiden artist, might reflect fashionable acquisitions around 1635, and the earlier works might have been inherited by Jan Rijcksen and Griet Jans. Only two items appear to be related to shipping and the sea: a seascape by Simon de Vlieger and a drawing by Willem van de Velde the Elder, a specialist in seascapes. Jan Rijcksen, a wealthy designer of ships, and his son, Cornelis Joan, a master carpenter in the service of the Dutch East India Company and the Dutch West Indian Company (V.O.C. and W.I.C.), were not avid collectors of art. Rather, they owned paintings that decorated the walls of their houses, and that demonstrated a variety of themes. These were family portraits, and paintings of landscapes, genre subjects, two seascapes, and several religious and historical subjects. They did not possess more art than would comfortably hang on view.

Occasionally Rembrandt's sitters were portrayed by several artists. In this case, we have no additional images with which to compare. We may assume that Jan Rijcksen and Griet Jans were content with their large double portrait by Rembrandt, and evidently were not inclined to have another artist render their features. They passed it on to their son who displayed it in the biggest room of his house. The second Rembrandt portrait is of "*Harder oom*" (literally, "uncle Harder," but indicating an older male relative). This would most likely be a portrait of the older son who died in 1637. Several portraits of young single men of the mid-1630s, otherwise unidentified, exist, and have been tentatively related to the Rijcksen young man by the Rembrandt Research Project.[7] A limited pattern of patronage is also suggested by the two portraits by Rembrandt, two heads by Jan Lievens, and landscape by Jan van Goyen—all Leiden artists. Rembrandt and Lievens were closely associated, and similar in age to both sons of Jan Rijcksen and Griet Jans. The older son, Harder, may well have become acquainted with the young Leiden artists, Rembrandt and Lievens, and had his own portrait made around the same time as that of his parents. However, identifying the couple does not provide insight into their spectacularly unconventional appearance in this double portrait.

The Man in his Study: Immediate Precedent and Fashionable Models

To help establish a visual context for this double portrait we may investigate Rembrandt's experiences in the art world of Amsterdam. After studying in Amsterdam with the painter Pieter Lastman for about six months around 1624-1625, Rembrandt established himself as an independent artist in his native Leiden. By 1631, however, he moved from Leiden to Amsterdam to further his career as a portraitist of prosperous merchants, devout clergy, and their spouses. During his Leiden years, he concentrated on historical figures and episodes, such as the 1628 *Two Old Men Disputing*, but at the same time, he studied current trends in portraiture. The surviving documents of the mid-1630s indicate that Rembrandt was a presence in the commercial milieu of the art dealing business of Hendrick Uylenburgh.[8] Rembrandt attended the Amsterdam auctions, where he was a buyer in quantity and a keen observer.[9] By 1656, Rembrandt possessed one of the largest art collections in the Netherlands, with spectacular paper art, a respectable number of paintings by foremost Italian and Northern artists, a quantity of large sculptures, and exotic specimens, medals, weaponry and other objects. His level of collecting belongs to those who formed *kunst-kameren*, or comprehensive collections of natural and fabricated objects. Documents, including the itemization of the collection in the 1656 inventory made on the occasion of his bankruptcy, reveal that Rembrandt himself acted as an art dealer repeatedly, in purchasing and selling artworks.[10] Such activity indicates a pattern of intense engagement with the commerce and collecting of art. Considering the tracing of Rembrandt's visual prompts in the works of other artists, as in his inspired use of Lucas van Leyden in the *Two Old Men Disputing*, we may recognize that Rembrandt, from his early career, was keenly aware of the art available on the market. We may also surmise that Rembrandt was keenly aware of the corollary of the art market: the ownership and display of art in the private houses of Holland.

The immediate precedent within Rembrandt's circle for a man interrupted while at his work is Thomas de Keyser's *Constantijn Huygens and a Servant* of 1627 (Fig. 4). This painting was surely familiar to Rembrandt, as Huygens had befriended the young artist and fostered his career.[11] As a general type, the depiction of a man with his secretary at a working desk has its genesis in Sebastiano del Piombo's *Ferry Carondelet Triple Portrait* (Fig. 5). With a third person as a shadowy servant entering at the left, the Carondolet composition implicitly included the interruption of work. Very well known in the seventeenth century, the Carondolet portrait was considered to be by Raphael, and acquired by Thomas Howard around 1608. On his visits to London in 1618 and later, Huygens visited the Arundel collection, and would have likely seen the *Carondolet* there. The portrait undoubtedly was in his mind when he commissioned Thomas de Keyser to portray himself and a servant. The spatial divisions of Huygens in his luxuriously-furnished study recall the colonnade and landscape of the *Carondolet*. In both, the main figure is framed by a background that emphasizes his stature: Carondolet, by the portal and colonnade, Huygens by the tapestry. But apart from their portrayals of men at work and framed by a background rectangular element, these two portraits have less in common than has been assumed in the literature. De Keyser showed the moment of interruption, while Sebastiano merely suggested such an interruption, as the main figure coolly regards the viewer as his secretary writes, and the third figure bearing a letter is hidden in the shadows. Other Italian portraits explore the potential for interruption more fully. Among these is Giovanni Battista Moroni's *Seated Man and Boy Bearing a Letter, Count Alborghetti and his Son* (Fig. 6). Moroni's portraits were often attributed to Titian. Huygens may have seen a similar painting during his travels to England (1618) and Italy (1620), but it is equally possible that he saw such a double portrait in the Netherlands. De Keyser most likely acted on Huygens' wishes to depict him seated, turning to respond to the entering servant.

Rembrandt's ship designer belongs thematically to the category of the professional man at work, interrupted by a messenger, but this grand painting departs radically from precedent by an intensity of gesture and action. For Griet Jans' sudden entrance to Jan Rijcksen's study, neither the *Huygens*, the *Carondolet*, nor the *Alborghetti*, would have sufficed as a point of departure. No earlier portrait, whether Dutch or Italian, prepares us for the wife as messenger who delivers the letter to the man at work. Griet Jans has urgent communication as her goal. The written, silent letter is not enough for her purposes and her open mouth imparts speech, to which Jan Rijcksen turns his attention. Thomas de Keyser's genteel interruption of the scholar-secretary Huygens at work, gracefully and quietly turning toward a deferential young man holding his hat in one hand and letter in the other, is a far cry from the noisy wife breaking the calm of her husband at work. The common theme of the letter-bearing and interrupting figure is insufficient to explain Rembrandt's unique solution to a marriage portrait. And indeed, it may have been so radical that it inspired no variations.

Rembrandt's Inspiration for Urgent Communication: Art in Amsterdam

We may suggest another visual prompt that was in Amsterdam and within Rembrandt's circle of contacts in the early 1630s. The emphasis on urgent communication in the *Shipbuilder and his Wife* has a kinship with the two figures in dynamic exchange of Guercino's *Semiramis Receiving the News of the Revolt of Babylon* (Fig. 7). The painting belonged to the Gerard Reynst collection in Amsterdam, from which it went to England with the Dutch Gift of 1660, a major group of paintings presented to Charles II by the Dutch Republic. Engraved for the *Caelaturae*, a selection of Reynst paintings begun c. 1655, Guercino's *Semiramis* would have been among the most prized of the Reynst paintings.[12]

Around 1630, Gerard Reynst (1599-1658) brought to Amsterdam much of the art that he and his brother Jan (1601-1646) acquired in Venice, and included the comprehensive Vendramin collection of sculptures, coins, precious objects, and paintings, most of which were by Venetian artists. Other paintings in the Reynst collection were familiar to Rembrandt, and inspired several appropriations, during the early 1630s and during the 1650s. From Bassano's *Lamentation*, Rembrandt adapted the figure of the fainted Virgin in his own *Descent from the Cross* of 1633, part of the Passion series commissioned by the Stadholder Frederik Hendrick.[13] From Palma Vecchio's *Courtesan*, Rembrandt appropriated the theme and compositional guide for his *Hendrickje at an Open Door* of ca. 1656.[14]

Guercino's *Semiramis* received a brief notice in the diaries of the Bolognese historian Carlo Cesare Malvasia (1616-1693). With access to Guercino's own account books and the records kept by his family, Malvasia is generally reliable, but in this case, his remarks require some interpretation. According to Malvasia, in 1624 Guercino painted *Semiramis* for Daniele Ricci, about whom nothing is known; the painting was exhibited in Bologna at that time as a *"maraviglia dell'arte;"* and the painting went to the King of England.[15] Malvasia, relying on a document presumably from Guercino himself, omitted the painting's whereabouts between Ricci and Charles II, that is, when the painting was in the Reynst collection. Malvasia was less well-informed from sources outside Italy, but was aware that the painting found its way to the English monarch; his informants did not place it in Amsterdam between 1624 and 1660. And yet, the sensational display of the painting in 1624 indicates that it was a striking image, even among Guercino's early and notable works.

If today Semiramis, Queen of Assyria, is a somewhat obscure figure, in the seventeenth century she belonged to the general historical material handed down from antiquity by Herodotus and other historians who may have blended fact and fiction in their accounts.[16] The pertinent episode from the life of Semiramis does not appear within their narratives, but is added by Valerius Maximus. He included it in his compendium of notable actions (*Facta et Dicta Memorabilia*), which was frequently published in Latin and in the vernacular after 1500.[17] Semiramis is having her hair coiffed when she is interrupted by a messenger who brings news of the revolt of Babylon. Semiramis reacted so immediately that she went straight into battle with her hairdo half-done, and did not complete her coiffure properly until after the revolt was successfully put down.

During the seventeenth century, the episode was rare in the visual arts, although it had some currency in Rembrandt's circle. Mattaeus Merian engraved it for an illustration in the historical compendium by J. L. Gottfried (1629), a book used in Rembrandt's studio. Pietro da Cortona's painting of Semiramis, ca. 1623, was owned by the Uylenburgh firm in Amsterdam, somewhat later but certainly by 1675. For his painting for Daniele Ricci, Guercino evidently had no pictorial precedent, and followed the account in Valerius Maximus.[18] Each of the three figures—the queen, messenger, and maid—plays a crucial role in illustrating the narrative. The queen sits, crowned and dressed in richly brocaded and bejeweled robes and a cape; she rests one hand upon the arm of the chair, and the other cups her ear as she listens to the words of the agitated messenger. He points with one hand to the left, presumably to the direction of the Babylonian insurgence, and holds a cap with the other. The maid combs Semiramis' hair, already tied up on one side of the queen's head but loose on the other. The hair is essential to the narrative, as the half-done coiffure is the identifying feature of the queen. Guercino crafted an intense confrontation between the queen and a messenger, in gaze and gesture, with the calm attendant emphasizing the hair as the queen's attribute.

Guercino's *Semiramis* was among the extraordinary Italian paintings in Amsterdam around 1630. These included Caravaggio's *Madonna of the Rosary* which arrived in Amsterdam 1616, and was taken to Antwerp ca. 1620; Louis Finson's copy remained in Amsterdam. The impact of the *Madonna of the Rosary* on the painters in Amsterdam was powerful. For Pieter Lastman (1583-1633), who had seen Caravaggio paintings in Italy during his years there (1603-1607), the study of the *Madonna of the Rosary* decisively affected how he composed his later historical paintings.[19] In his remark to Huygens that some of the best Italian art was to be seen north of the Alps without the bother of travel, Rembrandt indicated how thoroughly he knew the Italian art in Amsterdam. Indeed, he had studied the Caravaggio altarpiece, and it guided his figural arrangement in his 1629 *Judas Returning the Silver* (Private Collection). Much of the Italian art in Amsterdam was of the highest quality, and was accessible to artists, especially Lastman and Rembrandt.[20]

Three aspects of Guercino's *Semiramis* appealed to Rembrandt. One was the psychological and physical movement, so strikingly conveyed by the two main figures. The second was the theme of speech and its consequences: one active figure, arriving suddenly with a serious message, and a passive figure, attentive to this news. Guercino's messenger communicates by speech and gesture, while Griet Jans communicates by speech and letter. As we have seen, these are constant interests of Rembrandt, appearing throughout his oeuvre.

The third aspect was the compositional organization of a seated figure who turns to receive an arriving messenger. In reversing Rembrandt's *Shipbuilder and his Wife*, the formal similarities are emphasized (Fig. 8). Both paintings feature two main figures, whose bodies form essentially a right angle; the arms of the Shipbuilder and of Semiramis loosely form counterparts: Jan Rijcksen's hands rest on the table and chair armrest, and compare to Semiramis' hands, one of which rests on the armrest and the other holds her ear. The messenger's arms and hands form an upward diagonal, loosely corresponding to Griet Jans' arms, which extend from the door handle at the edge of the painting to the center. In his early paintings, Guercino typically rendered arms, hands, and bodies in dynamic and occasionally confused patterns, as if such physical attitudes could impart an intensified expressiveness.[21] Rembrandt would have found Guercino's solutions appealing.

However, the Guercino example in Amsterdam was also a theme of a strong woman from antiquity. Guercino rendered her seated and listening, in a relatively passive pose, contrasting to an arriving male messenger. By transferring the active role to the female and the passive role to the male, Rembrandt reformulated the Dutch pair portrait. Perhaps Griet Jans actually participated as a partner in her husband's business, as suggested by David Smith.[22] Dutch women assumed responsibilities within family businesses, as the shipping industry demanded that men be often away at sea. Yet given that the pattern of active wife and passive husband was not imitated in other Dutch marriage portraits, that explanation does not sufficiently explain Rembrandt's singular portrayal of the couple.

Nonetheless, it is tempting to view this role reversal in this grand double portrait as a nod to the power of women. At just this time, Rembrandt explored the character of the ancient queen Artemisia, who, with her husband Mausolus, was renowned for building a massive tomb; after Mausolus' death, Artemisia had his body cremated and she daily mixed his ashes in a drink. She was consistently represented as the exemplar of wifely devotion by drinking this mixture. Less recognized is Artemisia's patronage of the literary arts in commissioning eulogies to honor Mausolus, who predeceased her by a short time. In 1634, Rembrandt portrayed Artemisia with a large book that contains these eulogies (Fig. 9).[23] In so doing, he emphasized how Artemisia patronized the art of oratory to serve the memory of her husband. While other artists portrayed the queen only as ash-drinker, Rembrandt uniquely rendered her as both ash-drinker and arts patron.

In general, Rembrandt's portraits of contemporary women conform to the passive and conventional type, and his historical women are unfortunate targets of male lust, as Callisto, Susanna and Bathsheba, or duplicitous characters avenging men, as Delilah.[24] Exceptional for emphasizing the active roles of women both within conventional portrayals and within Rembrandt's work are Griet Jans and Artemisia. As a strong character in history, Guercino's *Semiramis* may well have suggested to Rembrandt to show another historical woman, Artemisia, as active in her role as arts patron. For Rembrandt's *Shipbuilder and his Wife*, Guercino's model provided a dynamic solution for a double portrait, by transferring the messenger to the wife, and the monarch to the husband. Blurring the boundaries between formal portrait and narrative, Rembrandt created a moment of work interrupted, by taking the sudden action of an arriving messenger from a history painting.

The relationship between Rembrandt and Guercino is not limited to the Dutch artist studying the Italian's art in Amsterdam in the early 1630s. Twenty years later, the Sicilian nobleman Antonio Ruffo acquired Rembrandt's canvas *Aristotle and the Head of Homer* of 1653 (New York, The Metropolitan Museum of Art). Ruffo wished Guercino to paint a pendant for the *Aristotle*. The Italian artist interpreted that work as a physiognomist, and planned a cosmographer to go with it. In one of his many letters to Ruffo, Guercino noted that Rembrandt's etchings *"riuscite molto belle, intagliate di buon gusto e fatte di buona maniera"* ("succeed very beautifully, [they are] engraved with good taste and made with a good manner").[25] Sharing an appreciative patron in Ruffo, the relationship between Rembrandt and Guercino is better understood, at least around 1660, as collaboration at a distance.

Conclusion

For portraiture, Rembrandt appropriated poses from various sources. On the one hand, he was pragmatic, and selected models that served his purpose. Given the commission for a marriage double portrait, he looked at the latest solution for a double portrait in Thomas de Keyser's 1627 *Huygens and a Servant*. But he wished a more dramatic effect. Just arrived from Italy were the Reynst paintings. These included fine examples by Palma Vecchio, Jacopo Bassano, and Guercino. Rembrandt regarded these works as touchstones for his own compositions. The Guercino was among the newest examples of Italian art available in Amsterdam. It provided a stunning guide for a dynamic portrayal of two figures in one frame, and resonated with Rembrandt's already-formed interests in representing movement and speech. For the commission of a married couple, he took inspiration from a source that offered a solution, if he reversed the typical gender roles and portrayed the woman as the active messenger and the man as the passive draughtsman. If we could reconstruct more biographical details of Jan Rijcksen and Griet Jans, we might craft a narrative into which this dramatic moment fits. What letter with news of family or commerce might arrive to elicit Griet Jans' swift and immediate response? For all we know, and it is highly speculative, this news might even have some resonance with Semiramis' own story of urgent communication, as a notice of a sea calamity, a business loss, or a family event.

Lack of more thorough factual information has not prevented such fictional recreations of those portrayed in Dutch paintings. Susan Vreeland, Tracy Chevalier, and others have seized on Vermeer's imagery to construct sweeping narratives and poignant stories about figures in Vermeer's paintings. Rembrandt's paintings, whether real or imagined, have figured prominently in fiction. But the domestic life and business collaboration of Jan Rijcksen and Griet Jans are stories waiting to be told.

End Notes

[1] I'd like to acknowledge funding from Lycoming College, which contributed to my research for this article.

[2] A. Blankert et al., *Rembrandt: A Genius and His Impact*, exhibition catalogue, Melbourne, National Gallery of Victoria/Canberra, National Gallery of Australia, 1997, 90. Josua Bruyn et al., *A Corpus of Rembrandt Paintings* (The Hague: Stichting Rembrandt Research Project, 5 vols., 1982-2010), II:1631-1634, A 77, 367 ff. (Abbreviated here as *Corpus*).

[3] J.S. Held, "Rembrandt and the Spoken Word," in *Rembrandt Studies* (Princeton: Princeton University Press, 1991), 164-83.

[4] For the *Shipbuilder and His Wife*, see *Corpus* II, A77. Rembrandt's more conventional marriage portraits, especially as regards the active man and

passive woman, include the *Man Rising from his Chair* and *Woman* (Cincinnati, Taft Museum; and New York, Metropolitan Museum of Art; *Corpus* A 78 and 79), the Beresteijn pair portrait (New York, Metropolitan Museum of Art; *Corpus* C 68 and 69), the 1633 *Couple in an Interior* (Boston, Isabella Stewart Gardner Museum; *Corpus* C 67), and the 1641 *Cornelis Anslo Speaking to his Wife*, in which Rembrandt inserted the narrative element of a speaker and a listener (Berlin, Gemäldegalerie; *Corpus* A 143). For the tradition of marriage portraiture, see David R. Smith, "Rembrandt's Early Double Portraits and the Dutch Conversation Piece," *The Art Bulletin* 64 (1982) 259-288; E. De Jongh, *Portretten van echt en trouw: Huwelijk en gezin in de Nederlandse kunst van de zeventiende eeuw* (Waanders/Zwolle and Teyler's Museum/Haarlem, 1986).

[5] I. H. van Eeghen, "Jan Rijcksen en Griet Jans," *Maandblad Amstelodamum* 57 (1970), 121-27.

[6] For the inventory of their son Cornelis Joan Reyxse (d.1659), of 7 November 1659, see The Montias Database of Sixteenth- and Seventeenth-Century Inventories of Dutch Art Collections from the Gemeentearchief Amsterdam, Nr. 125 (Access through the Frick Art Reference Library, New York).

[7] See *Corpus* IIA, 77.

[8] For the Uylenburgh documents, see F. Lammertse and Jaap van der Veen, *Uylenburgh & Son: Art and commerce from Rembrandt to De Lairesse 1625-1675*, (London and Amsterdam: Dulwich Picture Gallery/The Rembrandt House Museum, 2006).

[9] For Rembrandt at auctions in Amsterdam, see Walter Strauss and Marjon van der Meulen, *The Rembrandt Documents* (New York: Abaris Books, 1979), especially 1635/1; 1637/2; and 1638/2.

[10] For the 1656 inventory, see Strauss, *Rembrandt Documents*, 1656/12. Among Rembrandt's best known art dealing activities is his 1637 purchase of a Rubens painting, which he sold it at a profit seven years later; see Strauss, *Rembrandt Documents*, 1637/6. But he made many other purchases and sales, including a sale of plasters to the Elector Karl Ludwig Palatine; see Strauss, *Rembrandt Documents*, 1658/31.

[11] For Huygens and Rembrandt, see, among other sources, Strauss, *Rembrandt Documents*, 1630/5. Thomas de Keyser's portrait of Huygens clearly is the most famous example of the motif in Rembrandt's circle. However, another example was most likely known to Rembrandt; see Nicolaes Eliasz Pickenoy, *The Governors of the 'Spinhuis,'* 1628, Amsterdam Historisch Museum; see *Corpus* III, 129, under A 44, fig. 7. However, the Pickenoy example has none of the urgency so striking in Rembrandt's *Shipbuilder and his Wife*, and merely indicates the prevalence of the motif of letter-bearer in Amsterdam portraiture.

[12] For the Dutch Gift and the Reynst collection, see Anne-Marie S. Logan, *The 'Cabinet' of the Brothers Gerard and Jan Reynst* (Amsterdam, Oxford, New York: Koninklijke Nederlandse Akademie van Wetenschappen Verhandelingen, 1979), 124. For the possibility that Rembrandt was prompted by another Italian model in his first commissioned portrait, see A. Golahny, "Rembrandt's 'Ruts' and Moroni's 'Bearded Man,' *Source* 10 (Fall 1990), 22-25.

[13] For Rembrandt's use of the Bassano figure, see Lammertse and Van der Veen, *Uylenburgh & Son*, 280.

[14] For Rembrandt's *Hendrickje at an Open Door* and its guide in the Palma Vecchio *Courtesan*, see K. Clark, *Rembrandt and the Italian Renaissance* (New York: New York University Press, 1966), 132.

[15] For Guercino, see Carlo Cesare Malvasia, *Felsina Pittrice. Vite dei pittori bolognesi* (Bologna: Guida all'ancora, 2 vols., 1841) II, 251; see also D. Mahon, "Guercino's Paintings of Semiramis," *Art Bulletin* 31 (1949), 217-23. I am grateful to Giovanna Periti and Shilpa Prasad for their insights into Guercino's *Semiramis*.

[16] From about 1600, Semiramis became popular on the stage, and belonged to the broad canon of personages in series of strong women. See further Jane O. Newman, "Sons and Mothers: Agrippina, Semiramis, and the Philological Construction of Gender Roles in Early Modern Germany (Lohenstein's *Agrippina*, 1665)," *Renaissance Quarterly* 49 (1996), 77-113.

[17] D. Schackleton Bailey, trans., Valerius Maximus, *Memorable Doings and Sayings*, 2 vols. (Cambridge MA and London: Harvard University Press, Loeb Classical Edition, 2000), Book 9, cap. 3, ext. 4. Valerius compiled his material from various sources, including Diodorus Siculus and Herodotus, but only he presented the coiffure anecdote.

[18] J. L. Gottfried, *Historische Chronica, oder, Beschreibung der furnembsten Geschichten, so sich von Anfang der Welt biss auff unsere Zeitten zugetrage* ... (Frankfurt: Caspar Roeteln, 1629-1634), I, 17. The Gottfried chronicle was used by artists, including Rembrandt; see A. Golahny, *Rembrandt's Reading: The artist's bookshelf of ancient poetry and history* (Amsterdam: University of Amsterdam Press, 2003), 138 ff. Merian's illustration of Semiramis and the accompanying text would have provided a ready reference for this anecdote. The near-contemporary portrayal of Semiramis by Pietro da Cortona may have some bearing on Guercino's choice of subject. However, Cortona depicted the moment when Semiramis swears to quell the revolt, while Guercino portrayed the earlier moment of the news. See Lammertse and Van der Veen, *Uylenburgh & Son,* 241, for Cortona's *The Oath of Semiramis*, ca. 1623-1624 (Oxford, Ashmolean).

[19] For Lastman's regard and adaptation of Caravaggio's *Madonna of the Rosary*, see A. Golahny, "Rembrandt and Italy: Beyond the disegno/colore

paradigm," *Jahrbuch der Berliner Museen, Neue Folge* 51 (2009), 113-20, Special volume: *Rembrandt – Wissenschaft auf der Suche. Beiträge des Internationalen Symposiums Berlin 4/5 November 2006.*

[20] See Strauss, *Rembrandt Documents*, 1630/5 for Rembrandt's remarks to Huygens. For Rembrandt's *Judas* and Caravaggio, see Golahny, "Rembrandt and Italy," 117.

[21] Shilpa Prasad, *Guercino: Stylistic Evolution in Focus* (San Diego and Seattle: Timken Museum of Art/University of Washington Press, 2006).

[22] Smith, "Rembrandt's Early Double Portraits," 273.

[23] See A. Golahny, "Rembrandt's 'Artemisia': Arts Patron," *Oud Holland* 114 (2000), 139-52.

[24] Eric Jan Sluijter, *Rembrandt and the Female Nude* (Amsterdam: Amsterdam University Press, 2006).

[25] This is my translation, which does not fully convey Guercino's measured enthusiasm in Italian; see further Jaco Rutgers, *Rembrandt en Italië. Receptie en verzamelgeschiedenis* (privately printed, 2008), 14; Strauss, *Rembrandt Documents*, 1660/7.

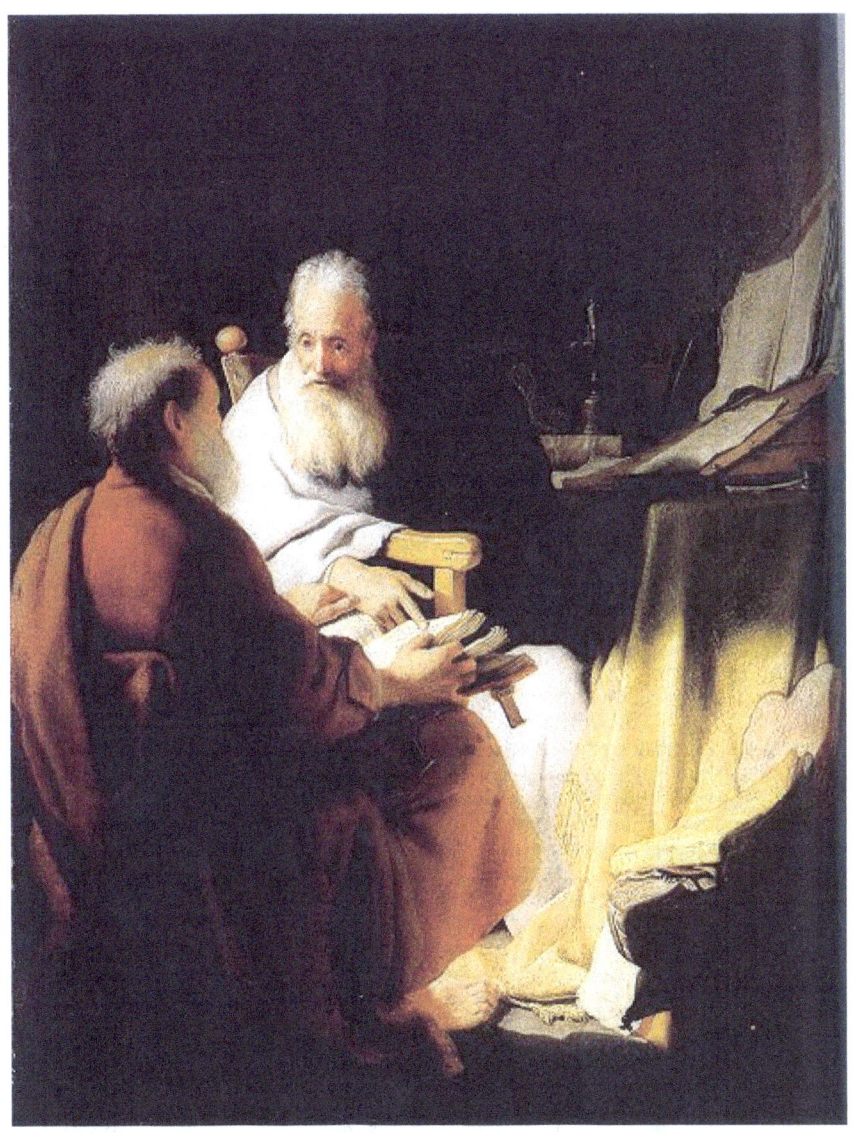

1.1. Rembrandt van Rijn, *Two Old Men Disputing (Peter and Paul?)*, 1628, oil on canvas, National Gallery of Victoria, Melbourne, Felton Bequest.

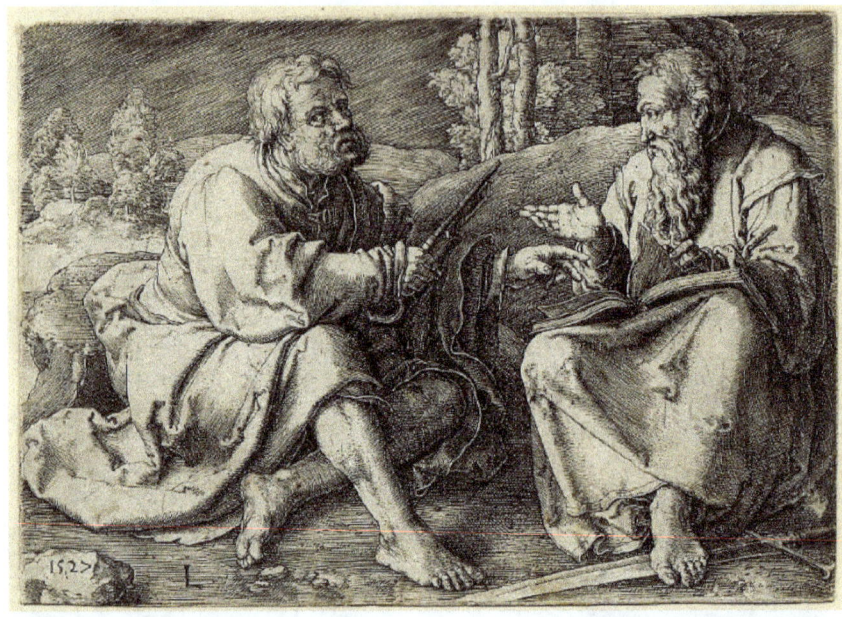

1.2. Lucas van Leyden, *Peter and Paul in a Landscape*, engraving, 1527, British Museum, London.

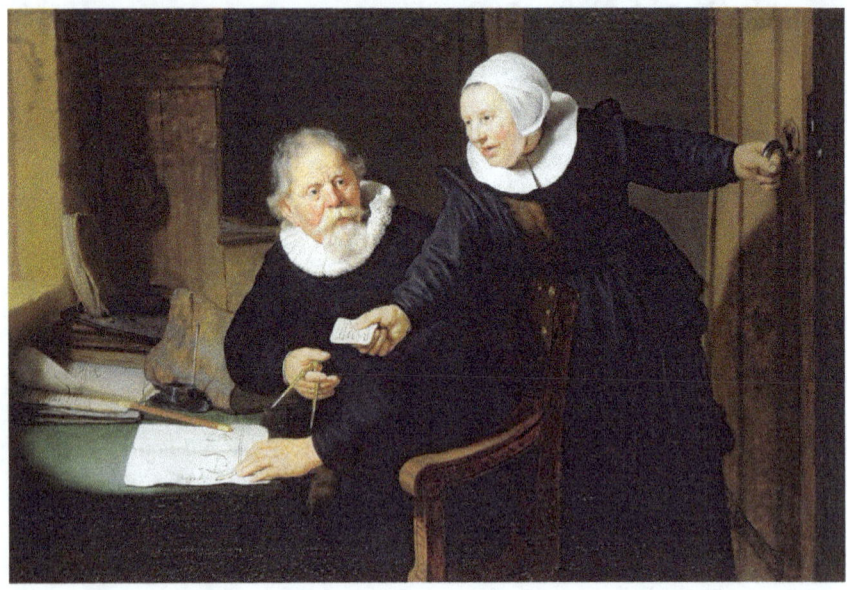

1.3. Rembrandt van Rijn, *Double Portrait of Jan Rijcksen and Griet Jans ('The Shipbuilder and his Wife')*, 1633, oil on canvas, The Royal Collection © 2011, Her Majesty Queen Elizabeth II.

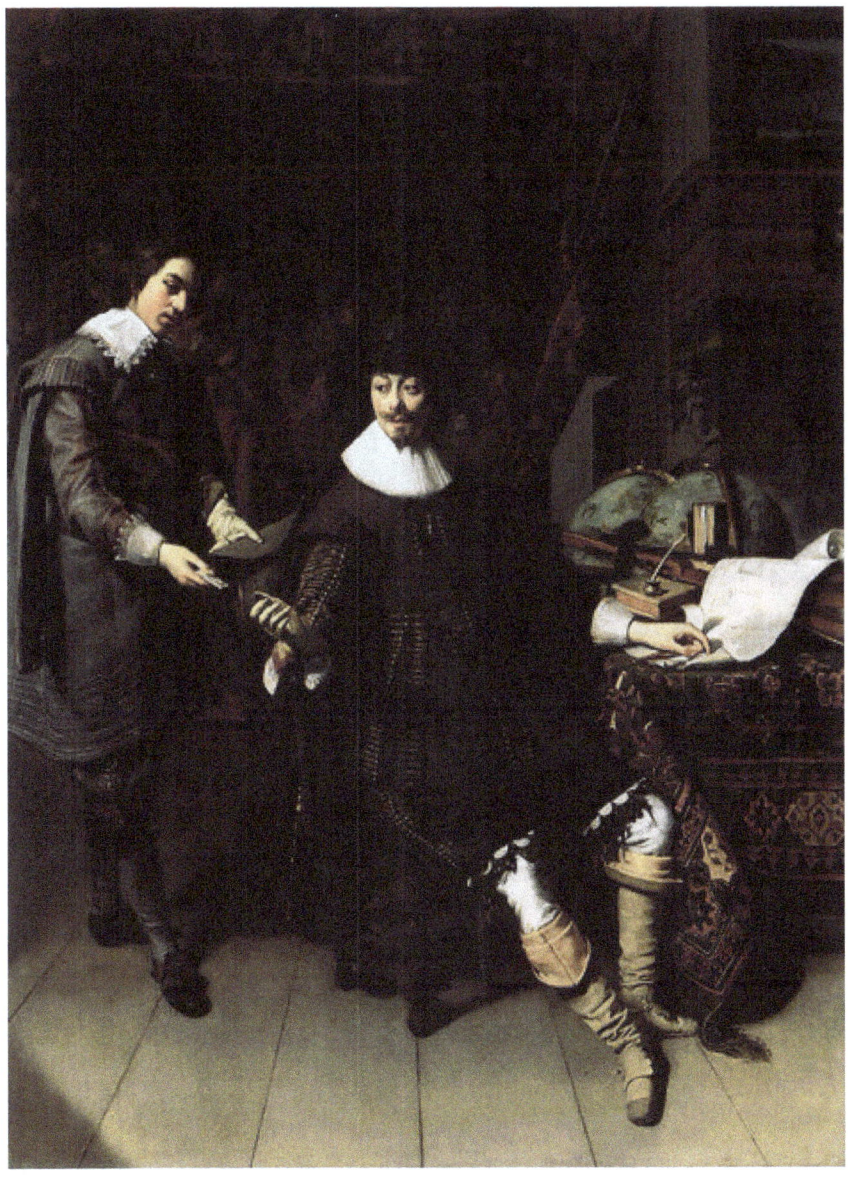

1.4. Thomas de Keyser, *Portrait of Constantijn Huygens and a (his?) Clerk*, 1627, oil on canvas, © The National Gallery, London, Bequeathed by Richard Simmons, 1847.

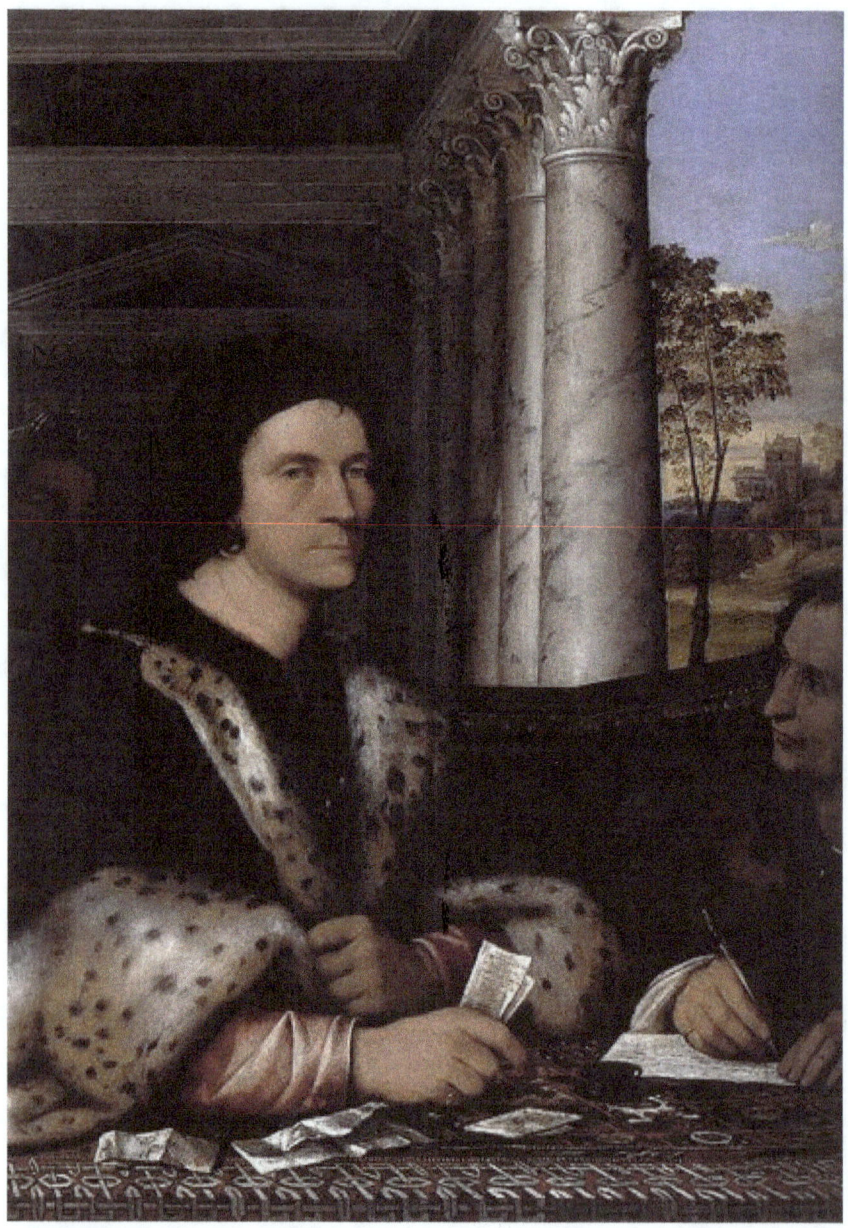

1.5. Sebastiano del Piombo, *Ferry Carondolet*, ca. 1515, oil on canvas, Thyssen-Bornemisza Museum, Madrid.

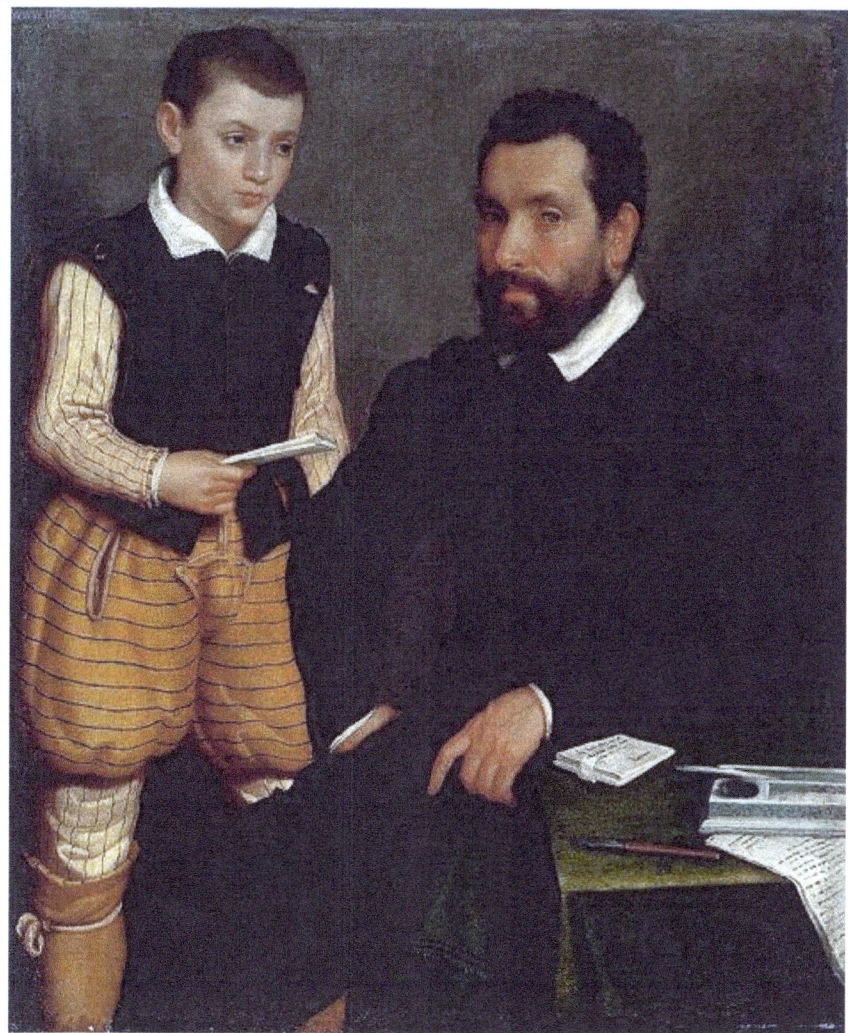

1.6. Giovanni Battista Moroni, *Seated Man and Boy bearing a Letter, Count Alborghetti and his Son*, ca. 1545, oil on canvas, Museum of Fine Arts, Boston, Museum purchase with funds donated by Mrs. Turner Sargent (Amelia J. Holmes), Turner Sargent Fund.

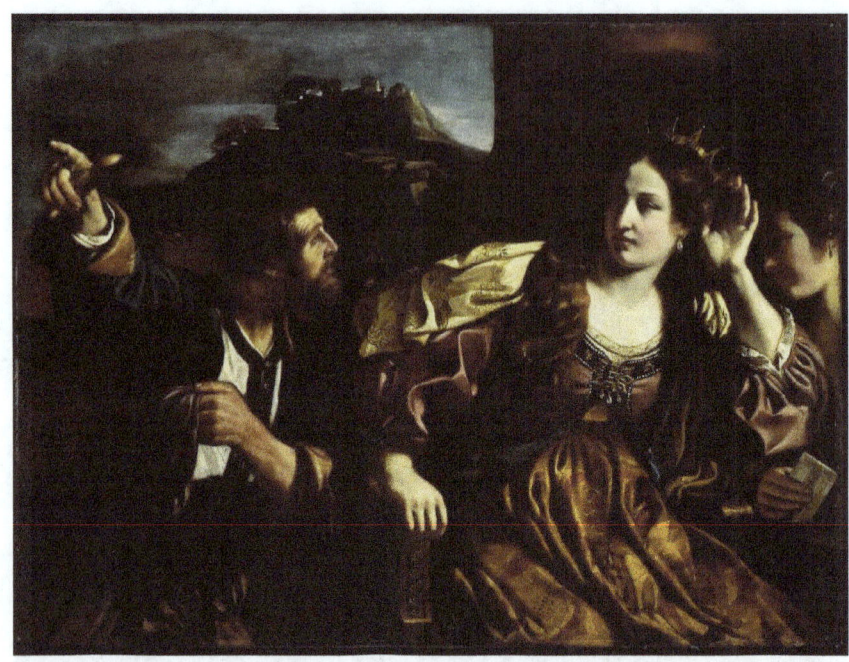

1.7. Guercino, *Semiramis Receiving the News of the Revolt of Babylon*, 1624, oil on canvas, Museum of Fine Arts, Boston, Francis Welch Fund.

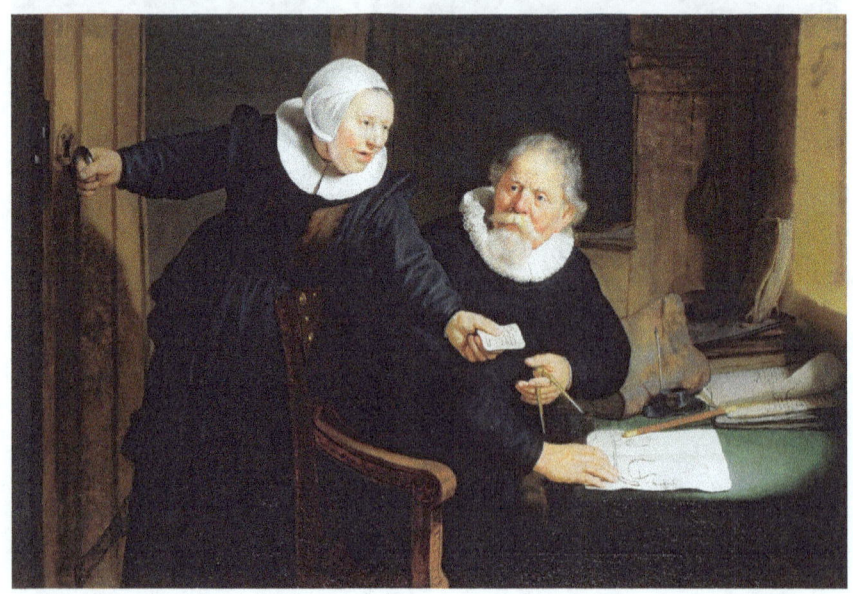

1.8. Rembrandt van Rijn, *'The Shipbuilder and his Wife'*, reversed.

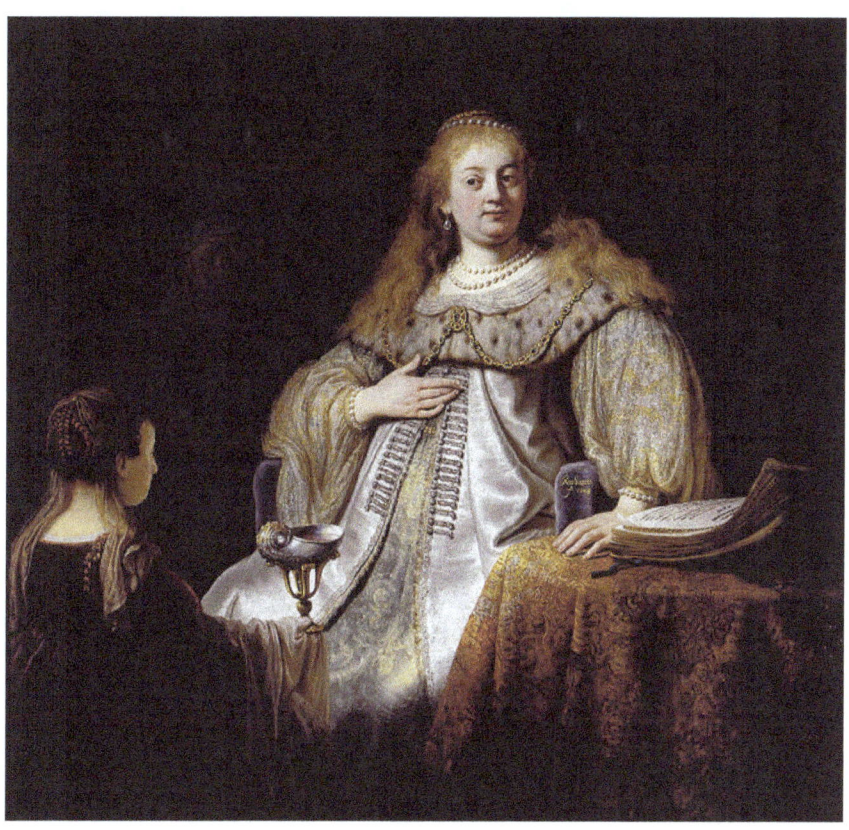

1.9. Rembrandt van Rijn, *Artemisia*, 1634, oil on canvas, Museo del Prado. Madrid.

2
Breeding and Bridling:
The Equestrian Marriage Portrait
in Georgian England

Margaret A. Hanni

Marriage portraits from Georgian England are often exceptionally fine pictures as well as fascinating social documents. William Hogarth, Thomas Gainsborough, Joseph Wright of Derby, Francis Cotes and George Stubbs are just a few of the artists who distinguished themselves with especially creative solutions to the demands of representing the husband and wife in the same canvas. A survey of British museums and National Trust houses demonstrates today that marriage portraits were a specialty of eighteenth-century England, and suggest the variety and quality of what was produced then in this idiosyncratic, charming and socially-charged genre.

The special popularity of the eighteenth-century marriage portrait in England is one of many indicators of Georgian society's near obsession with the "Question of Marriage." Texts of all sorts from the period disseminated arguments and ideals about the proper basis for marriage, who should control it, and for whose benefit. Many graphic examples satirized the aristocratic anxiety over diluting its ranks (or its coffers) through alliances from outside the nobility. Sermons, novels and plays presented prescriptions for happy unions and caricatures of unfortunate choices. Periodicals advised on polite courtship behaviors, complained about the costs of matrimony, and listed the amounts of marriage portions recent brides had brought to their husbands' families. Conduct literature and private letters offered advice on how to navigate the marriage market, as well as evidence of the negotiations that governed it. Even the law that regulated marriage changed in England, when Lord Hardwicke's Marriage Act was passed in 1753, making it more difficult for children to wed without a parent's knowledge. The upper ranks of English society literally couldn't afford to ignore the business of matrimony, for family privilege and power depended on the kind of assets that marriage often transmitted, including land, money and status. Parents made agreeable unions and settlements for their children far more often than fiction, drama and satire would have us believe, but such texts foreground anxieties and fantasies about marriage that point toward common concerns. Especially for those in the merchant and gentry ranks, an advantageous match represented the most effective means of upward mobility, while the aristocracy predictably employed wedlock as a mechanism to preserve and solidify its place within the social and political hierarchy, to retain, not disperse key assets. Portraits of spouses participated in this diverse, amusing, and sometimes cacophonous public discourse as many hundreds of marriage portraits joined family picture galleries; some were exhibited as art, and a few were engraved and widely disseminated.

Some of the most intriguing and idiosyncratic examples from the period are equestrian marriage portraits, in which the couple is shown riding, preparing for the hunt, or enjoying their estate from a carriage. This specialty must count as one of the most characteristically English of productions, with its inscription of the specifically rural possessions and recreations savored by the Georgian elite, new and old. The public conversation from the eighteenth century rehearses horsemanship—the art of riding, carriage-handling and breeding horses—eagerly and often, presents it as Englishness itself and as a specifically manly recreation, a defining pastime of the country gentleman. Equestrian marriage portraits, by artists like George Stubbs, Joseph Wright of Derby and others, should be viewed as performances that employ the symbols and language of horsemanship in the process of articulating something, not only about possessions and social status, but also about eighteenth-century marriage and family. Through the inclusion of images and ideas that held cultural currency, these portraits privilege the controlling role of the husband, inscribe the benefits of good breeding and bloodlines, equine and human, ratify the role of marriage as something that properly tempers the passions and underlines the stability that a well-made match promises to families and society.[1]

Numerous pamphlets, conduct manuals, and prints from the eighteenth century share the notion that marriage is useful in the tempering of passions, which—left unchecked—poses a threat to the material well-being of individuals or property, and thus families. Only by adhering to the proper laws or customs can temptation and other disruptive behaviors be held in check. A variety of texts from the period use the metaphor of the bridle, or bridling, to connote the moderation of passions fundamental to the successful marriage and its role in the ordering of society. Used in this context, the bridling metaphor signals a conservative ideology of marriage, one in which temperance and reason held sway over passion, so good matches were made based on their benefit to the future of the family, rather than individual affection or preference, and where the family was properly overseen by the guiding influence of the father, followed by the husband. These layers of potential meaning accrue to the eighteenth-century equestrian marriage portrait, and complement quite comfortably the ideals of privilege and good management that horsemanship also construed.

Therein lies the difficulty for the twenty-first-century viewer. What is fair to read into these images? How much can we posit for an eighteenth-century understanding of them? Is it plausible that patrons actually had in mind, say, the tempering of passions when they commissioned George Stubbs or Joseph Wright of Derby to create a portrait of their marriage? It seems very unlikely. The process of producing meaning from these images is more complex than a direct correlation of symbol to sitter. The subjects and the artists who portrayed them made pictorial choices that clearly possessed particular cultural currency. Horsemanship, breeding and bridling as they intersected with ideologies of marriage and family did represent a legible discourse in Georgian England, one that was widely recognized, especially among the ranks with the discretionary income to commission portraits. It is impossible to reconstruct the conversations of artists and sitters around these pictures. But it is fair, I think, to acknowledge the codes through which the couples chose to be represented, and the fact that the images were intended for display, typically in a family home and sometimes in more public spaces. The portraits spoke in culturally legible terms that encouraged or permitted inflections of privilege, prudence, good breeding and good management by the male, desirable means of framing a family alliance among the elite.

The early history of the imagery of horses and marriage yields emblems of rulership and order, dynastic genealogies and cautionary maxims about control. Renaissance and baroque equestrian marriage portraits all represent members of the ruling nobility. Their mounts mark their privileged stature and endorse their right to maintain it, by demonstrating the rider's ability to control his horse, and by extension, his people.[2] The hunt, too, was a significant motif in equestrian portraits, with its connotations of landed and aristocratic privilege. One especially relevant example is Daniel Mytens' *Charles I and Henrietta Maria*, from 1630-1632.[3] Charles I and his Queen stand hand-in-hand on a terrace, their horses and dogs nearby. The accoutrements of the hunt denote their status and the grand scale of the portrait leaves no doubt as to their singular importance. The Mytens portrait even suggests a quite direct precedent for the eighteenth-century; scaled down to a conversation piece size, this format was used with great success for equestrian marriage portraits of the Georgian aristocracy, and even more commonly, of the gentry.

It is easy to see how the assertions of rulership and landed privilege prominent in earlier equestrian marriage portraits appealed to the propertied ranks, new and old, in Georgian England. The mechanisms for social control and governance, linked to marriage, were now vested in landedness, inherited or purchased. The hunt maintained its associations with nobility, even as it became a more generalized marker of country life and the sport of well-to-do gentlemen. Good breeding became a metaphor for the quality of one's family alliances, as well as for polite behavior, even as it showed off the excellence of one's stable. Tailored once to the ruling class only, the equestrian marriage portrait in eighteenth-century England offered an engaging vehicle through which a gentry family might place itself on a visual par with the traditions of nobility.

Sports of the field animate a number of marriage and family portraits from Georgian England, even those that are not equestrian. Thomas Gainsborough's marriage portrait, *Mr. and Mrs. Andrews*, ca. 1750, (Fig. 1) displays Robert Andrews as a hunter, accompanied by his hound and presumably having delivered the game bird to

his young wife, Frances, which she holds in her lap, the only unfinished portion of the canvas. Robert's ability to provide for his new
bride is underlined in the painting by his up- to-date farming technique, the planting of wheat in rows rather than scattered. Hunting
and fowling figure in a variety of manuals on the art of being a
gentleman published throughout the century. These defined a class
and quality of person, explicitly male, by his recreational pursuits.
According to Richard Blome, author of *The Gentleman's Recreation*,
1710, the horse is crucial to many aspects of "manly recreation."
His introduction explains, "Horsemanship is a very Great Accom-
plishment in a person of Quality, or Gentleman."[4] It denoted status,
but also proper attention to male responsibilities. Thomas Fairfax,
in the preface to his 1795, *The Complete Sportsman*, locates the roots
of hunting for sport in the historical necessity of supporting one's
family, and points to "those manly performances...[as] essentials of
education." He compares the "laudable" pastime of hunting to the
"false pleasures that consume both health and fortune," and concludes, "There is nothing supports the dignity of man more than a
thorough acquaintance with the diversions of the field."[5] In *Persuasion*, Jane Austen points to the pretensions associated with these
non-productive, pointedly-gendered sports, "The Mr. Musgroves
had their own game to guard and destroy, their own horses, dogs
and newspapers to engage them, and the females were fully occupied in all the other common subjects of housekeeping, neighbors,
dress, dancing and music."[6] Just as the inclusion of an up-to-date
landscape garden as the background in a marriage portrait com-
mented upon the quality of the man who had sufficient taste and
resources to devote to such delightfully unproductive beauty, the
equestrian motif was capable of asserting the husband's proper
management of the land and the family through his avid or well-
appointed pursuit of expensive equestrian pastimes.

   George Stubbs' equestrian marriage portraits mark a high point
in English painting and are intriguing in their ability to present just
this sort of exposition, while at the same time suggesting Stubbs'
keen observations of the sitters who are pictured. Stubbs' career
coincided with the period when the English thoroughbred was
finally developed, and with it, the heyday of horse breeding and
racing in Britain. Hunting and horse racing had become so much

a part of the rural lifestyle of the landed classes that a distinctive iconography emerged in connection to it. This drew upon elements of both portraiture and sporting art, and in this particular context, the horse became a prominent attribute of upper-class Englishness itself. Especially after 1750, the horse assumed a more prominent role in portraits and conversation pieces, not primarily as sporting subjects, but as signs of the gentleman himself.[7]

Stubbs' style of painting, too, enhanced the expository power of his portraits. His restrained classical compositions embody order and control. Carriage wheels and horses' coats garner as much attention as the faces of the spouses. The intense legibility of his images renders them convincing as statements of fact. *His Lady and Gentleman in a Phaeton,* 1787 (Fig. 2) and *The Milbanke and Melbourne Families,* 1769-1770 (Fig. 3), both now in the National Gallery, London, demonstrate superbly Stubbs' ability to fashion images that celebrate, and appear to document, the idiosyncratic relationship of English landed society to its horses. His portraits assert for the sitters a status in society defined by its equestrian pastimes. So, too, the visual language of horsemanship inflects them with ideas about marriage that at the time had cultural currency.

George Stubbs, for all the care he lavishes on horses and harnesses, nonetheless provides a rather animated image of spouses, in his *Lady and Gentleman in a Phaeton,* 1787. The picture places the couple--probably well-to-do gentry--their horses and carriage in the immediate foreground with a generalized landscape behind them. We are invited to focus on the fine horses and the phaeton they will pull, and through them, to appreciate the status of the couple. But the image also comments on the man in particular. This phaeton was likely designed especially for this as-yet-unidentified Englishman, as it became popular for gentlemen to drive their own custom-made carriages. "Driving became a form of sport in which gentlemen prided themselves on driving as well as a coachman, and in which elegance of turnout was as important as display of skill."[8] The man holding the reins is active as he leans forward in his seat, and, though his wife seems inattentive to him, she engages the viewer. Stubbs accentuates the lightness of her face, framed with dark curls and topped with the marvelous hat whose plumes echo the shape of the trees behind. The woman's outward look encourages us to engage her, to appreciate her fashionable attire and how it perfectly suits her husband's fine horses and equipage. Though the portrait revolves around a well-rehearsed sign of the husband-in-control, the artist and presumably his patrons, chose to give the lady an unusual "speaking" role, but one that underlines typical gender roles of the period. Stubbs' meticulous treatment of animals and equipment just adds to our desire to believe that the picture records, rather than invents, a real situation; his legibility adds authority to the image.

Stubbs' remarkable care in describing horses' harnesses coincides with his close observation of the subjects he painted and signals his desire to articulate as precisely as possible the mechanics of horsemanship at the time. But the image of the bridle or reins as a symbol of temperance and controlled desire or passions has a long visual and literary history that continued into the eighteenth century. The image appears in an English emblem book as early as 1635, in which a woman holds a bridle in one hand and a ruler in the other, while beyond her a horse is being tamed by two men. The accompanying verse reads, "Doe not the golden Meane, exceed,/ In word, in Passion, nor in deed."[9] Dutch emblems, too, associated the bridle with proper behavior, and presented it specifically in the context of marriage. Jacob Cats' *Spinster's Coat of Arms*, 1625, indicates that matrimony is the only acceptable way for a man to make a maiden his own, and shows the young woman on the left, identified by the inscription as "Modesty," standing before a bridle.[10] In Cesare Ripa's *Iconologia*, first translated into English in 1709, the figure of Temperance holds a bridle, which, according to the attached text, restrains the appetites. Joseph Spence, in his *Guide to Classical Learning*, 1764, a manual intended for "those who wish to have a true taste for the beauties of Poetry, Sculpture and Painting," explains the bridle in hand as the symbol for temperance.[11]

One also finds many references in eighteenth-century literature to the bridling of passions, specifically in the context of the necessity for marriage to serve and maintain the social order. In a *Spectator* essay of 1712 about husbands' expectations and how to manage one's family, Richard Steele referred his readers to Socrates' comments about living with his difficult wife, Xantippe, "That they who learn to keep a good Seat on horseback, mount the least manageable they can get, and when they have master'd them, they are sure never to be discompos'd on the Backs of Steeds less restive."[12] The model for princes and kings in the Renaissance Steele translates to the husband's governance of his wife.[13] Tancred Leman, in his essay in support of the Lord Hardwicke's Marriage Act of 1753, argues that people simply need to be controlled. Men especially, in his construction, abandon themselves to ardor, and laws are necessary to replace that drive with prudence. In order to "bridle the passions," he recommends "... the ceremonies and rites connected to marriage, through which one becomes entitled to privileges and protection of the community."[14] Another advocate of the 1753 Marriage Act, Joseph Sayer, argued that the only way to protect property is to restrain temptation, though, in his view, women are more likely to be swayed to make imprudent decisions than are men. In either case, the control of this flaw is crucial. Sayer uses an equestrian metaphor to explain himself, writing that "...passion is a high mettled colt, which if at first well broke affords his master many delightful rides; but for want of this is all his life long unruly, vicious and dangerous."[15] The use of an equestrian metaphor to describe gender roles in marriage also appeared in *A Series of Genuine Letters between Henry and Frances*, a several volume set by Richard and Elizabeth Griffin, published in several editions between 1757 and 1770. In one example, Henry writes to his wife, "The Husband should hold the long Reins in his Hand and *seem* to drive; it looks manly, and saves Appearances; but the Wife should always *underhand* be allowed to take the *leading Rein*."[16] Here, the writer satirizes the stereotype of the husband in control, more evidence, I think, that this sort of equestrian metaphor was widely recognized at the time to connote a properly managed marriage.

George Stubbs' *The Milbanke and Melbourne Families*, 1769-1770 (Fig. 3), presents just such an image. The couple is literally embedded in the context of the larger family and the equestrian milieu asserts that order and affluence mark this match. The portrait commemorates the April 1769 marriage of Elizabeth Milbanke, age 16, to Sir Peniston Lamb, 24, 2nd Baronet, later 1st Lord Melbourne in the Irish peerage (1770). In eighteenth-century terms, the match represented a promising union of two socially well-suited families. Sir Ralph Milbanke, MP, Elizabeth's father, was 5th Baronet, his merchant grandfather having been created first baronet by patent in 1661 by Charles II. Lord Melbourne's family had been admitted to the peerage only fairly recently, in 1755, with the elevation to baronet for his father Matthew Lamb. Melbourne's family's shorter history in the peerage would likely have been more than made up for by the considerable fortune he inherited at his father's death in 1768, estimated at half a million in property and again as much in sterling.[17]

Stubbs' portrait, entitled *A Conversation* when it was exhibited at the Society of Artists in 1770, seduces us with a sense of privileged leisure and restrained propriety. We detect no personal engagement between Elizabeth, at left in her pony cart, and her husband, Lord Melbourne, opposite and facing her astride his expensive Arabian horse. While Lord Melbourne fixes his attention upon his young wife, it is her father, Sir Ralph Milbanke, standing beside her, who glances toward Melbourne, while Elizabeth looks out at the viewer, as she holds a whip in one hand and reins slack in the other. Whether Stubbs intended it or not, her placement in the cart seems an apt metaphor for this kind of eighteenth-century marriage, in which the woman passes from her father's family to her husband's. She is the person in the picture, and in the family, who migrates. In the middle ground, standing beside his horse in the conspicuously fashionable cross-legged pose is Elizabeth's brother, John Milbanke, who, like her, looks at the viewer. There is an ordered progression from one figure to the next. The three Milbankes are grouped under the majestic tree, while Melbourne stands just outside its shade. His spaniel points us to him, and we follow his gaze and his horse's arched neck across the back of John Milbanke's horse to Elizabeth's stocky pony, whose harness leads us to her and to her father. The small, dark spaniel next to her cart balances Melbourne's white dog, just as he and Elizabeth complement each other, his dark shape against light sky balancing the brightness of her face and clothing set into the dark foliage behind her. Despite this careful arrangement, the figures remain quite separate, articulated individually, but unengaged with one another; no conversation or personal attention is evident.[18]

Surely, though, this equestrian portrait makes a positive statement about the marriage it presents. For the eighteenth century, we might posit something like this: Good breeding and prudence direct this merger between two similarly endowed families. Order promises continued prosperity and privilege for all. Clarity and legibility argue persuasively that what we see is true.[19] As it turned out, the union proved to be more successful on a financial than a personal level. Within months of the marriage, Lord Melbourne was a client of the courtesan Sophia Baddeley, in whose memoirs he figures. And Elizabeth, Lady Melbourne, for her own part, seems to have had liaisons with three especially powerful men, the Prince of Wales, the Earl of Egremont, and the Duke of Bedford. Family histories remind us that portraits like the Stubbs construct an ideal, no matter how realistic the representation.

In an example from several years later, in which his sitters are well-to-do gentry rather than aristocracy, George Stubbs unknowingly presents us with a fascinating opportunity to consider how the language of horsemanship translated ideas of family and breeding into a portrait of wedlock intended for Colwick Hall's picture gallery. In his *John and Sophia Musters Riding at Colwick Hall*, 1777, (Fig. 4) the couple rides across the foreground of the picture, mostly in profile, set against a carefully rendered backdrop of John Musters' newly renovated home, Colwick Hall. The year before, Musters had married Sophia, eldest daughter and co-heir of James Modyford Heywood of Maristowe, Devon, and soon after, he had become High Sheriff of Nottingham, an important post in local politics.[20] The choice of George Stubbs as the artist, and an equestrian double portrait for the format surely reflect Musters' own well-documented interest in horse breeding and racing and suggest his eagerness to document his newly-elevated status. In fact, during 1777-1778, Stubbs had been commissioned to create seven pictures for Musters, more than from any other of Stubbs' patrons, including two equestrian portraits with Sophia, three separate portraits of his horses, and two of Mrs. Musters' spaniels, an overall grouping that fully characterized the "man of property" of the day.[21]

In one portrait, the placement of Sophia and John on a hill higher than the level of the country house underscores Musters' proprietary relationship to the land. The regular divisions of the classical facade behind the figures are echoed in the intervals at which Stubbs places the white dog and the two horses, subtly conveying a sense of orderly procession. Sophia leads the way. In her scarlet riding habit and fashionable black hat, she is the standout focus of the work. We might well read Sophia here, too, in her economic role, as one of the many valuable assets that John Musters has acquired, a sign of his affluence, literally trotted out for display alongside the other possessions that mark his status. In this sense, the image seems conventional in focusing on the man as the definer of the couple's position. But Sophia's prominence argues that she is a more active agent in the portrait. Stubbs departs from the convention of showing the man directing the action, not just by placing Sophia in the lead, but also by having her engage the viewer. In the orderly parade of possessions, Sophia interrupts things. Her gaze invites the viewer's conversation and appreciation. The variation, of course, is not enough to undermine the gender hierarchies implicit in the image. John Musters' profile portrait keeps him aloof; he is clearly understood as the proprietor here, among other things, of an especially spirited wife. The Musters, as it turned out, lived much of their married life separately, with John preferring country life and Sophia residing primarily in London.

Reynold's extravagant *Mrs. Musters as Hebe*, from 1785, now in the collection at Kenwood House, portrays Sophia as cupbearer to the gods. With its grand scale, mythological theme, elegance and sensuality, it announces very boldly Sophia Musters' role as a London hostess, and departs quite radically from earlier portraits of her as the country gentlewoman. John eventually became convinced of his wife's infidelity and, though he never divorced her, he drastically altered the two Stubbs portraits that commemorated their marriage. In the portrait where the couple rides in front of their country seat, (Fig. 4) Musters had an unknown artist paint out the figure of Sophia. Once Sophia's figure was covered by horse and clouds, the solitary Musters followed a riderless horse, which must have been an unsatisfactory solution, so John had his own figure over painted as well, and grooms leading the horses were added. The over painting was not removed until the 1930s.[22]

In another other equestrian marriage portrait by Stubbs, *John Musters and the Rev. Philip Story riding out from the Stable Block at Colwick Hall*, 1777, still in a private collection, John was pictured in the lead, his wife behind him on her grey horse, situated before the stable and kennel block Musters had recently built. At their feet are four of Musters' famous pack of foxhounds—no doubt portraits of specific dogs—and a hunt servant brings up the rear.[23] In this case, Musters had George Stubbs replace Sophia with a portrait of the Reverend Philip Story, the Vicar of Lockington, a fox-hunting friend of John. This picture retains the changes made by Musters. In each painting, an image of marriage and family is translated quite readily into a commemoration of the "good breeding" of horses and hounds for which Musters was well known.

Ronald Paulson interpreted Muster's action as an acknowledgment that Sophia was essentially his property, that he therefore controlled her presence (or absence) in the image, a view that the visual language of the portrait entirely supports.[24] It is easy to imagine that Musters, angry and disappointed, found it impossible to live with a portrait that suggested his vision of a particular kind of married life, one in which Sophia had starred in some way that we see expressed in the original vivacious portrayal by Stubbs. Sophia's role there is tempered by the order in which it is imbedded. It is not implausible to see this painting, in eighteenth-century terms, as an image that calls attention to an especially beautiful and sociable wife, while it presents her as safely and properly in step with her husband. Once Musters believed that order compromised, he took steps to excise his wife from the images. The removal of Sophia from the Stubbs' double portraits neatly transformed them from significant pictures of a rising gentry family into documents of John's expensive manly pursuits. The ease of the translation is telling; analogies between the good breeding of horses and a distinguished family genealogy seemed quite natural in the upwardly mobile milieu in which Musters' lived. Once "the marriage" was obliterated from the painting, a desirable order was restored to it.

The omission of Sophia from two paintings likely hardly changed what Musters' picture gallery recited *ensemble* about his family. The alteration would primarily affect how viewers saw him. Without Sophia, the pictures' now-purely equestrian and hunting themes still framed the family in the legible and desirable light of the country gentleman. The two altered portraits have nearly identical measurements with another picture by Stubbs, *John Musters' Brood Mares in Colwick Hall Park*, 1777, something that suggests that

Musters at one time hung the three works together or intended to do so. If that were the case, the parallels between the good breeding of family and of horses would have been explicit; the beautiful bride who promised progeny to carry on John Musters' estate and name hanging beside the brood mares whose offspring likewise elevated Musters' status and standing. The possibility that such a picture hanging was planned or executed is evidence of the active dialogue that existed more generally in eighteenth-century England between portraits, living subjects, and a family's cumulative picture of itself.

Despite the dramatic alterations to the Musters' pictures and the fact that he gave the women unusual roles in which they engage the viewer, Stubbs produced typical eighteenth-century marriage portraits, in that propriety, order and markers of family status tend to supersede emotional content. But a handful of equestrian portraits demonstrate a different approach, one that foregrounds the sense of a personal relationship. One of the most evocative is *Mr. and Mrs. Thomas Coltman*, ca.1771 by Joseph Wright of Derby (1734-1797), (Fig. 5) in which the artist balances signs of the privileged milieu of the country gentleman with a lively characterization of the young couple's affection for one another. Wright situates the Coltmans in front of Gate Burton, a country home that they leased at the time. Thomas inherited the family seat, Hagnaby Priory, near Boston, Lincolnshire, after the death of his elder brother, but the couple did not move there until the 1780s.[25] As Wright presents him, one would never guess that Coltman was relatively new to the gentry, his great uncle, a successful London merchant, having purchased his estate only in 1715.[26] Wright carefully articulates Coltman as a country squire and sportsman, impeccably and fashionably dressed, at ease with the land, his horse and his wife.

Wright, too, conveys a great deal of information about the Coltmans' relationship. Thomas is primary here. He stands at the center, his right hand in a directing gesture, his pose the very picture of confidence and control. The blue of his waistcoat and white frock coat are repeated in the sky, and his yellow breeches echo the color of the earth around him. Wright literally connects him to the countryside that denotes his status and his pleasure. Mary stands out for the rosy red of her riding habit and her height, enhanced by the white of her hat against the trees behind her. But her focus, too, is on Thomas, and if we are initially drawn to her, she then directs us to him, with the tilt of her head and her affectionate expression as she attends to what he says.

Wright's portrait of the Coltmans stands out among Georgian marriage portraits for its very personal quality, a result, perhaps in part, of the fact that the artist was a friend of his patrons. He lived near the Coltmans, had done charcoal portraits of them in 1769, and included them in one of his most innovative subject pictures, *An Experiment on a Bird in the Air Pump*, 1768. There he shows them looking quite intently at each other, not at the dramatic experiment taking place in their presence.[27] In addition to the portraits, Coltman owned two candlelight pictures by Wright and also a self-portrait, probably a gift of the artist.[28] In depicting the Coltmans, Wright demonstrates his command of the visual codes of privilege in rural England, but he introduces an interaction between the figures that is quite new to the equestrian portrait, and unconventional for marriage portraits in general at the time. Unlike the examples by Stubbs, the horses here remain subordinate to the people in visual interest. Signs of property and all it implies, they provide an activity that husband and wife share and enjoy, directed, naturally, by Thomas. Wright presents their marriage as a picture of affection and pleasure, underpinned by order and propriety.

The equestrian marriage portrait seems to have been uniquely suited to the landed classes of Georgian England, for it developed in that culture as it did nowhere else. Its special popularity with the gentry makes sense in a society where the country life, and horsemanship in particular, articulated a quintessential upper-class Englishness that seemed to be ancient and aristocratic even when it wasn't. Traditional associations between horses and marriage, breeding and bridling, migrated to eighteenth-century England, where they, too, participated in the public conversation over purposes and paradigms for wedlock. Because of the cultural codes they tapped, and the visual language they employed, these images of horsemanship made spirited arguments for a conservative ideology of matrimony, one governed by fathers and husbands, marked by order and restraint that preserved estates and possessions for future generations. With its ability to inscribe privilege, prudence, and good management, the equestrian marriage portrait presented an especially English way to frame a well-made match and the stable family prosperity it promised.

End Notes

[1] For other equestrian marriage portraits, see Arthur Devis, Francis Wheatley, Johan Zoffany, and Sawrey Gilpin.

[2] For an excellent history of the equestrian portrait, see Walter Liedtke, *The Royal Horse and Rider* (New York: Metropolitan Museum of Art, 1989) and also Horst Janson, "The Equestrian Monument from Cangrande della Scala to Peter the Great," in *Aspects of the Renaissance,* Archibald R. Lewis, ed. (Austin: U. Texas Press, 1967).

[3] See also Adriaen Van de Venne, *Frederick V of the Palatinate and his Wife Elizabeth Stuart on Horseback*, 1628. Both are reproduced in Liedtke; the Mytens is cat. 128, and the van de Venne is cat. 175.

[4] Richard Blome, *The Gentleman's Recreation* (London, 1710), 1. Liedtke notes that the equation of horsemanship with the idea of the gentleman goes back to Castiglione's *The Courtier* (1516), 79.

[5] Thomas Fairfax, Esq. *The Complete Sportsman; or Country Gentleman's Recreation* (London, 1795), np.

[6] Jane Austen, *Persuasion* (1818) in *The Complete Novels of Jane Austen* (New York: Modern Library, nd), chapter 6.

[7] Ronald Paulson, *Emblem and Expression* (Cambridge, MA: Harvard University Press, 1975), 160 and 165. Taylor, 12.

[8] Judy Egerton, *George Stubbs, Painter: Catalogue Raisonné* (New Haven: Yale University Press, 2007), 502.

[9] George Wither, *A Collection of Emblemes, ancient and moderne* (London, 1635), 169.

[10] Jan Baptist Bedaux, *The Reality of Symbols* ('s-Gravenhage/ Maarssen: Gary Schwartz, 1990), 141 and figure 73.

[11] Joseph Spence, *A Guide to Classical Learning; or Polymetis Explained* (London, 1764), 205.

[12] [Richard Steele] *The Spectator* no. 479 (9 Sept. 1712)

[13] For example, a sixteenth-century emblem by Alciati titled *In Adulari Nescientum*, pictures a prince on horseback. Liedtke translates the title "To him unable to flatter," and explains that it alludes to the fact that ability, not flattery, is the only way to control a horse. As a horse learns to respect a man for his skill as a ride, not his rank, so the people respect a king for his ability to govern, Liedtke, 42-43.

[14] Tancred Leman, *Matrimony Analysed* (London, 1755), 7 and 60-61.

¹⁵ Joseph Sayer, *A Vindication of the Power of Society to Annull the Marriages of Minors, entered into without the Consent of Parents or Guardians in Which the Objections made thereto, in tow Pamplets lately published by the Reverend Dr. Stebbing are fully considered* (London, 1755), 43-46, 55-56.

¹⁶ Richard and Elizabeth Griffith, *A Series of genuine Letters between Henry and Frances* (London: W. Johnston, 1767-1772), V, 244.

¹⁷ DNB, 13/369 and 11/432.

¹⁸ Judy Egerton, *George Stubbs, Painter: Catalogue Raisonné* (London: Paul Mellon Center for Studies in British Art, 2007), 319 and n. 5.

¹⁹ Malcolm Elwin, *The Noels and the Milbankes. Their letters for twenty-five years* (London: MacDonald, 1967), 19.

²⁰ Judy Egerton, *George Stubbs 1724-1806* (London: Tate Gallery, 1984), 156.

²¹ Egerton, *George Stubbs, Painter: Catalogue Raisonné*, 57.

²² The alteration and restoration of the painting were first described by H. Wilberforce Bell, "The Vicissitudes of a Picture by George Stubbs," *Country Life* (26 Sept. 1936), lii-liii. Were it not for the fact that Musters had his wife's face over-painted in another work by Stubbs, one might assume that Musters simply disliked the double portrait, and tried to make it into something different. Egerton notes the similar treatment of the second painting, and suggests what seems a plausible explanation for the alterations. Egerton, *George Stubbs 1724-1806*, 157-158.

²³ Egerton, *George Stubbs, Painter: Catalogue Raisonné*, 392.

²⁴ Taylor observes that it was Stubbs who painted out the figure of Mrs. Musters. Basil Taylor, *Stubbs* (London: Phaidon, 1971), 211. Paulson concurs, noting that Stubbs did so in a way that it made it possible to recover her when the painting was restored in 1935-6. Ronald Paulson, "Hambletonian, Rubbing Down: George Stubbs and English Society," *Raritan* 4 (Spring 1985) 36-37.

²⁵ David Fraser, "Joseph Wright's portraits of Mr. and Mrs. Coltman and Colonel Heathcote," *Christie's Review of the Season* (1985), 48 and Judy Egerton, *Wright of Derby* (London, Tate Gallery, 1990), 73.

²⁶ Henry Coltman purchased Hagnaby Priory, and after his only son died, entailed the property on his nephew John, Thomas's father. Thomas was the fifth child, and second son. Benedict Nicolson, *Joseph Wright of Derby; Painter of Light*, 2 vols. (London, Routledge, Kegan Paul, 1968), I. 107.

²⁷ The charcoal heads are published in Nicolson, II, plates 118 and 119. Egerton, *Wright of Derby*, 59. The work is in collection of the National Gallery, London, and reproduced in Egerton, *Wright of Derby*, 59.

²⁸ Nicolson, 107-108.

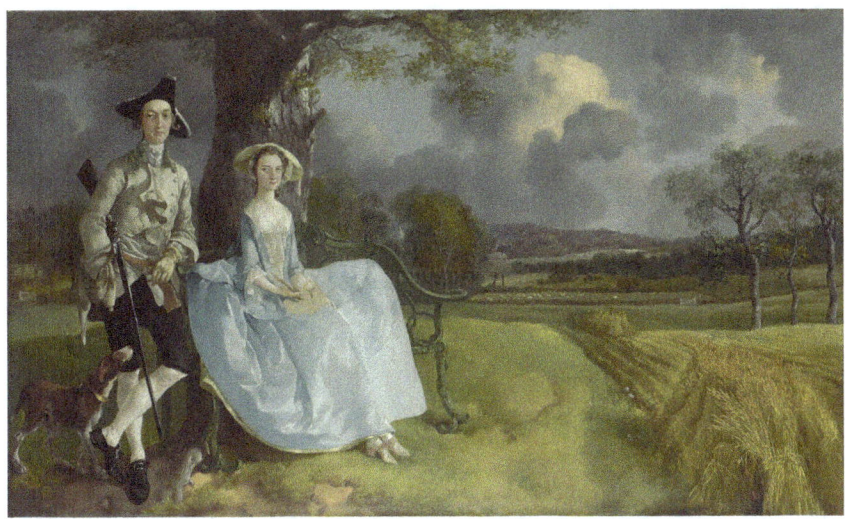

2.1. Thomas Gainsborough, *Mr. And Mrs. Robert Andrews,* ca 1750, oil on canvas, photo credit: ©The National Gallery, London.

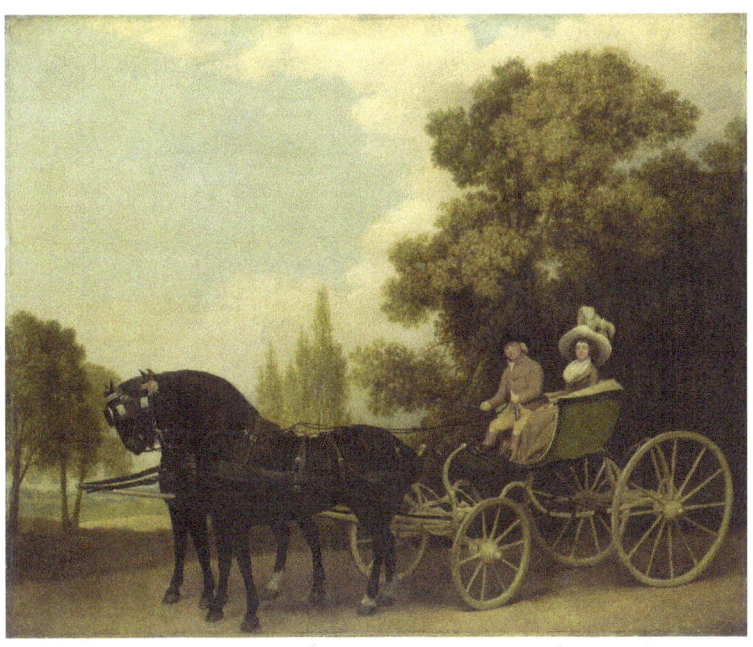

2.2. George Stubbs, *A Gentleman Driving a Lady in a Phaeton,* 1787, oil on canvas, photo credit: ©The National Gallery, London.

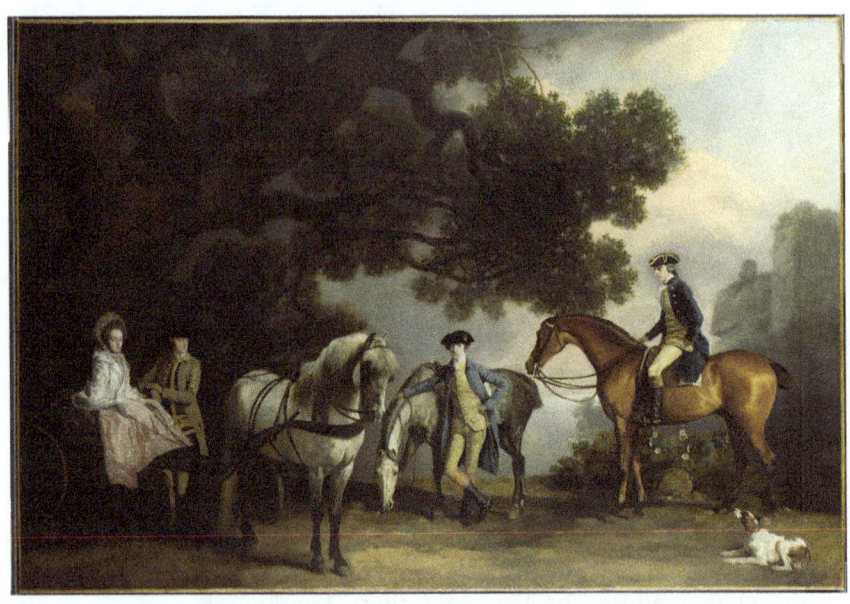

2.3. George Stubbs, *Sir Peniston and Lady Lamb, Later Lord and Lady Melbourne, with Lady Lamb's Father, Sir Ralph Milbanke, and Her Brother John Milbanke ('The Milbanke and Melbourne Families')*, 1769-70, oil on canvas, photo credit: ©The National Gallery, London.

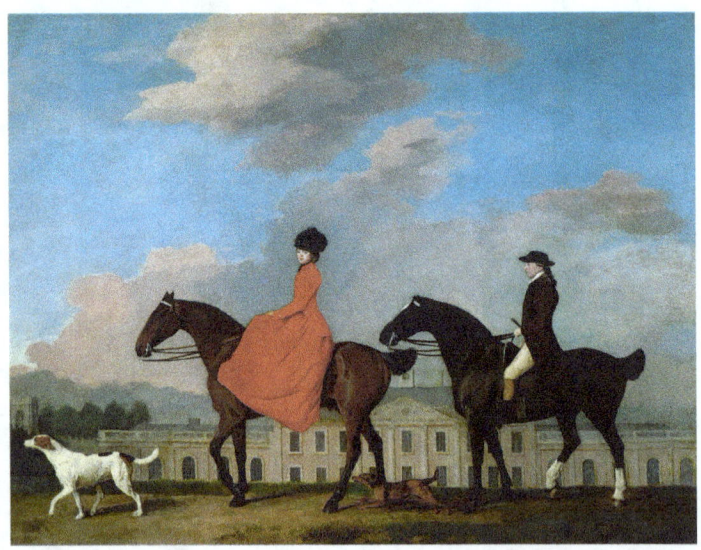

2.4. George Stubbs, *John and Sophia Musters at Colwick Hall*, 1777, oil on canvas, private collection, photo credit: the Bridgeman Art Library.

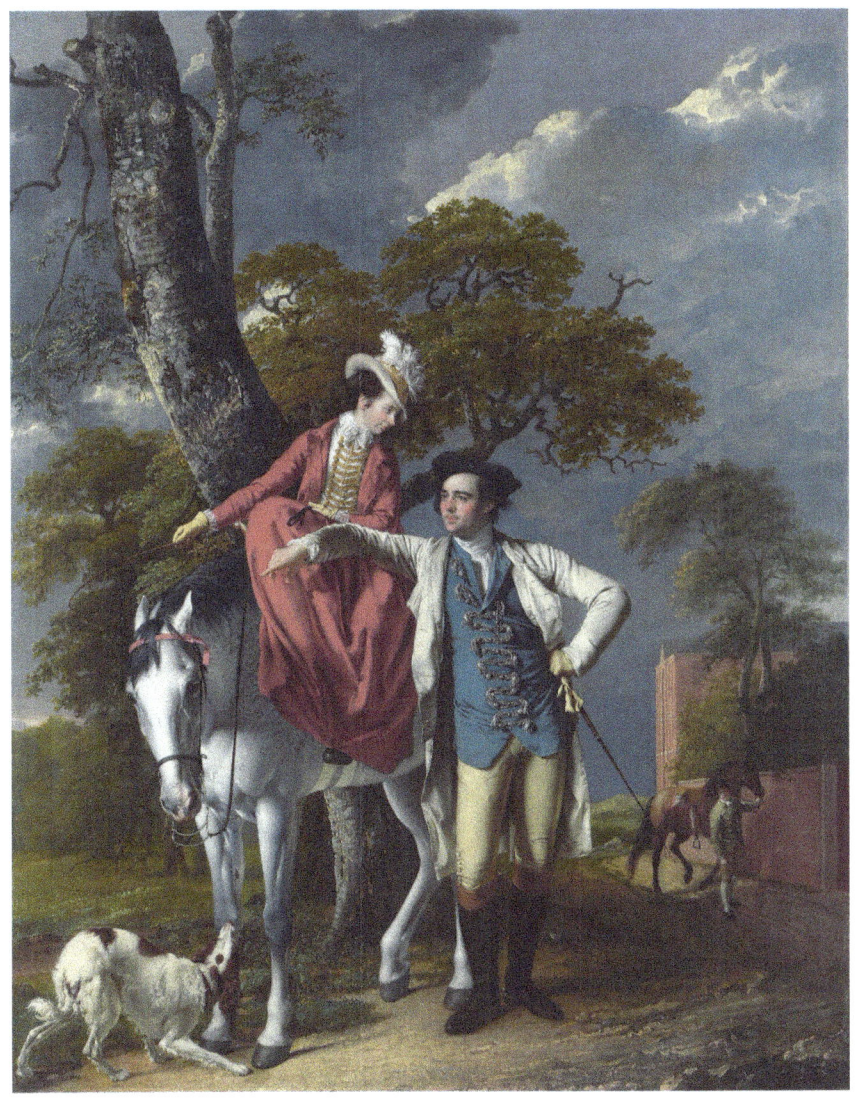

2.5. Joseph Wright of Derby, *Mr. and Mrs. Thomas Coltman,* ca.1771, oil on canvas, photo credit: ©The National Gallery, London.

3
The Pre-Raphaelization of
the Modern Literary Heroine

Susan P. Casteras

Pre-Raphaelitism remains a phenomenon that generates a tenacious holding power, popularity, and longevity in the twenty-first century, and among the hitherto unexplored aspects of this subject is its impact on late twentieth and early twenty-first century fiction. Thus far, there has been no in-depth examination of how modern writers have, in the realms particularly of the mystery genre as well as historical and contemporary fiction, incorporated Pre-Raphaelitism, especially in regard to femininity, into their writings. While some authors assign only occasional descriptive traits indebted to Pre-Raphaelitism to their female characters, others make this a driving force behind their stories and dramatis personae. This essay will investigate the content, significance, and linkage among several key works and motifs, comparing and contrasting these as well as indicating which specific images, principally by John Everett Millais, Dante Gabriel Rossetti, and Edward Burne-Jones, recur most often in authorial constructions of the Pre-Raphaelite female.

Before progressing, it is compelling to ask whether this current affection for Pre-Raphaelite artists, pictures, and heroines might have been predicted. Just why does this art continue to fascinate the public, in online blogs and eBay as well as in literature, films, and fashion? Why does Pre-Raphaelitism still permeate cultural consciousness while other types of nineteenth-century art movements (excepting Impressionism) have not? Pre-Raphaelite paintings and characters now penetrate most media, and it is revealing to consider how the very term "Pre-Raphaelite" has not only been stretched, but also sometimes misunderstood, misinterpreted, and degraded to a near breaking point of absurdity and, at times, hilarity.

In modern literature, championing the "Pre-Raphs" has proven a major international industry, privileging this band of artists above others and creating a "brand" to market and for consumers to "own" by merely purchasing a book. This process and awareness perhaps can be traced back to Victorian precedents like Mary Elizabeth Braddon's 1862 sensation novel *Lady Audley's Secret*, which today is matched by current authors keen to sell Pre-Raphaelitism in literary products that define femininity in a dazzling cast of characters from murder victims to seductresses, detectives, flappers, museum curators, and ladies of the drawing room.

The Pre-Raphaelite cult in the mystery genre is an apt place to start, for example, with P.D. James, who cites Millais, Holman Hunt, Rossetti, and William Morris in various books. In *The Skull Beneath the Skin* (1982), there are numerous such references to a "...six-foot tapestry...almost certainly by William Morris" and a cabinet by him as well, works by Holman Hunt, and a Millais double portrait in which the girls strike poses that "...were awkward, almost angular, and the faces with their bright, exophthalmic eyes...."[1] Years later, in James's *Death in Holy Orders* (2001), there are more extensive remarks registered by detective Adam Dalgliesh, who notices a disjunction between "aggressively modern" furnishings in a refectory with Victorian elements. Besides a Burne-Jones decorated sideboard, above the fireplace "...was a Burne-Jones oil, a beautiful romantic dream...Four young women, garlanded and wearing long pink-and-brown dresses of flowered muslin, were grouped round an apple tree..."[2] Later James notes other Pre-Raphaelite works there: "One, by Dante Gabriel Rossetti, showed a girl with flaming red hair seated at a window and reading a book...."[3] The second is Burne-Jones's aforementioned painting, "...and the third and largest, by William Holman Hunt, showed a priest outside a wattle chapel baptizing a group of ancient Britons."[4]

Arguably the most prolific contributor to the "Pre-Raphaelizing" of mystery fiction is Anne Perry, who since the 1980s has responded to the demands, even the voracious appetites, of the reading public for increasing amounts of modern Victorian fantasies and "goods." Her books are rife with references to Pre-Raphaelitism—

e.g., Millais is mentioned in *Death in the Devil's Acre* (1985), while in *Bethlehem Road* (1990) Rossettian traits define Africa, for whom "Rossetti could have used her perfect Pre-Raphaelite face in one of his Arthurian romances; she had all the earthy naïveté and the unconscious strength of his subjects."[5] In *Cardington Crescent* (1987), Perry describes a character as "...holding forth on the chivalry of the Pre-Raphaelite painters, their meticulousness of detail and delicacy of color...but..., she totally misunderstood what he believed to be the concept."[6] *Farrier's Lane* (1993) recycles this feminine type, positing the character Caroline as "...in the romantic vision of the Pre-Raphaelites, her gown with a design of flowers and leaves."[7] Perry even alludes in *Half Moon Street* to what becomes the main visual prototype appropriated by modern writers, Millais's *Ophelia* (Fig. 1). She even opens this novel with a drifting boat containing a dead male in female drag, "...like some obscure parody of Millais's painting of Ophelia."[8] Ultimately detective William Pitt concludes that a death had been "...perpetrated by a person of high emotion and a great deal of imagination, and presumably a familiarity with art, to mimic Millais's painting of Ophelia so closely."[9] As these examples attest, Perry typically brandishes Pre-Raphaelitism as a convenient and compact literary symbol for a type of Victorian woman understood by her readers to be identifiably "Pre-Raphaelite" in appearance and spirit.

The Pre-Raphaelite aura and legend are often invoked to enhance the visuals not only of people, but also interior spaces and scenes. P.D. James in *The Private Patient* (2008) supplies copious detail about a town house in word-pictures worthy of John Ruskin: "...There was a certain feminine elegance about the facade, and... it was in this part of London that Victorian and Edwardian gentlemen provided houses for their mistresses. Remembering Holman Hunt's painting *The Awakening Conscience*, he brought to mind a cluttered sitting room, a young woman starting up, bright—eyed, from the piano, her lounging lover, one hand on the keys, reaching out to her."[10] Perry too declares the interior and decorative aspects of Pre-Raphaelitism, and in *Bethlehem Road*, police detective Thomas Pitt (who has married a woman of a higher class and thus presumably absorbed her aesthetic tastes through osmosis) wonders whether the aristocratic owners chose the paintings, which were

"...cool, romantic, after the style of the Pre-Raphaelites; women with enigmatic faces and lovely hair, knights in armor, and twined flowers."[11] Similarly, in the same author's *Belgrave Square* (1992), a ladies' boudoir is filled with "...pre-Raphaelite paintings, all brooding and passionate faces, clean lines of design and dark, burning colors. Figures of legend and dream...depicted in noble poses...."[12]

Increasingly in the 1990s and beyond, mystery writers became obsessed with reincarnating the Pre-Raphaelite female. In Gillian Arscott's *Absent Friends* (1999), the author describes Lucinda Sollers as an auburn-haired, Burne-Jonesian mermaid who "gave the impression of bonelessness like a victim in a Pre-Raphaelite painting."[13] Katherine Hall Page's *A Body in the Big Apple* (1999) traces the adventures of a rich girl named Emma Morris Stanstead, who "looked like a model for one of the Pre-Raphaelite painters, Jane Morris—an ancestress?—in an outfit by Donna Karan."[14] Nancy Atherton's light-hearted *Aunt Dimity Beats the Devil* (2000) puts forward a passive Victorian-style female, Nicole Hollander, who, with "a wavy mane nearly to her waist", looked like "a wild-haired damsel from a Pre-Raphaelite painting."[15] The best-selling author Elizabeth Peters, whose series on the exploits of an extraordinary family of Egyptologists has been a huge success with fans and critics, includes in *The Falcon at the Portal* (1999) this emotion-charged encounter:

> They faced one another across the cage, and...the tableau would have made a splendid subject for one of the pre-Raphaelite painters like Holman Hunt, or the great Dante Gabriel Rossetti. On one side the maiden, crowned with the coils of her golden hair; on the other, the tall dark-haired youth...Rossetti would probably give the maiden robes of forest-green velvet...[16]

Another author, Claire Berlinski, in *Loose Lips: A Roman à Claire* (2003) envisions Selena Keller, a CIA agent, being drawn by someone during a lecture: "In his portrait I had no flaws...my hair cascaded in Pre-Raphaelite ringlets down my back...It was the way I LIKED to think I looked, but deep down I knew better."[17] Berlinski's heroine seems to enjoy her moment of being a Pre-Raphaelite female, despite the fact that in her own time she personifies hard-nosed, tough street smarts rather than a ladylike demeanor. Like Berlinski, there are writers such as Carole Nelson Douglas who sprinkle Pre-Raphaelite nuggets like pinches of seasoning in literary recipes. She sustains these through several books, beginning with *Good Night, Mr. Holmes* (1990). Here Irene Adler Gordon, a free-spirited American singer and detective who was one of Sherlock Holmes's few strong female adversaries, is depicted as she "leans against the faded brocade armchair, looking so much like one of Mr. Burne-Jones's languishing painted ladies that I was quite surprised to hear her actually speak."[18] In the same book Irene throws herself on a sofa à la "Sarah Bernhardt or the painted ladies of the Pre-Raphaelites."[19] In the sequel, *Good Morning, Irene* (1992), she and her free-flowing hair are paid the compliment "that Burne-Jones would want to paint her."[20] *Castle Rouge* (2002), on the other hand, features a woman with a Lady of Shalott-like "explosion of unbridled hair" that makes her look like "...one of Burne-Jones's medieval maidens..."[21]

Beyond Pre-Raphaelite flavorings of texts with certain clichéd descriptors, there are signs that some modern writers utilizing "Pre-Raph" traits really do not fully understand the movement or the art. Sometimes the misconceptions are amusingly incongruous; in Nicholas Kilmer's *Harmony in Flesh and Black* (1995), e.g., it seems as if Kilmer, despite his words, is actually describing non-Pre-Raphaelite artists and themes. Accordingly, a man named Fred pontificates that:

> The Pre-Raphaelites eschewed representing such common and depressing contemporary themes as coal mines, hangings, or the profession of collecting night soil, and instead chose imagined ancient scenes to elevate the spirit and demonstrate morality. The subjects are often nude except for their suppressed genitals—Burne-Jones used the airbrush long before it was invented—or they wear Roman dress, or medieval dress based on the Roman. Except for Rossetti, all of these painters depict the traditional British stiff upper lip, though other exposed parts remain flaccid. William Morris had an extraordinary thing for feet.[22]

This passage elicits a chortle today because of how it discloses a limited and imperfect knowledge of Pre-Raphaelite subject matter, including a mention of supposed podiatric defects in Morris's figures.

The first of the more complex referencing of the Pre-Raphaelite Brotherhood is arguably Mollie Hardwick's *The Dreaming Damozel* (1995), a Doran Fairweather mystery with an engraved version of Millais's *Ophelia* on its cover. This inside/outside dual testimonial to Pre-Raphaelitism signals how particular images, above all Millais's interpretation of Shakespeare's heroine, have been perceived as effective marketing tools, with high recognizability to buyers. Hardwick devotes myriad paragraphs about the Pre-Raphaelites, discussing Elizabeth Siddal's fate as a "born victim" and "...one of their ideal Stunners, with red-gold hair, and thin enough...to suit medieval gowns."[23] There is furthermore a conversation partly devoted to Siddal's modeling for *Ophelia*: "'Millais' *Ophelia*, wasn't she?...Floating in that stream, singing snatches of old songs as she dies.'" The companion then explains the staging of Millais's painting with "a bath in Millais' studio, and the water heated by a lamp underneath...Lizzie in that heavily embroided [*sic*] dress, lying there obediently and getting icier and icier. She got pneumonia, and her father sued..."[24]

This dialogue occurs between a reporter and the heroine Doran, an antiques dealer, who is the first of a steady stream of orphaned waifs who identify with "Lizzie" Siddal and are fixated upon the Brotherhood, especially Rossetti. Journalist Rodney deliberately compares Doran with Siddal, saying "Like Lizzie Siddal, she hadn't known where or who she was. He wishes the picture hadn't turned up to reincarnate the waif; especially at a time when she often looked too thin and pale herself for his liking."[25] Hardwick wittily hails the group as a "rum lot" and views an all-consuming Pre-Raphaelite obsession as a craving analogous to "eating pounds and pounds of something agreeable with garlic on it. One ultimately feels deliciously satisfied but slightly nauseated."[26] She also assails the "wretched frightened" animal model in Holman Hunt's *Scapegoat* and disparages Ford Madox Brown's *Work*, retitling it "'...How to behave with absolute uselessness in Hampstead.' I'd sooner watch endless catfood commercials."[27] In lieu of adulation she proffers a welcome and rare dose of acerbic humor: she thus asserts that Hunt's *Hireling Shepherd* is a canvas "people saw as a trollopish peasant girl on the point of getting seduced by a lout in rope leggings."[28] And even though the book on some levels functions as a quest for Rossettian information, the author uses tabloid journalists as an "...excuse for a discussion of the painter's sexuality."[29] As a result, Rossetti's *Astarte Syriaca* becomes a half-page supplement in the Sunday newspaper and is described as "a goddess, gazing, or rather glaring, at her worshippers....The head is too small for the body, even with its fall of frizzled hair....The 'love-freighted lips', as Rossetti called them....look as though Astarte has just enjoyed an aperitif of human blood. The bare shoulders are strapping enough for an old-style docker...."[30]

But it is Siddal/"Lizzie" who proves the superstar again and again, in Hardwick's seminal text and others, above all as the model for *Ophelia* and as a doomed victim in general. While the main protagonist pretends to be dead, the first actual corpse is found in the river and explicitly compared with *Ophelia*. The model, dubbed "another dead damozel" or "dreaming damozel," is both dressed and posed like Ophelia.[31] Yet another body materializes, this time a Jane Morris look-alike, with "Jane as Proserpine, Astarte, Guinevere...One couldn't mistake her with the long ripply hair..."[32] But this turns out to be a man, "made up as a horrible caricature."[33] Doran brings the police proof that these corpses deliberately connect to the Pre-Raphaelites, and an Inspector named Claybourne initiates an inquisition (which itself recalls what happened after Siddal died from an overdose of laudanum). The Pre-Raphaelite links pique the national press, which revels in reproducing images of *Ophelia* and Rossetti's *Astarte* and lavishes countless pages chronicling Rossetti's sexual conduct. There is an unexpected touch when Doran is interviewed about Rossetti's *Beata Beatrix* at the Tate Gallery, and a reporter asks, "You have quite a thing about Lizzie, haven't you?"[34] Doran agrees but castigates Rossetti as "a total wimp. He didn't have the moral courage to save himself from drink and drugs, and he certainly didn't save poor Lizzie..."[35]

In the narrative Doran meets the elusive, enigmatic Ralph Janner, who occasionally—and conveniently, from the perspective of plot—impersonates Burne-Jones as well as Morris and owns a drawing ascribed to Rossetti. But Janner is a malevolent force, drugging Doran and trying to kill her in a car crash, thereby adding to Pre-Raphaelitism a new dimension, violent crime. His accomplice is Ancilla, a woman obviously named after Rossetti's early painting *Ecce Ancilla Domini*. The complicated interwoven narratives end with several Rossetti drawings, underscoring the lengths to which Hardwick goes to imbue Pre-Raphaelitism into her fiction.

Another novel in this category is Joanne Harris's *Sleep, Pale Sister* (1994), which bases its whole narrative structure on legendary Pre-Raphaelite sexual notoriety. Set entirely in the nineteenth century, the tale foregrounds Henry Chester, an artist whose works are described as "quite Pre-Raphaelite", a sobriquet which, he said, "delighted me, and I took care to nurture this similarity, even taking subjects from Rossetti's poetry...."[36] Chester becomes infatuated with a nine-year old girl named Effie, who in name (and in situation—she later weds a frigid man) explicitly alludes to Ruskin's obsession with little girls, especially Rose LaTouche, as well as his marriage to Euphemia "Effie" Gray, whose second husband was John Everett Millais. Chester's first painting of young Effie was "... *My Sister's Sleep,* from the Rossetti poem."[37] In this she is depicted "lying on a little narrow bed, light from the window "promising redemption in death, the purity of the innocent who dies young", a central theme in Chester's oeuvre.[38] But Effie detests such roles like the *Little Beggar Girl* and *The Convent Flower* (reminiscent of Marie Spartali Stillman's painting *Convent Lily*). Neither childlike nor passive, Effie resents posing for Chester and that her mother forced her at age seventeen to marry him, thereby relegating her to a loveless, sexless marriage. Chester, who considers sex disgusting, perceives Effie as a *femme fatale,* seductress, and sorceress. To keep her pure and inaccessible, he imprisons her physically and mentally, often drugging her with laudanum.

Harris orchestrates both male and female voices/viewpoints that shift back and forth in the plot. Effie resents Henry's controlling ways and his imposition of mutual chastity. Besides including a female brothel keeper named Fanny (alluding to Fanny Cornforth, one of Rossetti's paramours), who develops an intense relationship with Effie, Harris creates a rival for Chester. Effie has an affair with

Moses Zachary Harper, an artist and cad who despises his nemesis. The author moreover sets up various vignettes which, as in Fiona Mountain's *Pale as the Dead*, visually re-position the female protagonist as a Burne-Jonesian Sleeping Beauty. Thus, Chester envisions his wife as "...Sleeping Beauty on her couch, all twined round with climbing roses...."[39] Harper is, with his lusty behavior, more Rossettian and certainly the antithesis of the frigid Henry, who envies his friend's success in the art world (and perhaps in the bedroom). Harper brags of Ruskin's (unlikely) praise of his *Sodom and Gomorrah* and archly recounts the opening of Chester's art exhibition and how "Pre-Raphaelite idols...Hunt and Morris...Mrs. Morris", attended.[40]

Shelly Reuben's *Spent Matches* of 1996 escalates the percentage of Pre-Raphaelite content and places the Brotherhood center stage in the mounting of a fictional exhibition dedicated to Pre-Raphaelitism. The show is curated by Georgiana Weeks, whose first name coincidentally is that of Burne-Jones's wife. Even without a Pre-Raphaelite image on its cover, *Spent Matches* is nonetheless one of the most Pre-Raphaelite-centric novels imaginable. Unlike certain previous books with their judicious sprinkling of references, this novel completely revolves around a Pre-Raphaelite exhibition and continually mentions members of the Brotherhood. As if Weeks's passion for the Brethren were not enough, her assistant Camden Kimcannon is equally devoted and claims to "know everything about the...Pre-Raphaelites...I live them. I sleep them. I study them. I breathe them."[41]

There is even a detailed exhibition (complete with catalogue entries) entitled *Artists, Lovers, Poets, Friends: The Pre-Raphaelites — A Passionate Grouping*; the description of its evolution as a project furthermore confirms the author's awareness of the work involved organizing and installing of a show. Readers are given a checklist of the show at the fictional Zigfield Art Museum. Thus, Burne-Jones's *Love Leading the Pilgrim*, *The Sleeping Princess*, *The Rock of Doom*, and *Depths of the Sea*, along with Rossetti's *Blessed Damozel* and *The Beloved*, are among the coveted paintings theoretically on loan. *The New York Times* theoretically both previews and reviews the show, an unusual approach on several levels. In outlining the exhibition, Reuben insightfully and unexpectedly captures the problematic status of Victorian art at most universities and thus notes that "...19th-century British Pre-Raphaelites were neither taught nor respected" when Georgiana went to school.[42] Solid details like Weeks's inspiration from works by Rossetti and Siddal and particularly the Bancroft collection at the Delaware Art Museum reinforce the "reality" of the curatorial undertaking, although it should be pointed out that the likelihood such objects would be lent is minimal and unrealistic. Overall, Weeks has a fascination with the Brotherhood that borders on compulsion. Nevertheless, she suggests why the Pre-Raphaelites so impressed her, and perhaps the reader too. She explains,

> The energy and the originality and the unparalleled beauty of these paintings; the talent; the passions; the sheer, inescapable DRAMA of it all; and the connections, always the connections. These Pre-Raphaelites...are fascinating...glamorous, gorgeous, and sexy. They are larger than life. They are dream people...I have to find out EVERYTHING about them.[43]

Another highly-evolved, intricately Pre-Raphaelite-centric work is Fiona Mountain's 2002 *Pale as the Dead*, the first installment of a Natasha Blake mystery. Siddal again resurfaces and is linked to a modern young woman named Bethany Marshall. When Bethany, who had been abandoned at birth and was later adopted, disappears, her boyfriend Adam hires Natasha (a genealogical consultant with sharp detective talents). This novel too is Ophelia-laden, from its cover to its convoluted plot. The first scene depicts Bethany (who is predictably obsessed with Siddal and in the end turns out to be a descendant) about to re-enact Millais's *Ophelia* for her photographer boyfriend. Bethany also aspires to write a biography of Siddal, conveniently ignoring that in real life Jan Marsh has already produced an excellent one. Such an interest in Siddal's life—and death—is made plausible because Bethany's grandmother told her about the exhumation of Sidall's body. Old Granny also maintained that for *Beata Beatrix*, Rossetti "used Lizzie's corpse as a model, which makes it a kind of mortuary painting."[44]

However, Bethany is not the only Pre-Raphaelite enthusiast in this mystery; Natasha owns well-known, real publications like *The Pre-Raphaelite Dream* by William Gaunt and admires *Beata Beatrix* and Rossetti's *Proserpine*. Like Bethany, she too almost swoons over Pre-Raphaelite images; e.g., she "...turned the pages to find Lizzie Siddal in Millais' *Ophelia*. A beautiful, haunting painting, the colours of the dense foliage and Lizzie's face as realistic as a photograph."[45] She is mirrored by Margaret, a similarly-inclined minor character preoccupied with Siddal and works like *Clerk Saunders*. Margaret's commentary provides useful background for the non-Pre-Raphaelite reader. It is she who invents the title of "pale sister" (the deceased Lizzie), since it was easy "...to imagine a pale hand rising from the grave" when Rossetti retrieved his book of poems.[46] Natasha even visits Siddal's grave, and Adam joins the fan club with his own reasons for the appeal of the Pre-Raphaelites: "They've got it all. Sex and death and drugs as well."[47]

The plot continues with another old woman named Marion, who owns the house where Siddal allegedly died. Virtually everyone seems associated with the Pre-Raphaelites; even Adam, prior to the project with Bethany as *Ophelia*, admits he was a "groupie" who in college joined a secret society, the Ravens, which "modelled ourselves on the Pre-Raphaelites...[and] took it all very seriously, drew up a code of conduct and voted in members."[48] Towards the end Natasha searches for evidence at Bethany's family home and finds her bedroom bedecked with Pre-Raphaelite posters, notably *Ophelia* and Hughes's *April Love*. As if all this accumulated detail were not enough, Reuben adds to the clues a locket with a coil of red gold hair belonging to Bethany's great-great-great grandmother, Siddal. In her quest, Natasha travels to the Ashmolean Museum to see images of Siddal along with photographs, drawings, and poems preserved in solander boxes. (This is only a minor error, since the boxes with Siddal's treasures are instead owned by the Fitzwilliam Museum.) Besides Lizzie's writings, there is—in private hands—supposedly a diary that surfaces which once belonged to Jeanette Marshall, whose father was the physician Rossetti summoned on the night of Lizzie's death. The finale exposes how Dr. Marshall supposedly raised Siddal's baby daughter and named her Eleanor (part of Siddal's original name), thus making this child Bethany's future great-grandmother.

Another Brotherhood-focused novel is Elizabeth Hand's *Mortal Love* (2004), which like some other counterparts features a cover with a work by Rossetti, his *La Ghirlandata*. Hand explicitly acknowledges her indebtedness to the Brotherhood in the foreword and with a unique twist names various chapters after famous Millais canvases, e.g. *Chill October, The Eve of St. Agnes, Ferdinand Lured by Ariel,* and *The Order of Release*. Hand's boldness furthermore lies in integrating real Victorians—e.g., Algernon Swinburne—into the nineteenth- and twentieth-century portions of the story. In the past, Swinburne meets Radborne Comstock, an American artist who is moved by the sight of Millais's *Ophelia* and its "...emerald glamour, the astonishing veracity of his bluebells and mashwort" and agrees to work at a private asylum run by a strange doctor.[49] The twentieth-century protagonist Daniel Rowland is an American journalist seduced by Larkin Meade, a modern femme fatale. She exerts lethal effects on Rowland's body, literally searing and scarring his flesh and soul. Not surprisingly, she is repeatedly described as a *belle dame sans merci* and Pre-Raphaelite/Rossettian stunner. To add to these elements, she moreover owns a collection of Pre-Raphaelite works and is designated by the author to be a collector of souls as well as a reincarnation of one of Comstock's patients, Evienne Upstone. Upstone thus experiences a second life as her doppelgänger Meade, who is endowed with a blend of overtly Pre-Raphaelite, Siddalesque, and Jane Morris-like attributes. These are a "...square cheekbones, heavy, nearly black eyebrows; wide, red-lipped mouth—a face that should have looked masculine but asserted itself as a kind of beauty Daniel knew only from paintings. Not modern paintings, either; he thought of...Jane Burden or Lizzie Siddal...."[50] The tale moves repeatedly between modern and Pre-Raphaelite intersections—from Burne-Jones's paintings of his mistress Maria Zambaco, to Georgiana Burne-Jones, and Rossetti's house (which Larkin says was occupied by John Paul Getty in the 1970s). And Comstock's own canvases sound as if they are Pre-Raphaelite compositions, his *Love Philtre* mimicking Frederick Sandys's painting of the same title.

There are other permutations of the Pre-Raphaelite heroine in modern literature, and this essay does not aim to exhaustively cite every example. Mention might nonetheless be made of Michel Fa-

ber's *The Crimson Petal and the White* (2002), in which the main figure, "Sugar," a kept woman who (like Hunt's model Annie Miller
for *The Awakening Conscience*) aspires to be a lady. In her case, her
education includes learning about Pre-Raphaelite art, although her
mastery of such information seems minimal, as the author implies:
"Oh, she's read about the Pre-Raphaelites in journals, but that's as
far as it goes; she wouldn't know Burne-Jones or Rossetti if they
fell on top of her."[51] On the other hand, Marion Chesney's *Sick of
Shadows* (with its Tennysonian-inflected title) consciously channels
the floating Ophelia strand of imagery. In this mystery Lady Rose
Summer finds a woman's body in London: "A rowing-boat was
moored in the water by the bridge. In it lay Dolly dressed like the
Lady of Shalott in the Pre-Raphaelite illustration to Tennyson's famous poem...."[52] Elsewhere, in A.S. Byatt's well-received novel *The
Children's Book* (2009), there are some fleeting references to a book
with illustrations by Burne-Jones and a young woman,"...a Stunner
from Margate...[who] had been painted by Burne-Jones and Rossetti."[53] And the 2010 novel *The Swan Thieves* by Elizabeth Kostova
briefly tantalizes readers with portraits that are "...highly realistic,
in places nearly photographic...It reminded me...of the Pre-Raphaelites and their detailed portraits of women; it had that mythical
quality, too..."[54] Additional examples would most likely resemble
and reinforce preceding ones that have already established the fundamental trends and dominant traits of grafting Pre-Raphaelitism
onto modern literature.[55]

A final category is quite distinctive and attests to the Pre-Raphaelite literary presence in the atypical visual and narrative format of
comic books and graphic novels. There are numerous examples,
among them Charles Vess's *The Book of Ballads* (2004), replete with
pages recollecting Burne-Jones's designs for Morris's Kelmscott
Press tomes and to some of Rossetti's heroines. For example, the
long-haired women with flowing hair in Vess's publication invite
comparison with counterparts in works like Rossetti's 1855 drawing *The Maids of Elfen-Mere*.

An outstanding example is *Of Pre-Raphaelite Persuasion* (1991),
a Canadian publication subtitled "A Look at the Pre-Raphaelite
Brotherhood with two illustrated stories by Mark Murphy." The
writers offer a bland, error-laden guide to the Brotherhood accom-

panied by thirty-eight small, grainy reproductions of paintings at the Tate Gallery and elsewhere. The first tale, "Buried Poems," melodramatically updates Rossetti's decision to bury his poems in Siddal's coffin—and later to exhume them. In this re-telling, the authors portray moments in which Rossetti anguishes about what to do. Curiously, Ford Madox Brown physically resembles Ruskin, yet it is intriguing to see important Pre-Raphaelite events reduced to the telegraphic text, style, and classic panels of a comic book. The most creative dimension has Lizzie haunting Rossetti by sending back her burned letters as he awaits the delivery of the exhumed poems.

The second story, "Pre-Raphaelite Persuasion", focuses on Lizzie's modeling for Millais's *Ophelia* and sustains a cinematic dream sequence (Fig. 2). While floating in the bathtub, she sinks into a fantasy realm or state of unconsciousness in which she enters a seeming forest of canvases, one of which depicts rival Jane Morris in Rossetti's *La Pia de Tolomei*. Janey, or her clone, begs for help from the tower where she is imprisoned. To rescue her, Lizzie re-enacts the male role of savior in the Sleeping Beauty myth by entering an enchanted garden. Lizzie ignores warnings not to do this, but is unable to resist and is plunged into eternal slumber. Her fate is a scene strikingly indebted to Burne-Jones's famous *Sleeping Beauty* canvases (Fig. 3), in which Janey—not the Prince—cradles the beautiful, sleeping woman, Lizzie. The final pages fast forward to Janey posing for *La Pia* and, like Lizzie, experiencing a nightmarish dream world, now, with fitting reciprocity, imagining Lizzie's endurance posing for *Ophelia*.

As these selected examples all attest, the interpretation of the Pre-Raphaelite heroine varies significantly. Many women are merely lightly endowed with Pre-Raphaelite physical traits like long hair, smoldering eyes, sensuous airs, and languid poses and occasionally called stunners. These uses of Pre-Raphaelitism are rather two-dimensional, much like the paintings that inspire the authors. Perhaps even a majority of references falls into this more superficial category of representation. However, a few writers dare to poke fun at Pre-Raphaelite characteristics, alleging, as Hardwick does, that the bodily proportions are exaggerated, the heads hydrocephalic, and the lips overly large. Others deal more with the phenomenon of Pre-Raphaelitism itself, whether intense overkill in Reuben's hypothetical exhibition or Kilmer's misunderstood yet amusing litany of attributes. In addition, there are instances of almost total, single-minded absorption of Pre-Raphaelitism, as with Hardwick, Harris, Reuben, Mountain, and Hand.

Whether mysteries, historicizing romances, paranormal fiction, or otherwise, most of these novels seem driven not just by the desire to describe decorated interiors or anesthetized stunners, but instead to explore the idiosyncratic, haunting impact of Millais's *Ophelia*. Ophelia is mentioned in Perry's *Half Moon Street,* and with more urgency by Hardwick in the character Doran. Harris, on the other hand, almost equally invokes Hunt, Burne-Jones, and Millais. But for Mountain, it is Siddal—as the model for *Ophelia* and other canvases like *Beata Beatrix*—who serves as the catalyst and primary source of inspiration. Mountain's creation and Hardwick's are both so permeated by Ophelia that they share a dual force of what might be called "Siddalization" and "Pre-Raphaelization." In contrast, Hand offers a different, more evil creature—the Rossettian, hyper-dangerous femme fatale Larkin Meade. Despite sundry references to Millais's paintings in chapter titles and the text, it is Rossetti's presence that is mostly felt. Meade is definitely one of his offspring and injects a supernatural element paralleled in lesser doses in other novels. Finally, *Of Pre-Raphaelite Persuasion* combines several of these components by having Lizzie and Janey interact in a spellbinding series of events. Compared with real life, all these female protagonists share a two-dimensional quality, although Hardwick, Reuben, Harris, Mountain, and Hand orchestrate more complex, melodramatic narratives with Pre-Raphaelite elements that sometimes overpower. The very last image in this graphic novel (Fig. 4) about Pre-Raphaelitism depicts Janey walking as if in a trance past a huge (oversized) painting of *Ophelia*, a fitting finale to this riveting strand of imagery.

These literary incarnations reinforce how the cultural fantasies and adaptations of Pre-Raphaelitism are remarkably widespread and pervasive, reflecting an ongoing obsession with the Victorian past which continues to mount as audiences both aestheticize and even fetishize the past. How can this explosion of Pre-Raphaelization be explained? What is it that consumers, whether readers or

viewers, doggedly pursue and find so appealing about the Brotherhood? Is it the sense of their lives as theatrical, sexualized morality
plays-cum-soap operas, the volatile romances, or the juggling of
respectability with impropriety, rebelliousness with acceptance?
Do current audiences like them because they are so similar—or so
different—from the present? Is it the necrophiliac beauty of *Ophelia*
and the indelible memory of her corpse and flowing red hair or the
aggressive qualities of viragos like Meade that beckon? Do modern
women readers in particular identify with these extremes of femininity; if so, why?

Some might maintain that the Pre-Raphaelites have been
tamed and drained by all this literary commodification, commercial branding, and the endless iterations in books that perpetuate
red-haired maidens and phlegmatic femmes fatales in the public
imagination. Have these phenomena made these artists and their
canvases more commonplace or vulgarized their contributions?
Scholars may be repulsed, entertained, or even gratified by these
developments, but perhaps also astonished by how "elastic" the
fabric of Pre-Raphaelitism has proven in expanding its material influence into mainstream post-modern culture. Admiration is one
response to how this broad range of literature—from lowly comic
book to popular mysteries and historical fiction—has reinvented
and revitalized Pre-Raphaelitism. It turns out that the Brotherhood
can withstand constant adaptations, interpretations, and usage, ac-
commodating in fiction traits from brief amalgams of Pre-Raphaelite features to total absorption, along with tolerating the sensation-
alizing of past historical events. What remains to be seen is whether
future generations will share this literary and visual preoccupation
and continue to transform and re-forge Pre-Raphaelitism in these
forms or new ones.

End Notes

[1] P.D. James, *The Skull Beneath the Skin* (London: Penguin Books, 1982),
74 and 108.
[2] P.D. James, *Death in Holy Orders* (New York: Alfred A. Knopf, 2001), 57.
[3] James, *Death in Holy Orders*, 149.
[4] James, *Death in Holy Orders*, 149.
[5] Anne Perry, *Bethlehem Road* (New York: Fawcett Books, 1991), 118.

[6] Anne Perry, *Cardington Crescent* (New York: Ballantine Books, 1987, 46.

[7] Anne Perry, *Farrier's Lane* (New York: Fawcett Columbine, 1993), 330.

[8] Anne Perry, *Half Moon Street* (Boston: Houghton Mifflin, 1984), 1.

[9] Perry, *Half Moon Street*, 140.

[10] P.D. James. *The Private Patient* (New York: Vintage Books, 2008), 283.

[11] Perry, *Bethlehem Road*, 9.

[12] Anne Perry, *Belgrave Square* (New York: Fawcett Columbine, 1992), 99.

[13] Caroline Arscott, *Absent Friends* (New York: Delacorte Press, 2004), 26.

[14] Katherine Hall Page, *A Body in the Big Apple* (New York: Morrow, 1999), 19.

[15] Nancy Atherton, *Aunt Dimity Beats the Devil* (New York: Viking, 2000), 79.

[16] Elizabeth Peters, *The Falcon at the Portal* (New York: Avon, 1999), 263.

[17] Claire Berlinski, *Loose Lips: A Roman à Claire* (New York: Random House, 2003), 119.

[18] Carole Nelson Douglas, *Good Night, Mr. Holmes* (New York: A Tom Doherty Associates Book, 2990), 37.

[19] Douglas, *Good Night*, 97.

[20] Carole Nelson Douglas, *The Adventuress (Good Morning, Irene)* (New York: A Forge Book, 1992), 105.

[21] Carole Nelson Douglas, *Castle Rouge* (New York: Tom Doherty Associates, 2002), 296.

[22] Nicholas Kilmer, *Harmony in Flesh and Black* (New York: Henry Holt and Co., 1995), 59.

[23] Mollie Hardwick, *The Dreaming Damozel* (New York: St. Martin's Press, 1990), 25.

[24] Hardwick, *The Dreaming Damozel*, 25.

[25] Hardwick, *The Dreaming Damozel*, 26.

[26] Hardwick, *The Dreaming Damozel*, 24.

[27] Hardwick, *The Dreaming Damozel*, 79.

[28] Hardwick, *The Dreaming Damozel*, 25.

[29] Hardwick, *The Dreaming Damozel*, 134.

[30] Hardwick, *The Dreaming Damozel*, 134.

[31] Hardwick, *The Dreaming Damozel*, 68.

[32] Hardwick, *The Dreaming Damozel*, 123.

[33] Hardwick, *The Dreaming Damozel*, 123.

[34] Hardwick, *The Dreaming Damozel*, 136.

[35] Hardwick, *The Dreaming Damozel*, 136.

[36] Joanne Harris, *Sleep, Pale Sister* (New York: Harper Perennial, 2005), 12.

[37] Harris, *Sleep, Pale Sister*, 15.

[38] Harris, *Sleep, Pale Sister*, 15.

[39] Harris, *Sleep, Pale Sister*, 16.

[40] Harris, *Sleep, Pale Sister*, 51.

[41] Shelly Reuben, *Spent Matches* (New York: Scribner, 1996), 68.

[42] Reuben, *Spent Matches*, 59.

[43] Reuben, *Spent Matches*, 166.

[44] Fiona Mountain, *Pale as the Dead* (New York: Thomas Dunne Books, 2004), 115.

[45] Mountain, *Pale as the Dead*, 19.

[46] Mountain, *Pale as the Dead*, 101.

[47] Mountain, *Pale as the Dead*, 115.

[48] Mountain, *Pale as the Dead*, 110.

[49] Elizabeth Hand, *Mortal Love: A Novel* (New York: Harper Collins, 2003), 103.

[50] Hand, *Mortal Love: A Novel*, 194.

[51] Michel Faber, *The Crimson Petal and the White* (London: Harcourt, Inc., 2002), 39.

[52] Marion Chesney, *Sick of Shadows* (New York: St. Martin's Minotaur, 2005), 16.

[53] A.S. Byatt, *The Children's Book* (New York: Alfred A. Knopf, 2009), 45. This author's prize-winning *Possession* (1999) arguably began the trend to "Victorianize" contemporary fiction, although it is not as laden with specifically Pre-Raphaelite components as the novels in this essay.

[54] Elizabeth Kostova, *The Swan Thieves* (New York: Little, Brown and Co., 2010), 125.

[55] A separate classification and essay might be devoted to recent works mentioning William Morris, e.g., Diane Meier's *The Season of Second Chances* (New York: St. Martin's Griffin, 2011) and Carol Goodman's *Arcadia Falls* (New York: Ballantine Books, 2011).

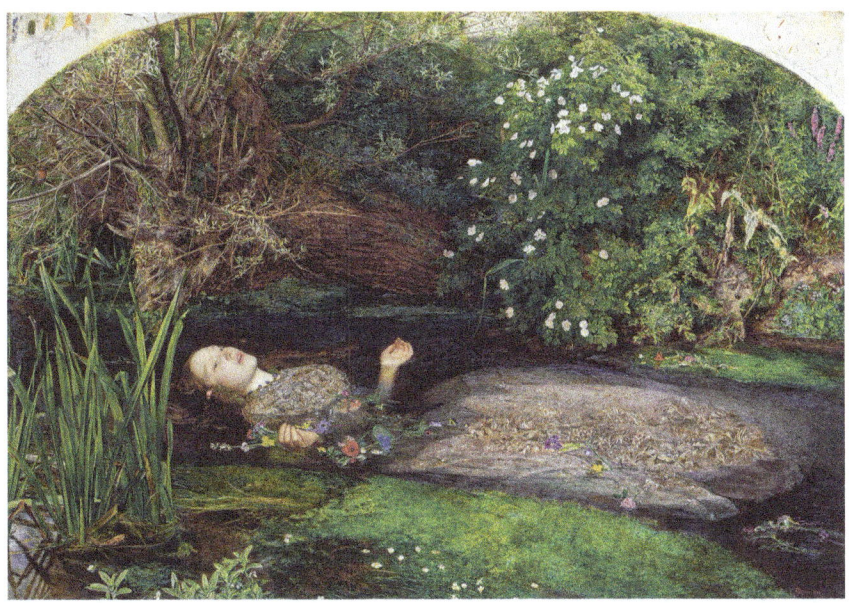

3.1. Sir John Everett Millais, Bt., *Ophelia*, 1851-2, oil on canvas, Tate Britain, London.

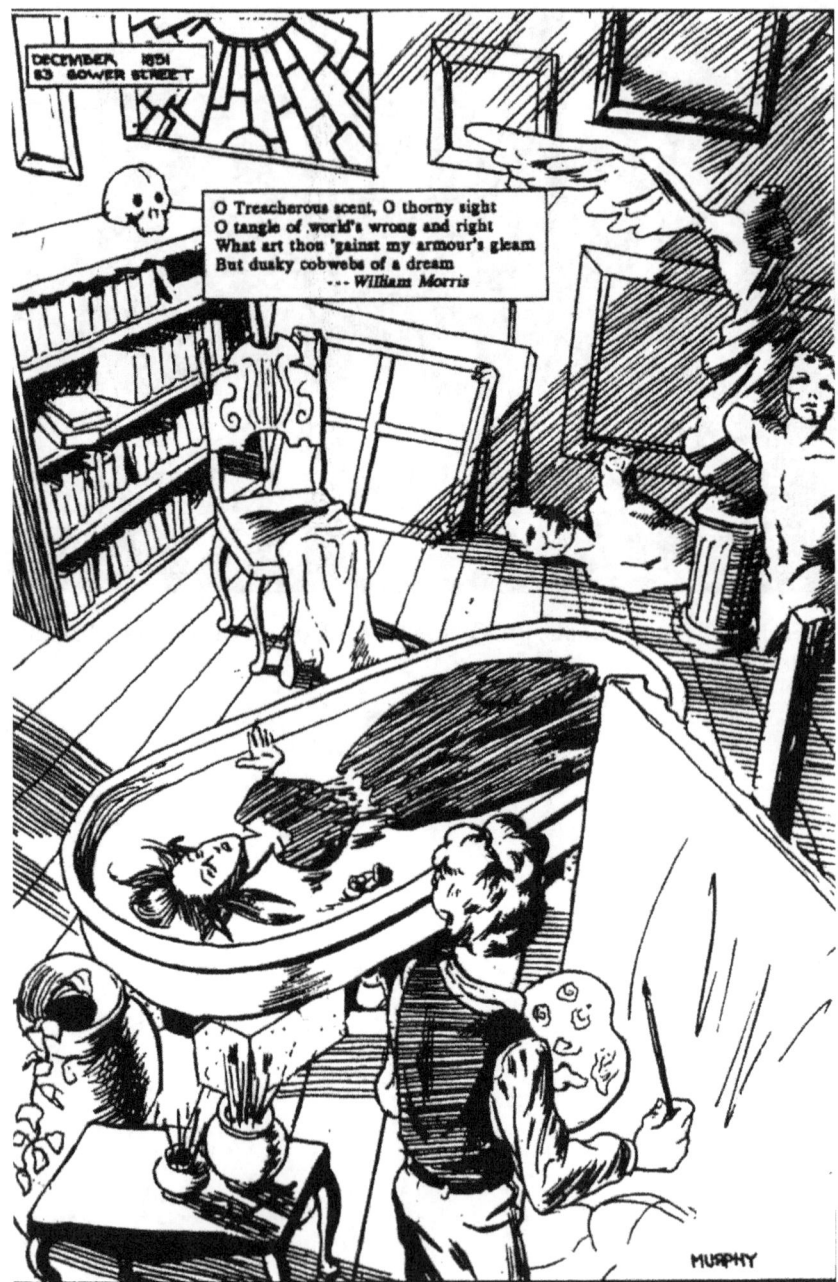

3.2. Mark Murphy (illustrator), *Of Pre-Raphaelite Persuasion*, Plymouth, MI: Tome Press, 1991, author's collection.

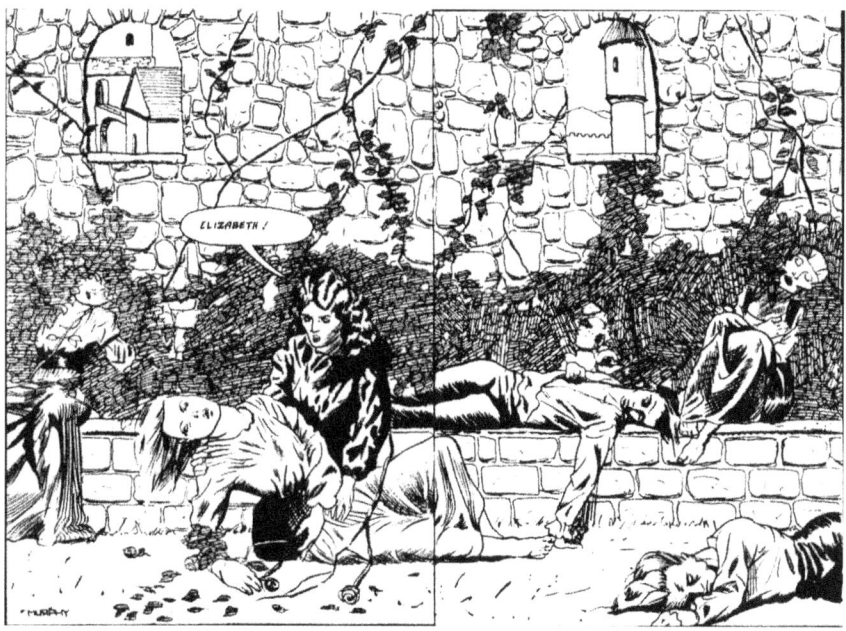

3.3. Mark Murphy (illustrator), *Of Pre-Raphaelite Persuasion*, Plymouth, MI: Tome Press, 1991, author's collection.

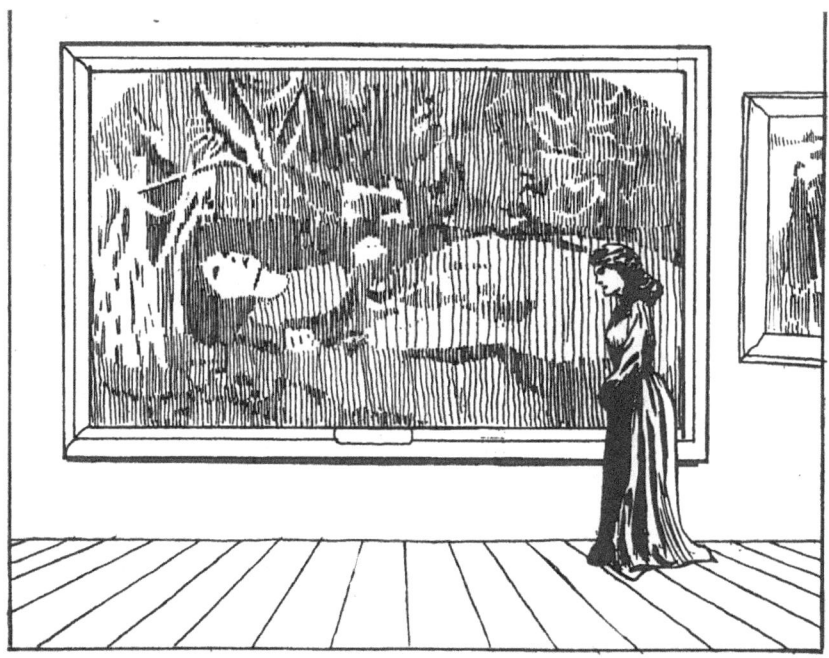

3.4. Mark Murphy (illustrator), *Of Pre-Raphaelite Persuasion*, Plymouth, MI: Tome Press, 1991, author's collection.

4

Edward Burne-Jones's Love Songs: Art, Music and Magic

Liana De Girolami Cheney

Heart, thou and I are here, sad and alone[1]

The magical world of Edward Burne-Jones (August, 28 1833 – June 17, 1898) is reflected in his paintings, in particular, his love song paintings including *Lament* of 1865-66 (Figs. 1 and 3-7) and *Le Chant d'Amour* (*The Love Song*) of 1868-77 (two versions, Figs. 8 and 9, and studies Figs. 10-11). He explains what painting means to him: "I mean by a picture a beautiful, romantic dream of something that never was, never will be—in a light better than any light that ever shone-in a land no one can define or remember, only desire-and the forms divinely beautiful—and then I wake up."[2] These paintings reveal Burne-Jones's endless and unresolved love for the beautiful, wealthy and accomplished Greek sculptress, Maria Zambaco (*Portrait of Maria Zambaco* of 1870, Figs. 12-14). She is his model, muse and sorceress. Burne-Jones composed paintings that are depictions of music scenes that capture a poetical world of ardent and endless love, as well the world of the senses, a physical realm, and the world of aesthetics, a metaphysical realm.

Most of the Pre-Raphaelite artists embrace some of the principles of the Aesthetic Movement, "art for art's sake,"[3] considering art devoid of moral or sentimental signification and narrative purpose. The quest is to emphasize beauty as the only concern for art. The leading exponents of this movement are the literati John Ruskin, Walter Pater[4] and Oscar Wilde.[5] Influenced, in particular, by John Ruskin's writings and his moral and aesthetic rejection of modern civilization, artists such as William Morris and Edward

Burne-Jones embraced the Aesthetic Movement but for different reasons. Both artists pursue beauty through art because they are animated by nostalgia for the medieval world. Under its spell, these Pre-Raphaelite painters rediscover the Celtic myths, Arthurian legends, and are deeply absorbed in the fairy-tales of Shakespeare's comedies. Burne-Jones's paintings create a whole world of legends and myths whose spiritual origin lies not only in the Middle Ages but also in antiquity. He rejects contemporary reality, desperately escaping in dreams and fantasy, thus transmitting in his painting metaphysical, moral, and aesthetic ideas dear to his heart, which binds him intensively to the use of the world of legends and myths. Burne-Jones combines in his imagery his personal quest for the narrative, while paralleling the Aesthetic Movement for the artistic pursuit for beauty, a visual necessity, a code to live by, and an aim to live beautifully and to be surrounded by beautiful things. His cultural symbolism is a consequence of his professional knowledge of the ancient mythologies bequeathed to him by the classical tradition of his English cultural milieu, i.e., his training in the classics at Oxford and his visual familiarity with the extensive classical collection displayed at the British Museum. Personally, his affair with the Greek sculptress Maria Cassavetti Zambaco also facilitated the mythical imagery of beauty portrayed in his paintings.

Burne-Jones's cultural milieu provides him with an understanding of the classical revival in the arts of the Renaissance drifting into mannerism, the baroque, the rococo, and gaining greater momentum in the nineteenth century as a result of the excavations of Herculaneum and Pompeii.[6] In England, the love for the antique led to collecting. The continuous British interest in antiquity is manifested in commissioning excavation, purchasing and collecting ancient art, such as found in the British Museum's classical collection of the Elgin marbles (the Athenian reliefs from the Parthenon).[7] The Society of Dilettanti in England, and the British Art Colony in Rome, to further the knowledge of the Antique world, commissioned and financed exploratory expeditions in order to understand the Grecian taste and Roman Spirit, and to encourage artists and collectors to visit, explore and excavate the ancient sites. Both societies function to further the knowledge of antiquity in England.

Obviously, Burne-Jones's art reflects his familiarity and interests in the classical tradition experienced through his cultural milieu and era. In addition, his affinity with classical ideals can be seen from his early schooling at Oxford (1853-1856),[8] his numerous trips to Italy (1859, 1862, 1871 and 1873)[9] as well as a manifestation of his patronage by wealthy Greek families residing in London, such as the Ionides and Burne-Jones's amorous involvement with well-known Greek sculptress, Zambaco, further contributed to his fascination with the antique.

Moreover, Burne-Jones appropriates historical and literary themes from ancient and medieval texts into his visual imagery. His aesthetics reflect the interaction between art and literature, and his paintings reveal the power of the images and the power of love. Central to this shared aesthetic view, for example, is the fact that both Burne-Jones and the Pre-Raphaelite painters viewed woman as a symbol of love and lust. His images of women reflect or correspond to the various embodiments of the *femme fatale*. Paradoxically, on the one hand, for Burne-Jones woman is the embodiment of purity (Galatea, Psyche or Andromeda)[10] but on the other hand, she appears as a temptress (Circe or the Sirens).[11] Thus, this type of imagery reveals Burne-Jones's unresolved love and passion for Zambaco.

Burne-Jones searched for a classical metaphor to express his dreams and existence, i.e., in pursuit of a canon of art that results in his adage: *To love beauty*. His aesthetic quest is reminiscent of Renaissance aesthetics or Neoplatonism. In this philosophy, "beauty consists of a certain charm" as something spiritual that transcends sensual experience and makes us long for the origin of what we perceive.[12] In Renaissance art, a visual example is Botticelli's imagery, *Primavera* of 1475 (Uffizi Gallery, Florence), which emphasizes this spiritual concept of ideal beauty rather than the physical reproduction of beauty, as it exists in nature. Favoring this concept, Burne-Jones elaborates on the Neoplatonic aesthetic ideal by creating an idealized image that combines beauty and arouses love. "Only this is true, that beauty is very beautiful and softens, and comforts, and inspires, and rouses, and lifts up, and never fails," he says.[13] These paintings portray more than a study in formal relationships, that is to say, a canon of beauty, but also a personal fear or quest for love.

In his search for other visual sources for his love song paintings,

Burne-Jones seeks inspiration in the literary tradition of love and death tales. He consults the illustrated manuscripts and emblematic books narrating romantic storytelling, such as Guillaume de Lorris and Jean de Meun's *Romance of the Rose* (1236-1276), Francesco Colonna's *The Dream of Poliphilo* (1499) and Otto Vaenius's *Amorum emblemata* (English edition, 1615-20). In 1859, an illustrated edition of the *Romance of the Rose* was on view at the British Museum. Burne-Jones was so enamored with this tale that he would take friends such as George Boyce to admire the saga of love because it represented the art of love as a discipline beset with difficulties, requiring the slow development of self-knowledge.[14] For example, toward the end of the *Romance of the Rose,* an illustration depicts the hero-poet arriving in the rose garden after traveling a series of trails, and selecting the rose of his choice. Burne-Jones's painting is compositionally influenced by the enclosed rose garden, as well as by the symbolism of the rose as visualized in *Lament.*

Francesco Colonna's *The Dream of Poliphilo* (*Hypnerotomachia Poliphili*) is another fairy tale dealing with the tribulations of love.[15] Burne-Jones owned a copy and praised it for its magical illustrations.[16] Colonna's *The Fountain of Adonis* likely influenced the décor of the rose garden in Burne-Jones' *Le Chant d'Amour.*

In the seventeenth century, the romantic emblematic heritage fused the classical, medieval and Renaissance traditions of romantic fairy tales in a compendium illustrated in *Amorum emblemata* by Otto Vaenius.[17] This collection of love emblems relates the story of an amorous counterfeit enacted by a mischievous, playful and winged putto, cupid. As for the personification of love, Vaenius's putto-type derives from Vincenzo Cartari's Cupid images in his mythographic compendium, *Imagini delli Dei de gli Antichi.* In his paintings of love songs and allegories of music, Burne-Jones fuses these textual and visual traditions.

Burne-Jones paints two versions of *Lament* (Fig. 1). The first one (1866) is executed in watercolor, with body color on paper laid down on canvas. It is signed and dated in the lower left as an emblematic coat-of-arms: *EBJ 1866.* A year earlier, he completes *Lament*, which is exhibited in 1869 at the Old Water-Colour Society in London.[18] Originally, John Hamilton Trist, a wine merchant and an avid collector of Pre-Raphaelite painters, owned this version. He bought it from the artist in 1867 and sold it to Christie's London on April 9, 1892 (Lot 15). Sir Frank Brangwyn subsequently purchased it and later donated it to William Morris Gallery in 1941, where it is presently on view. A second version of this painting exists in oil with a landscape. In July 4, 1967, Christie's London sold it to a private collector (Lot 57, current whereabouts unknown).[19]

Lament is a complex painting, in which Burne-Jones experiments with several artistic quests and indirectly begins to formulate his art theory of the beautiful. He considers classical references, Renaissance compositions and Pre-Raphaelite decorative designs, and symbolically he refers to ancient myths, Renaissance ideals and Pre-Raphaelite conceits.[20]

Burne-Jones's trips to Europe, in particular, Italy (1859 and 1862), and his constant visits to the British Museum to study and draw the Elgin Marbles sculptures as well as to consult its literary collection, provided him with an imaginative and intricate composition for *Lament*. The painting is composed of a series of sets of two, e.g., two architectural structures, two columns, two round windows, two doorways and two seated figures. The architectural design is based, in part, on Italian Renaissance palaces with interplay of open and closed spaces; diffuse and contrasting light effects, and symmetrical and asymmetrical ornamentation. In the exterior, the decoration of uneven windows ornaments the façade, while in the interior, the courtyard structure with hexagonal fountain and large stepped areas enclose an intimate and recreational space. With the architectural compositional design, Burne-Jones orchestrates a contrast between the architecture in the background, which is somewhat in ruins, recalling the exterior of Renaissance palaces, with the foreground, which is unspoiled, portraying private English dwellings.[21] In the background, there is no foliage in the trees, but in the foreground a rosebush blooms and rose petals are scattered about. The motif of the flowering rose branch or bush remains a constant in Burne-Jones's paintings, e.g., the cycle of *The Legend of the Briar Rose* of 1885-1890.[22]

In *Lament*, Burne-Jones reveals his Italian influence in the conception of spatial relations and structures. He orchestrates a composition in a series of geometrical designs, first creating three parallel, horizontal rectangles, from background, to middle ground, to foreground. He also composes three vertical rectangles that separate the background from the foreground, thus achieving an elegant spatial and optical recession. To accentuate the importance of the figures, Burne-Jones monumentalizes them by positioning them in triangular spaces as well as depicting them *all'antica* (in the classical manner). In the foreground of *Lament*, two simulated sculptural figures are enclosed in a small courtyard. They share an intimate and suspended moment of beauty: a song, a recollection and feelings. The female figure plays a psaltery (an ancient Near-Eastern instrument) while chanting, and her eyes are filled with tears as she gazes at the reaction of her male companion. At the sound of music and her voice, he recoils in an act of devotion and prayer. To accentuate this dramatic scene, Burne-Jones selects primary colors for the garb of his figures: the female musician is in red, the arouser of the emotion through the plucking of psaltery's chords. Her male companion is clothed with a blue mantel that tightly envelops him. His intense clasped hands parallel the cloth wrapping tightly around his body. The clinching of his hands contrasts with the musician hands, which openly embrace the instrument of bright golden color. A blue ribbon around the breast of female musician, matching in color the garment of her companion, loosely hangs. The ribbon's string forms a "S" shape, an intended initial for the word sound (an artistic whim).

Burne-Jones conveys two different types of reflections: artistic and metaphysical. The artistic reflections are manifested through the effects of the light, which are displayed throughout the composition, e.g., the brick and marble pavement, sitting platform, and the porphyry column. The metaphysical reflections are revealed through the gestures of the individuals, e.g., crying, singing, playing, meditating and grieving. These emotional expressions of the spirit are provoked and evoked by the sound of music or of a voice, thus a lament of the soul conveyed through imagery, and in turn revealing the signification of the imagery. At one level, this artistic or visual meaning is an impact of the Greek and Italian Renaissance styles in Burne-Jones's conception of creating beauty in art, revealing the Aestheticism of the nineteenth century in England. At another level, at the conceptual or metaphysical level, the arousing the spirit for beauty's sake or arousing the spirit to comprehend art through human emotions represents Burne-Jones's manifestation of his art theory of expression. Masterfully, he further alludes to an expressive theory of art, where the senses arouse the spirit, e.g., the sense of touch (playing), hearing (male listening to the song), smell (the perfumed rose bush) and seeing (the viewer observing the scene) provide a manifestation of the inner state of the artist and a fictive stage for the interaction of the imagery with the audience's psyche.

Burne-Jones consciously explores the treatment of the figure in order to provide a visual rendering of the emotional reaction to the sound of music. In doing so, he selects for his creations Greek sculptures admired and studied in London. Inspired by the Elgin Marble statues at the British museum, and under the encouragement of John Ruskin, Burne-Jones executes numerous renderings of these ancient sculptures.[23] His sketches and drawings are assembled in notebooks in various English collections: at the Birmingham Museums and Art Gallery, in Birmingham; the Victoria and Albert Museum in London; the Ashmolean Museum in Oxford; and the Fitzwilliam Museum in Cambridge.

In *Lament*, Burne-Jones portrays a seated muse, dressed in red, playing a musical instrument, in a private courtyard (Figs. 1 and 7). The treatment of the figure, in terms of the seated position and handling of the drapery reveals how Burne-Jones examines closely the sculpture of Phidias' *Demeter* of 447 BCE, in the East Pediment of the Parthenon at the British Museum (compare Figs. 1 and 2). Evidence of this parallelism is found in his drawing of a *Study for Lament* (*Seated Figure* of 1865) at the Birmingham Museums and Art Gallery (compare Figs. 2 and 3) [24] and another drawing, *A Copy of Mars*, from the Parthenon Frieze of 447 BCE, at the Victoria and Albert Museum (compare Figs. 3 and 4).[25]

Burne-Jones's musical figure is the muse Erato, traditionally considered the most famous of all the Muses. She is the muse of lyric and love poetry. The lyre and roses are her attributes and a *putto* at her feet accompanies her performance.[26] Burne-Jones portrays Erato holding a type of psaltery, which Greeks called *psallein*, meaning an instrument plucked with fingers. He does take liberties in depicting the instrument that the muse holds vertically as if playing a harp or lyre. Although recalling types of muses' sarcophagi, where each of them holds their corresponding attributes, e.g., Erato plays the lyre as seen in the *Muses Sarcophagus* of 2nd century AD at Musée du Louvre, MR 880, (originally found in Via Ostiense, Rome), Burne-Jones changes the attribute of the personification of music or Erato from a lyre to a psaltery. Also, he displaces the rosette decoration from the traditional center to the top on the instrument. Perhaps, he selects this ancient Near Eastern instrument because of its expressions of warm sound, enhancing a reflecting and personal mood. In the painting, the muse is playing the psaltery, holding it with the left hand, while plucking with the right hand. As she sings—indicated by her parted lips—and plays, she gazes at her lamenting companion, the *putto,* seated across from her. A feeling of grief is aroused; her moist eyes manifest her discomfort.

Familiar with Chaucer's writing, in particular, *The Miller's Tale,* from his Oxford schooling, Burne-Jones recalls a refrain: "He kitse hire sweete and taketh his sawtrie, And pleyeth faste, and maketh melodie," where a psaltery is played to accompany a song.[27] He also incorporates the Celtic tradition of employing the harp in musical performance to capture a variety psychological moods and modes. The conventional three modes are sleep, laughter and grief; with grief being the most dramatic and emotional. Burne-Jones captures these raptures in the scene where Erato cries and her *putto* companion laments.

Dressed in blue, the *putto,* a recoiled figure, or lamenter, is engaged in deep meditation or profound sadness, resting his head with closed eyes on his clasped hands. Could he be a personification of tragedy? There are several studies pertinent at the Birmingham Museums and Gallery (Figs. 4 and 5).[28] The earlier studies depict the lamenter as female nude figure (Fig. 5). A later drawing is closer to the painting rendition, the now-clothed female figure is posed meditating, as pleading in her prayers (Fig. 6). The classical treatment of the dress's drapery is inspired by the seated figures in the pediment of the Parthenon and the previous drawing for the Muse (compare Figs. 2 and 6). Another similarity among these drawings for *Lament* is their seated base. This cubical support for the seated figures reveals Burne-Jones's careful attention to the spatial structure of the Elgin Marbles (compare Figs. 2 with 1, 3-6).

In *Lament,* Burne-Jones is depicting three different types of perceiving. The first one is a physical seeing, as the natural light permeates through the scene, colors selections of blues and reds creating a visual mood, and architectural compositions to differentiate interiors and exterior spaces. The second perception is psychological or intuitive as the muse experiences the anguish of her companion, and moved by seeing his grief, she cries and ceases playing and chanting. And the third perception is metaphysical or spiritual, an internal apprehension or state of mind conveyed by the expressions of the lamenters, recoiling and with suspended posture.

Perhaps the most intriguing aspect of *Lament* is the vertical statue located behind the Erato. The columnar shape is contrasted with the porphyry column behind the lamenter. Raised on a pedestal, the greenish statue emerges from foliage of palms. The body is treated as a classical terminal figure, while the upper part of this architectural term depicts a human form. Burne-Jones depicts this type of architectural ornamentation that he observed in wall decorations and furniture in Italian Renaissance palaces as well as in the illustrations of his favorite Italian book, *The Dream of Poliphilo*.[29]

Burne-Jones's term is unusual and paradoxical in that the figure depicted is a pseudo-*kore* figure, dressed in classical garb. The figure appears to be holding serpents in one hand, an attribute of Ceres, the Goddess of Agriculture, Regeneration and Death.[30] Her headdress is decorated with a *corona spicea*, while her lower body is filled with foliage. In classical tradition, in particular, during the Augustan era, Ceres is portrayed emerging as plant-like from the earth, her arms entwined with snakes and her head crowned with fruits.[31] Burne-Jones composes the vertical shape with the ornamental design to allude to the shape of a torch, perhaps alluding to Ceres' torch employed in the search for her daughter Proserpine in the underworld or to a dormant or dead love as in Italian Renaissance funerary art.[32] Another attribute included here is a musical instrument, a syrinx or a pan flute, which is traditionally considered to be a pastoral instrument (Plato, *Republic*, Book III, Chapter 10),[33] as well as a sexual symbol for its shape.[34] The inclusion of these two types of musical instruments, the psaltery or lyre, a string instrument, and the syrinx or flute, a wind instrument, suggests that Burne-Jones is subtlety alluding to the musical contest between Apollo playing the lyre, an urban instrument, and Marsyas playing the syrinx, a pastoral instrument.[35] He conflates in these classical themes, one dealing with an allusion of deception (Apollo's contest) and the other relating to a story of love and grief (Ceres' predicament), with his artistic and intellectual ability of injecting classical references in his Pre-Raphaelite paintings.

During his painting of *Lament,* Burne-Jones begins to illustrate with William Morris, Geoffrey Chaucer's *Canterbury Tales*, focusing on the story of *Merchant Tale.* Chaucer narrates a moral story of inner blindness or visual deception, referring to the month of May, the month of the goddess Ceres (Demeter).[36] Is this why Burne-Jones depicts the image of Ceres with eyes cast down? Is Ceres lamenting the loss of her daughter, Proserpine? Traditionally, the recollection of her tragedy is reflected in Ceres' creation of the winter season, but in Burne-Jones' *Lament*, the blooming roses allude to a spring season. Is Burne-Jones alluding to another tale?

In observing closely the herm figure, an enigmatic and problematic imagery, it is possible to identify the figure as a male rather than a female. The figure is crowned with pointed ears, has a long beard hanging from his chin, and wearing unusual attire, a composite classical garb. The instrument held is still a syrinx. The ambiguity of the gender further suggests Burne-Jones's fascination with symbolism and his desire to conflate classical legends with medieval tales. At this time, Burne-Jones is illustrating several of the *Canterbury Tales*, including *The Wife of Bath,* a moral story of avarice, ignorance and folly. In this story, the wife narrates Ovid's tale of King Midas, who is known for his love of the pleasures of life and his pristine rose garden. The focus in Chaucer's tale, however, is on Midas' punishment for offending the God of Music, Apollo, for false judgment and lack of musical taste in the music contest with Marsyas or Pan. Apollo changes Midas' ears into donkey's ears (Ovid, *Metamorphoses*, Book 11).[37] Perhaps Burne-Jones is depicting the garden of Midas with the rosebush and the herm as the figure of Midas. The herm's holding of a syrinx recalls Marsyas' musical contest with Apollo. Burne-Jones is visualizing Midas's punishment and fate in depicting Midas' pointed donkey's ears and his bodily transformation into large foliage leaves.

Or, is Burne-Jones combing the Chaucerian tale with Algermon Charles Swinburne's verse play on *Rosamond* (1860) in his painting? Swinburne befriends Burne-Jones at Oxford in 1857. Both are fascinated with the medieval tale of the *Roman de la Rose*, where the symbol of the rose reveals that "love is a necessary consequence of beauty,"[38] and the immortality of love and beauty is attained only through death.[39] Swinburne chants:

Ah; and love
That makes the daily flesh an altar cup
To carry tears and rarest blood within
And touch paired lips with feast of sacrament
So sweet it is, God made it sweet.[40]

For Swinburne, the name Rosemund or *"Rosa mundi, non Rosa munda"* refers to Rosamund Clifford, the famous mistress of Henry II, who is murdered by his wife, Eleanor of Aquitaine. Burne-Jones is also inspired by this poem in an early depiction in gouache of *Fair Rosamund and the Queen Eleanor* of 1861 (Private Collection in England).[41]

In *Lament*, Burne-Jones depicts a lovely rosebush of pink and salmon blossoms behind the lamenting *putto*. This forms an interesting contrasting tone between the flourishing rosebush behind the lamenter and artificial palm leaves behind the muse. Again, Burne-Jones plays with the paradoxes in his imagery, keeping the visual tension and aesthetic contrast between the real and the artificial realm in life and art. Here he captures Horace's motto, *"ut pictura poesis"* ("as is painting, so is poetry") and adds another aesthetic flavor *"ut musica poesis"* ("as is music, so is poetry or painting"). Combining the sister arts in this delicately-woven painting, Burne-Jones will continue to pursue these connections through his artistic career.

Burne-Jones loved music.[42] In a trip of 1862 to Venice with Ruskin, he listens to the Italian songs of the seventeenth century; at Oxford, he views the performances of musicologist Henry Ellis Wooldridge and, at Wooldridge's home, his wife, Georgie, a pianist and singer, entertains their friends with "older English airs and French chansons."[43] An indication of Burne-Jones's interest in music is visualized in two versions of the painting, *Le Chant d'Amour* (*The Love Song*). The theme is based on a refrain from an old Breton song: *"Hélas! je sais un chant d'amour, / Triste ou gai, tour à tour"* ("Alas, I know a love song, / Sad or happy, each in turn"). Burne-Jones is enamored with the subject and paints numerous versions on this theme. The focus here is on a small painting in watercolor with bodycolor on paper, mounted on panel, and signed and dated on a tablet in the lower left as *EBJ* 1865 (now at the Museum of Fine Arts in Boston, MA, Fig. 8),[44] and a larger version in oil on canvas, signed *EBJ* and dated 1868-77 (now at the Metropolitan Museum of Art, NY, Fig. 9).[45]

There are numerous drawings for the Metropolitan version, including a complete cartoon, perhaps executed by Burne-Jones, and another of the Love or Cupid in the nude (Figs. 10 and 11).[46] The theme of this painting elaborates on the musical theme of *Lament* and explores the power of music and love. Burne-Jones reveals this parallelism and the signification of this painting for him in the *Portrait of Maria Zambaco* of 1870 (on gouache at Clemns-Sels-Museum, Neuss, in Germany, Fig. 12), where Maria is depicted opening an illuminated manuscript where at the top of the page the Boston *Le Chant d'Amour* is illustrated. To emphasize his amorous liaison with Maria, Burne-Jones depicts a plumed peacock arrow pointing to the musical love imagery. He enwraps the arrows with a *cartellino*, with the inscriptions, *"Mary Aetat XXVI, August 1870 EBJ pinxit"* ("Mary at aged 26, August 1870, painted by *EBJ*"). Several allusions and associations of love are depicted, such as the Cupid pulling aside the curtain to reveal the beautiful woman, Maria, a type of a Greek Aphrodite, as well as the inclusion of flowers, such as the pink primrose and the blue iris. The primrose alludes to the renewal of love and devotion. Maria is holding the flower in her hand and pointing to the miniature of the *Love Song*. The blooming blue iris, too, conveys deep sentiments of affection. Not by accident, the Greek word for rainbow is iris. Burne-Jones conveys his subliminal passion for Maria through the application of the intense blue color in the background, e.g., the curtain, the iris and the lapis lazuli necklace. The *putto* unveils not only the beauty of the model, but also the signification of the model for the painter. The gemstone and the flowers both allude to sentiments of friendship, truth and unending love, as well as spiritual communion of the mind and body. Similar to the image in the miniature, the *Love Song* is a suspended melody, an allegory of music; so is the painted portrait of Maria, which is a poised similitude of Burne-Jones's loved one, an unveiling of image of love as well as an allegory of painting. Burne-Jones, here, is assimilating and modifying the ancient Greek motto of Horace's *ut pictura poesis* into *ut pictura musica.*

Burne-Jones and his teacher, Dante Gabriel Rossetti, are fascinated by the power of music in evoking physical and metaphysical states. In their paintings—Burne-Jones's *Le Chant d'Amour* and Rossetti's *The Blue Closet*—both artists convey emotions and aesthetic experiences through "unheard melodies."[47] Although intrigued by Walter Pater's comments on music in "The School of Giorgione" (1877) as an art that must be "constantly aspire,"[48] in their paintings, Burne-Jones and Rossetti portray the poetic evocation of sounds as well as sight, whose aims are to arouse the senses and the soul of the perceiver.

In both versions of *Le Chant d'Amour*, the pastoral composition, the evening light, subdued coloration, and the romantic mood represent an assimilation of Venetian Renaissance paintings, in particular, the works of Carpaccio, Giorgione and Titian. But in the architectural design, Burne-Jones combines his romantic medieval quest with his present Pre-Raphaelite living areas, creating a utopian setting.

The design of both *Le Chant d'Amour* is similar. The composition is divided into three horizontal bands. In the background, there is a similar sunset with an Oxford medieval village (the Metropolitan version expands the village and sharpens the brick texture of the building); in the middle ground an idyllic landscape where sheep rest on a green pasture; and in the foreground on an elevated platform, there are three figures engaged in the sound of music. Before them, a frieze with a bed of flowers, tulips, red and yellow tiger lilies, and periwinkles, associated with the setting of the sun, encloses the scene.

When comparing these two pictures, *Le Chant d'Amour*, it is in the foreground where the major variations occur. In his analysis of these paintings, the author John Christian focuses on the stylistic improvements in figure treatment, light and color effects in the second version (Metropolitan version) revealing Burne-Jones's assimilation of the Renaissance style during his repeated visits to

Italy. Christian also elaborates on Henry James's positive exhibition review, where the Metropolitan version was in displayed in 1877. "No English painter of our day has a tithe of his distinction," James writes.[49]

Both paintings are extraordinary in their aesthetic beauty and in their unique signification. In both foregrounds, the three figures (knight, musical muse, and personification of Love) are designed in separate triangular spaces in the manner of the Italian High Renaissance style. But they are united on a horizontal and rectangular platform. The two lovers, knight and musical muse, are separated from the personification of Love by an organ. With the exception of the knight, the other two figures are different in both action and signification.

In the Boston *Le Chant d'Amour*, the muse is playing an organ while singing, indicated by her parted lips. As she chants, she turns the pages of the musical score book with one hand, with the other, she plays the organ. Both knight and muse are rapt in the magic moment of the power of music. The knight is particularly engaged in perceiving both sounds, one from the muse's voice and the other from the organ played by the muse. For the muse, the enthrallment is in her performance of playing, but mostly of singing for her lover, the knight. On the other side of the simple wooden organ, the personification of Love is bellowing the instrument. He performs blindly, as love itself is without sight. Flickering flames of love encircle him and indicate his mercurial nature, while also identifying his function, which is to evoke ardent love. Crowned with roses, Love rests his bow and arrows on a bed of flowers. His deed of igniting love is achieved; the knight is in love with the muse of music. Of the three figures, Love is most active participant as he eagerly bellows the organ. Burne-Jones parallels Love's blowing action with his windblown veil. But, most significantly, he masterfully paints Love surrounded by glimmering flames, which are readily burning despite residing on a marble platform. The other two figures, the musical muse and the knight, are receptive of the gifts of passion and music provided by Love.

Burne-Jones parallels the power of music with the power of love, the arousal of the senses through hearing and seeing is elevated to the abstract and aesthetic concepts of Platonic beauty and love. The Boston *Le Chant d'Amour* reveals the sensation of love through the senses of touch, sight, and hearing. In this painting, Burne-Jones manifests the dazzling of love in its early stages. Burne-Jones is indicating that the visual depiction of the triumph of love parallels with the aesthetic manifestation of beauty in art. "Only this is true, that beauty is very beautiful and softens, and comforts, and inspires, and rouses, and lifts up, and never fails."[50]

The Metropolitan *Le Chant d'Amour* symbolizes another type of love. The transformation is from ardent love into devotional love. In the foreground, there are several transformations. Burne-Jones's most dramatic transformation is in the personification of Love, from the depiction of a young, blind Cupid (Boston) to an angelic type of Cupid (Metropolitan). The flames and the bow and arrows have disappeared to be replaced by a meditative figure of Love, crowned with laurel and surrounded by myrtle, plants sacred to Apollo and Venus.

Among the various studies for this painting, two stand out. In 1868, Burne-Jones composes a unique nude study of the Cupid (*Study for Le Chant d'Amour: Seraph* at Aberystwyth University, School of Art Gallery and Museum, Wales, Fig. 11), as well as a female's portrait, (*Study for Le Chant d'Amour: Woman's Head*, also at Aberystwyth University, School of Art Gallery and Museum, Wales), or the drawing of *Maria Zambaco* of 1868 (Birmingham Museums and Art Gallery), which is reminiscent of Maria Zambaco's features (Figs. 12-14). During this period Burne-Jones employs Maria as a model for his paintings, while conducting his amorous interlude with her. This period, in part, parallels the beginning and ending of Burne-Jones's execution of the painting; starting in 1868, constantly working throughout the years, and completed circa 1873.

In the painting, the knight, the lover, continues admiring the figures of Cupid and the muse. He appears untransformed in comparison with the Boston version. But in this painting, the muse plays the organ and does not chant. She seems to have become the personification of Love as well as the personification of Music. Laurel and myrtle plants, the attributes of Venus, the Goddess of Love, surround her. Burne-Jones's type of foliage is reminiscent of the plants in Botticelli's *Birth of Venus*, where Venus is an allegory of

Love. Here, Burne-Jones may be inverting as well as reverting the roles between the muse and Cupid. The knight may be gazing at the organ's decoration. Unlike the Boston version, the Metropolitan painting depicts a very elaborate ornamentation on the frame of the organ. Burne-Jones decorates the wooden frame of the organ, at the level of the metal pipes, with acanthus leaves and vases where flowers and birds reside. However, at the lower part of the organ, below the level of the bellows, in a niche, a standing classical figure is surrounded by laurel, with his head surrounded by sunrays. It is likely that Burne-Jones is depicting Apollo, also a god of Love and Music. The laurel recalls the myth of Apollo and Daphne. In addition to the power of music and love and it transformation in the human psyche, the knight may be contemplating the transformation of the myth as well. Burne-Jones may be reversing the mythic gender roles in depicting his own transformation into Daphne, being unable to follow through his interlude with Maria, and recoiling into his Victorian marriage. He portrays Apollo in despair in the organ's decoration, likely alluding to himself, while the knight contemplates the personifications of Love and Music in the depiction of the muse (Maria) and Cupid. Burne-Jones evocative and enigmatic paintings of *Le Chant d'Amour* and *Lament* arouse in the viewer complex and personal feelings, as well as intricate aesthetic perceptions in art. The visual imagery and its signification becomes a catalyst for comprehending metaphysical notions about creativity. He is able to immortalize them in an aesthetic form of beauty. In these paintings, Burne-Jones manifests the intricacies of, and bonds within, the creative arts, poetry, painting and music, as well as the reflections of the human spirit.

End Notes

[1] Georgiana Burne-Jones, *Memorials of Edward Burne-Jones* (London: McMillan Company, 1904), Vol. 2, 1.

[2] See David Cecil, *Visionary and Dreamer: Two Poetic Painters, Samuel Palmer and Edward Burne-Jones* (Princeton: Princeton University Press, 1969), 143, quoting from a letter Burne-Jones wrote to Morris.

[3] A term based on the French slogan, "*l'art pour l'art,*" coined by French philosopher Victor Cousin, see Gene H. Bell-Villada, *Art for Art's Sake &*

Literary Life: How Politics and Markets Helped Shape the Ideology & Culture of Aestheticism, 1790-1990 (Lincoln: University of Nebraska Press, 1996), Introduction.

[4] Burne-Jones is likely aware of Walter Pater's philosophical writings, particularly *Plato and Platonism* (London, 1893), 241-44, where Pater discusses Plato's notions of Beauty and Nature. See also Robin Spencer, *The Aesthetic Movement: Theory and Practice* (London: Studio Vista Ltd., 1972), 37, and Liana De Girolami Cheney, "Burne-Jones : Mannerist in an Age of Modernism," *Pre-Raphaelite Art in Its European Context*, Susan Casteras and Alicia Faxon, eds. (Cranbury, N.J.: Fairleigh Dickinson Press, Associated University Press), 103-16.

[5] John Ruskin, The *Elements of Drawing* of 1852 (New York: Dover Publications, 1971); *The Stones of Venice* of 1853 (Cambridge, MA: De Capo Press, 2003); *Modern Painters of* 1843-1853 (New York: Knopf, 1998), *Pre-Raphaelitism* of 1851 (Baltimore: Penguin Press, 2010); Walter Pater, *Studies in the History of the Renaissance* of 1869-73 (New York: Dover Publications, 2005); and Oscar Wilde, *The Picture of Dorian Gray* of 1890 (New York: Modern Library, 1998). See also Stephen Calloway and Lyn Federle Orr, *The Cult of Beauty: The Aesthetic Movement 1860-1900* (London: Victoria and Albert Museum 2011), Introduction.

[6] John Hale, *England and The Italian Renaissance* (London: Fontana Press, 1996), 1-81.

[7] Viccy Coltman, *Classical Sculpture: and the Culture of Collecting in Britain since 1760* (Oxford: Oxford University Press, 2009), 117-58.

[8] Martin Harrison and Bill Walters, *Burne-Jones* (London: Barie and Jenkins, 1973, 9-32; Stephen Wildman and John Christian, *Edward Burne-Jones: Victorian Artist-Dreamer* (New York: Harry N. Abrams Inc., 1998), 41-47; and Ann S. Dean, *Burne-Jones and William Morris in Oxford and the Surrounding Areas* (Malvern: Heritage Press, 1991), 1-61. See also M. A. Goldberg, "John Keats and the Elgin Marbles," *Apollo* (November, 1965), 374-78; Frank M. Turner, *The Greek Heritage in Victorian Britain* (London: Yale University Press, 1981), 1-14; Caroline Clifton-Mogg, *The Neoclassical Source Book* (New York: Rizzoli, 1991), 16-26; and Sam Smiles, *The Image of Antiquity in Ancient Britain and the Romantic Imagination* (London: Yale University Press, 1994), 1-8.

[9] See Harrison and Walters, *Burne-Jones*, 56-57, and John Christian, "Burne-Jones's Second Italian Journey," *Apollo* (November 1975): 334-37, for a discussion of the Italian, Flemish and German paintings and manuscripts that influence Burne-Jones during the time of his first two journeys to Italy; namely, the Italian painters, Giotto, Fra Angelico, Piero della Francesca, Giovanni da Matteo, Luca and Andrea della Robbia, Carpaccio, Signorelli, Mantegna, Giorgione, Correggio, Tintoretto and Veronese,

and, in particular, Botticelli. In addition, Burne-Jones spends a great deal of time viewing manuscripts at the British Museum, National Gallery of Art and then the newly opened South Kensington Museum (Victoria and Albert Museum). He also develops a special interest in Flemish and German painters and prints, namely Jan van Eyck, Lucas Cranach, Lucas van Leyden, Hans Memling, and, in particular, Albrecht Durer's prints of *Melancolia, Knight, Death and the Devil*, and *Adam and Eve*. In viewing Burne-Jones' sketchbooks of this period, one observes his impressions of Thomas Hope's *Costumes of the Ancients* (1809) and Henry Shaw's *Dresses and Decorations of the Middle Ages* (1843) in his paintings.

[10] The cycles of *Pygmalion and Galatea* of 1868-78 and *Paris and Helen of Troy* of 1870-unfinished, at Birmingham Museums and Art Gallery, *Cupid and Psyche* of 1874-1876, at the Manchester Art Gallery, *Perseus and Andromeda* of 1875-1878, at the Graves Art Gallery, Sheffield.

[11] *The Sirens* of 1870-189, at the Ringling Museum, Sarasota, Florida.

[12] Marsilio Ficino, *Symposium, I. 3*, in *Opera* (Basel, 156l), and for a study on the impact of Marsilio Ficino's Neoplatonism and Renaissance art, see Liana Cheney, *Botticelli's Neoplatonic Images* (Potomac, MD: Scripta Humanistica, 1993).

[13] William Gaunt, *The Pre-Raphaelite Tragedy* (New York: Harcourt, Brace and Company, 1942), 152, and Robin Spencer, *The Aesthetic Movement: Theory and Practice* (London: Studio Vista Ltd., 1972), 37.

[14] Penelope Fitzgerald, *Edward Burne-Jones* (London: Hamish Hamilton, 1975), cfr. n. 5, 68.

[15] This book, which was published in 1499 by the Venetian Aldine Press, was considered the most beautiful book printed in the Renaissance. See L. Fierz-David, *The Dream of Poliphilo: The Soul in Love*, Dallas 1987, and Joscelyn Godwin, *The Strife of Love in a Dream* (London: Thames and Hudson, 1999), ed. and trans. English edition.

[16] Fitzgerald, *Edward Burne-Jones*, 108, note 5. Burne-Jones admires these woodcut illustrations and so he appropriates them for the imagery of *Cupid and Psyche*. See Harrison and Walters, *Burne-Jones* (London 1973), 82, for a discussion of the close parallels of Morris' *The Earthly Paradise* and Colonna's *Hypnerotomachia Poliphili*.

[17] Otto van Vaenius, *Amorum Emblemata* (Antwerp 1608). In 1609, Vaenius publishes an early English edition with a dedication to two English noblemen, William Herbert, the third Earl of Pembroke, and his brother, Philip Herbert, Earl of Montgomery. These two nephews of Sir Philip Sidney were known as the greatest literary patrons in England in their time. See a recent reprint of Otto Vaenius, *Amorum Emblemata* with an introduction by Karl Porteman (London: Scholar Press 1995), 7.

[18] GBJ, *Memorials*, Vol. 1, 273.

[19] Maria Teresa Benedetti e Gianna Piantoni, *Burne-Jones: dal preraffael-lismo al simbolismo* (Milan: Mazzotta, 1986), 156.

[20] See Benedetti and Piantoni, *Burne-Jones*, 155-56, for a information on the provenance of the painting as well as its sources. See Stephen Wildman and John Christian, *Edward Burne-Jones: Victorian Artist-Dreamer* (New York: Metropolitan Museum of Art, 1998), 131-33, for a discussion on the merits of this painting only—aesthetically devoid of any subject matter.

[21] Burne-Jones's interior setting design recalls the architectural design for chambers in Francesco Colonna's *Hypnertomachia Poliphili* (Venice 1499), edited and translated in English by Joscelyn Godwin, *The Strife of Love in a Dream* (London: Thames and Hudson, 1999), 443 and 446.

[22] Burne-Jones created three series with this topic. The subject derives from the Grimm Brothers' story of the *Sleeping Beauty* (1812). The first Briar Rose series paintings (*The Briar Wood, The Council Chamber* and *The Rose Bower*) are in the Muse de Arte de Ponce in Puerto Rico. The second Briar Rose series paintings (*The Briar Wood, The Council Chamber, The Garden Court* and *The Rose Bower*), is located at Buscot Park in Oxfordshire, United Kingdom; and the third Briar Rose series of paintings have been divided into three collections, *The Garden Court* is in the Bristol City Museum and Art Gallery, *The Council Chambers* is in the Delaware Art Museum in Wilmington, Delaware, USA, and *The Rose Bower* is in the Hugh Lane Gallery of Modern Art in Dublin, Ireland. The series in Buscot Park was first exhibited at Agnew's Gallery in Bond Street in 1890. Alexander Henderson, later known as Lord Farringdon, acquired the series for his residence in Buscot Park. When Burne-Jones saw them in their salon setting, he makes adjustments by filling in the gaps to continue the rose motif from wall to wall.

[23] British poets were impressed by the Elgin Marbles, see M. A. Goldberg, "John Keats and the Elgin Marbles," *Apollo* (November 1965): 370-78.

[24] When flipping the imagery, the association becomes more obvious.

[25] The Victoria and Albert Museum in London owns six notebooks of Burne-Jones's sketchbooks (No. E-I-1955-E-6-1955).

[26] Guy de Tervarent, *Attributs et Symboles dans L'Art Profane* (Geneva: Droz, 1997), 305, and James Hall, *Dictionary of Subjects and Symbols in Art* (New York: Harper and Row Publishers, 1974), 217.

[27] Burne-Jones is familiar with Chaucer's writings since his schooling at Oxford. With Morris, he planned to illustrate many of the Chaucer's works. See Christopher Wood, *Burne-Jones* (New York: Steward, Tabori & Chang, 1978), 36-38, and Stephen Wildman and John Christian, *Edward Burne-Jones: Victorian Artist-Dreamer* (New York: Metropolitan Museum of Art, 1998), 308-10.

[28] There are numerous drawings for *Lament*, mostly located at the

Birmingham Museums and Art Gallery. (Study for the Lamenter are Accession number: 1904P203; Accession number: 1904P205; and, here are included: Accession number: 1904P207; Accession number: 1904P206; Accession number: 1904P204; and Accession Number: 1904P188).

[29] See Godwin, *The Strife of Love in a Dream*, 344, for an illustration of a terminal figure.

[30] Barbette Stanley Spaeth, *The Roman Goddess Ceres* (Austin, TX: The University of Texas, 1996), 63-65.

[31] Spaeth, *The Roman Goddess Ceres*, 37, illustrated in figs. 7 and 29.

[32] Hall, *Dictionary of Subjects and Symbols in Art*, 305.

[33] Thomas J. Mathiesen, *Apollo's Lyre: Greek Music and Music Theory in Antiquity and the Middle Ages* (Nebraska: University of Nebraska Press, 1999), 222 and note 142.

[34] Apostolos N. Athanassakis, "Music and Ritual in Primitive Eleusis," *Platon* 28 (1976), 86-105.

[35] According to ancient tradition, the syrinx is viewed as a foreign instrument, some claiming that Marsyas discovered the syrinx and learned to played it (Athenaeus' *Deipnosophistae* 4.82), while others maintains that the Celts, the islanders in the ocean, invented it (Pollux's *Onomasticos* 4.77), Mathiesen, *Apollo's Lyre*, 223, notes 144 and 145.

[36] Raymond Preston, *Chaucer* (London: Sheer and Ward, 1950), 472; Peter Brown, *Chaucer and the Making of Optical Space* (London: Peter Lang Publishers, 2007), 152; and Benedetti and Piantoni, *Burne-Jones*, 221-22.

[37] Raymond Preston, *Chaucer* (London: Sheer and Ward, 1950), p. 246, and Benedetti and Piantoni, *Burne-Jones*, 221-22.

[38] Anthony H. Harrison, *Swinburne's Medievalism-A Study in Victorian Love Poetry* (New Orleans: Louisiana State University Press, 1979), Chapter 2, note 4, and Benedetti and Piantoni, *Burne-Jones*, 278-79. In 1870s, Burne-Jones illustrates Chaucer's partial translation of the *Romaunt of the Rose* for the Kelmscott Press; however, his major source of inspiration is the Quattrocento manuscript (Mr. Harley 4425) acquired by the British Museum, whom he consults numerous times because he admires the *hortus conclusus*, garden decorations, in the illustrations (GBJ, Memorials, 104, II, 217).

[39] Anthony H. Harrison, "The Swinburnean Woman," *Philological Quarterly*, LVIII (1979), 90-102.

[40] Harrison and Walters, *Burne-Jones*, 64-65.

[41] Harrison and Walters, *Burne-Jones*, Fig. 11.

[42] Fitzgerald, *Edward Burne-Jones*, 16, Malcolm Bell, *Sir Edward Burne-Jones* (London: George Bell and Sons, 1901, reproduced in 2010), 1-10, discussing his educational years. See Denys Sutton, "Celtic and Classical Dreams," *Apollo* (November 1975): 314-20, for an analysis of Burne-Jones's artistic influences and musical interests, in particular, his musical atten-

dance at Lord Leighton's home, where well-known musician Joachim performed with great enthusiasm.

[43] Wildman and Christian, *Burne-Jones*, 99.

[44] See Wildman and Christian, *Burne-Jones*, 100, for all the commentaries made when the watercolor painting is displayed at the Old Water-Color Society in 1866.

[45] William Graham, an important collector and patron of Burne-Jones, purchases the Boston version from the artist, likely before 1868. In 1906, the painting is acquired by the Boston Museum of Fine Arts (Inv. 06.2432). The watercolor is exhibited at the Old Water-Color Society of London in 1865. Graham also commissions the Metropolitan version in 1868. It is then exhibited at the Grovesnor Gallery in 1878. The panting is acquired by the Metropolitan Museum of Art in 1947 (Inv. 47.26). Henry James highly praises it, describing it "as a group of three figures, seated, in a rather unexpected manner upon the top of a garden wall." See Wood, *Burne-Jones*, 78, for records which document the early design on this subject, *Le Chant d'Amour*, created for a decoration of a small upright piano made by F. Priestley of Berners Street in London (now in the Victoria and Albert Museum, London). The American walnut piano is given as a wedding present to Burne-Jones in 1860. Burne-Jones paints the lid of the piano in monochrome in 1863. The subject is of a lady playing the organ with a figure of Love (Cupid) at the bellows. Then, in 1865, Burne-Jones paints the Boston watercolor adding the lovesick knight in armor, the Arthurian landscape in the background, and the wallflowers and tulips in the foreground. A year later, in 1866, he paints a similar version sans the figure of Love. And in 1868, Burne-Jones revisits the theme and begins painting a large version in oils, which he finishes in 1877, now at the Metropolitan Museum of Art. See Wildman and Christian, *Burne-Jones*, 212-14, for a discussion of the reception of this painting during Burne-Jones's era.

[46] There is another drawing of the muse's face, signed and dated *EBJ 1878*; but it is executed after the painting was exhibited at the Grovesnor Gallery, or likely Burne-Jones reworks the drawing of 1864 and adds the date of 1878. See Sotheby's London, July 15, 2008, LO131; Lot 14.

[47] Patrick Blade, *Edward Burne-Jones* (New York: Parkstone Press, 2004), 27.

[48] Wildman and Christian, *Burne-Jones*, p. 98, quoting GBJ, *Memorials*, I, 302. See Burne-Jones' study of the knight at the Birmingham Museums and Art Gallery (Accession number: 1904P226).

[49] Wildman and Christian, *Burne-Jones*, 214, quoting Henry James.

[50] Gaunt, *The Pre-Raphaelite Tragedy*, 152 and Cheney, "Burne-Jones: Mannerist in an Age of Modernism," 103-16.

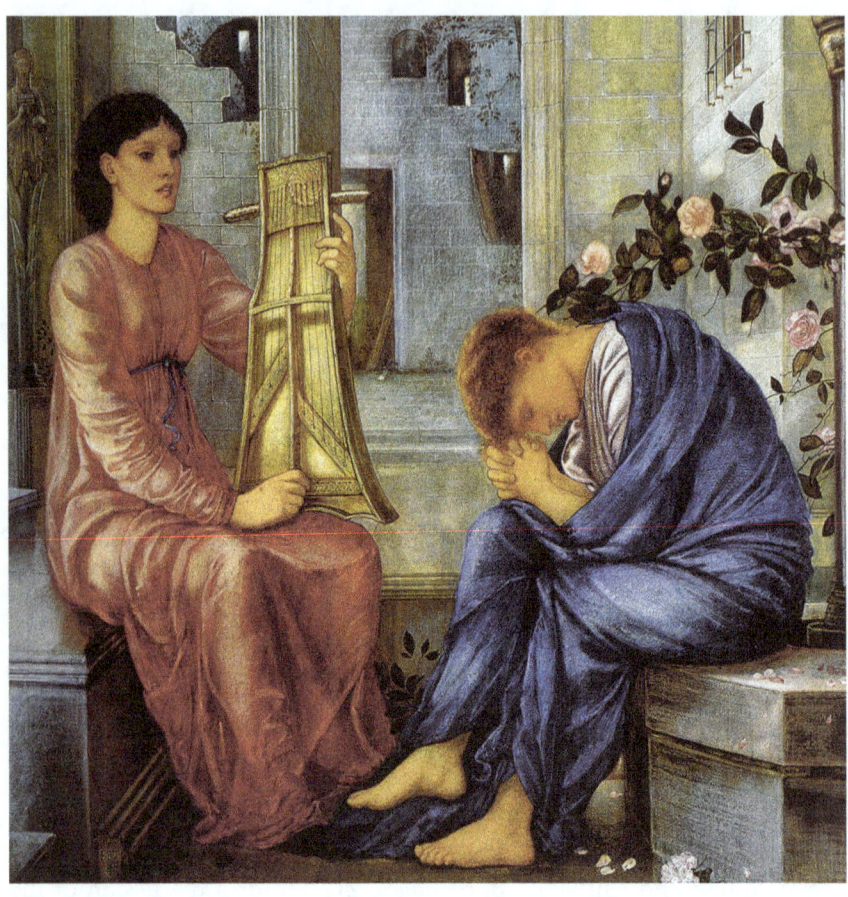

4.1. Edward Burne-Jones, *Lament*, 1866, watercolor, William Morris Gallery, Walthamstow, UK, photo credit: Art Resource/NY.

4.2. Phidias, *Demeter*, East Pediment of the Parthenon, 447 BCE, British Museum, London, photo credit: author.

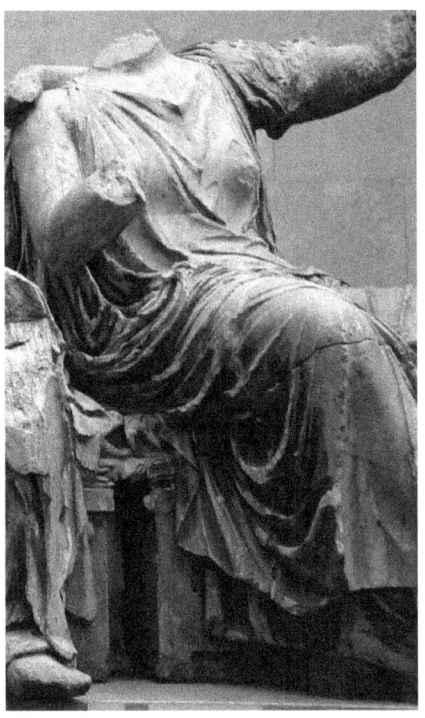

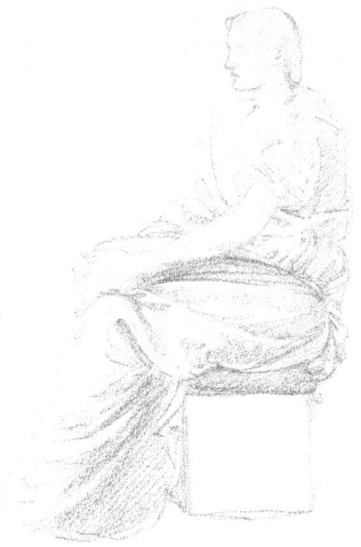

4.3. Edward Burne-Jones, *Study for Lament*, 1865, drawing, Birmingham Museum and Art Gallery, UK, photo credit: Birmingham Museums and Art Gallery, UK (Accession Number: 1904P207).

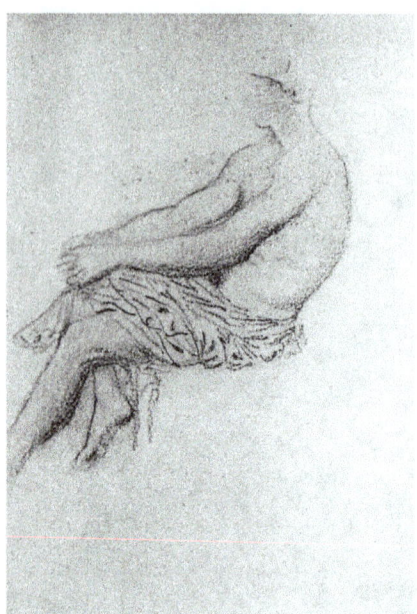

4.4. Edward Burne-Jones, *Copy of Mars* (Parthenon frieze), 1864, drawing, Victoria and Albert Museum, London, photo credit: Victoria and Albert Museum, London.

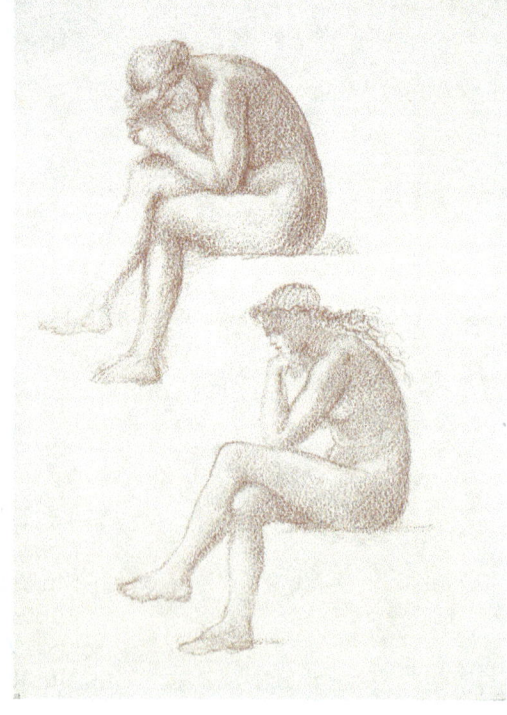

4.5. Edward Burne-Jones, *Sketch of Two Seated Figures: Lament*, 1864-65, drawing, Birmingham Museum and Art Gallery, UK, photo credit: Birmingham Museums and Art Gallery, UK (Accession Number: 1904P206).

4.6. Edward Burne-Jones, *Study of Lament: Lamenter,* 1865, drawing, Birmingham Museum and Art Gallery, UK, photo credit: Birmingham Museums and Art Gallery, UK (Accession Number: 1904P204).

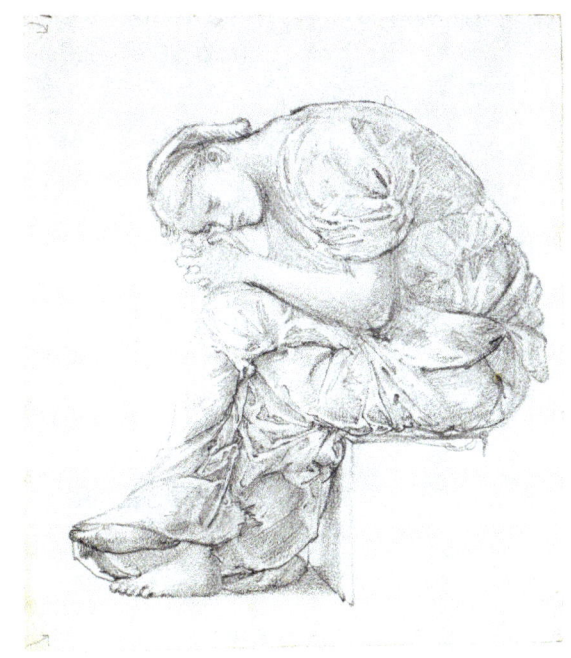

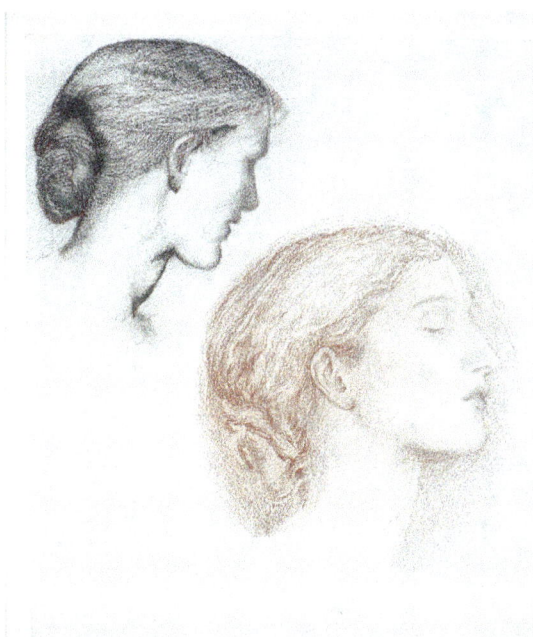

4.7. Edward Burne-Jones, *Study of Lament: Head of a Woman,* 1866, drawing, Birmingham Museum and Art Gallery, UK, photo credit: Birmingham Museums and Art Gallery, UK (Accession Number: 1904P188).

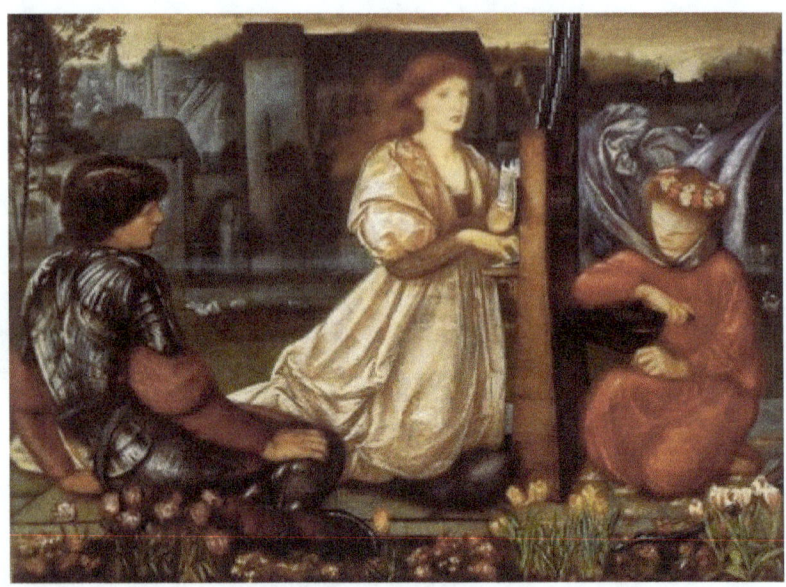

4.8. Edward Burne-Jones, *Le Chant d'Amour*, 1865, watercolor, Museum of Fine Arts, Boston, MA, photo credit: Museum of Fine Arts, Boston, MA.

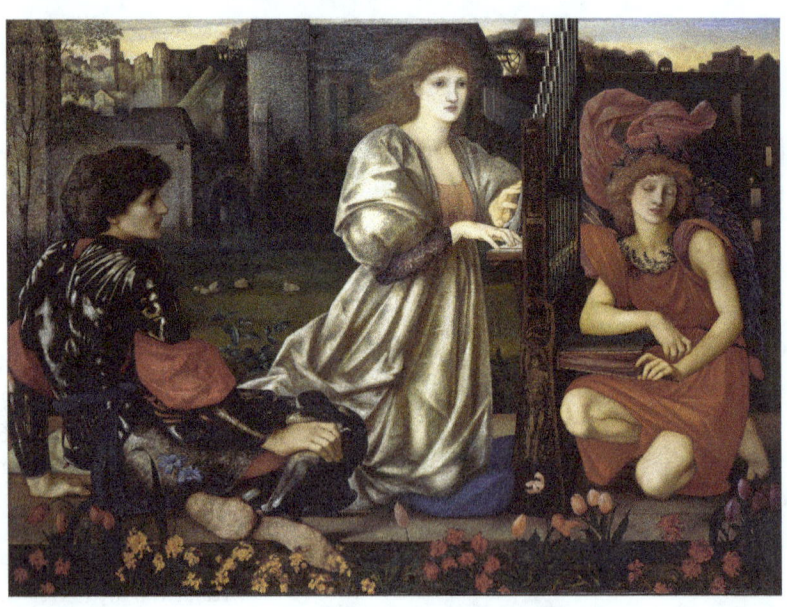

4.9. Edward Burne-Jones, *Le Chant d'Amour*, 1868-77, Metropolitan Museum of Art, New York, photo credit: Art Resource/NY.

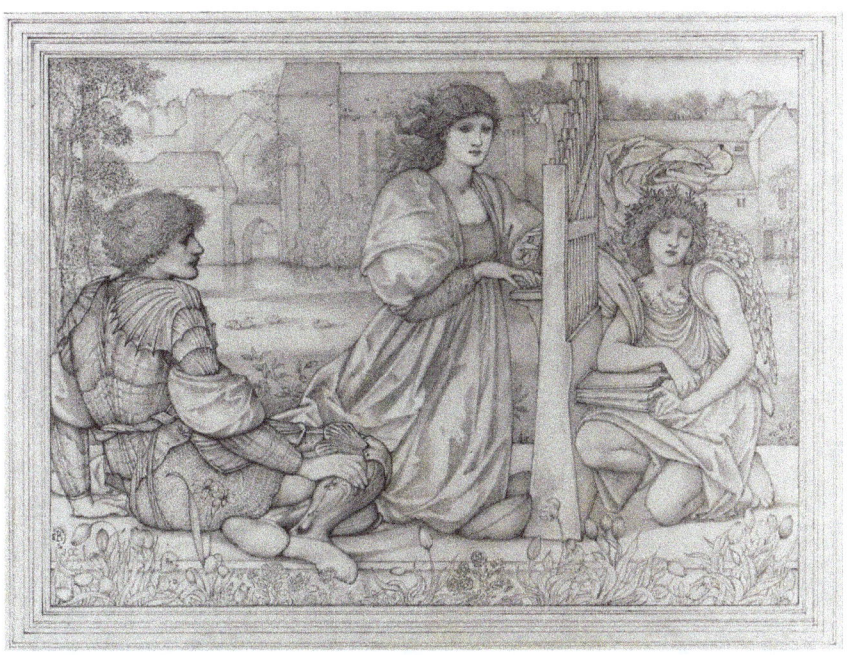

4.10. Edward Burne-Jones, *Le Chant d'Amour*, 1864, drawing, (Sotheby's London, July 15, 2008, LO8131; Lot 14), photo credit: Sotheby's, London, England.

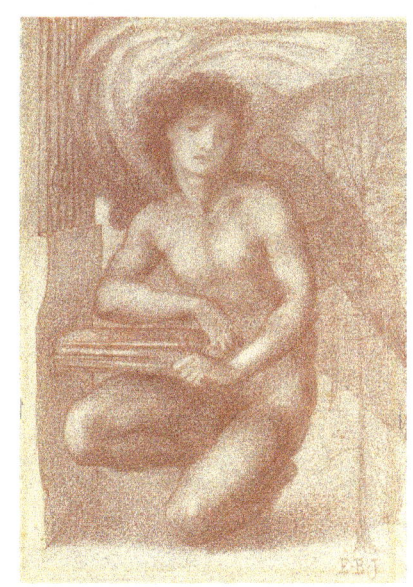

4.11. Edward Burne-Jones, Study for *Le Chant d'Amour: Seraph,* 1864, drawing, School of Art Gallery and Museum, Aberystwyth University, Wales, photo credit: Sotheby's, London, England.

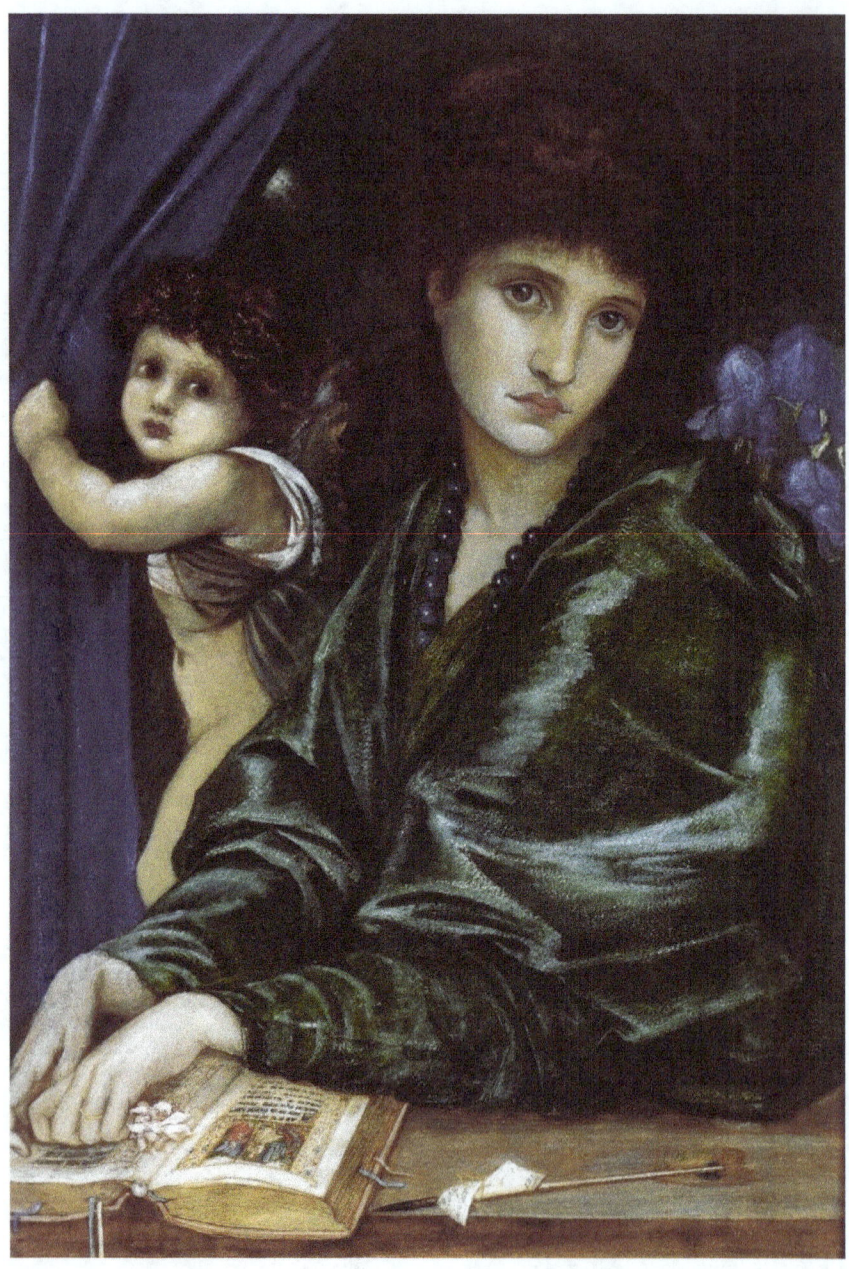

4.12. Edward Burne-Jones, *Maria Zambaco*, 1870, Clemns-Sels-Museum, Neuss, Germany, photo credit: Clemns-Sels-Museum, Neuss, Germany.

4.13. Edward Burne-Jones, *Maria Zambaco*, 1868, drawing, Birmingham Museums and Art Gallery, photo credit: Birmingham Museums and Art Gallery (Accession Number: 1927P451).

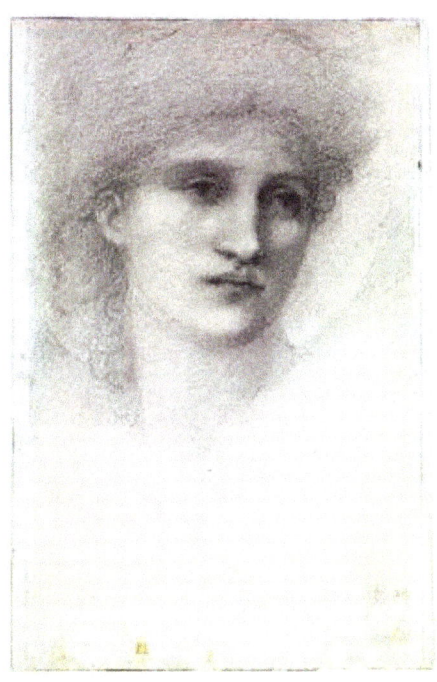

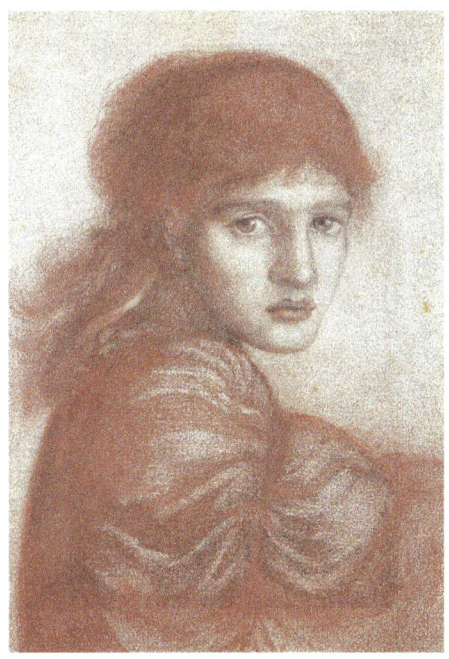

4.14. Edward Burne-Jones, Study of a Girl, Maria Zambaco, 1868, Wightwick Manor, Warwickshire, Great Britain, photo credit: National Trust Photo Library/Art Resource, NY.

5
The Waverley Oaks:
Something Borrowed, Something New

Lucretia Hoover Giese

Although Winslow Homer's Civil War paintings first brought him success and remain what is best known of his early career, they alone do not represent the extent of Homer's work before he sailed to Europe in 1866.[1] There is, for instance, *The Waverley Oaks* of 1864 (Fig. 1).[2] Though little discussed, this painting touches on fundamental problems Homer tackled in the 1860s: how to work out from under a variety of artistic influences; how to confront what were apparently opposing categories of genre and landscape; how to deal with the pervasive shadow of the Civil War (1861-1865). These involved choices, and Homer's decisions concerning them are the substance of this essay.

Homer began painting around 1862, in the midst of the Civil War (1861-1865).[3] Three years before, he had moved to New York from Massachusetts, seeking greener professional pastures for his work as an illustrator. Once in New York, he became acquainted with several artists through studios they maintained in the University Building, among them William J. Hennessy (1839-1917) and Eugene Benson (1839-1908).[4] Close in age, the three became friends.[5] By 1864, they were also linked professionally, to "the so-called 'genre' school" of painters that had "within the last few years, really taken root in America."[6]

Indeed, Homer's *The Waverley Oaks* of 1864 is at first glance a genre painting. Two young women stroll together apparently oblivious of anything but each other's company. Neither is greatly individuated apart from a costume accessory of red shawl or low

brimmed straw hat. Their pathway through a deeply wooded landscape follows a shaft of light that cuts nearly horizontally across
the painting, so sharp a contrast does its brilliance make with surrounding shadows. But the scene is not gloomy. Light strikes the
trees in the middle distance, and the sky, visible overhead through
the tree branches, is intensely blue and cloud-filled.

Upon closer inspection, if a genre painting, *The Waverly Oaks*
is an anomaly. Anecdote is all but absent. So, too, is the humor or
pointed relevancy associated with many Homers of the Civil War
decade.[7] Mood is unclear, as are the women's roles. Even the shaft
of light in *The Waverley Oaks* striking the figures does not impart
pastoral-like warmth. Several questions come to mind. Is the title
significant? Is the painting genre or landscape? Finally, there is the
question with which this essay began: what does the painting suggest about Homer and his connection to cultural issues of the mid-
1860s?

The painting's title, *The Waverley Oaks*, is of the period.[8] A grove
by that name of over twenty huge oaks stood in Belmont, Massachusetts. These trees, deemed "monarchs of the New England wilderness when Columbus discovered America," took their name
from the "village near which they stand" laid out by the Waverley
Land Company before Belmont's incorporation in 1859.[9] The development company in turn perhaps took its name from Sir Walter
Scott's Waverley Novels, then popular; in 1858, Boston publisher
Ticknor & Fields brought out a "household edition." The Beaver
Brook Reservation containing the oaks was created in 1893. In its
recommendation that "these grand old sentinels" be spared, the
Massachusetts Horticultural Society's Committee on Gardens gave
one tree's measurements as nineteen feet in circumference three feet
from the ground.[10] Some oaks, however, had been felled long ago
for shipbuilding, and other trees including "'large pines [within the
Reservation] were also selected and drawn out.'"[11] The Reservation
did protect the oaks, but by 1959, most were no longer standing, the
result of storm damage and decay.[12]

Belmont was known to Homer. He had relatives and, by 1858,
his parents also living there in a house rented by Charles, his older
brother. Homer's work provides proof of his own residency. Two
periodicals for which he worked in the late 1850s, *Ballou's Pictorial*

and *Harper's Weekly*, published respectively a panorama by Homer of Belmont in 1859, the year of the town's incorporation, and a series of wood engravings in the late 1850s, into which Homer slipped sly references to Belmont. "Belmont", for example, can be made out on the side of the provisions wagon in "Thanksgiving Day–Ways and Means," *Harper's Weekly*, November 27, 1858, and the town's name appears on a sign tacked to a tree in "May-Day in the Country," *Harper's Weekly*, April 30, 1859. Even after moving to New York, Homer produced works that pertained to Belmont.[13]

The very particular title *The Waverley Oaks*, then, argues for a very particular location and the activities the site must have fostered. A nineteenth-century photograph (1890) of the site features a sizable oak and two somewhat smaller ones in a park-like environment being enjoyed by visitors (Fig. 2).[14] The same oak captivated Homer, for he singled it out in a later drawing and watercolor (Fig. 3).[15] And his already mentioned "May-Day in the Country" of elegant women on horseback in the company of men and children reinforces the site's trees (the Waverley Oaks) as well as its suitability and attraction for light-hearted socializing. Lyrics for a song composed for festivities held at "Waverly [*sic*] Grove, Belmont, July 13, 1859," confirm the popularity of the site: "beneath the trees again/ In summer's glow we meet./…Our ceaseless music well accords/ With childish glee and noise,/ With youth's light laugh and earnest words/ And manhood's soberer joys."[16] The "two girls" in Homer's painting are without escort but, as noted by *The Nation* in 1866, they wear the "fashionable costume of the day."[17] Their poses also seem related to women's fashion plates in the popular press.[18] The reviewer rambled on about the painting's figures being "not more brilliant in color or more perfectly painted than other parts of the picture" and their being in a landscape, yet did not specify the site.[19]

Was it Belmont? The Waverley Oaks could have provided Homer a convenient and impressive wooded setting, yet nothing like the massive oak in Homer's drawing or those in later photographs figure in his painting *The Waverley Oaks*. What prompted Homer, then, to give that title to his painting and what did it connote in 1864? Homer provided no explanation, and contemporary authors Ralph Waldo Emerson and Henry David Thoreau are no help either as neither seem to have mentioned the Waverley Oaks. Harvard-based scientist Louis Agassiz in 1864 describing them in passing as "well known to all lovers of fine trees in our community."[20] But botanist George B. Emerson did not specify the Waverley Oaks in his Massachusetts-focused *A Report on the trees and shrubs growing naturally in the forests of Massachusetts* of 1846, nor did two other mid-century cataloguers of American trees, D. J. Browne and R. U. Piper.[21]

James Russell Lowell, however, did write of them.[22] He frequented the Beaver Brook Oaks area, his label for the Waverley Oaks, considering it "one of the loveliest spots in the world," and celebrating one giant specimen in his poem "The Oak" (1846).[23] Lowell's poem first appeared in the abolitionist journal, the *Anti-Slavery Standard* on December 31, 1846. After describing the qualities of the oak and observing, "all thy works are lessons," the poet asks God to:

Cause *me* some message of thy truth to bring,/Speak but a word through *me*, nor let thy love/Among *my* boughs disdain to perch and sing.[24]

Lowell's thrust is clear from lines in the poem's final stanzas. From his own "boughs", he hopes to articulate "some message of thy truth," a message, though not fully specified, appears drawn from the "lessons" of the steadfast oak's "rooted faith and oaken will."

Lowell's anti-slavery stance and dismay over the war, when it came, are clearly in evidence in a later poem of 1862. In Poem No. X, "*Mr. Hosea Biglow to the Editor of The Atlantic Monthly*," part of his pointed satire "The Biglow Papers," Lowell embedded a reference to Beaver Brook nearby the Waverley Oaks. Biglow, musing on the war, finds that its disruptions prevent even "Beaver" (Beaver Brook) from providing mental respite. He realizes "thet freedom ain't a gift /Thet tarries long in han's o'cowards!," and mourns the dead, longing for "Victory" and "Peace" to "bring fair wages for brave men,/ A nation saved, a race delivered!"[25]

Other American writings about America's woodlands occasionally had wartime resonance by the mid 1860s. For example, William Cullen Bryant's poem "My Autumn Walk," published early in 1865, is a meditation on the Civil War.[26] Bryant anguishes over the staggering numbers of "gallant dead" and contrasts them and their grieving families to the beauties of nature. In "woodlands ruddy with autumn" leaves fall "As fast, on the field of battle,/ Our brethren fall in death." Even though they "perish for the Right," the living left behind need consoling. Yet Bryant ends on a positive note. When the turmoil is over, life will begin again. For "The leaves are swept from the branches;/ But the living buds are there,/ With folded flower and foliage,/ To sprout in a kinder air." Bryant suggests solace comes from nature's rejuvenating force and indication that the nation will survive. Another instance is Thoreau's posthumously published *The Maine Woods*, which was interpreted by one reviewer in 1864 through the lens of war. Believing that the author's "sincere and careful book on Nature" would live forever, the reviewer took that assertion further to hope that "The infinite fascination of mountains and of forests will outlast this war and the next, and the race that makes the war."[27]

It cannot be assumed, however, that Homer considered the "forest" near him, Belmont's Waverley Oaks, in such terms. But he was doubtless aware of the oaks' impressive size and great age, perhaps considering them "a just symbol of fortitude," able to withstand "the wind and the storm," as one ante-bellum writer characterized the species in 1860.[28] The words tempt analogy with the country's situation in 1864 and 1865. Homer's views on the war are best gleaned from his visual "statements"—the countless drawings made while he was at the front (1861, 1862, and 1864), specific paintings (1864-1865)—and an isolated later written expression of the "horror" of "murder" performed by sharpshooters in 1862.[29] These indicate awareness of the issues and consequences of the war.

In 1864, Homer was once again at the front, this time in the contested terrain north of Richmond. The pinewoods there appear in several Homer paintings of 1864-1865 pertaining to the Civil War: *The Initials* (1864) (a young woman in a "pine-wood," so identified by a contemporary reviewer, traces initials carved in a tree of her dead or absent cavalry officer); *Old Woman Gathering Faggots* (1865) (in identical woods, an elderly woman burdened with faggots, drags them behind her, a subject linked to deprivation and hardship by a contemporary critic); *Trooper Meditating Beside a Grave* (1865) (in a comparable landscape, a young soldier gazes down at the solitary grave marker of a fallen comrade).[30] To this list, *Skirmish in the Wilderness* (combatants fight against the enemy all but invisible in the smoke of battle and tangle of trees and underbrush), exhibited with that location-specific title in November 1864, must be added (Fig. 4).[31] Significantly, the trees in *The Waverley Oaks* resemble those in the paintings just mentioned. Homer could have of course reused landscape components as a matter of convenience or to provide a certain gravitas to *The Waverley Oaks*. Its setting, as suggested, does relate to "America" at war, and its title, presumably chosen by Homer himself, strengthens association with America. Lowell, after all, among others, had considered the oaks "the largest, I fancy, left in the country."[32]

Should *The Waverley Oaks* then be considered a landscape painting, even though critics had identified Homer, Hennessy and Benson as genre painters?[33] The latter categorization makes sense, judging from Homer's *Boys on a Bough* (1864) (Museum of Fine Arts, Springfield, MA), *The Red Feather* (1864) (Wadsworth Athenaeum, Hartford, CN; Hennessy's *Girl Gathering Apples* (New York *Leader*, XI, 22 June 3, 1865), *Under the Pines* (*The Round Table*, March 5, 1864); and Benson's *The Autumn Walk* (*The New Path*, December 1863), *The Pensive Moment* (1865) (Christie's, NY, sale December 7, 1984).[34] Though similar in some respects, *The Waverley Oaks* is harder to pin down. A period commentator evidently had difficulty too, somewhat incoherently describing the

> two girls who are but a small part of the picture, and who are dressed in the fashionable costume of the day, and who are not more brilliant in color or more perfectly painted than other parts of the picture, are yet the picture, / taking proper precedence over the landscape, not because the landscape is subordinated, but because it is necessarily subordinate in the presence of human figures equally well painted with itself.[35]

"The landscape" is neither named nor described. Instead, figures have pride of place, so to speak, being more than mere staffage.

The major critic of the period, Boston-born James Jackson Jarves, had considered both genre and landscape painting in *The Art-Idea* (1864). In the chapter "The New School of American Painting Contrasted with the Old," Jarves approvingly noted the "dawn of a respectable school of *genre* and home painting" coming from "French [artistic] incitement."[36] One American practitioner singled out was Eastman Johnson, whose work expressed "those feelings, sentiments, and ideas" coming from American life. Jarves also discussed landscape painting, that "thoroughly American branch of painting, based on the facts and tastes of the country and people." It surpassed "all others in popular favor,…Almost everybody whose ambition leads him to the brush essays landscape."[37] In general, work in this category displayed "realism, vigor, enterprise, and freshness" but had little "poetry or ideas."[38] It had "barrenness of thought and feeling" and lack of "human association."[39] Were these due to American painters' "inaptitude" with figuration and the rendering of "strong passions and heroic action"? Using these deficiencies to explain why the "lofty character and vast issues of our civil war" had been largely overlooked, Jarves nevertheless urged an art commensurate with the noble aims of the current struggle.[40]

Benson's not-dissimilar position on this subject is evident in his reviews of the 1865 NAD Annual, the first after the war and President Lincoln's assassination.[41] (Benson began writing art criticism in 1864 under the sobriquets "Sordello" and "Proteus" for the *Round Table* and the New York *Evening Post*.)[42] In the "First Article," he acknowledged, "Our painters have worked in the midst of great events, and therefore subjected to the most tumultuous, shattering and ennobling [*sic*] experiences." His intent was to "discover" whether the Annual's offerings were forgettable or "a vital expression of our life," art, that is, that would "endure and be no mean attainment to remember as enriching a year that is memorable for the emancipation of a people, the supremacy of our arms, and a sorrow for the death of a good man [Lincoln].…" Clearly, Benson hoped to find the latter in what was exhibited. For he believed American art could not develop in isolation, "protected" from surrounding events.

In his "Second Article," Benson began by criticizing French painters for work that was "exquisite and expressive" in style but trivial in meaning. Although French painters may "have not much to tell, that little they tell so charmingly that we forget to ask more than they give."[43] Benson's position was that American painters, in contrast, attempted to "make us share something of their experience" even while speaking in "a language not yet acquired." Despite a certain awkwardness of style,

> seriousness and truth in *patois* ought to be more precious than folly and falsehood in the polished language of a French wit...Certainly we do not hanker after the graces, the seductions of French art. And if our sturdy reliance upon ourselves does not come from insensibility, we find cause to hope much of painters who would rather stutter in a language of their own that admits of a great development than impose upon themselves the letters of what is acquired and foreign.[44]

Indeed, some painting of "positive strength" had in fact materialized in the United States, notably at the hands of Homer. Benson was more specific about Homer in his "Concluding Article":

> It is invigorating to find boldness and truth amid the trivial and false...Homer is a young painter, but he has the manner of a practised [sic] hand, if we except refinement. We greet him as one of the most healthful among figure painters, and who brings to art just what redeems it from weakness and morbidness.[45]

Benson, however, concluded, echoing Jarves, that most painters had avoided the "agitating influences of this great epoch of our national life," having made in his opinion, art a "pleasant refuge from the toils and ardour [sic] of a sublime struggle." Benson did not label artists unpatriotic for giving "meager celebration of military triumphs" but suggested the times better suited to "imitate the Athenians than the Romans, better we honor the beautiful instead of covering our walls with battle-pictures to vie with Versailles."

Benson unhappily did not explain what he meant by the beautiful; however, he praised *Prisoners from the Front* (1866) in his review of that year's Annual as a "comprehensive epitome of the leading facts of this war."[46] This was what artists might create, not a histrionic war-machine but a painting in which figuration (three Confederate prisoners brought before a Union officer) and landscape (devastated by fighting) combined give meaning.

Benson did not discuss *The Waverley Oaks.* It did not appear in any NAD Annual and was not publicly shown until 1866 at the Athenaeum Club and at "Mr. Avery's [Samuel P. Avery, dealer] rooms in Broadway," and included in a Leeds & Miner sale on 16 November 1866. The painting did, however, garner some attention. *The World* considered it "a strongly painted picture;" *The Nation* described *The Waverley Oaks* as "particularly…full of power," even though Homer's work was thought to be "always so slap-dash."[47] And the painting was one of only three cited by title in *The Nation*'s review of the Leeds & Miner sale.[48]

But neither Benson nor Homer succeeded with the sale. Benson complained it had put him into debt, and Homer's *The Waverley Oaks* did not sell.[49] Homer deposited the painting with a friend, then wrote from Paris in 1867 to ask another if he would purchase the painting which "Perhaps you remember…"[50] Manner of painting may have been an issue. The unfinished quality of Homer's paintings had caused *The Nation* to question even the "propriety" of offering them for sale.[51] Or, although *The Waverley Oaks* had "human association" that Jarves sought in American landscapes, its lack of narrative clarity as a genre painting or specificity as a landscape may have been a hindrance. *The Waverley Oaks* does not tell an apparent story, unlike Homer's other pinewoods paintings of 1864-1865, or celebrate the landscape site its title identifies. Instead, the ensemble of towering, spiky trees (not oaks) and graceful female figures (seemingly merely ornamental) amid pronounced light contrasts is enigmatic.[52]

Benson had suggested, in reviewing the 1865 NAD Annual, art "of this great epoch of our national life" need not be of "wasted lands, clanging fights, and flaming towns." Pure landscapes were also "worthy of this great year," he posited, citing among those in the Annual, Worthington Whittridge's (1820-1910) "noble 'Twi-light'" on the Shawungunk (1865) or Homer Dodge Martin's (1836-1897) "vague mountains enfolded in mist and in the splendor of light."[53] Benson may well been thinking of Frederic Church's (1826-1900) *Twilight in the Wilderness* (1860), a visual premonition of the conflict ahead, or *Our Banner in the Sky* (1862), in which natural elements (solitary pine against red and blue streaked sky with star-studded patch of blue) comprise the nation's flag, understanding that landscapes could carry national symbolism. So could figural paintings. Benson would later label Homer's *Prisoners from the Front* a history painting.[54]

The Waverley Oaks, however, does not work this way. It remains in large part a Benson "home life" genre painting. One commentator, writing about the Homer/Benson sale in which *The Waverley Oaks* figured, declared the two artists' work revealed they were friends, who "have painted side by side," but went on to distinguish the two by considering Benson's "more carefully finished" pictures of generally "more home-like character" to speak to "the heart" whereas Homer's "appeal to the mind."[55] Perhaps this is so. Benson would soon choose criticism over art, but in 1866 Homer was only at the beginning of a long career of work. If *The Waverley Oaks* alludes to America and the Civil War by title and depicted forest, as proposed, landscape then is the signifier. In this respect, the painting begins to move from the "borrowed", the genre painting school to which Homer had early been linked, toward "new" possibilities of meaning achieved with landscape.

End Notes

[1] *The Waverley* [Waverly] *Oaks*, oil on paper mounted on panel (Museo Thyssen-Bornemisza, Madrid, Spain). Lloyd Goodrich, edited and expanded by Abigail Booth Gerdts, *Winslow Homer, Record of Works by Winslow Homer*, vol. 1, no. 248, 299-300. Museo Thyssen-Bornemisza uses the bracketed spelling and no article.

[2] Homer's wood engraving "The Army of the Potomac – A Sharpshooter on Picket-Duty," published by *Harper's Weekly*, 15 November 1862, bore the caption "From a painting by W. Homer." *Sharpshooter, Record of Works*, vol. 1, no. 187, 224-225.

[3] Thomas B. Aldrich in his early article on Homer ("Among the Studios. III," *Our Young Folks*, vol. 2, [July 1866]: 394) first provided this information.

[4] They were members of the Century Club of New York by 1864 or 1865; *The Century, 1847-1946* (NY: The Century Association, 1947), 366, 383, 384. Aldrich remembered meeting Homer and Hennessy after attending "The Gray Lady of Panarvon" at the Winter Garden in 1865 and walked home with them (Aldrich to his fiancée, letter of 22 May 1865 [Houghton Library, Harvard University, Cambridge, MA]). Benson characterized Hennessy and Homer as friends (Benson to William Conant Church, letter of 23 June 1868 [Church Papers, Rare Books and Manuscripts Division, New York Public Library]). The New York *Evening Post* (16 November 1866, 2) declared Benson and Homer to be friends. Homer may have been Benson's cousin; Homer's mother's maiden name was Benson. Elizabeth Johns (*Winslow Homer: The Nature of Observation* [Berkeley: University of California Press, 2002], 172, n. 53) is the latest supporter of this possibility. Cikovsky discusses Benson as a friend and colleague of Homer (Cikovsky, Jr. and Franklin Kelly, *Winslow Homer* [New Haven, CN: Yale University Press, 1995], 28, 36, n. 62, and 37, n. 66) but does not mention Hennessy. Nor does Johns, when citing Benson among artists Homer knew soon after moving to New York; see *Winslow Homer*, 27.

[5] Established artists Eastman Johnson and George Lambdin figured in the listing as well; see New York *Leader*, 10, 16 (16 April 1864): 4. Also, "Atticus," New York *Leader*, vol. 9, no. 22 (30 May 1863): l, and "E.[ugene].B.[enson]," *The Round* Table, vol. 3 (12 May 1866): 295. In this review of the National Academy of Design exhibition, Benson praised Homer, lambasted Lambdin, and vacillated on Hennessy. James Jackson Jarves earlier (*The Art-Idea* (Cambridge, MA: The Belknap Press of Harvard University Press [1864, reprint 1960]: 183), cited only Johnson and the today little-known James Crawford Thom (1842-1898).

[6] Examples are *Playing Old Soldier*, 1863 (Museum of Fine Arts, Boston, MA) and *In front of the Guard House*, 1863 (Canajoharie Library and Art Gallery, NY) or *Inviting a Shot before Petersburg, Virginia*, 1864 (The Detroit Institute of Arts, MI) and *The Bright Side*, 1865 (Fine Arts Museums of San Francisco, CA).

[7] The title appears in commentary in *The Nation*, vol. 3, no. 72 (15 November 1866): 395; *The World* (10 November 1866): 2 (as "Beverley Oaks by Homer Winslow"); and *The Nation*, vol. 3, no. 73 (22 November 1866): 416 (as "Waverley Oaks").

[8] Abbie Brown Farwell, "Notable Trees about Boston," *New England Magazine*, vol. 22, no. 5 New Series (July 1900): 522. Charles Eliot, Olmsted Landscape Architectural Firm and creator of the Metropolitan Parks Com-

mission, gave the age of the trees somewhat more conservatively as "of some size before the Pilgrims landed on the shores of Massachusetts Bay," in "The Waverly [note the spelling] Oaks," *Garden and Forest*, vol. 3, no. 104 (19 February 1890): 85. (This essay is given to Charles S. Sargent, Founding Director of the Arnold Arboretum when reprinted.) The spelling varies, as does the number of Waverley Oaks. Eliot cited twenty-three oaks and one elm, Lorin L. Dame cited twenty-five (*Typical Elms and Other Trees of Massachusetts* [Boston: Little, Brown, and Company, 1890], 78), but twenty-four is Joshua Kendall's figure ("Round about the Waverley Oaks," *New England Magazine*, 14, New Series [March-August 1896]: 232). I thank Lisa DeCesare, Botany Libraries, Harvard University Herbaria, Cambridge, MA., for her assistance.

[9] John J. Barker, "Report of the Committee on Gardens for the Year 1884," *Transactions of the Massachusetts Horticultural Society for the Year 1884* (Boston: Printed for the Society, 1885), II, 273.

[10] *Belmont Historical Society Newsletter*, vol. 31, no. 2 (December 1960): 6. Other tree varieties included plum, hickory, elm, ash, maple, and sycamore.

[11] *Belmont Historical Society Newsletter*, vol. 31, no. 2 (December 1960): 9. I thank Victoria Haase, Belmont Historical Society, Belmont, MA, for her assistance with BHS material.

[12] On Homer in Belmont after 1859, see *New York Daily Tribune*, 16 December 1864, 6 ("trying his hand this summer at painting country [presumably Belmont] boys," and *The World* [10 November 1860: 2] ["painting during the summer in Belmont"]). Works by Homer post-dating 1859 concerning the Waverley Oaks include: *Old Waterwheel in Waverley*, watercolor, inscribed "Win Homer/1861," *Record of Works*, vol. 1, no. 61, 149; *Orlando Mead* (cousin living in Belmont), two drawings inscribed "July 4th/64," *Record of Works*, vol. 1, nos. 239 and 240, 294 and 295; *The Waverley Oaks*, painting, n.d., *Record of Works*, vol. 1, no. 249, 304-305; *Waverley Oaks*, drawing, inscribed "Homer" recto, verso "Waverley Oaks/$10/No. 14" [1878], *Record of Works*, vol. 3, no. 738, 162; and *Waverley Oaks*, watercolor, inscribed "Winslow Homer 1878," *Record of Works*, vol. 3, no. 739, 163-164. Another drawing *Shepherdess Resting under a Tree*," inscribed "WH 1878," shows a similar landscape; see *Record of Works*, vol. 3, no. 738, 162. As these works lie outside concerns of this essay, they are not discussed here.

[13] This untitled photograph by W. H. Rollins accompanied Eliot's article on "The Waverly Oaks" (91) and subsequent pieces as well, including Kendall's "Round about the Waverley Oaks" (229) and Farwell's "Notable Trees about Boston" (516). A "picture furnished by Mr. Handyside, near whose house the [Beaver] brook flows" illustrated F.H. Underwood's essay "Ralph Russell Lowell" in *Harper's New Monthly Magazine*, vol. 62, no.

368 [January 1881]: 262, ill. 256). Herbert Wendell Gleason photographed a "Single Oak. Waverley Oaks" in November 11, 1903, to accompany Vol. 5 of Thoreau's *Excursions;* see Robbins-Mills Collection of Herbert Wendell Gleason Photographs, Concord Free Public Library, Concord, MA. Lorin L. Dame's *Typical Elms and Other Trees of Massachusetts* contains a few photographs by Henry Brooks of the Waverly [the text's spelling] Oaks; Oliver Wendell Holmes contributed the Introductory Chapter. He is also likely the author of the unsigned "Waverley Oaks," *The Atlantic Monthly*, vol. 40 (September 1877): 319-326. Lastly, artist and landscape architect Arthur Shurcliff sketched the site in 1890; see "'The Work of Our Own Hands:' The Evolution of the Arthur A. Shurcliff's Summer Residence at Ipswich," *Old-Time New England,* vol. 78, no. 268 (Fall/Winter 2000): 45, Fig. 2.

[14] Abigail Booth Gerdts (*Winslow Homer in Monochrome* [NY: M. Knoedler & Co., Inc., 1987], 27, no. 25) calls the drawing "unlikely...a direct study for the painting." Illustrated in *Record of Works*, vol. 3, no. 738, 162.

[15] F[ranklin] B[enjamin] Sanborn, "Song for the Festival of the Twenty-eighty Congregational Society, at Waverly Grove, Belmont, July 13, 1859," set to Auld Lang Syne. (MSS *74.676 Houghton Library, Harvard University, Cambridge, MA).

[16] "Fine Arts. The Seventh Annual Exhibition of the Artists' Fund Society of New York, I," *The Nation*, vol. 3, no. 72 (15 November 1866): 396.

[17] For example, "Dress of American Women" in *The Round Table*, vol. 1, no. 3 [2 January 1864]: 39) opened with the statement "Dress is undoubtedly a very important part of the business of a woman." Magazines such as *Harper's New Monthly Magazine* offered fashion illustrations in its pages throughout 1864.

[18] *The Nation* (15 November 1866): 396.

[19] Agassiz's point was that the Waverley Oaks "so well known to all lovers of fine trees in our community, stand on an ancient moraine, …"; see Louis Agassiz, "Ice Period in America," *The Atlantic Monthly*, vol. 14 (July 1864): 89. Agassiz was professor at the Lawrence Scientific School at Harvard University between 1849-73, when Homer's brother, Charles (1834-1917, class of 1855), studied there.

[20] George B. Emerson, *A Report on the trees and shrubs growing naturally in the forests of Massachusetts* (Boston: Dutton and Wentworth, 1846); D(aniel) J(ay) Browne, *Sylva Americana; or a Description of the Forest Trees Indigenous to the United States, Practically and Botanically Considered* (Boston: William Hyde & Co., 1832); R(ichard) U(pton) Piper, *The Trees of America* (Boston: A. Williams & Co., 1855).

[21] Lowell is presumably the "eminent New England poet" cited in *The Atlantic Monthly* article "Waverley Oaks" as having counted the rings of a

sizable fallen Waverley oak (n. 20, 323). In writing of Lowell for *Harper's New Monthly Magazine* (1881), Underwood mentioned the oaks as "the only group of aboriginal trees, probably, standing on the Massachusetts coast." (262). Lowell lent William James Stillman's painting *The Oaks at Waverly* to the Boston Athenaeum in 1858; see *The Boston Athenaeum Art Exhibition Index, 1827-1874*, compiled and edited by Robert G. Perkins, Jr., and William J. Gavin, III, (Boston: Boston Athenaeum, 1980), 132.

[22] James Russell Lowell, *Letters* I, 149, quoted in *The Complete Works of James Russell Lowell* (Cambridge: Riverside Press, 1924), 76.

[23] The italics are mine. *The Complete Works of James Russell Lowell*, 100.

[24] *The Complete Poetical Works of James Russell Lowell*, ed. Horace E. Scudder (Cambridge: Houghton Mifflin Co., 1911), 276-277. As early as 1842, Lowell penned to his friend G. B. Loring, "The horror of slavery can only be appreciated by one who has felt it himself, or who has imagination enough to put himself in the place of the slave, and fancy himself not only virtually imprisoned, but forced to toil, and all this for no crime and for no reason except that it would be *inconvenient* to free them…Are the slaves to be forever slaves because our ancestors committed a horrible crime and wrong in making them so? Only think for a moment on the miserable and outrageous lie and fallacy here." See Charles Eliot Norton, ed., *Letters of James Russell Lowell*, I (NY: Harper & Brothers, 1894), 67.

[25] Bryant called his poem a "trifle" and asked James T. Fields, Editor of *The Atlantic Monthly* (Letter to Fields, 13 October 1864) to provide a title for publication by that periodical (*The Atlantic Monthly*, vol. 15, no. 87 [January 1865]: 20-21); see William Cullen Bryant II and Thomas G. Voss, eds., *The Letters of William Cullen Bryant*, IV (NY: Fordham University Press, 1984), 412. The editors deem the poem "the most poignant of Bryant's Civil War poems." Bryant darkened one line in a subsequent letter to Fields (27 October 1864), changing "And the banks of the noble James" to "And the wasted banks of the James" (*Ibid.*, 418).

[26] *The Atlantic Monthly*, vol. 14, no. 83 (September 1864): 386.

[27] "Among the Trees," *The Atlantic Monthly*, vol. 6, no. 35 (September 1860): 259.

[28] For illustrations of Homer's passes to the front and discussion of probable return in 1864, see Marc Simpson, *Winslow Homer: Paintings of the Civil War* (San Francisco, Fine Arts Museums of San Francisco, 1988). fig. 3, 18; fig. 4, 19; and 21, 176; and *Record of Works*, vol. 1, 314-315. Homer to George C. Briggs, 19 February 1896 (Misc. Mss. Winslow Homer Papers, Archives of American Art, Smithsonian Institution).

[29] Commentary on *The Initials* appeared in the New York *Leader*, vol. XI, no. 24 (17 June 1865): 5. *Old Woman Gathering Faggots* had conjured up deprivation, albeit that of an English woman, in the mind of one reviewer

of Hennessy's 1862 painting of that subject; see Henry T. Tuckerman, *Book of the Artists* (1867) (NY: James F. Carr, 1966), 454. See *Record of Works*, vol. l, no. 247, 301; no. 265, 327; no. 274, 340-341.

[30] Mills and I both note a correspondence between the landscapes of *Skirmish in the Wilderness* and *The Waverley Oaks;* see Mills in Simpson, *Winslow Homer: Paintings of the Civil War,* 177. See *Record of Works*, vol. 1, no. 259, 314-315.

[31] Lowell, *Letters* I, 149, quoted in *The Complete Works of James Russell Lowell,* 76.

[32] Comparisons made on the basis of titles, scant descriptions in reviews, or works themselves are problematic at best and sometimes impossible since not all works can be located today. All three painters exhibited regularly at the National Academy of Design and elsewhere, but only Homer did not exhibit at the Boston Athenaeum in the 1860s as well (see Perkins and Garvin, *The Boston Athenaeum Art Exhibition Index,* 19 (Benson), 76 (Hennessy).

[33] See *National Academy of Design Exhibition Record, 1826-1860,* I (NY: New-York Historical Society, 1943), 31-32 (Benson), 222-223 (Hennessy); Marie Naylor, ed., *Exhibitions of the National Academy of Design Exhibition Record, 1861-1900,* vol. I, (NY: Kennedy Galleries, 1973), 52-54 (Benson), 423-424 (Hennessy). The Smithsonian Institution's National Museum of American Art Inventory of American Paintings, Artist Listings, unhappily incomplete, gives fifteen works to Hennessy plus two on which he collaborated with other painters (James A. Suydam and William S. Haselton) and thirteen to Benson. About Hennessy's participation in the Boston Sanitary Fair, I thank Meredith E. Ward of Hirschl & Adler Galleries, Inc., NYC (letter to author, 3 September 1996).

[34] *The Nation*, vol. 3, no. 72 (15 November 1866): 395-396.

[35] Jarves, *The Art-Idea,* (Cambridge, MA: The Beknap Press of Harvard University Press, 1960, reprint), 182.

[36] Jarves, *The Art-Idea,* 189. Landscape was seen as dominating official American art circles by the 1860s, a situation noted by contemporaries such as NAD President Daniel Huntington; (*New York Evening Post* [29 April 1865]: n.p.). See also discussion by Cikovsky (*Winslow Homer*, 27-28) in the context of Homer's early career.

[37] Jarves, *The Art-Idea,* 194.

[38] Jarves, *The Art-Idea,* 189-190.

[39] Jarves, *The Art-Idea,* 197, 208.

[40] "Sordello", "National Academy of Design Fortieth Annual Exhibition, First Article," New York *Evening Post* (3 May 1865): front page; "Second Article" (21 May 1865); and "Concluding Article" (31 May 1865).

[41] Robert J. Scholnick, "Between Realism and Romanticism: The Curi-

ous Career of Eugene Benson," *American Literary Realism,* vol. 14, no. 2 (Autumn 1981): 242-261, cites pieces only under the name Benson. See Scholnick, 254 (as Benson); Cikovsky, *Winslow Homer,* 28 (as "Sordello"); and H[arry] W[illard] French, *Art and Artists in Connecticut* (Boston: Lee and Shepard, 1879), 163 (as "Proteus"). Benson as critic and colleague knew Homer's work well. One commentator declared, "Each [Benson and Homer] has learned through years of friendly intercourse something from the other, ... A something you scarce know what, in their pictures show that they have painted side by side, and reveals to you the fact that they are friends." "An Interesting Exhibition of Pictures" (New York *Evening Post* [16 November 1866], page 2.

[42] "Sordello", "National Academy of Design Fortieth Annual Exhibition, Second Article," New York *Evening Post* (12 May 1865): front page.

[43] "Sordello", "National Academy of Design Fortieth Annual Exhibition, Second Article," New York *Evening Post* (12 May 1865): front page.

[44] "Sordello", New York *Evening Post* (31 May 1865): front page.

[45] "Sordello", New York *Evening Post* (28 April 1866): front page. *Record of Works,* vol. 1, no. 282.

[46] *The World* (10 November 1866), 2 ("S. P. Avery has lately added several new pictures to his collection. Among them ... a strongly painted picture called 'Beverly [*sic*] Oaks,' by 'Homer Winslow [*sic*]'"). *The Nation* 3 (11 November 1866): 395.

[47] *The Nation* 3 (22 November 1866): 416. The sale of "The Pictures Painted by Winslow Homer and Eugene Benson ..." was mentioned under "Special Notices" in the *New-York Commercial Advertiser* (16 November 1866).

[48] The painting's location remained unknown until 1965 (*Record of Works,* vol. I, 299).   Benson wrote the journalist William C. Church, "My 'sale' was not only a dead loss but put me in debt." (William Conant Church Collection N5, New York Public Library Manuscript Division, letter from Benson to Church, 6 December 1866). According to the New York *Evening Post* (16 November 1866): 2, the sale consisted of thirty-six paintings.

[49] Lloyd Goodrich (*Winslow Homer* [NY: MacMillan, 1945], 40) cites the letter (collection unknown) dated 26 August 1867.

[50] *The Nation,* vol. 3 (11 November 1866): 396.

[51] Another instance of unclear joining of figure and landscape occurs in *Croquet Player* of c. 1865 (*Record of Works,* vol. 1, no. 277, 343).

[52] New York *Evening Post* (31 May 1865).

[53] Anthony F. Janson (*Worthington Whittredge* [NY: Cambridge University Press, 1989], 92) has described Whittredge's *Twilight on the Shawungunk* as "a nationalistic rhetoric implicit in the brilliant sunset—." Church's

Our Banner in the Sky (1861) brought forth a "sudden and simultaneous outburst of patriotism...electrified the entire North, West, and East of America"(Angela Miller, *The Empire of the Eye: Landscape Representation and American Cultural Politics, 1825-1875* [NY: Cornell University Press, 1993], 131). Nature itself conjured up memories of the "Wilderness with Grant"; Spotsylvania, Cold Harbor, Petersburg, and comparisons between trees' "black shadows" and "weary soldiers in a bivouac" in the mind of one Civil War veteran on a trek of New Hampshire's White Mountains (Samuel Adams Drake, *The Heart of the White Mountains: Their Legend and Scenery* [New York: Harper & Brothers, 1882], 156). I thank Professor Janice Simon, University of Georgia, Athens, for this reference. Benson, "Historical Art in the United States," *Appleton's Journal of Popular Literature, Science, and Art*, vol. 1(10 April 1869): 46. See also Giese, "Prisoners from the Front," An American History Painting?" in Simpson, *Winslow Homer: Paintings of the Civil War*, 64-81.

[54] New York *Evening Post* (16 November 1866): 2.

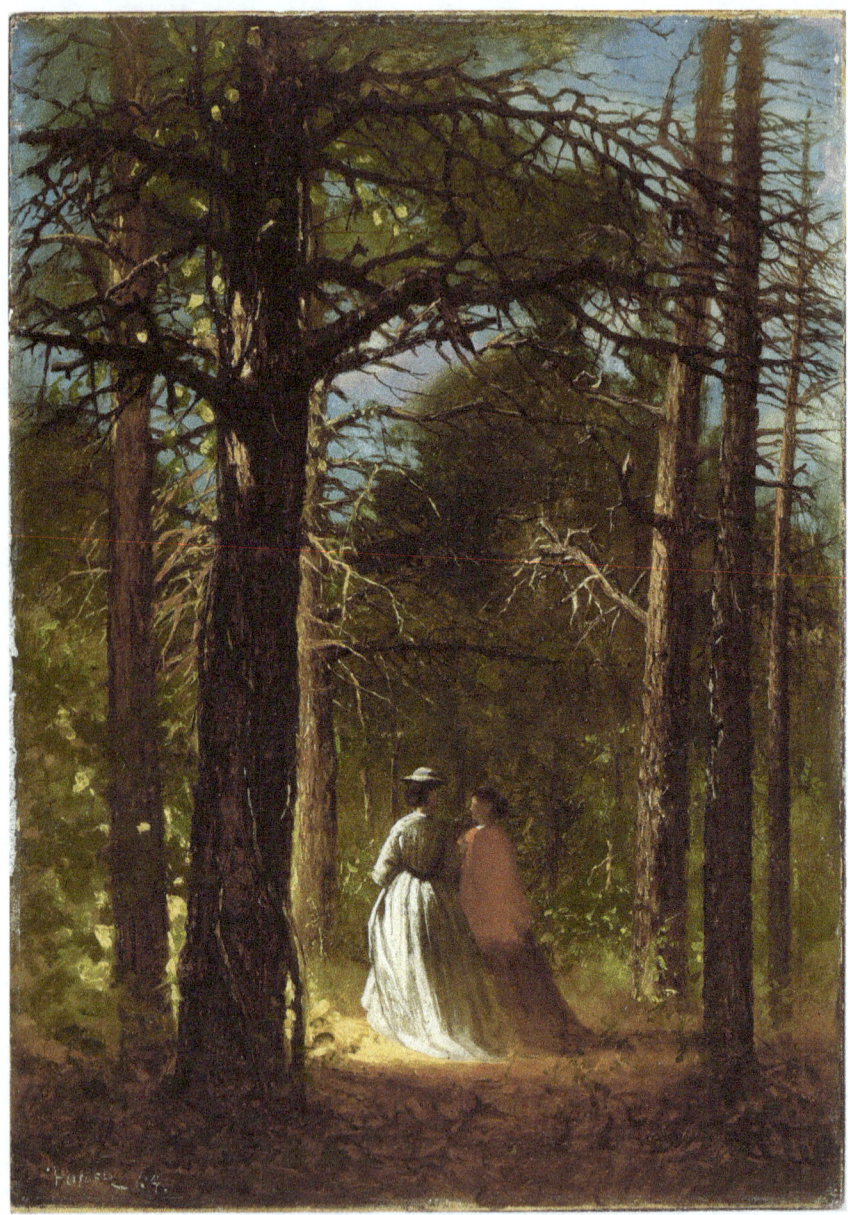

5.1. Winslow Homer, *Waverly Oaks* (owner's spelling), 1864, oil on paper mounted on panel, 13″ x 10″, Museo Thyssen-Bornemisza, Madrid.

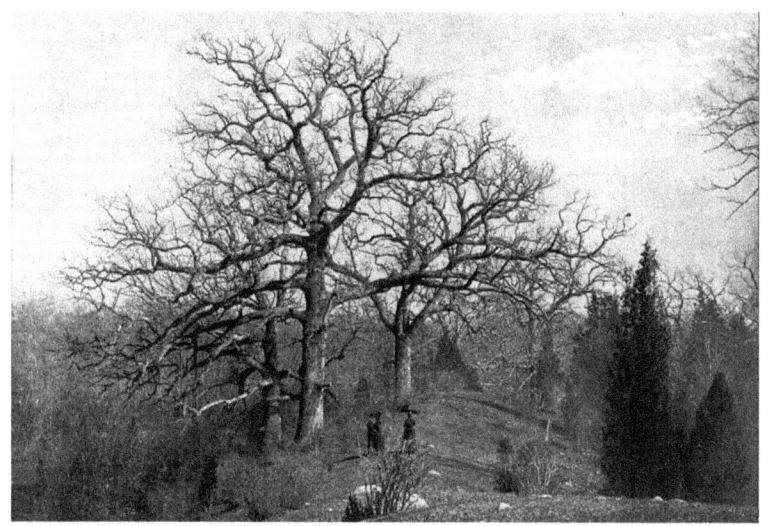

5.2. "The Waverly Oaks," 1890, photograph by W. H. Rollins. *Garden and Forest,* 3,104 (19 February 1890), 91, photograph courtesy of the Library of the Gray Herbarium, Harvard University, Cambridge, MA.

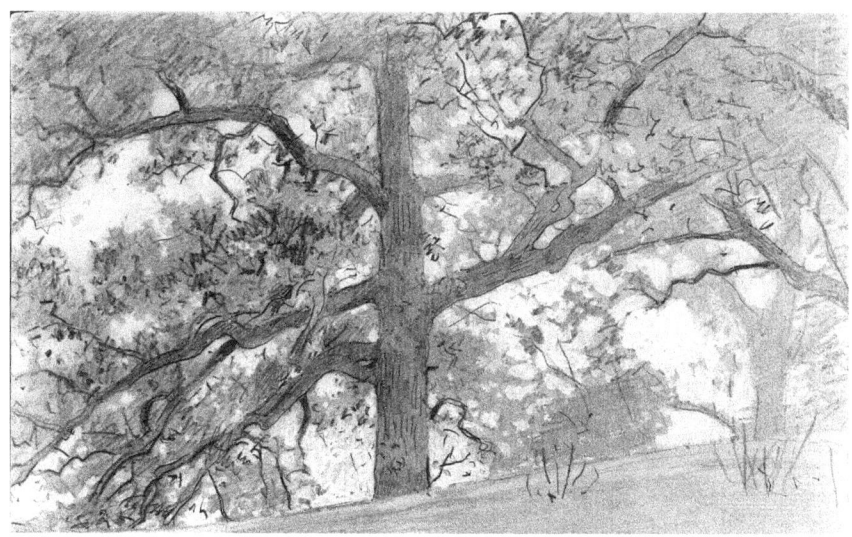

5.3. Winslow Homer, *Waverley Oaks*, 1878, graphite and watercolor on paper, 5 13/16" x 8 1/16", Cooper-Hewitt, National Design Museum.

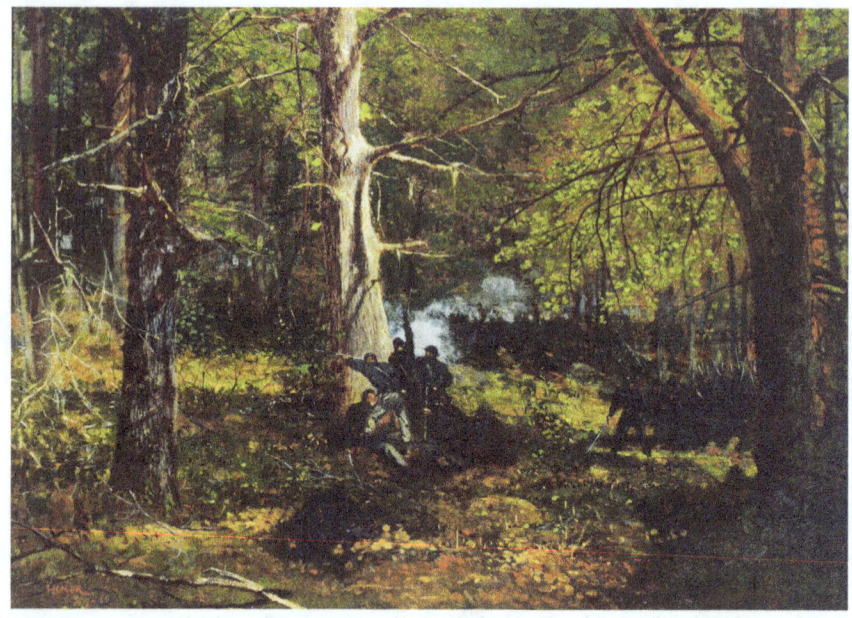

5.4. Winslow Homer, *Skirmish in the Wilderness*, 1864, oil on canvas mounted on masonite, 18" x 26", New Britain Museum of American Art, Harriet Russell Stanley Fund.

6
Maurice Prendergast: Confronting the Culture of Early Twentieth-Century Boston

Sister Ellen Glavin

Although Boston in the early twentieth century was not the center of the American art world, Maurice Prendergast was able to begin his career there.[1] In Boston he took his first formal art classes and had his first exposure to a great art museum. In Boston he found a job as a commercial artist and, after his student years in Paris (1891-1894), it was in Boston that he first exhibited his watercolors and monotypes. The enthusiastic reviews of local critics earned him the generous support of wealthy Boston patrons, and it was there that he began to enter his work in national exhibitions. The conservative art culture of Boston did not hesitate to welcome Prendergast in the early phases of his professional life.

When ten-year-old Prendergast arrived in Boston in 1868 from St. John's, Newfoundland, the city was undergoing dramatic changes in its geography and its commercial enterprises. It was a rapidly expanding metropolis, where powerful merchants were busy dredging and filling in the Back Bay, a malodorous tidal basin destined to become the site of elegant urban homes and many of the city's new civic buildings, including the Boston Public Library, Symphony Hall and the Museum of Fine Arts.

Boston merchants had realized that the outcome of the Civil War meant that manufacturing would be a major factor in the expansion of the Republic. Wealthy entrepreneurs, cautious and conservative, had turned to shrewd money management to protect and expand the fortunes of the founding families of the Commonwealth. The textile industry provided a secure place for these Boston business-men to invest their inheritance.

The textile mills flourished, but when Boston could not sell its cloth on either the domestic or the European markets, a comprehensive investigation was launched. The problem proved not to be the quality of the fabric but the quality of the designs. The merchants discovered that the English had earlier faced a similar problem in declining sales, and had solved it by introducing drawing into the school curriculum. This method of training students had insured a domestic supply of designers for the British factories. The Massachusetts investors, acting quickly to emulate the English, sent a petition to the State Legislature in 1869, and the following year the teaching of drawing and design became compulsory in Massachusetts public schools.[2]

Prendergast, a pupil in the Boston school system in 1870, benefited by these lessons in drawing, design, and color theory. On leaving grammar school, he took advantage of one of the provisions of the lawmakers and enrolled for several years in the free evening schools, where he continued his study of various types of drawing, principles of design, and theories of color harmony.[3] While the intent of the Legislature was to train home grown designers, Prendergast selected those night classes where the instructors emphasized individual development. When he had mastered the techniques, he went to work designing show cards for retail merchants.

The need for attractive textile patterns fortuitously made possible Prendergast's training in industrial design, which required skill in analysis of visual data, confidence in organizing compositions, and a command of line drawing and lettering. Prendergast, however, was preparing to visit Europe where he could refine his skills in the famous academies of France, study the old masters in the Louvre, and at the same time learn from the artists, some of whom were challenging the academic status quo.

In 1894 Prendergast returned from studying in Paris. His portfolio contained lively oil sketches, watercolors, monoprints, and drawings, all reflecting his animated, on-location sketches of the cafés, boulevards, and parks of the city. The views of fishing villages, boats at sea, and ladies with parasols enjoying the beach captured his summers spent painting on the coasts of Normandy and Brittany.

The Boston art critics praised Prendergast's Parisian and coastal scenes. The critic of *The Sunday Herald* declared, "His *Fishing Boats, Tréport, France* and his *Porte St. Denis* show a finely disciplined sense of pure and brilliant color, subordinated to a vivacious and accurate style of depiction."[4] William Howe Downes of the *Boston Evening Transcript* acknowledged "the sparkling piece of daring color, lively in style and action," that marked the *Fishing Boats,* and observed that the *Porte St. Denis* was a "first-rate street scene worthy of the best painters who have made such themes their specialties."[5] It was Maurice's command of color, representational drawing, and pleasing composition that had met the expectations of the critics. Conservative as the Bostonians might have been, they had visited Europe often enough to recognize and enjoy these delightfully original interpretations of familiar scenes.

To support himself, Prendergast accepted commissions from Boston publishers to illustrate their books and to create poster-style graphics for advertisements. At the same time he continued to paint on location in Boston's Olmstead parks and along the New England seashore. These new works delighted the critics, and brought about more sales than ever before. In 1897 *The Boston Evening Transcript* writer reviewed 200 watercolors in the Boston Art Club exhibition. The conclusion was that *People on the Beach* by Maurice B. Prendergast was "without a peer for brilliance in the exhibition…It glows; it flashes."[6] Conservative Bostonians had become Prendergast's loyal admirers and patrons.

At this time Maurice produced a number of works entitled *Franklin Park.* He was studying the new parks of Frederick Law Olmsted and his associates, where urban crowds flocked to enjoy the open spaces. In his watercolor *Franklin Park, Boston* (Fig. 1) Maurice used the skills he had developed in his quick studies of life in Paris to record celebrating groups of Boston families. Olmsted had envisioned the parks as pastoral landscapes where modern city dwellers would escape the isolation imposed by congested city neighborhoods and enjoy the refreshment of rural scenery in relaxed association with their neighbors. Maurice seemed to have caught the landscape architect's social ideal in these pictures of people enjoying the freedom of the open meadows. The well-organized composition gave structure to the recreating groups. He relied on color to control the visual harmony. The reds of the ladies' parasols and children's dresses led the viewer's eye into the depth of the painting, while the whites of gowns and hats set up the vertical and horizontal axes. Dark blue forms emphasize a contrasting frieze of white figures, while the greens of lawn and trees frame the picture. The Boston audience enjoyed these familiar scenes recording a time and place marked by flags and costumes, while critics praised the artist's mastery of color.

Prendergast's next trip in 1898-1899 was to Italy, where in Venice he had the leisure to study in depth the great Renaissance works of the Venetians. In this city, a favorite of traveling Bostonians like Mrs. Jack Gardner, he painted festive scenes of celebrating crowds. He discovered he could use the architecture of the city to frame his graceful and colorful spectacles of formal and informal processions. When he returned home, his new works were again greeted with approval. The *Transcript* review was ecstatic. "Maurice B. Prendergast, who has been in Venice, exhibits 11 sparkling and gay pictures of that aqueous capital in its most festive moods. Mr. Prendergast was born to paint fêtes, and he carries a whole Fourth of July in his color-box."[7]

In *The Grand Canal, Venice* (Fig. 2) Prendergast found crowds of people not organized by open pastoral landscapes but by the architectural constructions of a Renaissance city, that funneled crowds along the sides of canals, paraded them through arcaded squares, and packed them into the diminished spaces of balustraded bridges. The whole city now became a theatrical spectacle staged on the bridges and the squares between the elegant palaces and old churches. These watercolors were once again organized by color repetitions. In *The Grand Canal, Venice* the reds and greens of the dresses and the buildings carry the eye along the quay and across the canal. The vertical accents of the street lamps, pilings, windows, doorways, and chimneys anchor the diagonal sweep of the Grand Canal and the curve of the *Fondamenta del Vin*. Critics were again delighted by this fresh interpretation of the historic city. At the beginning of the new century, recognition of Prendergast by Boston art lovers had reached its highest point. Downes echoed the opinion of his fellow citizens when he proclaimed that Prendergast was "a brilliant and high pitched poet laureate of the picnic, the holiday, the park, the circus and the celebration."[8]

Had Prendergast continued to paint celebrations with his Fourth-of-July color-box, he would have achieved a comfortable living in Boston, but he had more challenging aspirations. He wanted to explore other techniques of painting, and other interpretations of his subjects. He painted now more often in oil, and he began to experiment with strong brushstrokes of color laid on small, heavily-underpainted wooden panels such as those he sent to the National Arts Club in New York in 1904. This series was entitled *Promenade on the Seashore 1, 2, 3, 4, 5, 6, 7.* The oil medium allowed him to capture the interaction of heavy *impasto* strokes distributed over layers of pigment. These panels not only represented his developing style of painting, but were also a new interpretation of one of his favorite subjects. His processions in parks and on seashores no longer represented a particular time and place. He had moved from recognizable scenes to a simplification of locale or a kind of ideal realm, which allowed him to stress color application over subject matter. Charles de Kay of the *New York Times* aptly noted this new reduction of realism, remarking that Mr. Prendergast "touches the sphere of the French neo-impressionists,"[9] thus placing the artist in the company of the radical French painters. Prendergast had given a clear signal to the Bostonians that he no longer would repeat the charming summer scenes of local places of recreation that had delighted them. The Boston critics had little to say. They were baffled by his new experiments.

Although we do not know exactly which panels Prendergast submitted to the National Arts Club in 1904, we have several examples of his style at this time, one of which is *Entrance to the Harbor* (Fig. 3). He had left behind his scenes of Boston parks and Venetian canals to experiment with generalized seaside subjects. This freed him from annotated details and allowed him to concentrate on compositions based primarily on color and texture. He selected wood panels to support extra layers of heavy pigment that he painted over designs prepared earlier, which gave the effect of colors built on other colors.

In 1907 Prendergast's visit to Paris confirmed these experiments, and gave him what he himself called a new impulse. He wrote about how wonderful he found the exhibitions during the spring, summer and fall of that year. In one of his notebooks he made a sketch of *Le Luxe I* by Henri Matisse, which had been shown earlier at the *Salon des Indépendants*. In June he saw for the first time a large group of Cézanne watercolors exhibited at the Bernheim-Jeune Gallery, which he described in a letter as "perfectly marvelous. He (Cézanne) left everything to the imagination. They were great for the simplicity and suggestive qualities."[10] What excited him was Cézanne's simplification of subject matter that Maurice had already introduced into his own work several years earlier.

But it was the Cézanne retrospective in October at the *Salon d'Automne* that aroused his total admiration. The power of the composition and the richness of color indicated that the French artist had resolved the problems with which Maurice had been grappling in his own work. In the same letter he wrote, "Cézanne gets the most wonderful color...I think Cézanne will influence me more than the others."[11] He compared the freedom and authority of the Paris exhibitions to the shows in Boston and New York, and described the American exhibitions as "monotonous." The question now was whether the art culture of Boston could move with the changes he was absorbing in France, so that it, too, would become dynamic and challenging.

Not unexpectedly, critics in Boston viewed Prendergast's latest paintings with dismay. The *Boston Evening Transcript* of March 15, 1911 merely noted that the artist's contributions to a group show at the Copley Gallery were "in his customary vein of whimsical and suggestive decorations."[12] In reviewing the same show, the critic for the *Christian Science Monitor* came closer to the truth, when he wrote, "It will be remembered that the painter was a pupil of the great Cézanne, whom the Post-Impressionists insist upon claiming for their own."[13]

Boston's tolerance was slowly coming to an end. In January 1913, the critic for the *Boston Evening Transcript* wrote in growing confusion of a show at the Brooks Reid Gallery: "Mr. Prendergast becomes more and more mannered in his work and his two figure compositions...are executed in his most incoherent style...The lightness that used to make his touch has given place to a heaviness which is not agreeable and his color, while it is more studied in its relations, is far less luminous and gay than it used to be."[14] Maurice, who would have been accepted, indeed welcomed, as a contemporary artist in Paris, found his experiments misunderstood and disparaged in his own city.

In the reviews of the March 1913 exhibition of Four Boston Artists at the City Club in New York, the difference between the Boston and the New York critics became evident. The *Boston Evening Transcript* critic again dismissed the Prendergast watercolors for making "no pretense at being more than amusing slight designs,"[15] while the critic for the *New York Times*, interested in analyzing the complexity of the artist's new style, observed that, "Prendergast, whose work is well known in the city, unites his reds and greens, his yellows and purples by graying the stronger colors and producing a smooth concord. His beach and river scenes are not sparkling but soothing, yet their effect is not at all of dead color, as he keeps his colors separated and unconfused, modifying but not mixing them."[16] This must have pleased Prendergast, who had admired Cézanne's colors, describing them as a "dusky kind of grey." Where New York saw creative development, Boston saw only decline.

The following year, the critic from the *Transcript* once again rejected the new style of the artist: "Of Mr. Prendergast there is nothing new to be said. He has become of late years more and more overburdened by his late mannerisms…The best that can be said of him is that within the boundaries of his own self-imposed conventions he is personal and piquant. His concoctions are an acquired taste and supply a sort of spicy hors d'oeuvre to go between the more substantial courses of the art feast."[17] The clear damnation rested on the faintest of praise.

The new style that distressed the Boston critics and intrigued the New York critics is evident in Prendergast's oil painting *Opal Sea* c. 1909-1910 (Fig. 4). By this time Maurice had changed his preference for working on wood panels to the more traditional canvas support. His promenade scenes are no longer identifiable as Franklin Park or the Grand Canal. The appeal of recognizing a particular place is no longer the focus of the painting. The subject is primarily the richness of color built on color and the rhythm of brushstrokes animating the surface of the canvas. Rather than the critics, it was the artists who understood and admired this new style. One of them bought *Opal Sea*. The new owner was Charles Hovey Pepper (1864-1950), under whose leadership the Boston Art Club had begun to show radical, as well as academic, contemporary artists. In an article published in 1910, Pepper, a painter and a friend of Maurice, explained Prendergast for the Boston critics, writing, "Pictures gay, joyous...Color powerful but not crude. Canvasses [*sic*] built up with overpainting—color dragged on color. A paint quality as delicious as an old tapestry...Such color. Now the opal...now a topaz, now a lapis. Trays of jewels."[18]

When the Armory Show came to Boston in 1913, the conservative art culture of the city once again manifested itself. Milton Brown, in his *The Story of the Armory Show*, sums up this resistance: "Boston simply ignored the intellectual and esthetic challenge of the Exhibition and, perhaps because it had arrived under so distinguished an aegis as the Copley Society, had the good manners not to question its decency."[19] The culture of Boston was not ready for change. It is no surprise, therefore, to learn that Maurice and his brother Charles decided in 1914 to move to New York.

Duncan Phillips, who had been one of Maurice's greatest champions for the decade 1914-1924, summed it up well: "To properly brought up Bostonians and to the pedantic craftsmen of the Boston School Prendergast was utterly incomprehensible."[20] The best summation, however, comes from Charles Prendergast, who fought by his brother's side for their entire lives. He wrote from firsthand experience, "People in Boston pride themselves on their intellect and talk about their cultural background, but I don't think they do much for art, you know. We'd have starved to death if we had stayed in Boston."[21]

End Notes

[1] I'd like to thank Cathy Ricciardelli, Registrar of the Terra Foundation of American Art for her kind assistance with obtaining images for this essay. The illustrations and captions are contributed by Terra Foundation.

[2] Arthur D. Efland, *A History of Education* (New York and London: Teachers College Press, Columbia University, 1990), 92-100.

[3] Ellen Glavin, "The Early Art Education of Maurice Prendergast," *Archives of American Art Journal* 33 (no. 1): 3-5.

[4] "The Boston Art Club's Fifty Second Exhibition," *The Sunday Herald*, 7 Apr.1895, quoted in Dominic Madormo, "The 'Butterfly' Artist: Maurice

Prendergast and His Critics," This essay contains a further discussion of the Boston critics and appears in Carol Clark, Nancy Mowll Mathews and Gwendolyn Owens, *Maurice Brazil Prendergast, Charles Prendergast A Catalogue Raisonné* (Williamstown Ma.: Williams College Museum of Art, 1990), 59-69.

[5] William Howe Downes, "The Fine Arts," *Boston Evening Transcript*, 15 Apr.1895.

[6] "The Fine Arts," *Boston Evening Transcript*, 3 Apr. 1897.

[7] "The Fine Arts," *Boston Evening Transcript*, 4 Mar. 1899.

[8] "The Fine Arts," *Boston Evening Transcript*, 3 Jan. 1900.

[9] Charles de Kay, "French and American Impressionists," *New York Times*, 31 Jan. 1904.

[10] Letter from Maurice Prendergast to Mrs. Oliver Williams, 10 Oct. 1907, Esther Williams Papers, Archives of American Art, Smithsonian Institution.

[11] *Ibid*.

[12] "Hopkinson, Pepper and Prendergast, Joint Exhibition," *Boston Evening Transcript*, 15 Mar. 1911.

[13] "Three Artists Exhibit at the Copley Society," *The Christian Science Monitor*, 18 Mar. 1911.

[14] "Four Boston Painters," *Boston Evening Transcript*, 8 Jan 1913.

[15] "Four Boston Artists," *Boston Evening Transcript*, 31 Mar 1913.

[16] "At Home and Abroad," *New York Times*, 30 Mar. 1913.

[17] "Brooks Reid Gallery, Four Boston Painters," *Boston Evening Transcript*, 13 Jan. 1914.

[18] Charles Hovey Pepper, "Is Drawing to Disappear in Artistic Individuality?" *The World To-Day* 19 (July 1910): 716-719.

[19] Milton W. Brown, *The Story of the Armory Show* (New York: Abbeville Press, 1988), 215.

[20] Duncan Phillips, "Maurice Prendergast," *The Arts* 5 (Mar. 1924): 126.

[21] Quoted in Hamilton Basso, "A Glimpse of Heaven-II," *The New Yorker* 22 (Aug. 3, 1946): 32.

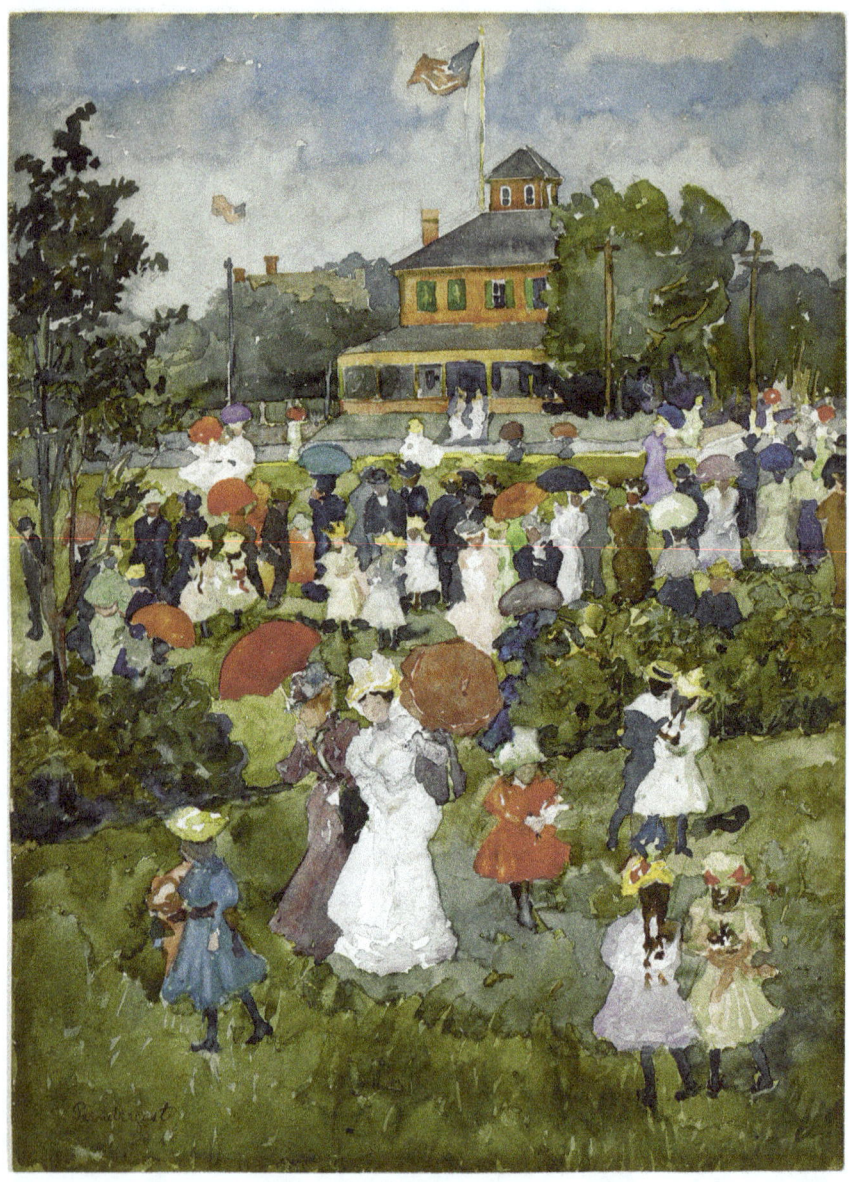

6.1. Maurice Brazil Prendergast, *Franklin Park, Boston*, 1895–97, watercolor over black chalk, on ivory wove, watercolor paper, 17 1/2" x 13 1/8" (44.5 x 33.3 cm), Terra Foundation for American Art, Daniel J. Terra Collection, 1999.111.

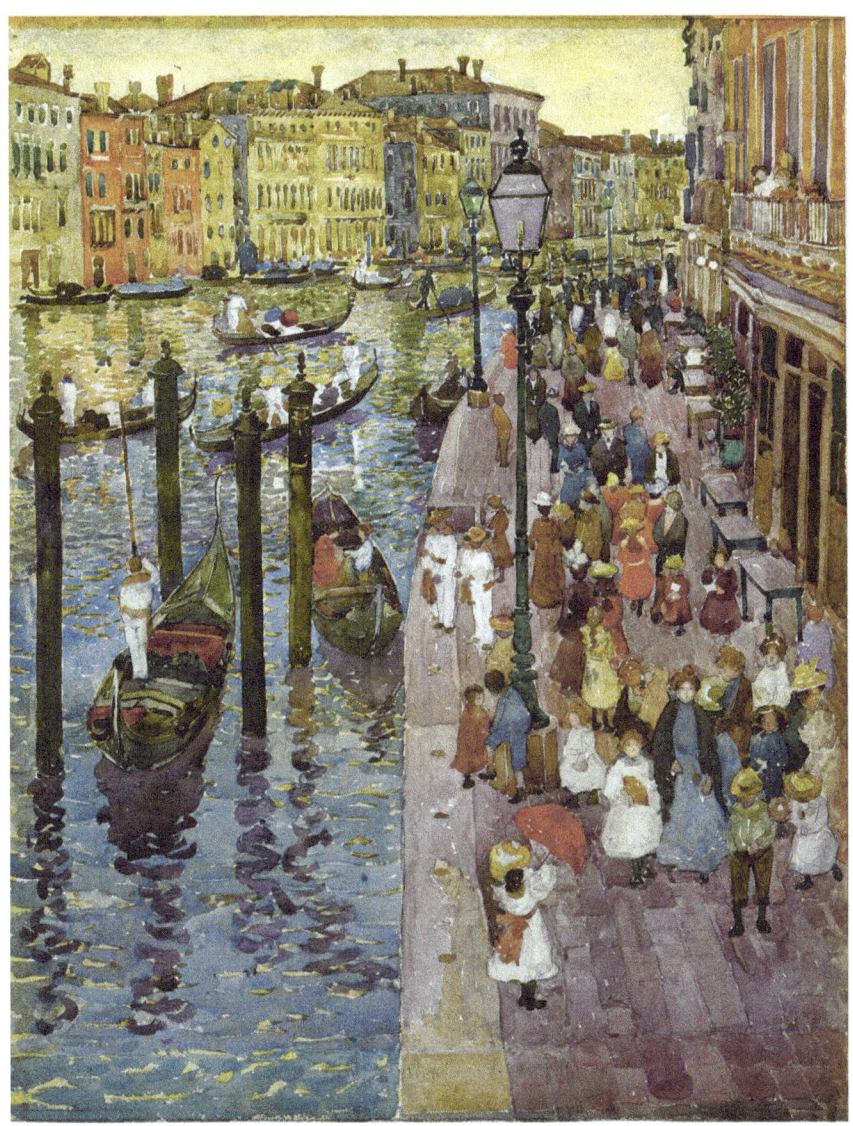

6.2. Maurice Brazil Prendergast, *The Grand Canal, Venice*, between 1898 and 1899, watercolor and graphite on paper, 18 1/8" x 14 1/4" (46.0 x 36.2 cm), Terra Foundation for American Art, Daniel J. Terra Collection, 1999.123.

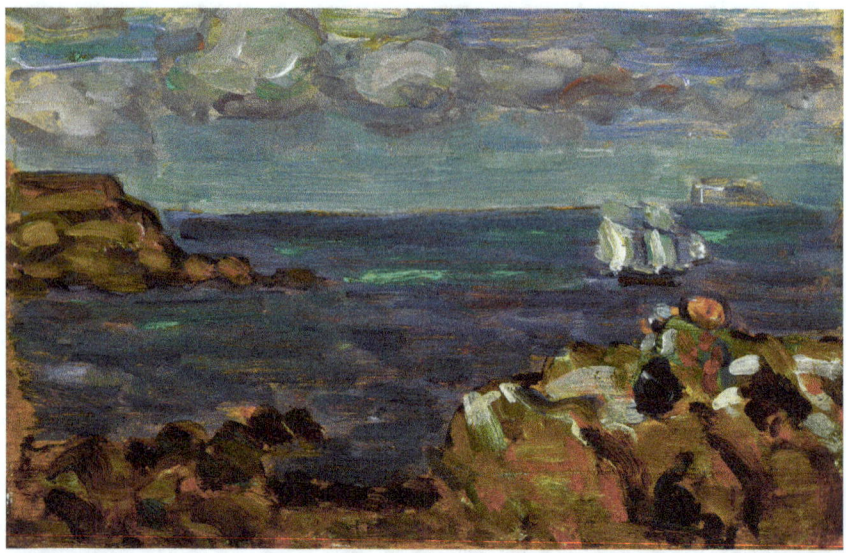

6.3. Maurice Brazil Prendergast, *Entrance to the Harbor*, c. 1907, oil on panel, 5 3/4" x 8 7/8" (14.6 x 22.5 cm), Terra Foundation for American Art, Daniel J. Terra Collection, 1989.23.

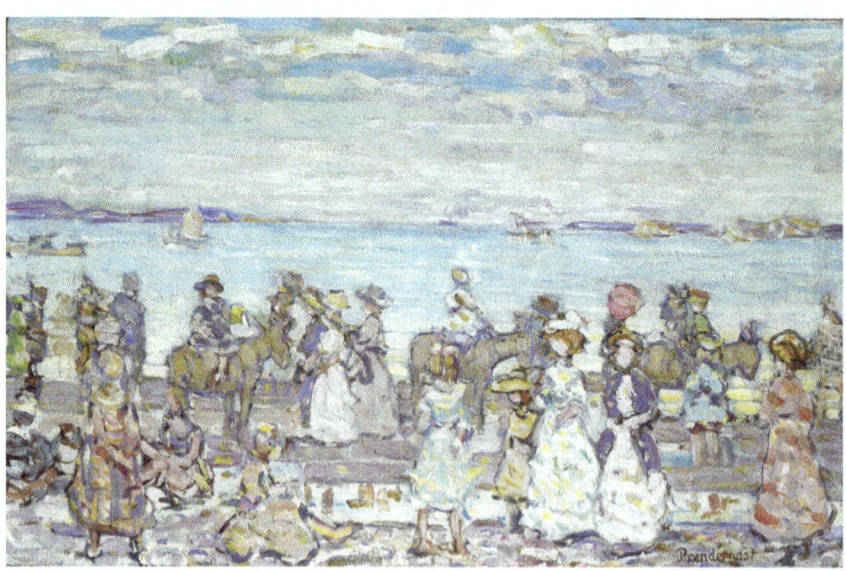

6.4. Maurice Brazil Prendergast, *Opal Sea*, between 1907 and 1910, oil on canvas, 22" x 34 1/8" (55.9 x 86.7 cm), Terra Foundation for American Art, Daniel J. Terra Collection, 1999.118.

7
Worpswede, Idyll and After: Creativity and Partnership in the Early Twentieth Century

Diane Radycki

Energy and possibility abounded in Worpswede at the turn of the century.[1] Under the genius of artistic creativity, a grey, heavy, flat landscape changed into "a beautiful piece of earth." In 1901 the art colony provided the young philosopher Martin Buber with the ultimate metaphor for transformation: "Jewish national life is the Worpswede of nations."[2]

Buber's "beautiful piece of earth" emerged out of a centuries-old moorland village lying south of the *Teufelsmoor* ("Devil's Moor") and northwest of the Lüneburg Heath, twenty-five kilometers (sixteen miles) outside the ancient Hansa city of Bremen, in northwest Germany. Worpswede sits at the foot of the Weyerberg hill, which, at less than two hundred feet, is the highest point in the low-lying landscape (Fig. 1). In the nineteenth century this was a sparkling, sparse landscape. The canals reflected the dramatic, ever changing northern skies and animated a landscape glistening with white birch trees and yellow hills of sand. Black-sailed barges, stacked with bricks of black peat, slowly plied the slowly flowing Hamme River.

Peat was the village economy, and the hard work of cutting peat shaped the people: thick heavy-set bodies, large gnarled hands, and blackened nails. Peasants housed together with animals in barn-size houses of redbrick and timber, with high-pitched thatched roofs. The village housed a church and a poorhouse, as well as cafés where locals gathered to play cards and bowl. These dour people, this moody landscape, all were considered picturesque at a time of rapid urban and industrial expansion. At the turn of the century enough of a tourist industry was generated to warrant postcards emblazoned "Greetings from Worpswede."

As an artists' colony, Worpswede dates from 1889 when two disaffected art students—Fritz Mackensen (1866-1953) and Otto Modersohn (1865-1943)—left the Dusseldorf Academy and settled in the remote village. Worpswede was one of several such back-to-nature ventures that sprung up in the late nineteenth century in Europe.[3] Whereas most art colonies were seasonal, Worpswede was a year-round settlement. (It is still active today.) The quaint village attracted artists who sought their truth in nature, romancing an idyll that was ever more peripheral in the fast-approaching twentieth century. Worpswede artists were in revolt: against the art academy, against its subject matter, against its techniques. Not for them the example of history and mythology, nor the heroics of the military, nor the doings of society, but a bucolic landscape and its folk were their subject matter. Painting out-of-doors and life-size was their revolution.

Within five years Mackensen and Modersohn were joined by a core of like-minded artists committed to lyric Naturalism. Around them a Worpswede "school" and utopian spirit developed: they shared an etching press, and promoted handcrafts, photography, and publishing. The art colony gained national recognition in 1895 when Mackensen won the gold medal at the Munich Glaspalast exhibition with his monumental painting of a sermon being given out of doors on the moor, and Modersohn received a lucrative 1200-mark prize for his painting of a storm on the moor. Following these successes, the Worpswede "Old Masters" soon found it easier to sell work and attract paying art students, among them, Heinrich Vogeler, Paula Becker, and Clara Westhoff.

Not surprisingly, teachers married students, artists married models, and young artists married each other. My investigation into creativity and partnership in the early twentieth century considers the most layered of partnerships—marriage—in an environment intended to foster utmost creativity—an art colony. I look briefly at three marriages, three couples who not only constituted a social circle at the heart of the Worpswede art colony, but also were intimate friends. They all attended parties together, concerned themselves with each other's work, and sharply observed each other's relationships. I trace the vicissitudes of these complicated harmonies as, over time, crises occurred, reputations fluctuated, roles and affections shifted, and art evolved away from Naturalism to Modernism.

Spring in Worpswede: 3 March 1901, the artist married his model; 28 April 1901, the poet married the sculptor; and 25 May 1901, the venerable landscape painter married the iconoclastic figure painter.

The Artist and His Model

The painter, designer, and architect Heinrich Vogeler (1872-1942), from a wealthy Bremen family, was idealistic and romantic. Slender, blonde Martha Schröder (1879-1961) was the daughter of a Worpswede school teacher (Fig. 2). Vogeler, the youngest of the core founding colonists, was different from the others artistically, temperamentally, and politically. He was something of an aesthete and a Utopian, and those features underlie both his early *Jugendstil* work and his post-WWI political art. In 1894 Worpswede spoke to him and he moved to the art colony to live his dream of an ideal society.

Heinrich was twenty-two years old; Martha was fourteen, and still in school. He determined to wait patiently for her to grow up. Meanwhile, he put her at the center of all his pictures (Fig. 3).

Committed to life in Worpswede, Vogeler brought a cottage that he enlarged into a stately house planted all around with birch trees, his *Barkenhoff* ("Birch Tree Cottage"). The Barkenhoff soon came alive with weekly parties, impromptu concerts, and recitals by those talents who regularly came through the art colony.

When the twenty-two year old art student Paula Becker first met Martha Schröder in 1898, she found her,

> …embroidering folding screens and mats for him (Vogeler) and living deep within the fairy-tale spirit of his art. She'll sit all day long in his atelier while he draws her endlessly, or he'll sit quietly next to her on the sofa in her Mother's living room and draw her. Soon she will be going to the Arts

and Crafts School in Berlin. Then what? He's had his house enlarged. For me, their relationship is too tender and too dream-like to have such an everyday ending.[4]

Whatever an "everyday ending" may be, they did not have one: marrying in 1901, having three daughters by 1905, estranged before World War I, separating shortly after the war, they divorced in 1926. After seven years of a picturesque courtship, one year of actual marriage introduced discord and tension into their relationship, or so it seemed to Paula (now Modersohn-Becker) in 1902: "I was at [the Vogelers] last night. I believe they're both going through a difficult time right now. I feel things may be strained because he can not talk to her about his ultimate concerns."[5] It was idealism stretched, tested, and aged by reality.

Vogeler's reality included World War I. He alone from the couples considered in this paper served in the military, from 1915-1918. In 1915 he was sent to the Eastern front, and his brother was killed in action. The war radicalized Vogeler, and led him resolutely, but not without difficulty, to embrace Communism. In 1919 he turned his manorial Worpswede Barkenhoff into an experimental school, with a pedagogical program directed at releasing the creative potential in children. Later he gave the house over to the Red Cross for a children's orphanage. Heinrich and Martha eventually found other partners: Heinrich and Zofia (Sonja) Marchlewska, with whom he had a son in 1923, married in 1926. (In his hunger for social progress, Vogeler immigrated to Russia in 1932. He was deported to Kazakhstan by Soviet authorities in 1941, where he died ignominiously in 1942 in a camp for political prisoners.)

After their separation in 1920, Martha Vogeler, with their three teen-age daughters, followed her own artistic dream (with financial backing from her estranged husband). Now no longer the object of his art, she became a maker of her own, and established a weaving workshop in Worpswede: *Haus im Schluh*. Martha, before she married, had learned weaving at school in Berlin, an undertaking that Heinrich had financially supported. He himself was active in the field of design: Vogeler had established the *Worpswede Werkstätte* ("Workshop") in 1908. Like other Jugendstil artists influenced by the English Arts and Crafts movement, he downplayed the difference between the creative individual and the ordinary craftsman.

Vogeler's most celebrated interior, however, remains the sumptuous Gold Room of the Bremen Town Hall, 1903-05, with its gilded leather wallpaper, chandelier, and unique door handles. Martha's more utilitarian handcraft was directed to domestic projects, such as the table runners that decorate the breakfast room of the pension Haus im Schluh, where Heinrich's wistful 1898 portrait of her as *Spring* hangs today (Fig. 4).

She was his model, he was her artist; they were spouses, parents, and exes; they were also each other's most enduring creation. While the idealist's life-long and brutally frustrated pursuit of a meaningful place for art in everyday life escaped his own practice and life, it attained concrete expression, without fanfare, in the achievement of a daughter of the moors, whose talent weaving provided a bulwark for her and her children against the vagaries of her knight errant. In turn, she wove more than table linen, her great success was to prove an idealist a visionary, and thereby weave him into the art historical record.

The Poet and the Sculptor

Vogeler, the social magnet of the art colony, traveled widely and invited the many writers, playwrights, musicians, and artists whom he met to his large and stately Barkenhoff. In 1898 he invited the poet Rainer Maria Rilke (1875-1926) and the artist Clara Westhoff (1878-1954) to Worpswede (Fig. 5). Vogeler met the twenty-three-year-old Rilke in spring 1898 in Italy. They had much in common artistically, to judge by their respective romantic juvenilia, and Vogeler proffered an invitation to his Barkenhoff, which Rilke took up for a few days in late December of that year.

Vogeler met the twenty-year-old Westhoff in Munich. She was studying painting, and he suggested she work with Worpswede's award-winning figure painter Fritz Mackensen. Westhoff arrived in the art colony in early spring; there she met Paula Becker, another Mackensen pupil at the time. It was Mackensen who redirected Westhoff away from painting toward sculpture. In August 1899 she went to Leipzig to study with the German Jugendstil sculptor Max Klinger, and in December to Paris to study at the *Institut Rodin*. Becker followed her new friend to Paris a month later.

They lived across from each other in bohemian Montparnasse, not far from *Le Dôme*, the big artists' café that was a known meeting place for Germans, and close to *Le Bal Bullier*, the big dance hall where they joined other students and artists in dancing their nights away. Come daytime, they attended anatomy lectures at the *Ecole des Beaux-Arts* together. The two girlfriends did not return to Worpswede until summer 1900, when, in late August, Rilke who was on his way back from Russia and Tolstoy stopped by to visit Vogeler for the second time.

In early September 1900 Rainer Maria met Clara—and Paula— at one of the weekly Sunday parties Heinrich hosted at the Barkenhoff, which famously lasted until dawn. Later the young poet visited both young artists in their respective studios, but he looked at the work only of the tall, dark sculptor. Rilke was already interested in the plastic arts, and in Rodin; and Westhoff had just spent seven months at Rodin's Paris atelier and his Institut. Rainer Maria and Clara became engaged seven months later, married at the end of April, and became parents on December 12th the same year. Ahead of them, as a married couple, were only a year and a half more of living together as a family, and a lifetime of friendship; ahead of them, as artists, were another twenty-five years of writing for Rilke, and another fifty-three years of sculpting for Rilke-Westhoff (Fig. 6).

Marriage and parenthood changed the Rilkes' situation quickly and irrevocably, and it alarmed their friend Paula who put her concerns candidly and forcefully to Clara, in a letter answered more formally by Rainer Maria. Their exchange articulates their respective positions on creativity and partnership, and I quote briefly from both:

> Dear Clara Westhoff ... Rilke speaks too strongly and too ardently in your words. Does love demand that one person become like the other? No, a thousand times no. Isn't the union of two strong people so rich and so rewarding for the very reason that both rule and both serve in simplicity and peace and joy and quiet contentment? I know little about the two of you, but it seems to me you have laid down too much of your old self, like a cloak spread for your king to

walk on. For your sake, for the world's, for art's, and for my own, I'd like you to put on your own golden cloak again. Dear Rainer Maria Rilke, I argue against you. I feel it necessary to argue against you—and I intend to do so with the thousand languages of love, against you and against those beautiful colored seals of yours that you stamp on more than just your elegantly written letters.[6]

Rainer Maria Rilke replied:

Dear Frau Modersohn, Permit me to say a few words about your letter to my dear wife, as it concerns me very closely… I hold this to be the highest task of the union of two people: that each should guard the solitude of the other. For, if it be in the nature of indifference and of the crowd not to respect solitude, then love and friendship exist for this purpose, continually to afford opportunities for solitude. This alone is true communion, which rhythmically interrupts deep isolation.[7]

His theory of marriage, as the mutual guardianship of the other's solitude, shaped the Rilkes' marriage. Rilke left for Paris that summer, in pursuit of paying work; Rilke-Westhoff soon followed and, once there, continued her studies with Rodin. Their eight-month-old daughter was left in the care of her maternal grandparents in Germany. The Rilkes infrequently lived together as a family with their daughter. Baby Ruth stayed with her mother, and often with her grandmother. Instead, they vacationed together as a family and, when apart, husband and wife corresponded frequently and at length, in beautiful letters revealing a deep mutual sympathy.

Over time, as each spouse sought patronage, they led lives that were not only detached from each other but also peripatetic. Rilke's extensive itinerary is well documented; less appreciated is the fact that Rilke-Westhoff too traveled widely for sculptural commissions, and with her patrons. She was back and forth between Paris and Germany; she spent a year in Italy in 1903-04; four months in Egypt in 1907; and so on. It was the Rilkes' correspondence that bridged geographical distances and unfolding years. Their letters reveal no traces of ordinary or extraordinary unhappiness with this accommodation. Instead, they engaged in an ongoing dialogue about art, art exhibitions, and artists (most notably, Cézanne), to the benefit of his poetic sensibility and her artistic consciousness.

These letters are often read in relation to his great ekphrastic poetry, as well as his two art monographs, *Worpswede* (Fig. 7) and *Rodin*; while, as concerns Rilke-Westhoff's sculpture, the letters are invaluable for understanding her artistic direction.

Something in this unexampled marriage worked for both of them, even as the arrangement inexorably loosened over time. Whatever other intimate allegiances they may have developed, they never sought a legal end to their marriage; nor did Clara remarry in the twenty-eight years after Rainer Maria's death. Of the three marriages I survey, this is the one of greatest mutual accord and artistic benefit, for both partners understood the ambition and energy of the other.

The Landscape Painter and the Figure Painter

The nineteenth-century landscape painter Otto Modersohn (1865-1943) and the twentieth-century figure painter Paula Becker (1876-1907) first met in 1897 (Fig. 8). At the time, Modersohn was thirty-two years old, co-founder of the art colony, a highly respected artist, married, and the father of a newborn; Becker was a twenty-one-year-old art student, in the colony between terms at art school in Berlin. They married in 1901. By the time their story was over in 1907 — with her untimely death — their tutorial roles had reversed.

Paula Becker, whose family lived in Bremen, went to nearby Worpswede to study figure drawing with Mackensen. New to the colony and to rural life, she recorded her impressions in her journal. Of Modersohn, she wrote:

> I've seen him only once and unfortunately very briefly. I didn't get a feeling for him. I remember only someone tall, in a brown suit with a reddish beard. There was something gentle and sympathetic about his eyes. His landscapes, which I've seen in exhibitions, have a deep mood. The hot,

brooding, autumn sun or the mysteriously sweet evening (Fig. 9). I'd like to get to know him, this Modersohn.[8]

No one need deny Otto and Paula their share of attraction and love, in acknowledging the pressures on each of them that argued strongly for speedy marriage. In June 1900 the thirty-six-year-old Modersohn had unexpectedly found himself widowed, with a motherless two-year-old daughter. At the very same time, the twenty-five-year-old Becker was being told bluntly by her father to prepare to earn her own living as a governess. Thus, the prospect of a husband to provide her support, of a wife to care for his child, and of spouses who understood the demands of art, could excite mutual hope, if not passion. Within three months, they were engaged, as we know from this laconic entry in Otto's journal: "Wed., 12th Sept. Afternoon boating—Paula Becker—Rilke. 5:30 p.m. engaged."[9]

Even before they were married, Otto was romantically disappointed in Paula. He complained that her letters to him were too little about love. Even before their first wedding anniversary, Paula was spiritually disappointed in Otto. She confided in her diary, "In my experience marriage doesn't make one happier. It takes away the illusion that previously sustained one's whole being, that there was a companion for one's soul." And even after they were married, they remained out of sync. This is made clear by the following diary entry by Otto, written less than a month after Paula's despairing of finding a soul mate in marriage: "In our taste, our art, and our thinking, Paula and I are very close…In our passions Paula and I fit together superbly."[10] Their differences are clear visually as well. In his painting of landscape, Otto adopted the worm's-eye view and looked up to all the glory he saw in nature; while Paula adopted the bird's-eye view and looked at the same landscape askew from on high, from a perspective diametrically opposed to the reigning Worpswede aesthetic. He—the lyrical Naturalist—valorized nature; she—the Modernist—questioned it.

While we know something of Paula's expectations of marriage from the above-quoted letter to her friend Clara, we do not know Otto's. He had been married before, for only three years, to a woman who had given birth within the first year of their marriage, and was ever after described as frail. Otto was "very nice," confided their friend Vogeler to Paula, "but perfectly blind to the horrible condition of his poor wife."[11] Paula did not take heed. She and Otto both thought marriage promising. (He thought so, as long as having children was not at issue—about which Paula was irresolute at the time.) Otto, the Worpswede Old Master, fast found that where art was concerned, Paula, the Worpswede Young Turk, did not hesitate to instruct him. She admired his drawings and urged him to continue to simplify form, work figures into their surroundings, and develop an expressive brushwork. After Paula fled in 1906, Otto, uncomprehending and in anguish, took her paintings to his studio and copied them, trying to understand better what it was that she was saying, seeing, painting.

Worpswede casts a dappled shadow on Modersohn-Becker. It discredits her to read her years in the art colony simply as the consequence of conjugal bonds. True, she had married into relatively comfortable circumstances. Although she had a young stepdaughter, she also had domestic help. She did not, for example, have to do the cooking. She was able to organize her day so that she worked in her studio from nine to one, and three to seven. And Modersohn-Becker found support in Worpswede for her presuppositions about art. Artists such as Modersohn and Vogeler were moving in the direction of a symbolic and expressive Naturalism, and their work interested her. Artists such as Rilke-Westhoff and Rilke provided her with the friendship of contemporaries seriously invested in Modernism. And her role as Frau Modersohn gave her the solitude to work through pictorial ideas that were inimical to all but a handful of those in the colony. Her husband predicted, the year after their marriage, "No one knows her, no one appreciates her—that will change."[12]

What changed, and changed continuously, was Otto's opinion. This, from his 1903 journal: "Paula has more intellectual interests than anyone else. She paints, reads, plays, etc. The household too is well run—only, her feeling for family and home is weak. I hope it will strengthen. I am very happy about the intellectual interests of my Paula—she could never play the simpleton—I only wish that our lives were a bit more enmeshed in each other, then I would call it ideal...Paula hates convention and now is falling prey to the error of preferring to make everything angular, ugly, bizarre, wooden. The color is wonderful—but the form? The expression! Hands like spoons, noses like knobs, mouths like wounds, looking like cretins. She loads on too much. Two heads, four hands in the smallest space, never less, and children at that! It is difficult to give her advice, as usual,"[13] so lamented the nineteenth-century Naturalist of the twentieth-century Modernist.

Five years after their marriage what had not changed was that Modersohn-Becker was still an unknown artist, and their marriage, she confided to her friend Rilke-Westhoff, was still unconsummated. "I couldn't stand it any longer," she wrote her mother, "and I'll probably never be able to stand it again either. It was all too confining for me and not what—and always less of what—I needed."[14] In the dead of a cold February night she left for Paris, without a word to anyone but the Rilkes. In Paris she painted furiously, pictures no one had ever painted before: children nude, mothers-and-children nude, self-portraits nude (Fig. 10). Today her legacy of female body imagery stretches through Frida Kahlo and Cindy Sherman.

There was, however, a dark side to independence: identity crises, isolation, a lack of money, depression, and—at age thirty—wracking irresolution about motherhood. After more than a year in Paris, Modersohn-Becker chose to return with her importuning husband to Worpswede. In early November 1907 she gave birth to their daughter; three weeks later she died from complications arising from the pregnancy.

Her untimely death shocked and haunted everyone. Rilke responded with a long and moving *Requiem For a Friend* in which he addressed her paintings, as well as her life. One incident in particular was especially telling. It happened when Paula and Otto were vacationing in the Frisian Islands. A sudden storm came up, and Paula decided to walk out into the North Sea on an old pier, heedless of Otto's ceaseless calls to come back, come back. Waves crashed over the pier, erasing it from sight, and, with the wind whipping at her drenched skirts, Paula from afar looked as if she were hovering above the furiously churning water, like some figurehead of a ship at sea. A virtual Venus of Samothrace who never once lost her footing.[15] Paula's daring and Otto's culpability surface in these lines from Rilke's *Requiem*:

Does the sea-captain still possess the figurehead
at his prow, when the mysterious lightness
of her god-like self lifts her high into the bright sea wind?
No more can one of us call back the woman
who does not see us any more,
who walks away from us as by a miracle,
on a narrow strip of her own being, without mishap;
unless guilt were indeed his calling and his pleasure.[16]

Yet return she did, and not at Otto's calling, but on her own terms. Something in the marriage, something in Worpswede, worked for her, as well as against her, just as did Paris. Storm and port both demand negotiation in this life.

As for the twentieth-century Worpswede idyll: before two decades were out, the Vogelers separated, the Rilkes' union faded, and Modersohn was left alone (a widower for the second time, now with two little daughters). These are marriages from an era when modernity was in the making, and an intimate union between artists held the promise of a home-front advantage in the heat of creating the new in design, poetry, and art. In like circumstance but with unlike success, what the Vogelers, the Rilkes, and the Modersohns made out of their very human desires for their respective artist-spouses was tested—bested—by their even stronger ambitions for a life in art.

End Notes

[1] A short version of this paper was presented at the German Studies Association conference, in Oakland, California, 2010.

[2] Martin Buber, "I.L. Perez: Ein Wort zu seinen fünfundzwanzigsten Schriststell-Jubiläum" (1901), in *The First Buber, Youthful Zionist Writings of Martin Buber*, ed. and trans. Gilya G. Schmidt (Syracuse: Syracuse University Press, 1999), 28-29.

[3] See Michael Jacobs, *The Good & Simple Life: Artists Colonies in Europe and America* (Oxford: Phaidon Press, 1985).

[4] Journal of Paula Becker, 18 October 1898, *Paula Modersohn-Becker in Briefen und Tagebüchern*, eds. Günter Busch and Liselotte von Reinken (Frankfurt am Main: S. Fischer, 1979), 139. Hereafter cited as M-B / Fischer 1979. All translations are by the author.

[5] Modersohn-Becker to Otto Modersohn, 7 November 1902, M-B / Fischer 1979, 330.

[6] Modersohn-Becker to Rilke-Westhoff, 10 February 1902, M-B / Fischer 1979, 309.

[7] Rilke to Modersohn-Becker, 12 February 1902, M-B / Fischer 1979, 310-11.

[8] Journal of Paula Becker, 24 July 1897, M-B / Fischer 1979, 102.

[9] *Otto Modersohn: Worpswede 1889-1907* (Fischerhude: Otto Modersohn Museum, 1989), 166.

[10] Paula Becker to Otto Modersohn, 4 March 1901; Journal of Modersohn-Becker, 30 March 1902; and Journal of Otto Modersohn, 25 April 1902, M-B / Fischer 1979, 293, 317, and 319.

[11] Heinrich Vogeler to Paula Becker, April 1900, M-B / Fischer 1979, 211.

[12] Herma Weinberg, in "Erinnerungen an Paula Modersohn-Becker," *Paula Modersohn-Becker: Ein Buch der Freundschaft,* ed. Rolf Hetsch (Berlin: Rembrandt Verlag, 1932), 16. Journal of Otto Modersohn, 15 June 1902, M-B / Fischer 1979, 323.

[13] Journal of Otto Modersohn, 25 June-26 September 1903, M-B / Fischer 1979, 369-70.

[14] Rilke-Westhoff to Rilke, 8 February 1906, in Renate Berger, *Malerinnen auf dem Weg ins 20.Jahrhundert* (Cologne: DuMont Buchverlag, 1982), 318-19. Modersohn-Becker to Mathilde Becker, 10 May 1906, M-B / Fischer 1979, 447.

[15] Virginia Woolf used a similar image in *To the Lighthouse* (1927): "It was an odd road to be walking, this of painting. Out and out one went, further and further, until at last one seemed to be on a narrow plank, perfectly alone, over the sea. And as she dipped into the blue paint, she dipped too into the past there."

[16] Rainer Maria Rilke, *Requiem (for a Friend)*, 1908, trans. Lilly Engler and Adrienne Rich, in *The Letters and Journals of Paula Modersohn-Becker*, trans. and ed. J. Diane Radycki (Metuchen, N.J., & London: Scarecrow Press, 1980), 325.

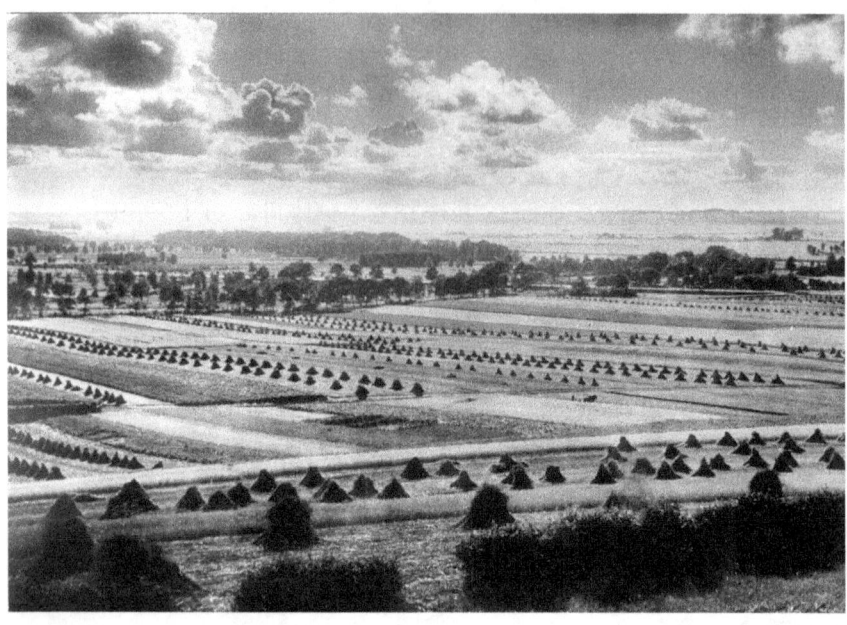

7.1. Worpswede, view of the Hamme River Valley from atop the Weyerberg.

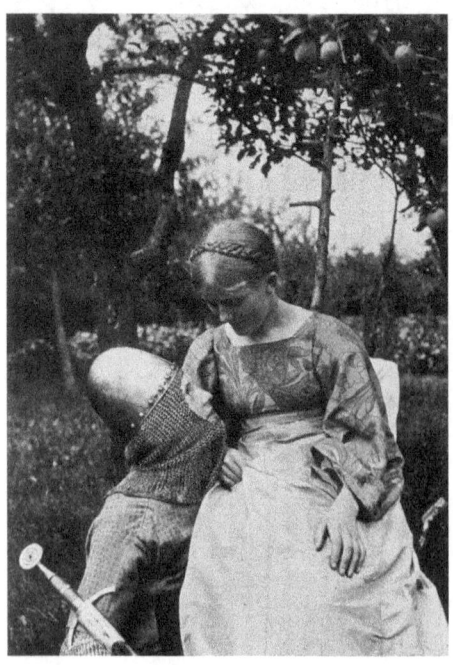

7.2. Heinrich Vogeler and
Martha Schröder, 1898.

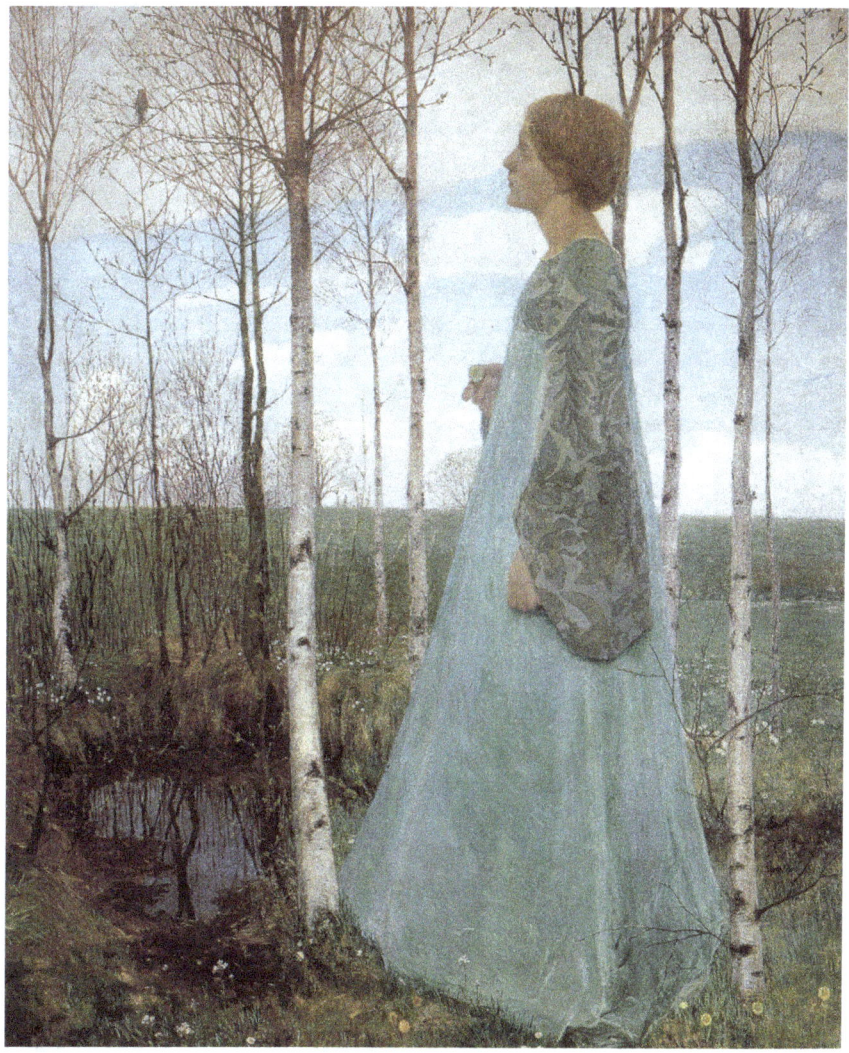

7.3. Heinrich Vogeler, *Spring*, 1898, oil on canvas, 42″ x 26″, Haus im Schluh, Worpswede.

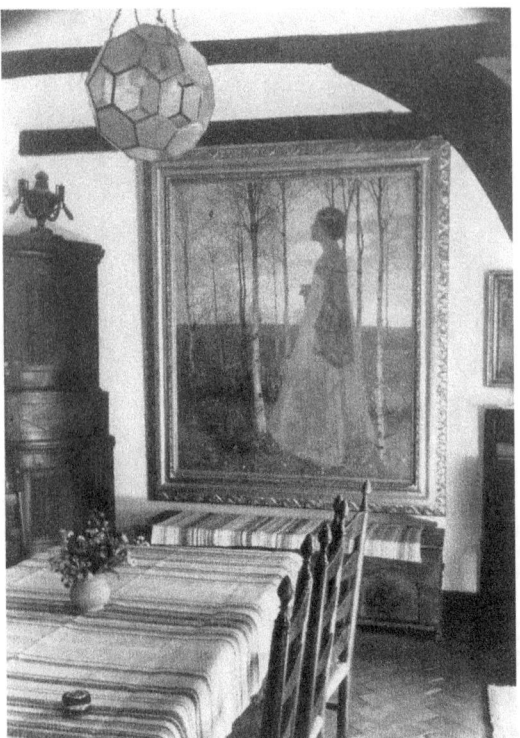

7.4. Breakfast Room,
Haus im Schluh,
Worpswede.

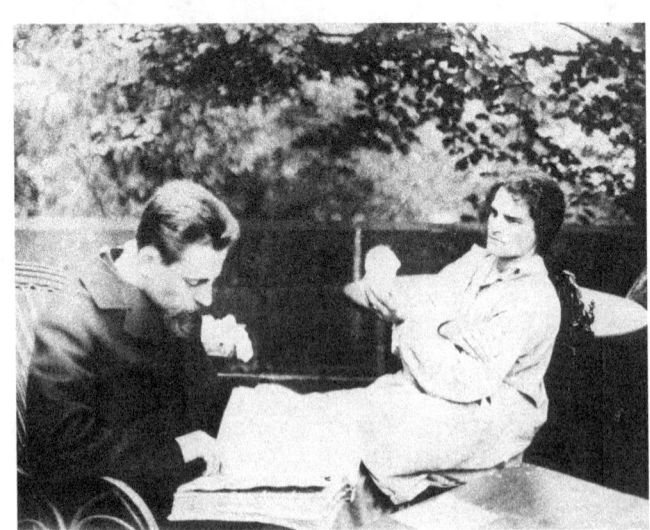

7.5. Rainer
Maria Rilke
Being Modeled
by Clara Rilke-
Westhoff, 1905.

7.6. Clara Rilke-Westhoff, *Rainer Maria Rilke*, 1936, bronze, h. 15″, Kunsthalle Bremen – Der Kunstverein in Bremen, photo credit: Lars Lohrisch.

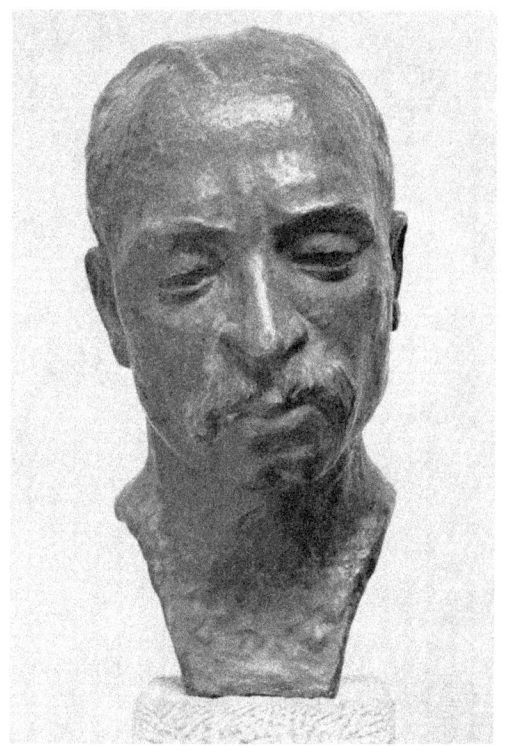

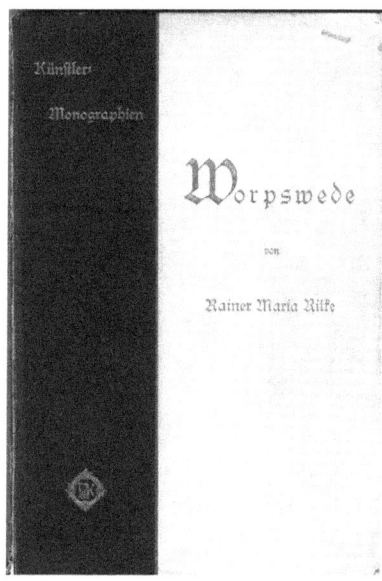

7.7. Rainer Maria Rilke, *Worpswede*, 1905 (2nd ed.), collection of the author.

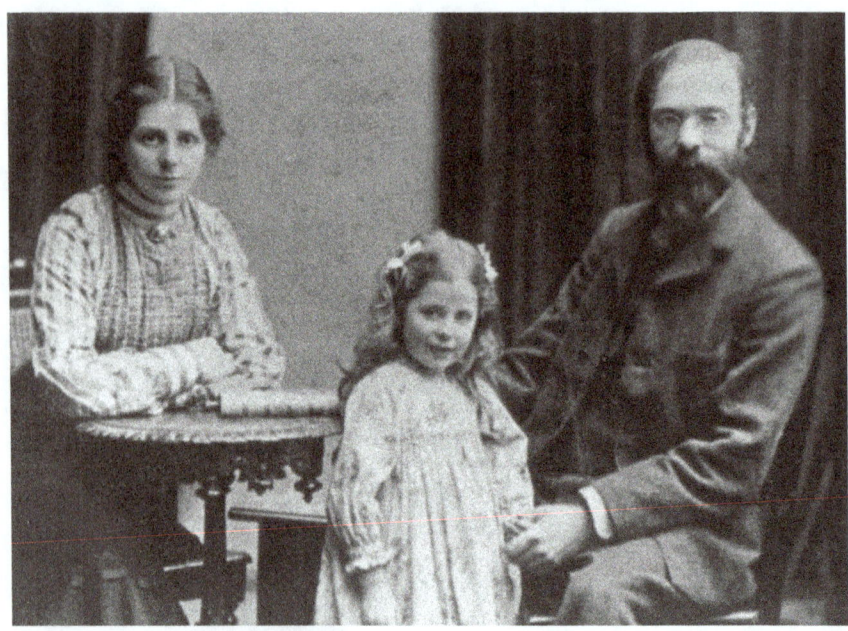

7.8. Paula, Elsbeth, and Otto Modersohn, c.1902, Otto Modersohn Museum, Fischerhude.

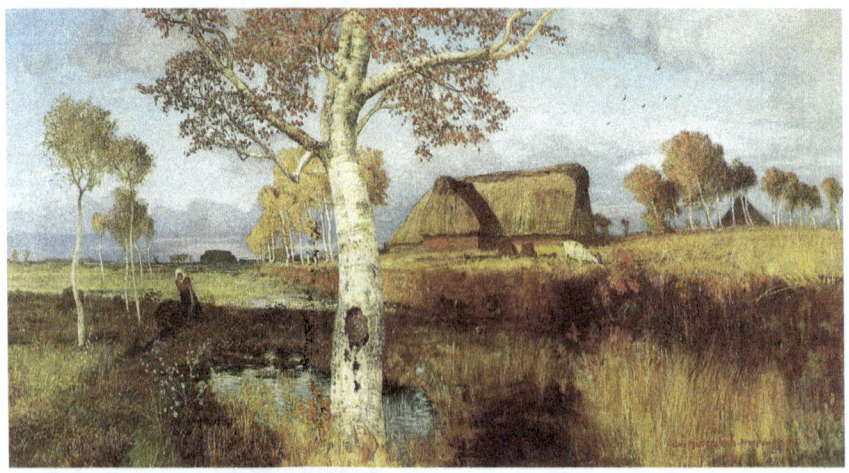

7.9. Otto Modersohn, *Autumn on the Moor*, 1895, oil on canvas, 32" x 59", Kunsthalle Bremen–Der Kunstverein in Bremen, photo credit: Lars Lohrisch.

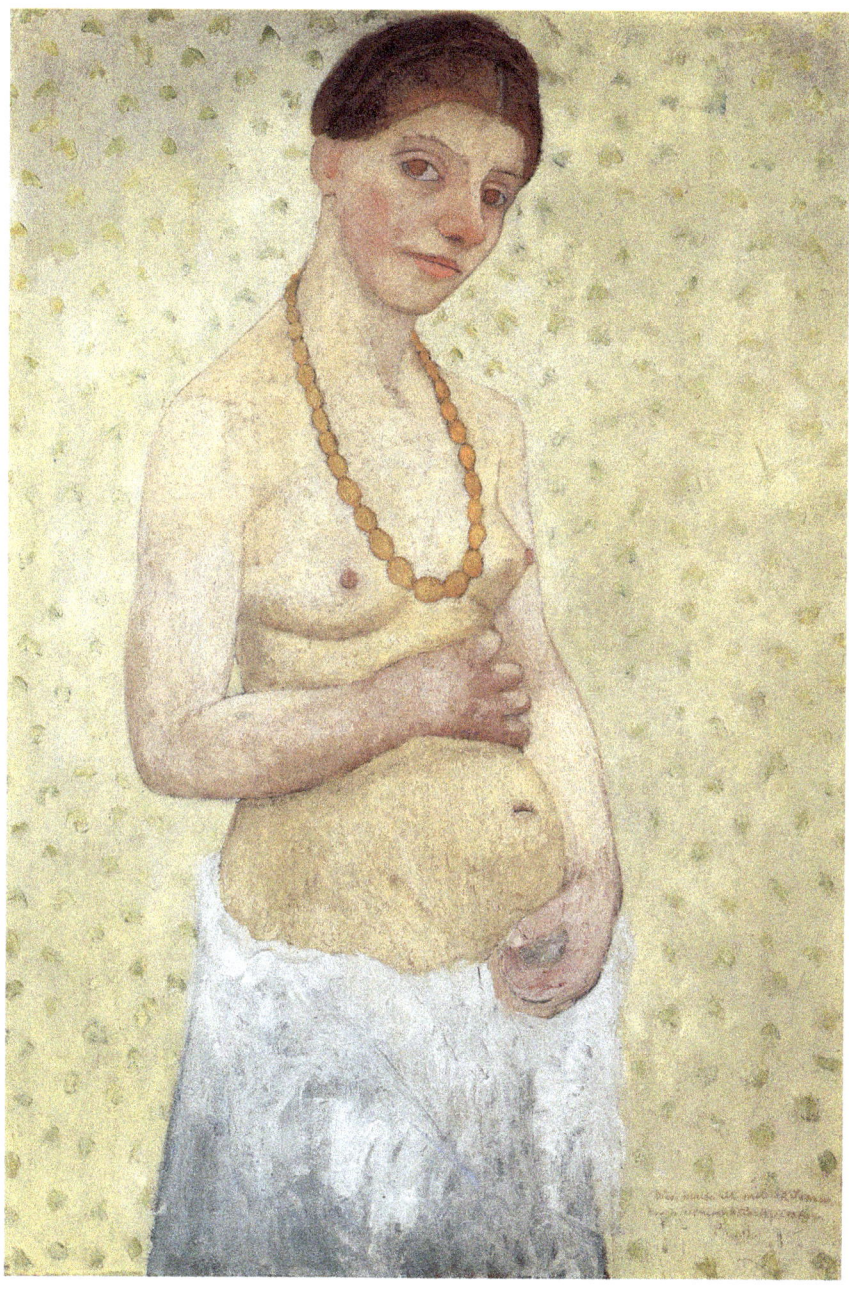

7.10. Paula Becker, *Self-Portrait, Age 30, 6th Wedding Day*, 1906, composite board, 40″ x 28″, Kunstsammlungen Böttcherstrasse, Paula Modersohn-Becker Museum, Bremen.

8
Home Sweet Home:
A Feminist Look at Nellie Mae Rowe

Joyce Cohen

The subject of house and home has a long history in American art. It can be found in paintings, quilts, rugs, coverlets, and samplers from the eighteenth to the twentieth centuries (Fig.1).[1] Many domestic images were the work of anonymous artists, women who learned needlework and passed these practices on to daughters and granddaughters.[2] The observation that for much of history "anonymous was a woman"[3] took on fresh significance in the wake of 1970s feminism as multiple eclipses based on gender and style were challenged by women artists and art historians. Today, because of feminist art we look at artists, domestic imagery, and craft traditions in new ways.

The art of Nellie Mae Rowe (1900–1982) overflows with references to traditional crafts as well as images of house and home (Fig. 2). Although she was hardly anonymous, her visibility has been limited for many of the same reasons that early female art makers remain anonymous. Rowe was a woman, African American and a self-taught artist working outside mainstream conventions. All these factors pushed her to the margins of the art world. Nonetheless Rowe has a fascinating relationship to twentieth-century feminism.

Many writers have pointed to the irony of Rowe's birth date—July 4th, 1900—Independence Day in the first year of a new millennium. She was the ninth child of Georgia sharecroppers descended from slaves. As the youngest girl she was given unusual freedom in her family; she had a habit of escaping from the hard work of the fields to bundle the family's laundry into cloth dolls—she tied the heads and drew faces on them. Whenever possible at the end of the day she would lie on the floor and draw. As an adult she often spoke about the fact that although both her parents worked the fields, they also made things with their hands. Her father was a blacksmith and basket maker. Her mother sewed dresses for her girls, made quilts, and taught needlecrafts to her children. It was also a family of storytellers.[4]

Like many young women of her social class, Nellie Mae Rowe had only four years of schooling and married young—at age seventeen, hoping to escape a life of grueling fieldwork. When her first husband died young, she remarried. At forty-eight she was widowed again and on her own, living in the four-room house that she had built with her second husband in Vinings, Georgia. At that moment Nellie Mae Rowe famously declared, "I ain't foolin' around no more. No more cookin'. No more marryin'. I'm going to get back to play—in my playhouse."[5] She said she had just "kept house long enough" and did not "want to be bothered by nobody 'cept myself."[6]

In recent years, a growing literature has documented how women like Nellie Mae Rowe—in different historical periods and in different countries—managed to negotiate the limitations of their lives and to forge identities as artists, often against crippling odds. From medieval cloisters of the twelfth century to twentieth-century America, their stories of discrimination and survival share notable features. Remarkable women found inventive ways to become artists even when they were denied education, had few role models, and received little or no support from their respective societies.[7]

Late in life Nellie Mae Rowe came to reflect on how she had always wanted to be an artist but it was unthinkable in her day.[8] Although she continued to work as a maid for another thirty years after her husband's death, she used every spare minute for creative activity. Over time, her little house at 2041 Paces Ferry Road—her "playhouse" as she called it—came to be an artist's studio and a work of art in its own right (Fig. 3). She embellished both interior and exterior spaces and made countless dolls and drawings. Over the forty-three years she lived in the playhouse, it evolved into a central image in her art.

Rowe's independent spirit and her embrace of play, reflects the remarkable power of the deep memory she retained of the little girl self, the small child who had discovered an identity through making dolls and drawings. "Play" was a psychic touchstone that directed Nellie Mae Rowe her entire life; however, the dichotomy between work and play was especially poignant for a middle-aged African-American woman in the late 1940s. She rejected the traditional roles available to someone of her race and social class, following the assertion that she was simply not "foolin' around no more."

In her book *Labor of Love, Labor of Sorrow: Black Women, Work and the Family*, the feminist historian Jacqueline Jones presents a compelling account of how working class Black women in the mid-twentieth century, despite the profound changes brought about by post-war industrialization, were virtually excluded from improvements in their work life. Their possibilities were restricted to domestic service and childcare in other peoples' homes or low-level jobs in factories and fields.[9] Rowe's pursuit of art was a unique choice for a woman of her social class and time, a deeply felt direction for an unusually independent woman. It was also a spiritual path. In interviews she repeatedly described how art was the fulfillment of a "gift" that God had given her when he blessed her with her talent.[10]

Dolls and drawings were made in the early 1950s but the yard at 2041 Paces Ferry Road became a focus of her creativity soon after her husband's death. The garden was always evolving and provided an important distraction from her loneliness. "I kept...I first started hanging things in trees and bushes in my yard. I'd put a wig on a head and sometimes have a shawl hanging on it and from up here it look like a person sittin' up in the tree. I'd color things with lipstick and crayon. The color would fade. But I like it when things keep changing, cause it keeps me busy."[11]

People would bring her things that she would transform and incorporate them into the yard in an inventive form of participatory aesthetics. She seemed to collect people in the same way she collected "stuff," as she called it. She scavenged for interesting objects and recycled everything. Friends gave her cast-offs and she incorporated these inside the house and outside in the yard.[12]

In 1971, a young Judith Alexander Augustine arrived at Rowe's doorstep and created one of the first records of her yard and playhouse (Figs. 4 and 5). Augustine was a student at Boston University, working on a photography assignment. Her mother passed Nellie Mae Rowe's house everyday and was the one who suggested that they "just knock on the door."[13] Augustine found an artist who "was very friendly and warm. She invited me inside where she was arranging some newly acquired plastic roses and paper Mache canaries and peppers. I was invited to look around, take all the pictures I pleased and she sat and told me about herself."[14] Later, Augustine's aunt (and her namesake, Judith Alexander) would come to represent the artist in her Atlanta gallery and introduce her to the world.

Augustine's photographs record the intimacy and visual complexity of Nellie Mae Rowe's yard in 1971. Hanging things in the trees, shaping topiary, making something out of nothing, recycling, and transforming the meanings of everyday fragments of life were the animating forces of this unique environment. Like many decorated yards of artists throughout the South, Rowe attended to the boundaries of her property, dressing up the fences and situating guardian figures at thresholds and doorways. Markers like these are hallmarks described by Grey Gundaker and Judith McWillie's in *No Space Hidden: The Spirit of African American Yard Work*, which describes a vast range of visionary sites and environments, like Rowe's.[15]

The artist's constructions were often fragile and therefore temporary, causing her to make constant additions and adjustments. She explained that she often had to transfer the dolls she made from chewing gum to the Frigidaire for a few days before they could go back outside and survive in the sun. She liked the way colors faded in the sun and objects dissolved; the way things were constantly changing.[16] Writing about these yards, Thomas McEvilley notes that such installations are not only "subject to continual alterations by their makers, they are also subject to the weather, constantly decomposing, and returning to the earth. "In their acceptance of organic processes" yards like Rowe's "manifest a balance between the interventions of culture and the cycles of nature."[17]

All this, of course, makes the destruction of Nellie Mae Rowe's playhouse after her death in 1982 all the more tragic. However, photographs that remain capture specific moments in an enterprise that was evolving over thirty years, freeze-frame the artist's amazing inventiveness, and reveal the complexity of what one writer has labeled "a deconstructor's paradise."[18] Sadly, there were tensions with some neighbors in the early years and the yard was routinely trashed by passers-by who taunted Rowe as a fortuneteller or "hoodoo" but throughout all this she remained receptive to visitors who were curious to see the playhouse, photograph it, and bring her objects that contributed to its evolution. "I just gain friends," she said. "I like livin' on the side of the road."[19]

Judith Augustine's visit and the notes she took reinforce what others who knew the artist have described as her generosity and eagerness to have her work seen. Her approach seems to foreshadow the popularity of participatory art projects of recent years, where viewers join to facilitate the meaning of an artistic space or concept and where the artist becomes part enchantress and part hostess.[20]

For someone who did not wish to be bothered by anyone except herself, Nellie Mae Rowe received a lot of visitors—over eight hundred people signed her guest book between May 27th, 1973 and March 15th, 1975. In 1975 Rowe's house was listed in the American Institute of Architect's Guide to Atlanta and people arrived in buses.[21]

Although "dressed yards" like Rowe's were, and still are, common in the South, it is worth noting that there are surprisingly few documented art yards attributed to women and even fewer large-scale visionary environments. In John Beardsley's catalog of vernacular sites, the author suggests that this gender difference may be due in part to economics—men being more likely to own their own spaces or to feel empowered to embellish even a rented plot. These yards, he notes "represent a form of public address" so men may feel more entitled to such a public voice, a sense of "male prerogative" perhaps while women's voices were more likely to find expression in interior spaces of the home.[22] None of these observations seem relevant to Nellie Mae Rowe's yard. The house was hers alone after her husband's death and she was not a shy woman reluctant to express herself.

Inside at 2041 Paces Ferry Road, another changing creation unfolded. J. Weiland, a photographer who visited Nellie Mae Rowe several times between 1977 and 1982 shows the artist inside her embellished rooms and how they too were a vivid extension of her efforts (Fig. 6). The recent book *The Saturated World: Aesthetic Meaning, Intimate Objects, and Women's Lives* by Beverly Gordon provides a useful way of looking at this rich environment.[23] Gordon draws from the history of material culture and women's craft hobbies to examine collecting, interior decorating, scrap booking, and doll making—all feminine enterprises typically dismissed as unworthy of academic study. Gordon has also extended her concept of "saturation" to vernacular environments and self-taught yard installations—personally created, over-flowing worlds of high sensory intensity and unique texture.[24]

Images of Nellie Mae Rowe in her playhouse speak for themselves as examples of a saturated environment. Hers is a densely embellished woman's space and a constantly compounding artwork. As dwelling, art studio, and display, Rowe's creation is multifaceted but also strangely cohesive. Like the yard, the interior rooms are alive and in flux. Pointing out the important relationships between the craft traditions of her family and Rowe's interiors and playhouse yard, Joanne Cubbs describes how for Rowe, "all content is subject to the potent authority of her strong decorative sensibility. She 'sewed' together complicated visual patters in the same formidable way that her mother, an accomplished quiltmaker, combined the multicolored pieces of fabric in her handiwork" (Fig. 7).[25]

Rowe compounds aesthetic intensity in ways that are highly personalized. Gordon speaks of the human impulse to "make things special" as something that transcends materials, class or race and is found in both the professional and amateur pursuits of women art makers.[26] Further, it is hard to ignore the way Nellie Mae made her space special at the very heart of her house and home, drawing on objects and images from and about the domestic domain.

When Rowe absorbs new elements into her saturated spaces— family pictures, stuffed animals, hand-made dolls, recycled and transformed objects—she is crafting a world of her own. She includes religious icons, art reproductions, posters, and calendars, along with posters of her personal heroes like Martin Luther King, shown making his "March on Washington" speech. All of this is positioned alongside her own drawings and sculptures. The elaboration of objects and textures reflect personal concerns, craft meanings, and build an identity. Rowe actually signs her wall, posting a painting, which is essentially a signature. Did she think of these surfaces as monumental drawings or installations that say, "This is mine? I am connected to all of this?"

Gordon also theorizes a phenomenon of "embodiment" common in saturated spaces, using the term to characterize ways creators are physically as well as psychically engaged in making and remaking their spaces. Embodiment speaks to the way things are touched, moved around, rearranged—actions guided by a personal vision rather than some abstract or informational logic.[27] Nellie Mae Rowe was an artist creating a world not an interior decorator or neutral cataloguer.

Embodiment is most overt with Rowe's hand-sewn dolls (Fig. 8). They are everywhere—inside and out, in trees, on the walls, resting on beds and chairs. The dolls include manufactured dolls that are frequently altered in some way. These float in the upper reaches of rooms or are part of tabletop tableaus. The dolls share her space. They keep company with her—intimate objects, extension of the body, and occasions for play and portraiture.

The young sons of the photographer J. Weiland, who made multiple visits to Nellie's playhouse with their father, show how visitors were also participants in the processes of embodiment. On this day in 1977, everybody gets to hold a doll. Through these photos we all get to play too. It is the nature of Rowe's aesthetic to encompass the viewer, to draw us into her world. Finally, we never forget that this interior is also a workspace—an artist's studio. In a unique construction, a collaged shoebox artwork, Rowe recycles photographs of herself working in the playhouse—an act of both recycling and self-representation (Fig. 9).

Since her death in 1982 and the destruction of the playhouse, Nellie Mae Rowe has come to be known primarily through hundreds of drawings she made, using mixed media and appropriated materials—crayon, felt-tip pens, acrylic paint on diverse available surfaces, including paper, cardboard, Styrofoam, and photographs. It is not surprising that these works are also filled with representations of her house and home. Familiar imagery, including many representations of the playhouse, serves all her major themes. The drawings are always about more than one thing but her subjects encompass spiritual matters, current events, and her life as an artist; they tell stories and explore the meaning of life and death.

In an important drawing the artist called *At Night Things Come to Me* (Fig. 10), Rowe's shows her playhouse as living space and as studio. She depicts herself asleep as visions hover above the bed. "I see what I draw in my mind at night," she said. "I can see everything like that. I don't care how crazy it is, I'll probably draw it. I can sit right now and look down there on the floor, I can see something. It looks like something I could draw. And I'll draw it."[28] She regarded her way of working as unique, reporting in interviews that she did not draw like other people. But her descriptions of process echo those of twentieth-century Surrealists, who sought to mine the unconscious, and bypassing the censoring mechanisms of logic.[29] From dream states these artists hoped to discover universal truths in new visual forms. André Breton wrote about the "superior reality" and "omnipotence of the dream."[30] Prescriptions like these were passed along to abstract expressionists like Arshile Gorky and Jackson Pollock who left a significant imprint on the identity of the New York School as well as contemporary assumptions about the sources of much abstract art.

Being true to such a process inevitably yields results that are difficult to decode and that even the artist may not be able to explain. Apparently, Nellie Mae Rowe resisted pinning down the precise meanings of her drawings, and while she loved to talk about her work, it is said that she could become quite testy when pressed for direct explanations of some drawings.[31] Engaging with her work requires viewers to surrender themselves to a world of incongruities and to struggle with idiosyncratic juxtapositions. Rowe was an artist who managed a complex array of symbols and unique tensions between the everyday, the literal, and the elusive.

At Night Things Come to Me is a double self-portrait. Rowe shows us the sleeping Nellie and the artist awake, perhaps to sketch the dream before it disappears. The visions that float overhead are familiar—both in Rowe's work and in the history of symbols. The dog, the rooster, the birds, and hybrid figures are very much the visitations that emerge in dreams, in the mythologies of many cultures, and throughout many storytelling traditions. They are watchful guardians with special powers, and mediators between the world of magic and the world of the everyday.[32] Another drawing, *Nellie's Playhouse, 1981* (Fig. 11) also positions the artist at home, working on a drawing that appears to be a tree, perhaps a tree of life. Outside the garden is filled with activity. Low hanging fruit has attracted birds, a dog, and a pig. Is this a tree of life or a feeding frenzy about to happen? Both are subjects of other Rowe drawings where she takes up biblical themes. The house itself is a triumph of patterning and decoration. Her signature, something she enjoyed experimenting with for decorative effect, is large and extravagantly drawn.

Nellie Mae's and Judith's Houses, 1980 (Fig. 12) has become one of the artist's best-known works. She combines a picture of her house (by this time a signature image in many drawings) with that of her dealer and friend, Judith Alexander. Both homes are colorful and decorated with patterns from African-American quilting, signs of Rowe's racial identity and her familiarity with craft traditions rooted in Africa. But, as always, there is a larger message in the representation of this architecture. Xenia Zed, who knew both Rowe and Alexander, has written that, "this fusion of the two...amounts to paying the highest visual compliment" to Alexander, a woman "who would ordinarily be considered an outsider in Rowe's world. It expresses the artist's desire to protect and enmesh her friend within her own personal and cultural universe."[33] Portraits of the two women appear above each house, although the homes themselves stand in for Judith and Nellie Mae.

In a charming photo collage in a Styrofoam frame, Nellie Mae Rowe shows herself trying on earrings with her dealer (Fig. 13). No feminist perspective could fail to mention the important role played by Alexander in promoting Nellie Mae Rowe's work and helping to give her a place in American art history. Alexander met the artist in 1978 after seeing her first exhibition *Missing Pieces: Georgia Folk Art, 1770-1976* in Atlanta.[34] Alexander later collected, catalogued, conserved, and promoted Rowe's work, eventually donating her personal collection of 130 Rowe works to the High Museum in Atlanta where today they form an important archive for continuing exhibition and study.[35]

The relationship between these two women is emblematic of an important pattern in which female dealers, collectors, and founders of cultural institutions have contributed to art history. A growing literature on women's leadership in the arts underscores the many ways these partnerships have influenced culture, from Isabella Stewart Gardner to Gertrude Stein and Peggy Guggenheim. The pioneer conceptual artist Joseph Kosuth, who has specialized in deconstructing institutions of art, notes that it has never been the artist alone who makes history. It takes the collector and the curator as well as the artist "to make culture visible."[36] The history of art would be incomplete without these relationships, many involving women philanthropists acting in defiance of social conventions to support unknown artists and to promote undervalued art styles.[37]

It is obvious from Rowe's construction that the two shared a relationship of trust and affection. We are shown two friends enjoying a girly moment. It looks as if Nellie Mae has just had her hair done! The phrase "Lord, we love you" and a sketch of the tree of life on the margin of the frame, are messages that all humanity is connected. Rowe obviously liked the photograph so much that she enshrined it in this specially ornamented frame tray, even affixing earrings at the top corners. A small image of the playhouse is in the lower corner as a gentle signature to the piece. Another notable tribute to her dealer and friend is Nellie Mae Rowe's portrait doll of Alexander in her signature red hat (Fig. 14).

2041 Paces Ferry Road, Vinnings, 1979 (Fig. 15) and *Nellie Mae Rowe House, 1981* (Fig. 16) are just two of many drawings sharing a device that became increasingly common in the late 1970s, and early 1980s, where a miniature image of the playhouse appears in the lower right hand corner of the drawing and contains the artist's signature. The playhouse drawing became a kind of "chop mark" and a stand-in for the artist herself. It is a unique signature and self-portrait.

Rocking Chair, 1981 (Fig. 17) is another drawing where the house is a unique container of meaning. It is believed to have been created soon after Nellie Mae Rowe learned that she was suffering from cancer. The empty chair (as memento mori) is used elsewhere in her work and it participates in a long art historical tradition of using a familiar, domestic object as a stand-in for the absent person. While the house is filled with activity, the artist is not at home. An angel, a black dog, and the dying plants reinforce the sense of impending absence. Greedy birds move in to eat the fruit while no one is at home to shoo them away.[38]

Peace, 1978 (Fig. 18) is another type of self-portrait, an indirect representation of the self in which the artist appears as protector of the innocent. We see a woman's hands (symbolic of female power and wisdom). In an assertion of artistic immortality, Rowe said, "When I'm gone they can see a print of my hand. I love that, to see a print of my hand. I'll be gone to rest, but they will look back and say, 'that is Nellie Mae's hand . . . There's some work I need to do before God take me. I ain't done my work—what he wants me to do. That's why the talent he gave me to do this work, he gave me that 'cause I didn't have no children and he give me something to do."[39]

Nellie Mae Rowe and 1970s Feminism

As Nellie Mae Rowe was developing her complex vocabulary involving images of house and home, she was certainly unaware that she was creating work within a highly contested realm of imagery that was personal and entwined with female domesticity. Beginning in the early 1970s, mainstream American art was at a crossroads in challenging the legitimacy of all these themes in art by women.

Since the 1940s abstraction and formalism had grown in dominance while subjectivity and materials of everyday life declined. In the 1950s the influential art critic Clement Greenberg, spokesman for a new American avant-garde, declared that any art that was not purely about color, line, and the flatness of the picture plane was not art—it was "kitsch." Storytelling, symbolism, and representation—these were out.[40] Art by women that reflected their daily experience was discredited by a powerful male-dominated art world of critics, curators, collectors, and artists themselves. Women's work, especially that rooted in traditional crafts, was relegated to a secondary status. Even in architecture, earlier notions of house and home suffered in the face of modernism's clean lines and stark white cubes.[41] Rigid categories separated art and craft. Critics in the

1950s and 1960s declared that avant-garde art had to be an art of hard edges, abstraction, minimal shapes, blank fields of color, and geometric forms.

Of course, women have always made art, despite the fashions of style and critical acclaim. But, throughout the early to mid-twentieth-century women artists survived mainly on the far margins of the art world. One exception to this pattern can be found in the years of the WPA art program when artists were employed in color-blind and gender-blind projects funded by taxpayer dollars. Projects hired near equal numbers of male and female artists as well as a higher proportion of African-American and Native-American artists than could be found in commercial galleries or museums at the time.[42]

In response to modernism's systematic exclusion of women in the early 1970s, feminist artists mounted an offensive that began in California at Fresno State College and Cal Arts but quickly spread across the country. Led by Judy Chicago and Miriam Schapiro, the feminist movement challenged the establishment's rejection of content and practices associated with women's work and women's lives—the very essences that defined Nellie Mae Rowe's work and made it so compelling.

Artists and students who gathered around Chicago and Schapiro found a cloistered setting in California where they questioned discriminatory practices of the studio, the gallery, and the museum and to confront the bias of critics and historians who had systematically rejected women. They critiqued patterns of male authority and tried to recover the histories of female artists. Their most visible product was the 1972 creation of *Womanhouse*, where the students and their teachers took over an abandoned house in LA, saved it from demolition and turned it into a collective studio, performance and exhibition space.[43] Miriam Schapiro collaborated with Sherry Brody to create *Doll House* (Fig 19), an edgy construction that recycled fragments of textiles the women had stockpiled for many years while they were paying their dues to the mainstream art world. Schapiro explained that, "feminism was the spur to the more important question for us. What would art look like if made in the image of domesticity by a group of women artists?"[44] These women made art about the structure of marriage and women's roles and they protested the absence of women's art in museums, galleries, and textbooks. But beyond subject matter, the most lasting legacy of the feminist movement was to reclaim practices associated with traditional crafts and domestic imagery (Fig. 20). For the first time since the advent of modernism, art viewers were seeing knitting, crocheting, and quilting—what one critic called "the soft, the sewn, the stitched."[45] These approaches, all practices advanced by anonymous women artists since the eighteenth century, were combined in the mid-twentieth century with political messages about the real lives of women and girls.

Part art showcase and part political theater, *Womanhouse* also fostered a higher consciousness about exclusions in the art world. In short, this group of teachers and students launched a movement that rippled throughout the 1970s and into the 1980s and 1990s, with the emergence of new feminist publications, exhibition spaces, and organizations like the Women's Caucus for the Arts. Miriam Schapiro established the Pattern and Decoration Movement and Judy Chicago's *Dinner Party* was created with the help of over four hundred women, celebrating women artists from history—Artemisia Gentileschi to Georgia O'Keeffe.[46]

Louise Bourgeois, one of today's most recognized artists, had been working in New York since the 1930s, but after 1970s feminism, she surfaced with drawings and paintings that reflected her own domestic imagery, work that she had hidden away for many years (Fig. 21). According to Bourgeois, she had suppressed these works from the 1940s, feared she would be ridiculed in the critical climate of the times.[47] A new multicultural awareness and attention to both sexism and racism empowered activists like Faith Ringgold—who began making dolls and quilts that were simultaneously political statements and beautiful domestic references. Ringgold and other African-American artists confronted the absence of Black women in the art world and supported each other to make objects that reflected their African-American roots.[48]

In recent years, the art critic Lucy Lippard has written lamenting the fact that "while feminist artists of the 1970s were rediscovering our mothers' and grandmothers' strategies for survival through beauty, marveling at quilts, china painting, hooked rugs, embroidery, and other homemade treasures, we should have also been discovering women who made paintings, sculptures, and yard shows in a vernacular context."[49] In addition to suffering racism and gender discrimination, self-taught women like Nellie Mae Rowe were largely overlooked by their contemporaries in the mainstream art world.

Self-Taught Women Artists in the Context of History

Imagine what first generation feminist artists might have learned from women like Nellie Mae Rowe, Clementine Hunter, Bessie Harvey, Sister Gertrude Morgan, or Gayleen Aiken—all their contemporaries, all self-taught, all artists who had worked for years in what Lippard called a "vernacular context." In the shadows of an art world defined by categories and dismissals, these artists had embraced the practices and materials of traditional crafts even while they created work expressing their lives as women. For Rowe it was not until after the 1982 *Black Folk Art Show*, in which she was one of only three female artists among the twenty featured in the show, that her work began to receive national exposure.[50] Alas, *Black Folk Art* opened just a few months before Rowe's death but by then her discovery of a rich vocabulary the 1970s feminists had fought so hard to bring about, had flourished for thirty years.

In 1989, the Guerilla Girls—"the conscience of the art world"— listed Nellie Mae Rowe among other important women artists in their now-famous poster—a long over-due emblem of inclusion signifying the dissolving boundaries between mainstream and self-taught art (Fig. 22). In her work on self-taught artists, the scholar Judith McWillie points out how the twentieth-century synthesis of African Art and European traditions heralded by shows like the Museum of Modern Art's 1985 *Primitivism in the 20th Century*, was a movement crediting white European artists for having "discovered" the primitive and adapted it to their own inventive purposes. McWillie argues instead that untrained African-American artists in the South had long-since accomplished this synthesis by combining elements from their own African pasts with twentieth-century artistic styles.[51]

Nellie Mae Rowe's playhouse and drawings prefigured an equally significant revolution in art. As early as 1950s she was representing a woman's life using the processes of traditional crafts and the materials of everyday life.

Although there will never be another Nellie Mae Rowe, we can only hope that with greater visibility of self-taught artists, the importance of their work will become better known and better understood in the context of twentieth-century art. At museums like the High Museum in Atlanta and the American Folk Art Museum, shows have begun to dissolve the barriers between mainstream and self-taught art. Thoughtful exhibitions, based on scholarship respecting the significances of each artist's origins, will begin to give artists like Nellie Mae Rowe their rightful place in art history.

End Notes

[1] I am grateful to Susan Crawley, Curator the Folk Art at Atlanta's High Museum from 2004 – 2013 for introducing me to Nellie Mae Rowe's artworks in their collection and for inviting me to give a public talk on Rowe in 2011. That lecture and a small exhibition I curated at the museum to accompany it were the inspiration for this article. I would also like to acknowledge the many private collectors who allowed their pieces to be reproduced here. In addition, I am indebted to Judith Alexander Augustine, and J. Weiland who shared their early photographs of Rowe and her Playhouse and enriched the visual impact of the photos with stories about meetings with the artist.

[2] Deborah Harding and Laura Fisher, *Home Sweet Home: The House in American Folk Art* (New York: Rizzoli, 2001), 11-15.

[3] Virginia Woolf, "A Room of Her Own" (lecture, Cambridge University, October 1929).

[4] Lee Kogan. *Ninety-Nine and a Half Won't Do: The Art and Life of Nellie Mae Rowe* (Jackson: Museum of American Folk Art and University Press of Mississippi, 1998), 16-18.

[5] Xenia Zed, "Nellie's Hagiography," *Nellie Mae Rowe* (Augusta, Georgia: Morris Museum of Art, 1996), 20.

[6] Kogan, *Ninety-Nine and a Half Won't Do*, 20.

[7] Norma Broude, "Introduction: Reclaiming Female Agency," in *Reclaiming Female Agency: Feminist Art History after Postmodernism*, Norma Broude and Mary D. Garrard, eds. (Berkeley: University of California Press, 2005), 1-25.

[8] Zed, *Nellie Mae Rowe*, 17.

[9] Jacqueline Jones, *Labor of Love, Labor of Sorrow: Black Women, Work and the Family from Slavery to the Present* (New York: Basic Books, 2010), 127.

[10] Bill Arnett, "Nellie Mae Rowe Inside the Perimeter," in *Souls Grown Deep: African American Vernacular Art of the South*, Vol. I, Paul Arnett and Bill Arnett, eds. (Atlanta, Georgia: Tinwood Books in association with the Schaumburg Center for Research in Black Culture, New York Public Library, 2000), 304.

[11] Zed, *Nellie Mae Rowe*, 21-22.

[12] J. Weiland, (phone interview with Joyce Cohen, March, 2009).

[13] Judith Alexander Augustine, *Nellie Mae Rowe: A Photo Essay* (with unpublished notes, 1971).

[14] Augustine, *Nellie Mae Rowe: A Photo Essay*.

[15] Grey Gundaker and Judith McWillie, *No Space Hidden: The Spirit of African American Yard Work* (Knoxville: University of Tennessee Press, 2005), 109-110.

[16] Augustine, *Nellie Mae Rowe: A Photo Essay*.

[17] Thomas McEvilley, "The Missing Tradition," *Art in America*, no. 9 (May 1997): 82.

[18] Zed, *Nellie Mae Rowe*, 24.

[19] Augustine, *Nellie Mae Rowe: A Photo Essay*.

[20] Ted Purves, *What We Want Is Free: Generosity and Exchange in Recent Art* (New York: University of New York: 2010), 1-20.

[21] Kogan, *Ninety-Nine and a Half Won't Do*, 18.

[22] John Beardsley, *Gardens of Revelation: Environments of Visionary Artists* (New York: Abbeville Press, 2003), 28.

[23] Beverly Gordon, *The Saturated World: Aesthetic Meaning, Intimate Objects and Women's Lives* (Knoxville, University of Tennessee Press, 2006), 1-35.

[24] Beverly Gordon, "Learning from Vernacular Environment Builders," symposium presentation, J. M. Kohler Arts Center, 2007.

[25] Joanne Cubbs, "New Geography: Mapping Meaning in Self-Taught Art," in *Let it Shine: Self-Taught Art from the T. Marshall Hahn Collection*, exh. cat., Lynne E. Spriggs, ed. (Atlanta, Georgia: High Museum), 25-26.

[26] Gordon, *The Saturated World*, 15-16.

[27] Gordon, *The Saturated World*, 17.

[28] Judith Alexander, *Nellie Mae Rowe: Visionary Artist 1900-1982* (Atlanta, Georgia: Southern Arts Federation, 1983), 5.

[29] Herschel B. Chipp, *Theories of Modern Art* (Berkeley: University of California Press, 1968), 417-419.

[30] Chipp, *Theories of Modern Art*, 412.

[31] Susan Mitchell Crawley, text of *Let It Shine: Self-Taught Art from the T. Marshall Hahn Collection*, exh. cat., Lynne E. Spriggs, ed. (Atlanta, Georgia: High Museum, 2001), 132.

[32] Hans Biedermann, *Dictionary of Symbolism: Cultural Icons & the Meanings Behind Them* (New York: Meridian Press, 1994), 97.

[33] Xenia Zed, "Makin a Way Outta No Way," *Raw Vision Magazine*, no. 32 (Fall, 2000): 28.

[34] Anna Wadsworth, *Missing Pieces: Georgia Folk Art 1770-1976* (Atlanta, Georgia: Georgia Council for the Arts and Humanities, 1976).

[35] Susan Crawley (Curator, High Museum Folk Art Collection), *Folk Art Society Magazine on-line*, Spring, 2005, website, www.folkart.org/mag/high/interview.

[36] Joseph Kosuth, interview with author on the occasion of the exhibition "Artist, Curator, Collector: James McNeill Whistler, Bernard Berenson, and Isabella Stewart Gardner –Three Locations in the Creative Process," Isabella Stewart Gardner Museum, Boston, Massachusetts, April 1, 2003.

[37] Kathleen D. McCarthy, *Women's Culture: American Philanthropy and Art (1830-1930)* (Chicago: Chicago University Press, 1991), xi-xvi.

[38] Arnett, "Nellie Mae Rowe Inside the Perimeter," 298.

[39] Kogan, *Ninety-Nine and a Half Won't Do*, 24.

[40] Norma Broude and Mary D. Garrard, "Introduction: Feminist Art in the 20th Century," in *The Power of Feminist Art*, Norma Broude and Mary D. Garrard, eds. (New York: Harry N. Abrams, 1996), 12-20.

[41] Christopher Reed, *Not At Home: The Suppression of Domesticity in Modern Art and Architecture* (London: Thames and Hudson, 1996), 14-15.

[42] Helen Langa, "Egalitarian Vision: Gendered Experience," in *The Expanding Discourse*, Norma Broude and Mary Garrard, eds. (New York: Harper Collins, 1992), 409-424.

[43] Arlene Raven, "Womanhouse," in *The Power of Feminist Art*, Broude and Garrard, eds., 32-65.

[44] Miriam Schapiro, *Femmages* 1971-1985, exh. cat. (St. Louis: Brentwood Gallery, 1985).

[45] Jane Delgado and Lydia Yee, *Division of Labor: Women's Work in Contemporary Art*, exh. cat. (New York: The Bronx Museum of the Arts, 1995), 9.

[46] Mary D. Garrard, "Feminist Politics: Networks and Organizations," in *The Power of Feminist Art*, Broude and Garrard, eds., 92-102.

[47] Delgado and Yee, *Division of Labor*, 10.

[48] Peggy Phalen, "Survey," *Art and Feminism*, Helena Reckitt and Peggy Phelan, eds. (New York: Phaidon Press, 2001), 68.

[49] Lisa Farrington, *Creating Their Own Image: The History of African American Women Artists* (New York: Oxford University Press, 2005), 235.

[50] Jane Livingston and John Beardsley, *Black Folk Art in America: 1930-1980*, exh. cat. (Washington, DC: Corcoran Gallery of Art, 1982).

[51] Warren Lowe and Shirley Lowe, *It'll Come True: Eleven Artists First and Last* (Lafayette, Louisiana: Artists' Alliance, 1992), 13.

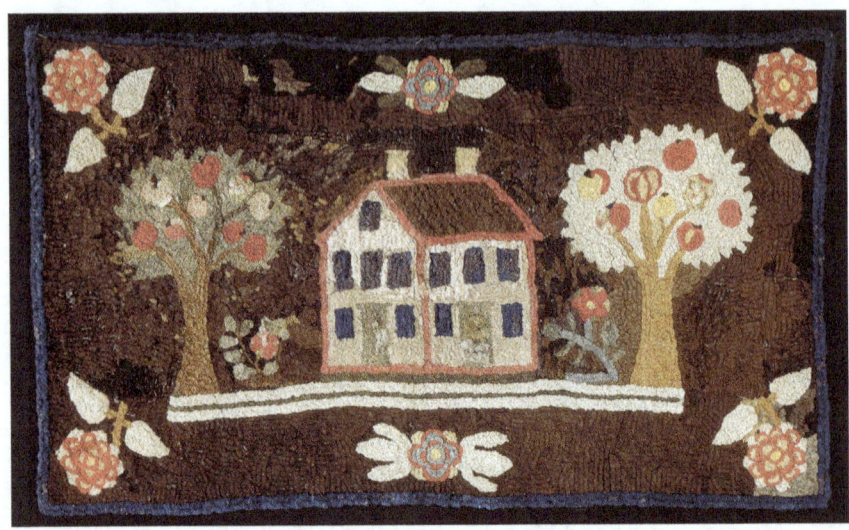

8.1. Artist unknown, probably New England, *Hooked Rug*, 1820-1830, linen, shirred wool, 35 " x 60", gift of Bertram K. and Nina Fletcher Little, courtesy of Historic New England, photo credit: David Bohl.

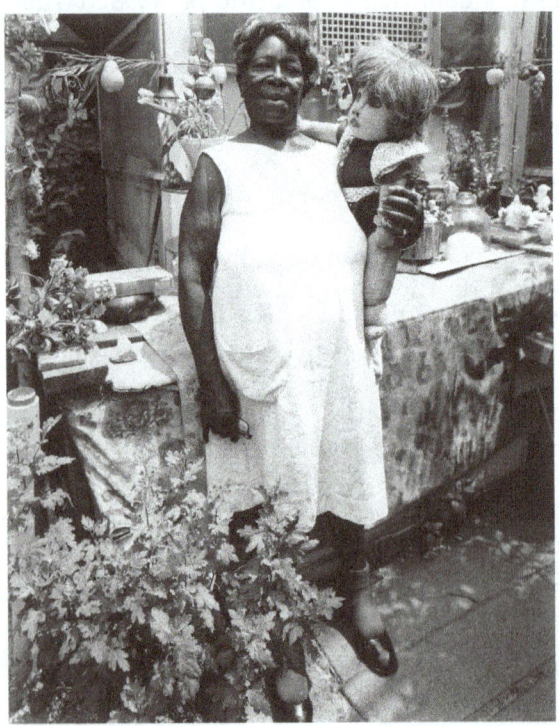

8.2. *Nellie Mae Rowe in her yard with "Little Nellie" doll*, 1978, photo credit: J. Weiland.

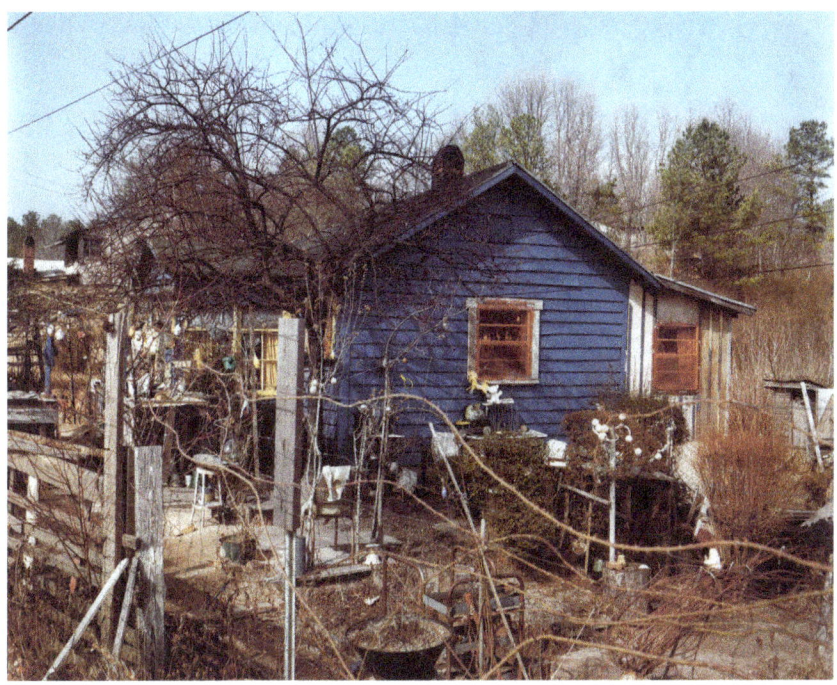

8.3. *Nellie Mae Rowe's house at 2041 Paces Ferry Road,* 1977, photo credit: J. Weiland.

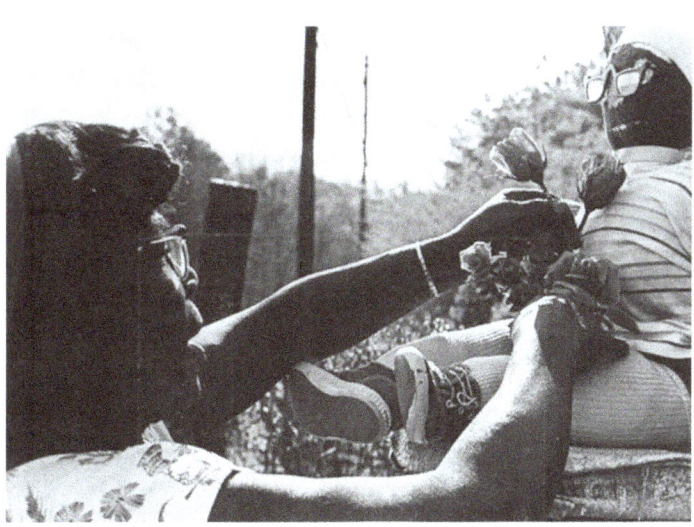

8.4. *Nellie Mae Rowe and "the ugly varmit" in her yard,* 1971, photo credit: Judith Alexander Augustine.

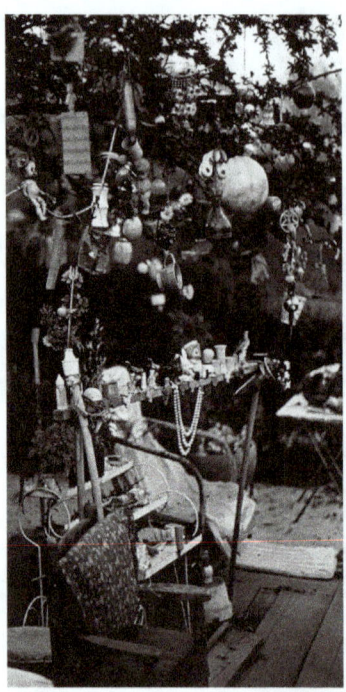

8.5. *Nellie Mae Rowe's Yard*, 1971, photo credit: Judith Alexander Augustine.

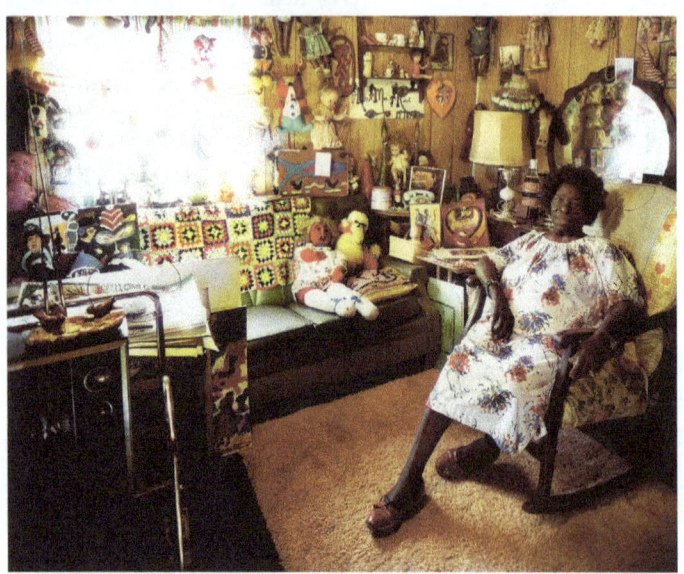

8.6. *Nellie Mae Rowe in her Living Room*, 1979, photo credit: J. Weiland.

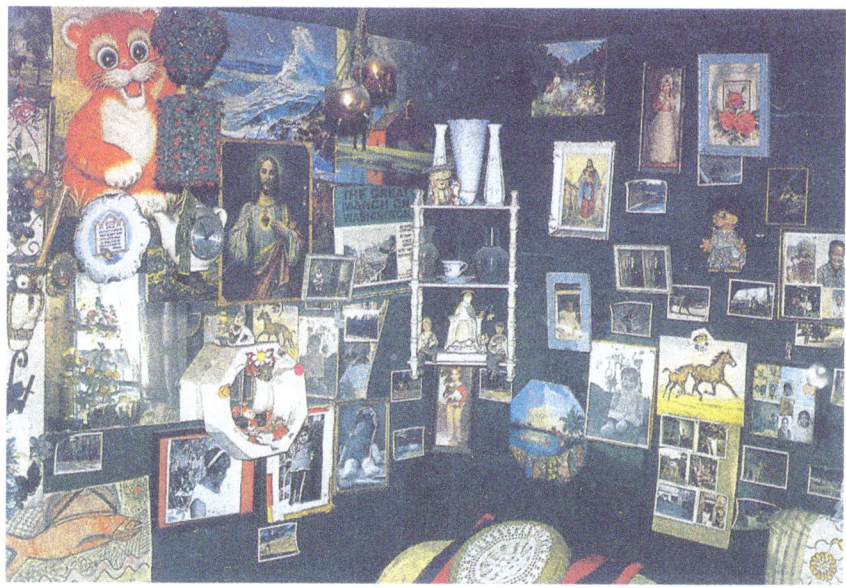

8.7. *Interior Wall in Nellie Mae Rowe's Playhouse*, 1976, photo credit: Andy Nasisse.

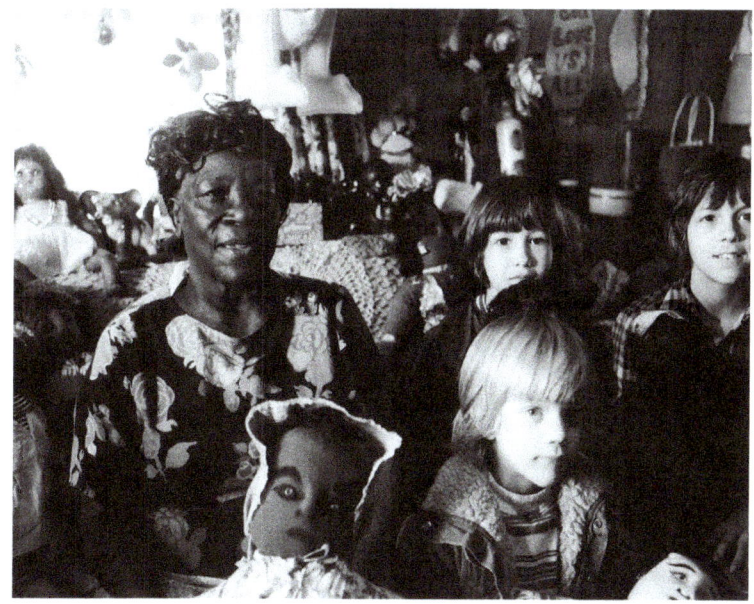

8.8. *Nellie Mae Rowe with David, Scott and Andy Weiland*, 1979, photo credit: J. Weiland.

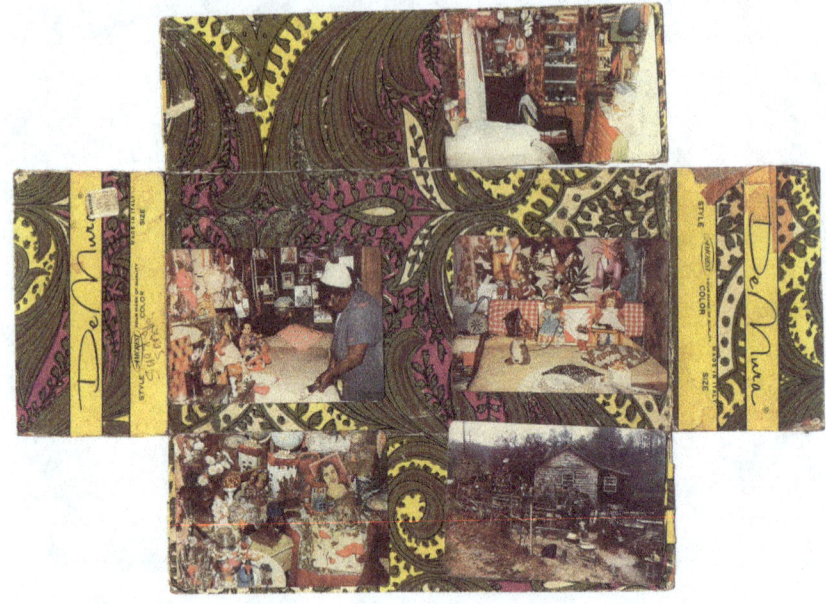

8.9. Nellie Mae Rowe, *Untitled (DeMura Shoe Box)*, ca. 1970s, photographs collaged on cardboard, 18″ x 13″, High Museum of Art, Atlanta, gift of Judith Alexander, 2003.234.

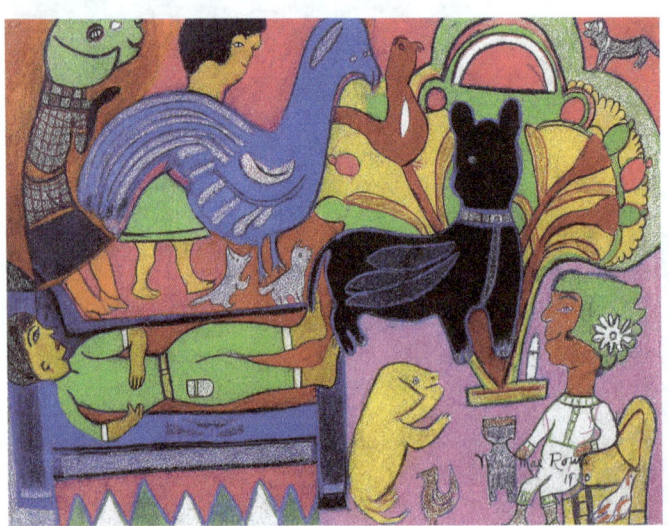

8.10. Nellie Mae Rowe, *At Night Things Come to Me*, 1980, crayon and pencil on paper, 18″ x 24″, High Museum of Art, Atlanta, gift of Judith Alexander, 2003.226.

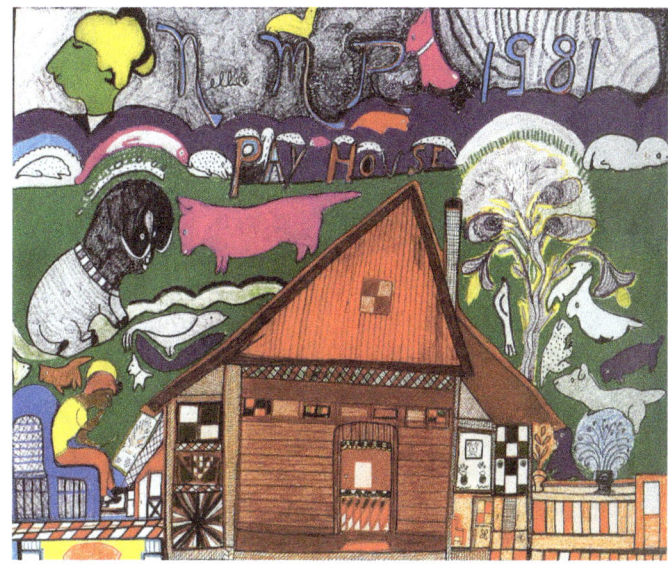

8.11. Nellie Mae Rowe, *Nellie's Playhouse*, 1981, crayon, felt-tip pen, and pencil on cardboard, 23" x 30", High Museum of Art, Atlanta, gift of Judith Alexander, 2003.217.

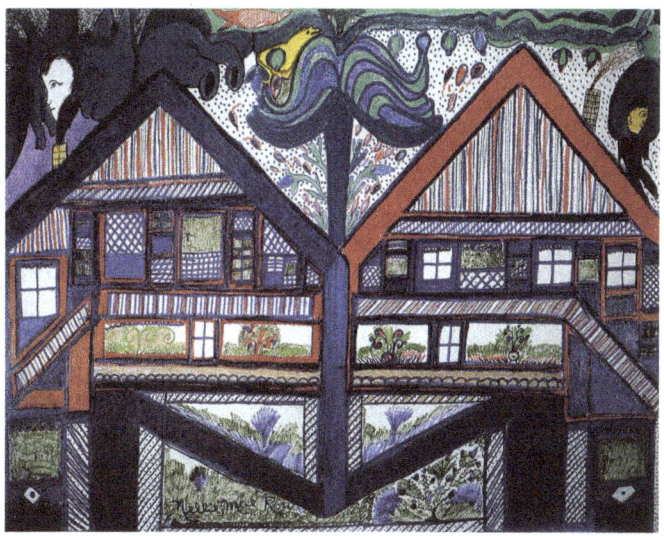

8.12. Nellie Mae Rowe, *Nellie Mae and Judith's Houses*,1980, crayon, felt-tip pen, pencil and gouache on paper, 19" x 24", High Museum of Art, Atlanta, gift of Judith Alexander, 2003.209.

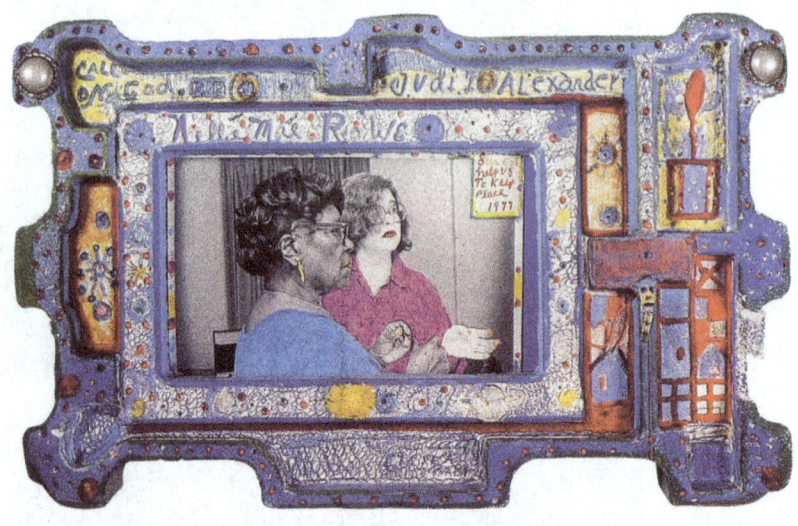

8.13. Nellie Mae Rowe, *Dear God Help Us to Keep Peace*, 1977, mixed media; photograph with marker, ballpoint pen, jewelry, and styrofoam frame with oil pastel, 13" x 20", High Museum, of Art, Atlanta, gift of Judith Alexander, 2002.236.

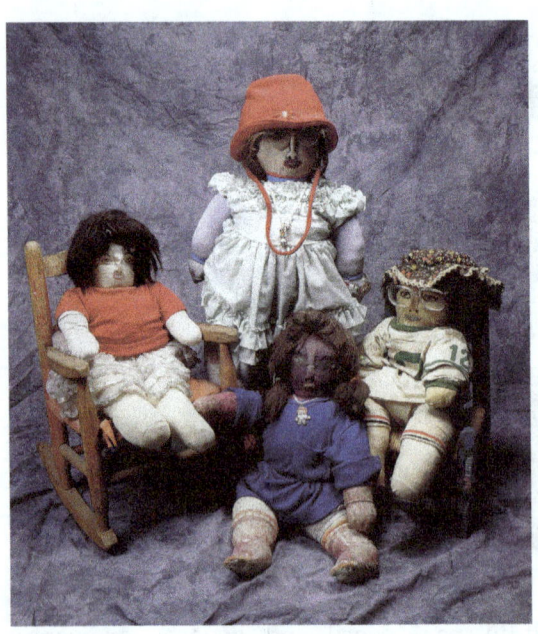

8.14. Nellie Mae Rowe, *Untitled (Hand sewn dolls)*, ca. 1981, cloth, fiber stuffing, glass, plastic, mother of pearl, wire, and pigment of unknown origin, wood rocking chair, 37" x 17" x 8', High Museum of Art, Atlanta, Gift of Judith Alexander, 2001.6a-b.

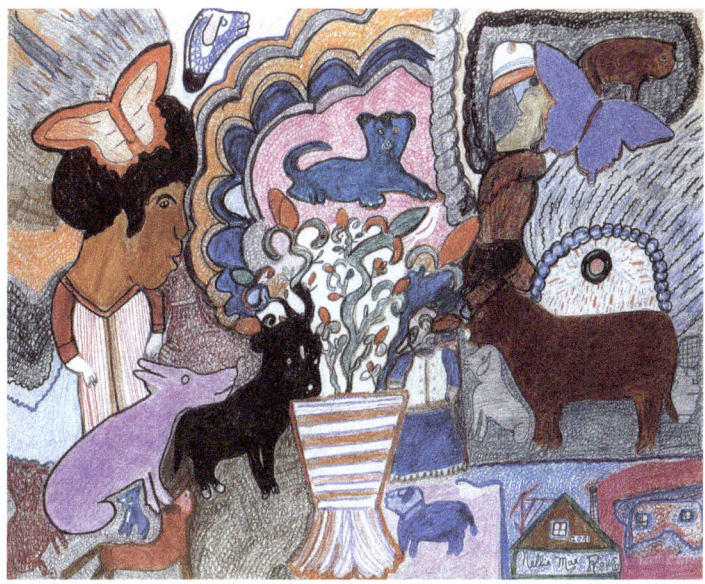

8.15. Nellie Mae Rowe, *2041 Paces Ferry Road, Vinings*, 1979, pencil, felt-tip pen, and colored pencil on paper, 19" x 24", collection of Judith M. Anderson.

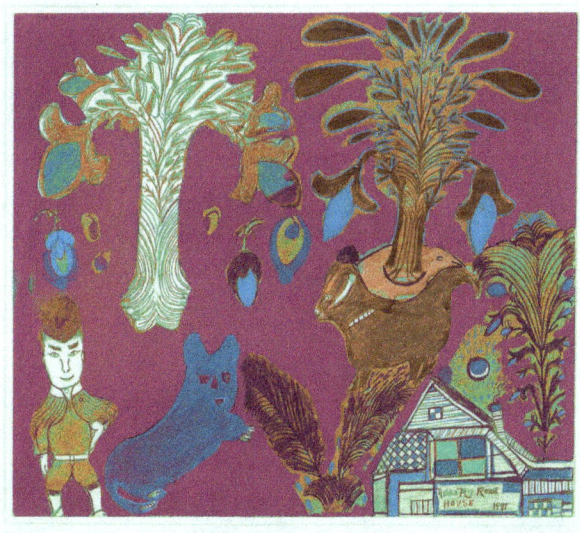

8.16. Nellie Mae Rowe, *Nellie Mae Rowe House*, 1981, colored pencil, ink, and oil on heavy paper, 24 7/8" x 28 7/8", collection of Carl W. Mullis III, courtesy of Georgia Museum of Art.

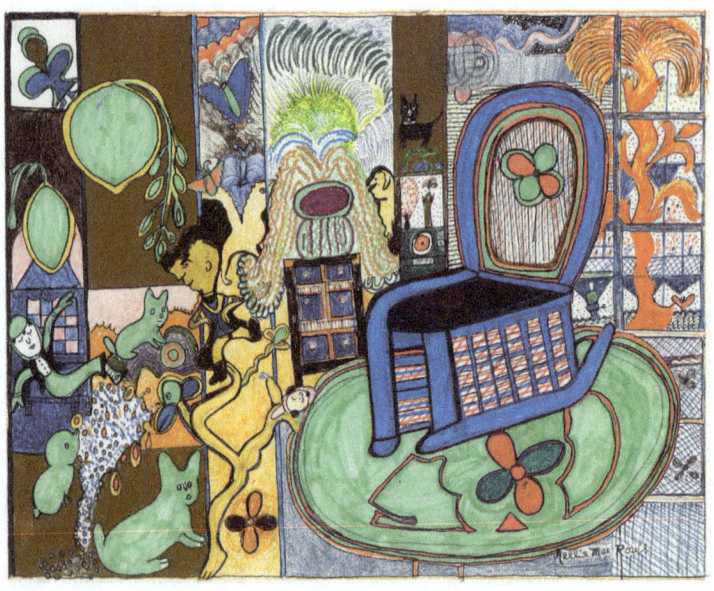

8.17. Nellie Mae Rowe, *Rocking Chair*, 1981, crayon, felt-tip pen and pencil on paper, 18″ x 23″, collection of Bill Arnett, courtesy of Tinwood Foundation.

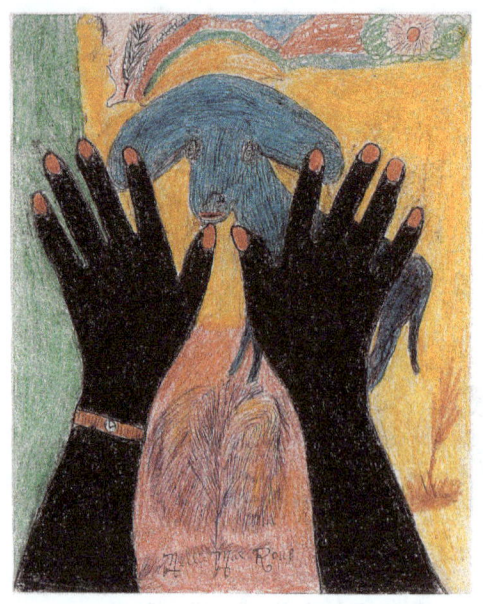

8.18. Nellie Mae Rowe, *Peace*, 1978, crayon and pen on paper, 17″ x 14″, High Museum of Art, Atlanta, gift of Judith Alexander, 2003.219.

8.19. Miriam Schapiro and Sherry Brody, *Doll House*, 1972, three-dimensional construction and mixed media, 48″ x 41″ x 8″, Smithsonian American Art Museum, museum purchase through the Gene Davis Memorial Fund, 1997.112A-B.

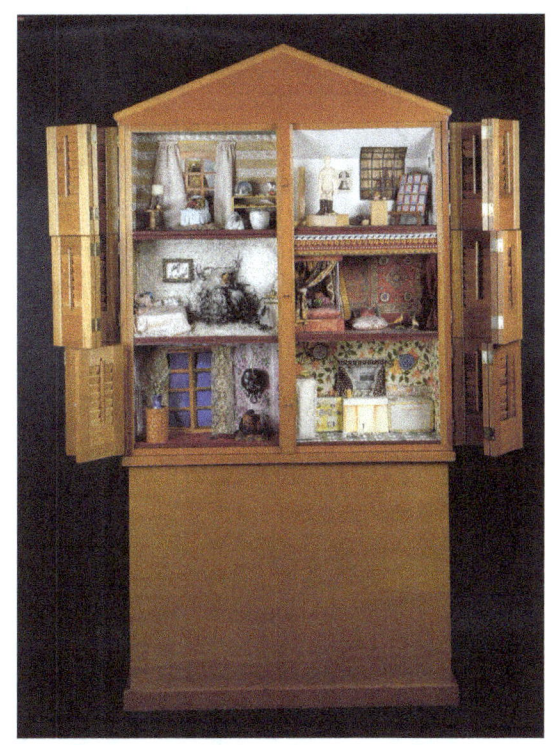

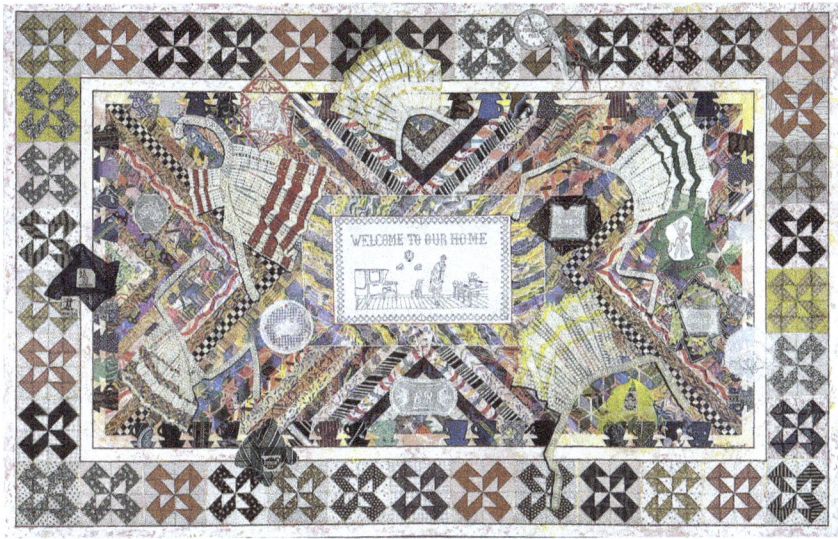

8.20. Miriam Schapiro, *Wonderland*, 1983, acrylic and fabric, 90″ x 144″, Smithsonian American Art Museum, gift of an anonymous donor, 1996.88.

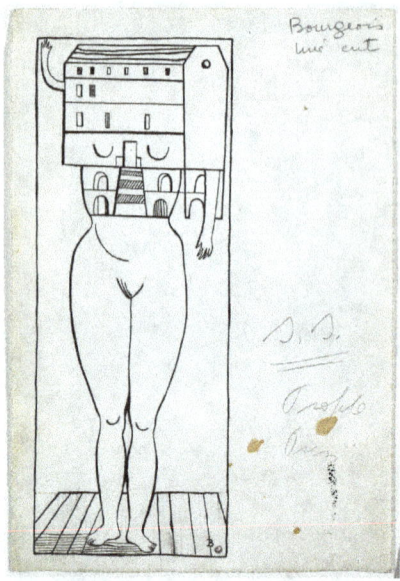

8.21. Louise Bourgeois, *Femme-Maison*,1947, ink and graphite on paper, 9 15/16" x 7 1/8", Solomon R. Guggenheim Museum, New York, 92.4008.

WHEN RACISM & SEXISM ARE NO LONGER FASHIONABLE, WHAT WILL YOUR ART COLLECTION BE WORTH?

The art market won't bestow mega-buck prices on the work of a few white males forever. For the 17.7 million you just spent on a single Jasper Johns painting, you could have bought at least one work by all of these women and artists of color.

Bernice Abbott	Elaine de Kooning	Dorothea Lange	Sarah Peale
Anni Albers	Lavinia Fontana	Marie Laurencin	Ljubova Popova
Sofonisba Anguisolla	Meta Warwick Fuller	Edmonia Lewis	Olga Rosanova
Diane Arbus	Artemisia Gentileschi	Judith Leyster	Nellie Mae Rowe
Vanessa Bell	Marguérite Gérard	Barbara Longhi	Rachel Ruysch
Isabel Bishop	Natalia Goncharova	Dora Maar	Kay Sage
Rosa Bonheur	Kate Greenaway	Lee Miller	Augusta Savage
Elizabeth Bougereau	Barbara Hepworth	Lisette Model	Vavara Stepanova
Margaret Bourke-White	Eva Hesse	Paula Modersohn-Becker	Florine Stettheimer
Romaine Brooks	Hannah Hoch	Tina Modotti	Sophie Taeuber-Arp
Julia Margaret Cameron	Anna Huntingdon	Berthe Morisot	Alma Thomas
Emily Carr	May Howard Jackson	Grandma Moses	Marietta Robusti Tintoretto
Rosalba Carriera	Frida Kahlo	Gabriele Münter	Suzanne Valadon
Mary Cassatt	Angelica Kauffmann	Alice Neel	Remedios Varo
Constance Marie Charpentier	Hilma af Klimt	Louise Nevelson	Elizabeth Vigée Le Brun
Imogen Cunningham	Kathe Kollwitz	Georgia O'Keeffe	Laura Wheeling Waring
Sonia Delaunay	Lee Krasner	Meret Oppenheim	

A PUBLIC SERVICE MESSAGE FROM **GUERRILLA GIRLS** CONSCIENCE OF THE ARTWORLD

8.22. Guerrilla Girls,*"When Racism & Sexism Are No Longer Fashionable,"* 1989, poster, courtesy of Guerrilla Girls (www.guerrillagirls.com).

9
Portrait as Performance: The Theater of the Self in Kathleen Gilje's Series of Curators, Critics and Connoisseurs*

Beth Gersh-Nešić

Portraits float between fact and fantasy.[1] The face should be based on fact: a person who actually lived. However, the clothes, setting, posture and possessions placed on view may be a complete or partial fantasy, or what we euphemistically call an "idealization." Kathleen Gilje's portraits of art historians, art critics, curators, and collectors have an added dimension: they are based on appropriations of masterpieces or well-known artists' styles. That several professional art aficionados (some of the most important art historians and critics of the late twentieth century and twenty-first centuries) collaborated with an expert art restorer-turned-artist, Kathleen Gilje, and an art historian-turned-art dealer, Francis Naumann, opens the door to the tantalizing speculation that these so-called "art historical" portraits may contain juicy iconographic content, encoded revelations or astute new readings of old chestnuts in art.

However, stepping back to consider Gilje's portrait project as of 2006,[2] we discover that these sitters refrained from secret revelations and instead opted for the opportunity to inhabit a role found in a work of art or dramatize a statement made by a revered art critique. The results became a form of theatre: performances or *tableaux vivants* arrested on canvas.

The Concept of Gilje's "Restorations"

Known for her "restorations" (the artist's term) of well-known masterpieces, Kathleen Gilje's appropriations grow out of a long and careful study of each work of art. She physically masters the artist's style, material, and execution. Then she scrupulously researches the iconography, artist's life and the socio-political context of the work in order to deepen her understanding of the artist's decisions. Often her academic investigations uncover background stories or encoded narratives embedded in the art or swirling around the artist's milieu that may inform her analysis.

Gilje's sly additions or adjustments in the works derive from her considerable research. Then, in an effort to break new ground, she paints revised art historical readings. Gilje calls this practice "restoration," because she fantasizes a restoration of the meaning of the work that may not be visible in the original work itself.

For example, in her 2001 "restored" version of Courbet's *Woman with a Parrot* (1866) she replaced the bird's perch with a nude male figure to emphasize the phallic symbolism of the original painting (Figs. 1 and 2). The parrot in the Courbet may represent the *petit ami* who is privileged to gaze upon the female model, or the Kamasutra.[3] Gilje painted her "restoration" of the artist standing over the frisky model and then painted an exact copy of the Courbet painting on top of her "restored" version. She had her exact copy x-rayed in order to show her faux "original" underneath the copy. Viewed as an installation, the 2001 copy of the Courbet painting placed next to the x-ray film of the "restored" version sparks a variety of associations. The perch clearly becomes the proxy for Courbet himself, who has eroticized his model for his own delectation.

Gilje's installation also comments on scopophilia: pleasure derived from the act of looking, an aspect of the male gaze.[4] In Gilje's "restoration" of Courbet's *Woman with a Parrot*, the artist enters into his own picture and experiences the pleasure of viewing the model directly. (The grainy texture of the x-ray also suggests that we are witnessing the artist's dream or fantasy as he paints the nude with ardent desire.)

Gilje's ability to alter the original iconography to serve her interpretation of the work elucidates what she believes lies beyond the physical evidence. In this way, she embarks on dialogues with art history's masters that seamlessly integrate her feminist readings and sometimes incorporate the very history of the work itself.

In her *Danaë, Restored* (2001), Gilje alludes to the vicious slashing and sulfuric acid attack on Rembrandt's painting, *Danaë* (1636), which occurred at The Hermitage Museum in St. Petersburg, on June 15, 1985 (Fig. 3).[5] In her *Danaë*, a puddle of acid flies through the air toward the nude heroine, instead of the supernatural golden shower of rain (Zeus' transmogrification in the myth) painted by Rembrandt in the original. Gilje explained in a conversation that the golden shower in the myth is the Greek deity's semen that impregnates Danaë with Perseus. Gilje views this sneaky sexual encounter as a romanticized act of nonconsensual sex: a form of rape.

Rape, the violation of another's body, is a perfect metaphor for the attack on the Rembrandt painting in 1985. Gilje noted that Danaë's gesture in the original painting was meant to welcome Zeus as the golden shower into her bower. In Gilje's "restoration," Danaë's raises an arm in a feeble attempt at self-defense, warding off the approaching acid. In the Gilje appropriation, Danaë's gesture emphasizes the vulnerability of the woman in the painting and the artwork itself during the violent attack at The Hermitage. The title of Gilje's work reminds us that Rembrandt's *Danaë* is now literally a restored work of art.

From Art Restorer to Artist in Her Own Right (1966 to the present)

Gilje came by her ability to reenact the masters' touch as an apprentice in Antonio DeMata's studio for restoration from 1966 to 1968. Then, she went to Naples with DeMata and his other assistants to restore masterpieces in the Museum of Capodimonte from 1968 to 1972. In 1973 she returned to New York City, her hometown,[6] to work for Marco Grassi, where she restored paintings for various collections, including the Thyssen Bornemizsa Collection in Lugano and Madrid and the Norton Simon Collection in Pasadena. In 1976 she opened her own studio, restoring works for numerous public and private clients, such as Stanley Moss, Eugene V. Thaw, and Robert Dance.[7]

Gilje's concept of the "restoration" painting (her Postmodern Appropriations) dates back to the early 1990s. Her *Bacchus, Restored* of 1992 (after Caravaggio's *Bacchus*, c. 1595) features plastic wrapped over the bowl of fruit with condoms strewn alongside the succulent choices Caravaggio depicted in his original (Fig. 4).

Gilje's "restoration" suggests that the beautiful young man in the seductively draped toga was indeed "forbidden fruit" for the patron Cardinal Francesco Maria Del Monte, who commissioned Caravaggio's work and delighted in beautiful young men.[8]

Gilje's *Bacchus, Restored* belongs to the horrific first wave of the AIDS epidemic and historically marks the overwhelming concern that gripped the arts community. Simultaneously, Gilje explored the iconography of homoeroticism in art, which had recently gained recognition as "queer" theory among academic art historians and critics.

The Series of Art Historians, Curators, Critics and Connoisseurs

After more than a decade of linking old masterpieces to contemporary issues, the 2004-2006 project of casting art historians, critics, curators and collectors in the roles of famous personages in art offered Gilje a new direction. Instead of social commentary, the series became a documentary of sorts, preserving the images of those whose texts drove modern and postmodern art commentary—and the art markets. However, the series did not evolve out of a deliberate decision to change direction. Instead, it began as one commission based on the artist's desire to paint the portrait of one particular collector and what that collector wanted Gilje to paint.

The renowned art collector, Toby Bevan Lewis bumped into Kathleen Gilje during a conference in Cleveland in 2003. The artist proposed painting Lewis's portrait in an Old Master style. Lewis already owned a portrait of herself by Andy Warhol, but in her heart of hearts, she imagined a portrait by John Singer Sargent (long dead, of course). Gilje's proposal solved the collector's dilemma. Lewis decided on her portrait as *Madame X*, originally painted by Sargent in 1884 (Fig. 5).

At this point, Lewis had not read Deborah Davis' novel *Strapless: Madame X and the Scandal that Shocked Belle Époque Paris* (published in 2003) and knew nothing about Virginie Amélie Avegno Gautreau, a New Orleans' beauty who captured the heart of French banker Pierre Gautreau and other members of France's high society (often as her lovers). Sargent, too, gravitated to this famous Southern Belle and asked to paint her portrait. Gautreau chose the Diana tiara to invoke references to this virgin goddess (perhaps, a reference to her name but not her true reputation). Sargent selected the table with legs carved as classical female figures denoting sirens (more fitting for this irresistible *femme fatale*).

Gilje explained to Lewis that Sargent originally painted the right strap dangling off Gautreau's right shoulder, which created quite a stir in the press. He later "corrected" the strap and left the revision to posterity. Lewis, who simply liked this Metropolitan Museum of Art painting, elected to have the right strap droop off the shoulder in the spirit of Sargent's original intention.

The result, *Toby Lewis as Madame X*, completed in 2004, performs Sargent's concept of erotic elegance as a combination of beauty and power. Poised and more authoritative in the turn of her body and head than Virginie, Lewis's portrait performs her self-assurance as a great patron of the arts.

Lewis left her portrait in Gilje's studio while she renovated her apartment in New York. During this period in 2004, New York University's art history professor and the Guggenheim Museum's curator, Robert Rosenblum, visited Gilje's studio and admired the work greatly.

Upon hearing Rosenblum's enthusiastic reception, Gilje proposed that she paint his portrait as a character in another work of art. Together they decided on Ingres' *Portrait of the Comte de Pastoret*, 1826, a painting many said bore an uncanny resemblance to Rosenblum, an eminent Ingres scholar (Fig. 6).

When Rosenblum's portrait was still an idea, Gilje discussed the encounter with her dealer Francis Naumann, who knew Rosenblum. Naumann offered to facilitate the process. By then Rosenblum was very ill. When Rosenblum felt strong enough, Naumann arranged for a photo session between the art historian and the artist. Gilje then used a photograph from this session for her Rosenblum portrait. She completed the portrait in 2005.[9]

The Project Begins

Becoming involved with the Rosenblum-Gilje collaboration sparked an idea for Naumann, a famous art historian in his own right.[10] Naumann saw the merit of a full-blown project that would celebrate the great art historians in their midst. He invited most of the sitters and Kathleen Gilje invited others, who in turn suggested mutual friends. Most, but not all, of the sitters taught at Hunter College and/or the City University of New York's Graduate School and University Center at one time or another.[11] Naumann, a graduate of the art history program (who taught a few courses as well) had developed close relationships with two of the three founders, European specialists John Rewald (1912-1994) and Leo Steinberg (1920-2011), and other members of the faculty.[12] With these contacts in mind (whom he revered), Naumann proposed a portrait project to Gilje that would record the likenesses of several important New York art historians, art critics, curators, and connoisseurs in the guise of art historical characters of their own choosing.

All of the portraits, except Toby Lewis', were at Francis Naumann's gallery in a one-person show from April 5 to May 24, 2006. The sitters were Robert Rosenblum, William Rubin, Arthur Danto, Linda Nochlin, Lowery Stokes Sims, RoseLee Goldberg, Robert Storr and his wife Rosamund Morley, Leo Steinberg, Michael Kimmelman, Charles Finch and Rosalind Krauss.

Behind the scenes, the sitters either posed for the photographs used specifically for Gilje's portrait series, selected existing photographs of themselves or had Naumann select an existing photograph of the sitter. Within this particular grouping, four portrait categories emerged: *doppelgängers*, iconographic associations, reenactments, and stylistic appropriations.

The Doppelgängers

The three *doppelgängers* are Robert Rosenblum as Ingres' Comte de Pastoret, William Rubin as Pablo Picasso and Arthur Danto as Socrates. These scholars chose a direct route: straightforward resemblance. Their choices were influenced by friends and relatives who pointed out the resemblances to them.

Robert Rosenblum confessed in his catalogue essay for Gilje's show: "...recognizing that the thirty-seven year old Count looked both handsome and intelligent, I naturally liked the comparison, but not having a drop of either blue or French blood, I didn't take it too seriously."[13] From this remark, we learn about the informed playful spirit that guided most of the choices in the project, much like dressing up for a masquerade ball. In each case, Rosenblum, Rubin and Danto virtually perform as their alleged art history doubles.

Fellow Picasso scholar William Rubin (1927-2006) immediately decided on a Picasso portrait, because he felt he looked more and more like the Spanish artist as he aged (Fig. 7). Rather than selecting a self-portrait, Rubin decided on a Henri Cartier-Bresson's photograph of Picasso taken in July 1967. The point was to draw attention to the physical similarities without appearing to identify with the artist himself. The choice, however, reminds us that Rubin was among the greatest Picasso scholars of his generation.

Francis Naumann took a series of photographs of Rubin in his home in Pound Ridge, New York, as he was not well.[14] Gilje selected the one she liked the best and painted her portrait of Rubin in *grisaille*, after Cartier-Bresson's black and white photograph.

Without any shred of evidence, we might wish to speculate that both Rubin and Rosenblum succumbed to identifying with their favorite subjects in art (Rubin on Picasso and Rosenblum on Ingres) or, more plausibly, they performed their deep affection for these artists through a nonverbal medium.

Arthur Danto, art critic and professor of philosophy at Columbia University, explained to me that over the years friends would send him postcards of Socrates' image and insist on his resemblance to the ancient philosopher. Gilje's portrait of Danto is based on a Roman copy of a Greek bust of the philosopher Socrates (Fig. 8). The painting of the bust is set against an appropriation of Leonardo da Vinci's floral fresco in the Sale delle Asse in Milan. Gilje decided on this particular background because it features knots that symbolized Danto's ability to tie philosophy in antiquity to contemporary art and ideas.

The original sculpture bears the words in Greek: "Socrates, philosopher of Athens." In Gilje's portrait, the depicted bust bears the words in Greek "Arthur Danto, Philosopher of New York."

Francis Naumann told me that Danto played Socrates on television, and Danto confirmed that he was in a 1996 Discovery Channel production about Plato's *Republic*.[15] In the portrait by Gilje, Danto reprises his role as Socrates, although this time without a voice.

Arthur Danto's choice performs the fact that he enjoyed hearing about his physical resemblance to one of his favorite philosophers. Kathleen Gilje saw to it that the iconography in Danto's portrait identified this twentieth-century aesthetician with Socrates and with his own contributions to philosophy and art.

Iconographic Associations

Linda Nochlin and Lowery Stokes Sims, two world-famous art historians and curators, as well as teacher and student through the City University of New York's Graduate Center, explored this golden opportunity to extend their commitment to social commentary through performing a concept in art history. They both chose personalities in art that could weave their likenesses—and by extension, themselves—into an iconographic narrative about their relationships to art and their professions.

Linda Nochlin chose one of her favorite paintings, "the beautiful and complex" Édouard Manet's *Bar at the Folies Bergère* of 1881-82 (Fig. 9). Here she enjoyed casting herself in the role of the seductive barmaid. "I could be both subject and spectator at once, in a wonderful setting," she wrote.[16]

Nochlin's portrait brings to mind this art historian's exceptional essay on Berthe Morisot's *Wet Nurse* wherein the Impressionist artist, a working woman, paints the nurse, another working woman.[17] In Manet's *Folies Bergère*, Nochlin becomes the subject of her own ruminations: a working woman whose job requires careful examination and interpretation of the world as she chooses to engage with it, visually interpreted by another working woman, the artist Kathleen Gilje.

However, Nochlin's portrait is not about class struggle and gender issues, her best-known contributions to art history—or at least, this was not her conscious intention. Instead, Nochlin tells us about herself: her passion for looking and absorbing everything that the world has to offer. Nochlin's slightly bemused smile (so different from Manet's careworn *serveuse*) performs her uncanny ability to size up any person or situation in a New York minute and apply her sharp wit to her perceptions. This clever wench is no bimbo and certainly does not suffer fools gladly. Though clothed in nineteenth-century garb and placed in a nineteenth-century setting, Nochlin at the Folies Bergère performs as a late-twentieth-century feminist: a free spirit who thrives on voluptuous sensuality and the theater of life.

Lowery Stokes Sims accepted Francis Naumann's invitation to join the portrait project and requested that Gilje paint her as Napoleon I with a gun (Fig. 10). Gilje decided on Ingres' imperial portrait from 1806. While completing the portrait, Gilje noticed that the pose and setting reminded her of the iconic 1968 photograph of Huey Newton, the Black Panther Minister of Defense, sitting on a rattan throne, holding a rifle in his right hand and spear in his left.[18] (Napoleon holds the scepter of the realm in his right hand and the hand of Charlemagne against his left thigh.) Sims also noticed the similarity when she viewed her image as Napoleon and liked it. "The lens is always working..." Sims wrote to me. "I love the portrait. It projects the hidden me. As an African American woman, I am always preoccupied with issues of power—both subtle and overt."[19]

The choice of Ingres is far and away different from her known specialty, Cuban artist Wilfredo Lam. Instead, this image firmly references male power and her ability to navigate successfully in a world dominated by white men. Here she reigns over her space with regal elegance and aplomb. For this art historian (who was a curator at the Metropolitan Museum of Art from 1972 to 1999, then ran the Studio Museum of Harlem from 2000 to 2007, and now curates for the Museum of Art and Design in New York) performs her imperial prerogative served up with a gun and faint grin—all the better to persuade effectively. Gilje's portrait of Sims also projects the art historian's natural warmth and accessibility, which Gilje perceived in Sims' photograph. They met in person after the portrait was completed.

Sims performs her commentary on the art world by implying that one either leads or follows. According to her portrait, she chose to lead and leave an indelible mark on history, much like the Little Corporal from Corsica.

Reenactments as Performance

Not all the sitters opted for costumed drama. RoseLee Goldberg, Robert Storr and Rosamund Morley wore their own clothes to pose in homage to the masterpieces they selected.

RoseLee Goldberg, director of Performa, a biennial festival of Performance Art in New York City (and a former dancer), posed as Édouard Manet's *Young Man in the Costume of a Majo* from 1863, which she knew very well from the permanent collection in the Metropolitan Museum of Art (Fig. 11). During an interview, she described her participation in the project as "performing the portrait."[20] Gilje recalled that the photo session required several hours of Goldberg working through the positions that led to the right one. Gilje explained: "It was about fantasizing the painting's image, the costume, and recreating the time when Manet made the painting. RoseLee really got into that."[21]

For Goldberg, the whole experience, from preparation to execution, increased her appreciation of the portraitist's role, especially in the planning stages. She became aware of the numerous choices that must take place between the artist and sitter. Her pose required some practice and tremendous self-control. It was exhausting and yet invigorating. Performing the painting helped Goldberg see Manet's work afresh. In addition, the task of modeling for Gilje's camera provided a kinesthetic understanding of Manet's nonchalant young man.

That Goldberg highlighted the performative aspect of Gilje's project reflects this curator's main interest in contemporary culture: Performance Art. As Manet's *majo*, Goldberg also performs her love of the style and panache, which these Spanish lower-class dandies cultivated throughout their lives.[22] She also performs her self-confidence as she emerges out of the darkness with a flashy red and black striped scarf draped over her shoulder. Somewhat saucy in posture and facial expression, Goldberg performs her genuine moxie as the doyenne of Performance Art in America and her love of the theatrical, which attracted her to performance artists in the first place.

Gilje's portrait Robert Storr captures this fellow artist, critic and dean of the Yale University School of Art as he listens to his wife Rosamund Morley play the viola da gamba in their home (Fig. 12). Self-consciously posed, Storr assumed a similar position to Édouard Manet's when the French artist listened to his wife Suzanne Leenhoff play the piano for their famous double portrait *Monsieur and Madame Édouard Manet* of 1868-69 by Degas. Here Storr leans casually toward his left side against the pillows of the white sofa, dressed in a black jacket and pants to approximate Manet's outfit worn nearly 140 years before.

Storr explained that he too, like Goldberg, perceived this occasion as a kind of performance. He and Morley decided to reenact the Manets seen through Degas' eyes for their Gilje portraits. They deliberately dressed in similar clothing, though not period costumes.[23]

The entire occasion, Kathleen Gilje recalled, was uncanny. "To this day I regret I was alone and didn't have somebody documenting the photo shoot," Gilje confessed during an interview. "It lasted several hours as I crawled under the baby grand piano to make room to photograph. Rosamund dressed in a long white skirt and white blouse and played the viola da gamba (sometimes we put on a disc of her performances), as Rob Storr lounged on the couch enjoying his wife's playing. It was about her music, his love for art and also, I think, about their relationship, all put together in the recreation of the Degas painting."[24] Here Gilje taps into the essence of both the Manet portraits and the Storr-Morley portraits: the performance of a couple's relationship. Both self-consciously consider how they would want to portray it and have others remember it in the future, while the viewer imagines the artist capturing a moment of unself-conscious intimacy, as indeed Impressionism tried to do.

The original portrait of Édouard Manet and his wife Suzanne Leenhoff suffered at Manet's own hand when he sliced off Suzanne's image, which displeased him (or maybe it displeased Suzanne).[25] Gilje also painted the two spouses on the same canvas and then sliced off Morley's image at the same point in the composition that Manet sliced off Suzanne's image. In this way, Gilje reenacted this hostile gesture with her own razor blade. She then had the larger portion of the canvas glued to another canvas that would extend and restore the size of the original double portrait of Storr and Morley. This French relined canvas was mounted on a stretcher by another professional restorer. The addition of raw canvas seems to infer that she might repaint Morley's portrait, but she never will. Again Gilje follows through on the Degas-Manet story. Degas added a strip of canvas to repaint Madame Manet—but never fulfilled his promise to revise the portrait.

Gilje saved the fragment of Rosamund Morley and mounted it on a separate stretcher by herself, so that both parts of the original portrait may be exhibited together.

(In this regard, Gilje departs from the object's true narrative, since the fragment of Suzanne Leehoff Manet seems to have disappeared into thin air.) Gilje's actions perform the violation and reconstruction of the Manets' portrait, referencing the object's history as she did in her appropriation of Rembrandt's *Danaë*.

Stylistic Appropriations

The four remaining portraits of art historians and art critics— Leo Steinberg, Michael Kimmelman, Charles Finch and Rosalind Krauss—display signature artistic expressions for reasons that have not been discussed so far. Loosely connected, these portraits tap into the sitters' personalities that seem to match the artistic temperaments exhibited in their respective styles. Leo Steinberg required something suave and Old Master – therefore Rubens was chosen for him. Michael Kimmelman needed a meditative vision and Eakins filled the bill. Charlie Finch's large personality could only be contained in a large figure—one that filled the picture plane: a Rembrandt self-portrait provided the formulation, but was not copied exactly. Kimmelman and Finch worked with Kathleen Gilje to arrive at an appropriate quotation. Rosalind Krauss decided on a younger version of herself (when she was considered quite glamorous) and the artistic style that she felt this particular photograph suggested.

Leo Steinberg agreed to be included in the series but left the selection of the appropriated art work and the photograph used for this appropriation to Francis Naumann's discretion.[26] Naumann and Gilje arrived at the decision to portray Steinberg as Peter Paul Rubens in the Flemish artist's self portrait of 1639 (Fig. 13). Robert Rosenblum's astute observation encapsulates the appropriateness of this choice best: the painting exudes "a cosmopolitan breadth, a verbal eloquence and an elegant, courtly demeanor" that truly characterized Steinberg in so many ways.[27] One could even make the case that Rubens and Steinberg were kindred spirits in certain areas: both excelled in several intellectual pursuits and mastered several languages. Rubens was an artist, businessman and diplomat who read, wrote and spoke Flemish, German, French, Italian, Spanish and Latin; Steinberg was an art historian and critic who read, wrote and spoke in all the major European languages and Russian.

Like Rubens, Steinberg led an international life and distinguished himself through his enormous breadth of knowledge in so many different disciplines (art, music, literature and classicism). He was born in Russia in 1920, moved to Germany in 1923 and then to England in 1933. He arrived in the United States after World War II. His command of English, his third language, is legendary. Precise and amusing, his erudition remains enviable. He was, like Rubens, a bona fide genius.

The Gilje portrait is based on Timothy Greenfield-Sander's photograph of Leo Steinberg taken in 1981. The art historian's expression in Greenfield-Sander's work seems candid, as if he had just turned to answer his companion in mid-conversation. Gilje transforms the look into a rakish façade emphasized by Rubens' gloved hand, studly sword and stylishly wide-brimmed hat arranged askew with the Flemish artist's personal flair.

Steinberg's left eye stares indulgently — almost disdainfully, but not quite. This nuanced difference between the photograph and the portrait performs Steinberg's charismatic European charm. It also performs Steinberg's proclivity for thinking about sex. These meditations have inspired his revolutionary analyses of Picasso's *Demoiselles d'Avignon* and Renaissance images of Christ, which he believed referred to sex and sexuality iconographically.[28] The work broke new ground in a manner that seemed as effortless as Steinberg's performance in his portrait: a gentleman whose comportment bespeaks superiority in taste and style. (In the gallery installation, one might wonder if Gilje intentionally meant to have Leo Steinberg leer at Linda Nochlin's décolletage.)

Michael Kimmelman's selection of Thomas Eakins' *The Thinker*

(Portrait of Louis N. Kenton) of 1900, which Gilje had suggested, performs this art critic personality as rather introspective (Fig. 14).[29] His job is to think deeply about art and all the influences that might inform it—or inform us about it.

A graduate of Yale and Harvard, Kimmelman started out as a music critic for *The New York Times,* since he trained as a concert pianist. Then the chief art critic John Russell invited him to try his hand at art criticism, because Kimmelman earned a graduate degree in art history. The assignment fit like a glove and Kimmelman remained in the job for decades.

In his portrait as *The Thinker,* Kimmelman wears his signature style—a sport jacket, open collar shirt and jeans—and performs his isolation as a critic, despite the highly social opportunities at openings, press previews and studio visits. Kimmelman's body language seems to perform an introvert's personality that speaks through his writing. Since 2006, Kimmelman has thought about Czech humor in political protest, bullfighting in Spain, Holocaust education in today's Germany and *négritude* in France, besides his reports on the art scene outside the United States.

Gilje's interpretation of Kimmelman makes sure that he quietly takes charge of his space as if to indicate this inwardness serves as armor against public scrutiny. Occasionally a guest on talk shows or panel discussions, it seems that this portrait offers insight into an intensely private person who would prefer to live without the klieg lights that come with the mantle of celebrity.

Charlie Finch, the infamously caustic and quite extrovert art critic, assumes the chocolate brown tunic and posture of Rembrandt's self-portrait of 1652 (Fig. 15). Finch smiles oh-so subtly in order to exchange a complicit glance with his viewer. He knows he is the bad boy of art critics: a mover and shaker who exerted his power through social networking way before Facebook's Mark Zuckerberg was born.

Rabelaisian in appetite of all sorts (food, arts, politics and gossip), Finch took on the art world in 1993 with fellow critic Matt Gleason in their short-lived publication *Coagula,* preserved in their book *Most Art Sucks: Five Years of Coagula* (Smart Art Press, 1998). In those days, Finch wrote under the pseudonym Janet Preston. Today he continues to skewer his victims with rapier wit in *ArtNet* magazine, an online publication. His primary mission is to target art world celebrities and their sacred cows.

Gilje's proposal of Rembrandt's mid-career self-portrait in 1652 has very little to do with Finch's public persona. Rather, it seems that Gilje decided to have Finch play the wise Shakespearian "fool" mouthing truthful witticisms that expose an "emperor" without his clothes. (In Finch's columns that would be hyped art without authentic merit.) In this role, Finch emerges out of a mysterious darkness to perform his kinder, gentler side that often goes unnoticed by his readers, but is indeed quite genuine.

Posing against Neo-Gothic windows in what appears to be an Ivory-tower setting, art historian and critic Rosalind (née Epstein) Krauss leans her chin upon her trusty typewriter in 1969 (Fig. 16). She is performing her interpretation of Clement Greenberg's famous quip: "Spare me smart Jewish girls and their typewriters." Krauss chose this Ann Gabhart photograph for Gilje's project; a photograph she regards as similar to Degas' early style. Gilje took that comment as a cue to look through early Degas paintings. She decided to appropriate the white floral with an impressionistic blue background wallpaper found in Degas' Bellelli family portrait of 1859, as a substitute for the windows behind Krauss's head in the Gabhart photograph.[30]

In Gilje's portrait, Krauss' penetrating stare performs her infamous penetrating personality as a scholar. The strong outline around the eyes trains like an eagle on its prey. Here is the meticulous scrutiny that informs her incisive writing. The photograph and portrait also capture Krauss' urbane gentility reflected in the carefully chosen clothes: a demure jewel-neck blouse tied at the nape of the neck. In 1969, this conservative attire belonged to women of discerning taste and self-discipline: no hippy fashions for this Harvard grad.

That Krauss selected Gabhart's photograph for Gilje's project clearly reveals how this art historian would like to be remembered. She had already selected the photo for the cover of her book *Perpetual Inventory* (2005), which is also posted on her website for Columbia University's Department of Art History and Archaeology. In an email response, Krauss wrote: "It was on one of the trips to New York I took to go to galleries that I visited Clement Greenberg and he made the comment (not about me but about someone else) 'Spare me smart Jewish girls with their typewriters!'"[31]

Apparently, Gabhart's photograph transformed Greenberg's egotistical remark into Krauss' own admonition or ammunition: this Jewish girl and her typewriter defer to no one. Greenberg's cocky slur might sound anti-Semitic and misogynist—two of Degas' well-known prejudices (as an anti-Dreyfusard, he broke off long-standing relationships with the Jewish Hélavy family and his Jewish colleague Camille Pissarro, while his unflattering depictions of women spoke volumes about his dim view of women). However, Clement Greenberg's biting remark actually reveals his own insecurity. For at that time, the rising stars of art criticism happened to be a clutch of young, Ivy-League-ish Jewish women: Rosalind Krauss, Barbara Rose, Linda Nochlin and Susan Sontag, among others.

That Krauss bothered to remember this revelation of desperation ironically pays homage to Clement Greenberg, the formalist guru, and casts Krauss as deeply flattered to be among those "smart Jewish girls" anointed by his comment. One might have expected something a bit more intellectually inspired from *October*'s cofounder, whose body of work has substantially challenged Greenberg and produced its own following in the field of critical inquiry. On the other hand, this choice seems to flirt with a bit of uncharacteristic wit and feminist pride. In 1969, she knew these aspiring "smart girls" (both Jewish and non-Jewish) who did light the art world on fire. This portrait will eternally perform that pivotal moment from the perspective of someone who had the smarts and dangerous typewriter.

The Visible and Invisible: A Portrait of Francis Naumann

Unfortunately, Gilje's portraits provide no secret messages or fodder for future gossip. Instead, most sitters gravitated toward simple amusement: physical likeness or *tableau vivant*. Only Nochlin, Sims, Goldberg and Krauss consciously played off of the iconography.

Linda Nochlin sought out a genre scene to refer to herself as an art historian: the observer and the observed (for indeed her mind is often on display as she lectures before colleagues, students and the general public). Lowery Stokes Sims aimed straight for an iconic image of power to portray herself in terms of art world politics, positioned metaphorically in the catbird seat. Krauss characteristically conveyed her encoded message to her Chosen People.

Among these art aficionado portraits, one invisible portrait deserves recognition, that of Dada art historian Francis Naumann, who organized this series of art-world luminaries. Here he performs his role as the connector among all the sitters selected for this series. As an art historian, he is both peer and ardent fan, eager to honor the legacies of those he had come to know. As an art dealer, this invisible portrait of Naumann performs his gallery's mission to sell art about art. To this end, Gilje's portrait series melds two sides of his art world personality, art historian and entrepreneur, with a lesser known facet of his career, that of an artist.

When asked why he did not choose to participate in the series as one of his fellow art giants, Naumann confessed that he felt uncomfortable with having a portrait of himself. This passing glimpse into the ego of an individual who participates in the study of portraiture (a requirement of any art history education) may serve as insight into the egos of the other art historians and critics in the series; for turning the spotlight on oneself is indeed a foreign experience for those who analyze humanity through art and know all the tricks of the trade that ascribe meaning to every little detail. Nevertheless, this series may well be Naumann's performance of the portrait that he resists in material terms. Instead, the series represents Naumann the artist, who, through the hands and eyes of another artist unwittingly curated/created an invisible portrait of himself.

Performing the Portrait: The Artist's Touch

Kathleen Gilje, on the other hand, knows her approach to appropriating art performs the process of making a masterpiece, as she summons to her aid the spirits of the artists who guide her. Her physical acts perform her study of the masters' brushstrokes, recipes, compositions, iconographic choices and formulae that successfully transmit a convincing psychological feeling. Through this process, she savors the history of making art.

During the two years of preparing for the exhibition at Francis Naumann Fine Art, Gilje assumed the role of the director who must interpret a shared vision. With the enthusiastic collaboration of Naumann and the sitters, she also shared their mutual love affair with the history of art. Gilje never lost sight of her subjects' trust as she embarked on their portraits. "I felt they were very brave and generous with their time," she emphasized during an interview.

On her own, she became aware of her own personality as a portraitist. The exercise clarified the nature of portraiture: the negotiations and tacit decisions required to arrive at a suitable likeness. Through this particular investigation, Gilje discovered the performativity of portraiture itself and the degree to which fact and fantasy converge through the choices of the pose, facial expression, clothes, furniture and setting.

Not surprisingly, she launched another portrait series of other famous people, entitled *Forty-Eight Sargent Women* (Fig. 17). For this project, she responded to Gerhardt Richter's forty-eight portraits of famous German intellectuals (1971-2) with an exercise in appropriating forty-eight images of well-known women found in John Singer Sargent's portraits, stripped of their clothes and luxurious surroundings ("neutralized," if you will, like the Richter portraits) in order to "restore" their identities as individuals, instead of decorative acquisitions. Her research yielded a treasure trove of information that attests to their accomplishments and contributions to the community—as well as their choices to decline professional careers because of their positions in society.[32] This series also cast a new light on the freedoms of the women portrayed in the arts-professionals series, because they benefited from the struggles of Sargent-era feminists.

The two series, *Art Historians, Curators, Critics and Connoisseurs*, plus *Forty-Eight Sargent Women* complement each other in terms of acknowledging that portraiture is performance arrested in time. Both acknowledge the portrait as a form of theater that integrates artifice and reality (fantasy and fact). The *Art Historians, Curators, Critics and Connoisseurs* series lays bare in Post-Modern fashion the artist's intention to conspire with the sitters to idealize the portrait through the fertile ground of imagination. *The Forty-Eight Sargent Women*, conversely, attempts to dismantle the portraitist's idealization in favor of revealing the real woman underneath the clothes and beyond the title of Mrs. Something or Other. Both exercises require digging deeper into the nature of art making in the Western canon.

Performing the Portrait: An Experiment in Non-Verbal Communication

In Naumann's Upper East Side gallery, the portraits loomed out from their respective environments like a rogues' lineup or an art history slide test on identification. These sitters know the source of their appropriations and require the audience to play along with their game. Consequently, these portraits work best before a well-informed crowd that knows the reputations of the sitters and the works of art selected. The portraits may also work best as an installation, since the conversation among these legendary art scholars becomes a sum greater than its parts—and will continue to improve with age as these faces cease to grace our earthly existence.

This wordless communication unfolds from those who normally communicate only through words, for all these people are writers, each and every one. Therefore, this portrait project offered an opportunity to speak in a new format: a forum without words that can also impart their knowledge. In so doing, they became artists and actors who relied on images to communicate their thoughts and feelings.

Moreover, these sitters had breeched the fortress of Otherness in the world of the artwork itself. Always examiners, they would be the ones who are now the examined, breaking the illusionistic "fourth wall" of the canvas's surface, they become part of the artworks themselves.

For, no matter how much one craves an exclusive connection with the beloved art object or artist, one rarely feels sufficiently satisfied or sure. Each work of art has its own protective moat that can be bridged but never completely filled in with solid ground. Performing the portrait erases that chasm as the exercise allows the arts writer to enter the work of art as a central figure and thereby become the author of and main character in the text.

End Notes

[1] This essay is dedicated to Professor Alicia Faxon, art historian and feminist *extraordinaire*, who hired me to teach the course on women artists at Simmons College in the fall of 1989 and again during the fall of 1991. Professor Faxon's books and articles on women artists (and dozens of other subjects) have been a tremendous source of inspiration. Above all, her constant encouragement and leadership has been a beacon of light through all the years I have known her. It is an honor to be among the great women artists and art historians represented in this collection of essays that celebrates Alicia Faxon's contributions to our field.

I also want to express my deepest gratitude to Kathleen Gilje, Francis Naumann and all the portrait sitters who generously responded to my queries and consented to the quotations printed here. Most of all, I want to thank Margaret Hanni, who worked so hard to bring this festschrift to completion and encouraged me to expand and clarify, which helped me think about this essay in a different way. Margaret, you are amazing and wonderful!

[2] Gilje's portrait series is an ongoing series.

[3] Mona Hadler introduced the notion that the parrot represents the privileged position of the male gazing upon the courtesan in her reading of her article "Manet's *Woman with a Parrot* of 1866," *Metropolitan Museum Journal*, v. 7 (1973): 115-122. Kam or Kamadeva, the god of love in Indian mythology, is best known for the *Kamasutra*. He flies through the air on his parrot. Therefore, the parrot can be associated with sensual love.

[4] Laura Mulvey, "Visual Pleasure and Narrative Cinema," *Screen* 16, no. 13 (1975): 6-18, was very much on the minds of feminist artists and art historians during the late twentieth century, as well as the feud between Linda Nochlin and Michael Fried on gender bias and artistic intentionality in *Courbet Reconsidered* (Brooklyn: Brooklyn Museum, 1988). Kathleen Gilje directed my attention to the two articles in this exhibition catalogue.

[5] The assailant slit the female figure across the stomach and thigh with a knife and then threw acid against the canvas. It took twelve years to repair. *Danaë* was put back on view in the Hermitage in 1997. (John Russell, *New York Times*, August 31, 1997.)

[6] Kathleen Gilje was born in Brooklyn.

[7] Information culled from the artist's website www.kathleengilje.com and interviews with the artist. Her own work belongs to collections all over the world, including the Musée Ingres, Montauban; the Weatherspoon Museum, North Carolina; and the National Museum of Women in the Arts, Washington, DC.

[8] Donald Posner, "Caravaggio's Homo-erotic Early Works," *Art Quarterly* 34 (1971): 301-24.

[9] Robert Rosenblum died on December 6, 2006. This recollection is based on interviews with the artist and Francis Naumann during the fall 2008.

[10] Francis Naumann is best known for his work on Marcel Duchamp, Man Ray and other members of the Dada and Surrealist circles in America.

[11] Most of the art historians in this group taught at or attended Hunter College, part of the City University of New York and its Graduate School and University Center: Leo Steinberg (1961-1975, who co-founded of the art history program at the Graduate Center in 1971), William Rubin (1960-67), and Rosalind Krauss (1974-1992). Linda Nochlin (1980-1990), Robert Storr (1990s) and Francis Naumann (early 1990s) taught only at the Graduate Center. Lowery Stoke Sims earned her Ph.D. from the Graduate Center in 1995. Francis Naumann earned his Ph.D. in 1988. I was introduced to Francis Naumann through a fellow Graduate Center student John Cauman. Naumann introduced me to Kathleen Gilje when I wrote a catalogue for his "Demoiselles Revisited" exhibition in 2007. I studied with Rosalind Krauss and Linda Nochlin at the Graduate Center and earned a Ph.D. in 1989.

[12] The third founder was Milton Brown, 1911-1998, whose work on the Ash Can School and the Armory Show remains a major contribution to American art history.

[13] Robert Rosenblum, "Kathleen Gilje's Reincarnations," *Kathleen Gilje: Curators, Critics and Connoisseurs of Modern and Contemporary Art* (New York: Francis Naumann Fine Art, 2006), 2.

[14] William Rubin died on January 22, 2006. This information is based on Francis Naumann's and Kathleen Gilje's recollections.

[15] Email exchanges with Arthur Danto on September 8 and 9, 2008 and conversations with Francis Naumann during the fall 2008. Arthur Danto died October 25, 2013.

[16] Email from Linda Nochlin to the author, September 22. 2008.

[17] Linda Nochlin, "Morisot's *Wet Nurse*: The Construction of Work and Leisure in Impressionist Painting," in *Women, Art, and Power and Other Essays* (New York: Harper and Row: 1989), 37-56.

[18] Photographer unknown.

[19] Email from Lowery Stokes Sims to the author, September 8, 2008.

[20] Phone interview with RoseLee Goldberg, September 17, 2008. Email from Kathleen Gilje, December 29, 2008 and interviews during fall 2008.

[21] Email from Kathleen Gijle, December 29, 2008.

[22] Édouard Manet, *Young Man in the Costume of a Majo*, 1863, Metropolitan Museum of Art, was painted in Manet's studio on the rue Guyot in Paris. The model was his younger brother Gustave. *Majos* are members of the lower-class who sported flamboyant fashions that influenced the other

classes, including the aristocracy. The critic Théophile Thoré noted that Manet introduced splashy colors through his art, inspired by his study of Francisco Goya (Charles S. Moffett, *Manet: 1832-1883* [New York: Metropolitan Museum of Art and Harry N. Abrams, 1983], 192).

[23] Phone interview with Robert Storr in October 2008.

[24] Email from Kathleen Gilje to author December 29, 2008 and interviews during fall 2008.

[25] Beth Archer Brombert, *Édouard Manet: Rebel in a Frock Coat* (Boston/New York/Toronto/London: Little, Brown and Company, 1996), 223.

[26] Leo Steinberg politely declined to discuss his portrait as Peter Paul Rubens' self-portrait of 1639 during a phone interview in September 2008.

[27] Rosenblum, [3].

[28] Leo Steinberg, "The Philosophical Brothel," *October*, vol. 44 (Spring 1988), most recent version; *The Sexuality of Christ in Renaissance Art and in Modern Oblivion* (Chicago: University of Chicago Press, 1997), previously published in *October*, vol. 25 (Summer 1983).

[29] Michael Kimmelman politely declined to comment on his portrait in an email exchange during the fall 2008. Kimmelman became the chief art critic of *The New York Times* in 1990. In 2007, he left New York with his family to write essays "from abroad" in Berlin. On July 5, 2011, *The New York Times* announced that Kimmelman would return to New York as the architecture critic and a "senior critic."

[30] Interview with Kathleen Gilje, fall 2008.

[31] Email from Rosalind Krauss, October 15 and 16, 2008. This remark appears in Rosalind Krauss, *The Optical Unconscious* (Cambridge, MA: MIT Press, 1994) and Rosalind Krauss, *Perpetual Inventory* (Cambridge, MA: MIT Press, 2010). The Gabhart photograph is on the cover of the latter. The quote also appears in Florence Rubenfeld, *Clement Greenberg: A Life* (New York: Scribner's, 1998).

[32] Kathleen Gilje's exhibition of *48 Sargent Women* took place in February 26 to April 10, 2009 at Francis Naumann Fine Art. Gilje's art historical portrait series continues. Her most recent addition was collector Melva Bucksbaum as Johannes Vermeer's *Girl with a Pearl Earring* (2010).

*This essay is based on a paper given at the College Art Association Conference in Los Angeles in February 2009 for the session "Battlelines: Painting Portraits Today" chaired by Brandon Brame Fortune, curator at the National Portrait Gallery in Washington, D.C. Thank you, Brandon, for accepting my proposal, supporting my work on Kathleen Gilje and so much more. I am deeply grateful for your guidance and friendship.

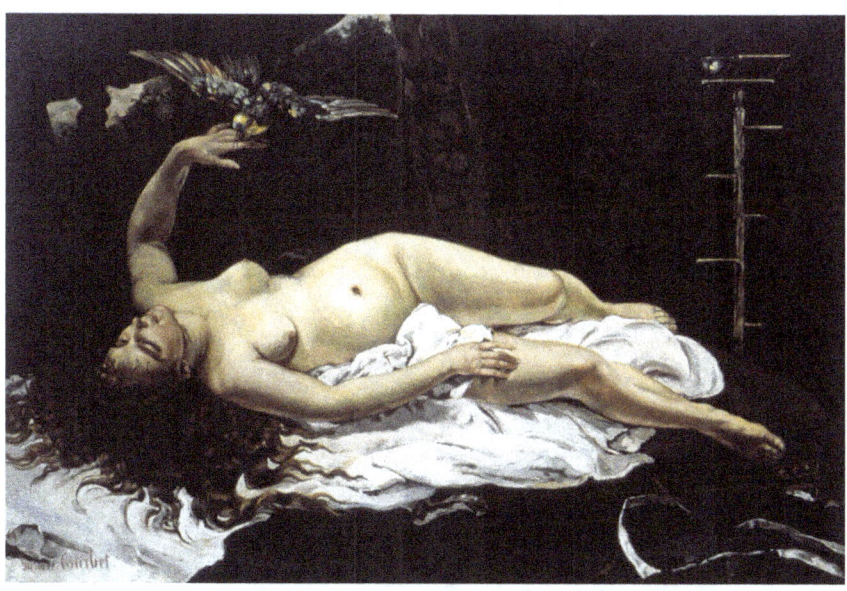

9.1. Kathleen Gilje, *Woman with a Parrot, Restored,* 2001, oil on canvas, 51″ x 77″ (After Gustave Courbet, *Woman with a Parrot*, 1863, Metropolitan Museum of Art, New York).

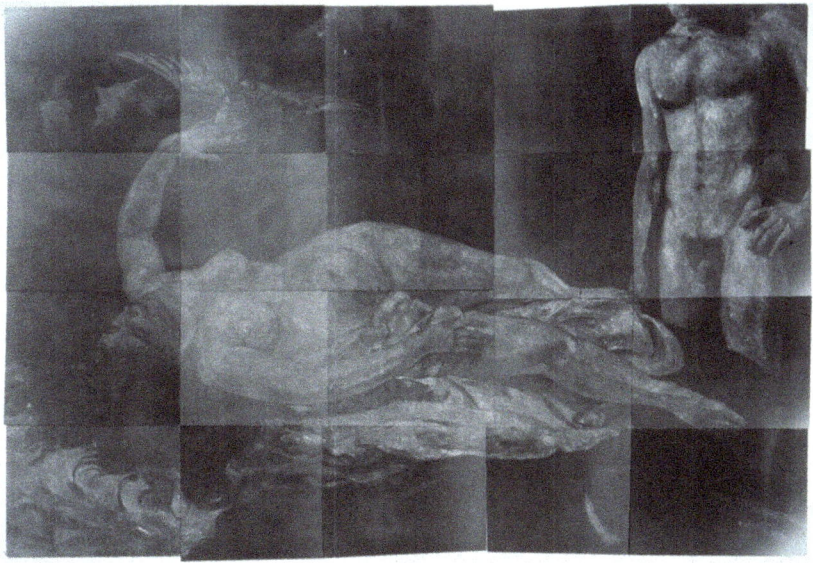

9.2. Kathleen Gilje, *Woman with a Parrot, Restored (Xray)*, 2001, xray film, 50″ x 76″.

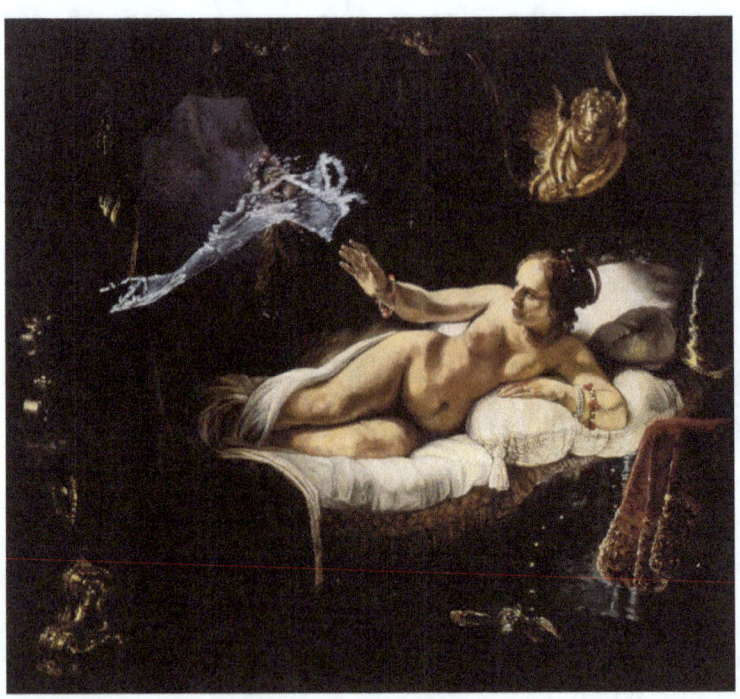

9.3. Kathleen Gilje, *Danaë, Restored*, 2001, oil on canvas, 72 1/2" x 80 1/2" (After Rembrandt van Rijn, *Danaë*, 1636, The Hermitage Museum, St. Petersburg).

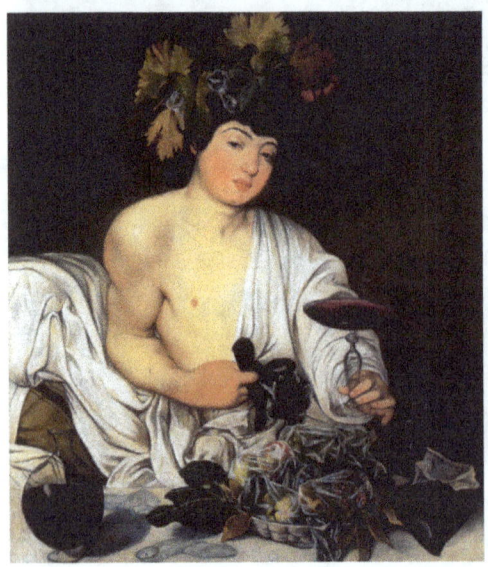

9.4. Kathleen Gilje, *Bacchus, Restored*, 1992, oil on linen, 37 1/2" x 33 1/2", collection of David Wilkinson, New Jersey (After Caravaggio, *Bacchus*, c. 1595, Uffizi Gallery, Florence).

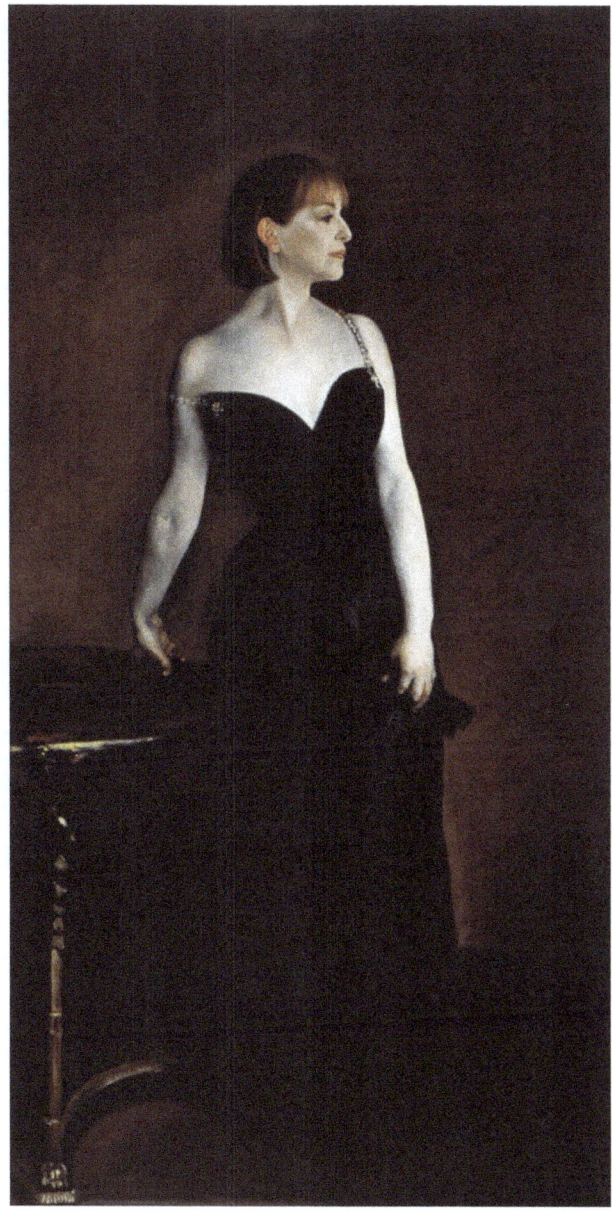

9.5. Kathleen Gilje, *Toby Lewis as Madame X*, 2004, oil on linen, 82 1/2″ x 43 1/4″, Toby Bevan Lewis Collection, New York (After John Singer Sargent, *Madame X*, 1884, Metropolitan Museum of Art, New York).

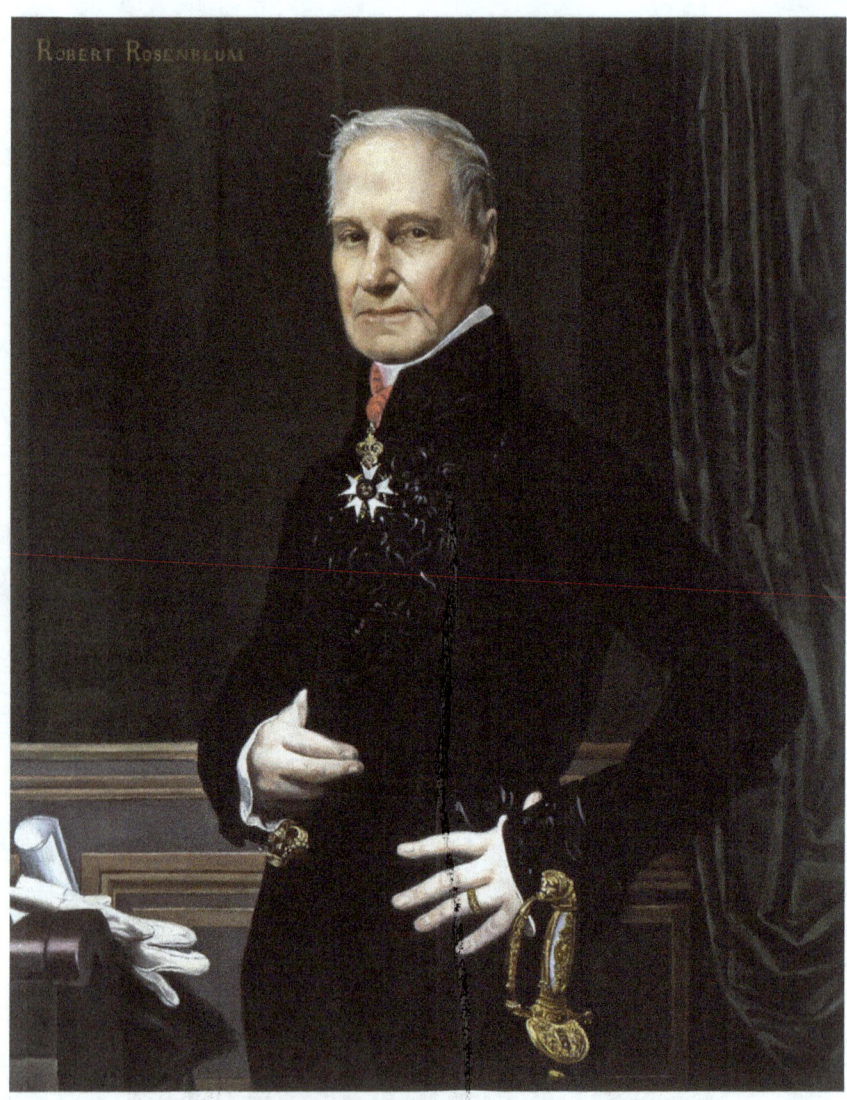

9.6. Kathleen Gilje, *Robert Rosenblum as the Comte de Pastoret*, 2005, oil on linen, 40 1/2" x 33" (After JAD Ingres, *Comte Amédée-David de Pastoret*, 1826, then Comte and later Marquis in 1840, Art Institute of Chicago).

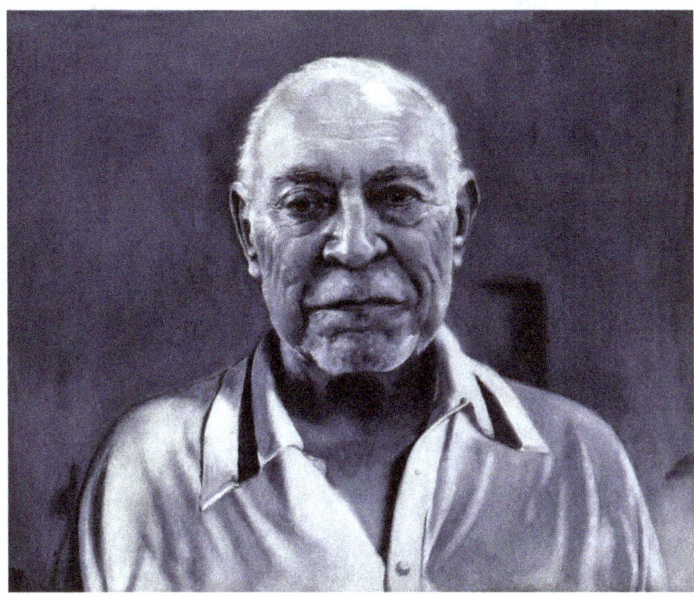

9.7. Kathleen Gilje, *William Rubin as Picasso Photographed by Cartier-Bresson (Notre-Dame-de-Vie, Mougins, July 1967)*, 2005, oil on linen, 31 3/4" x 35 1/2".

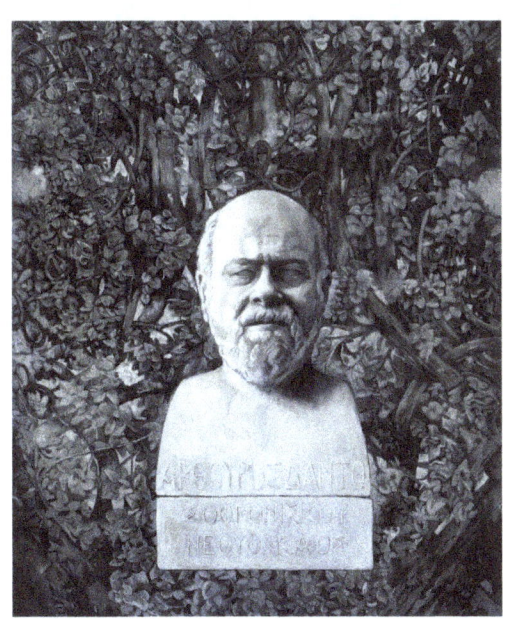

9.8. Kathleen Gilje, *Arthur Danto as the Bust of Socrates*, 2005, oil on linen, 37 1/4" x 31 1/2" (After a Roman copy of a 4th century BC Greek bust of Socrates, Vatican Museum, Rome).

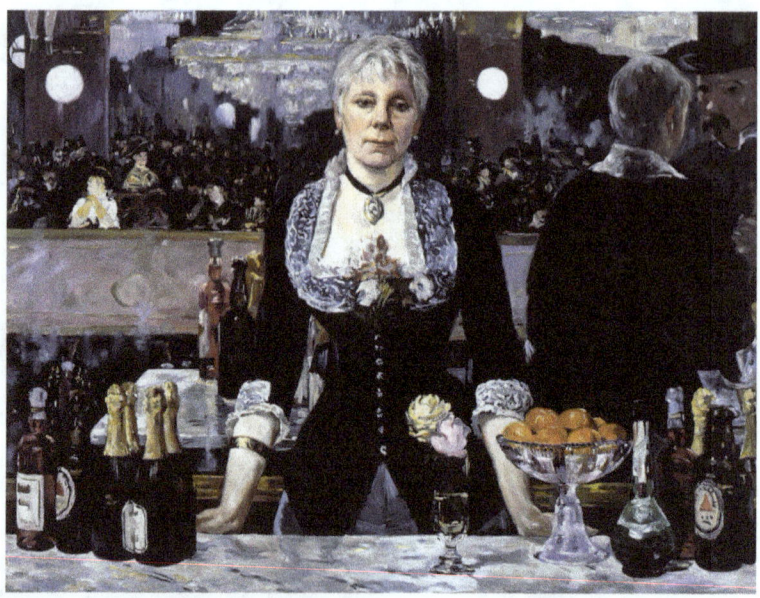

9.9. Kathleen Gilje, *Linda Nochlin at the Bar of the Folies Bergère*, 2005, oil on linen, 37 5/8″ x 51 7/8″ (After Édouard Manet, *At the Bar of the Folies-Bergère*, 1882, Courtauld Gallery, London).

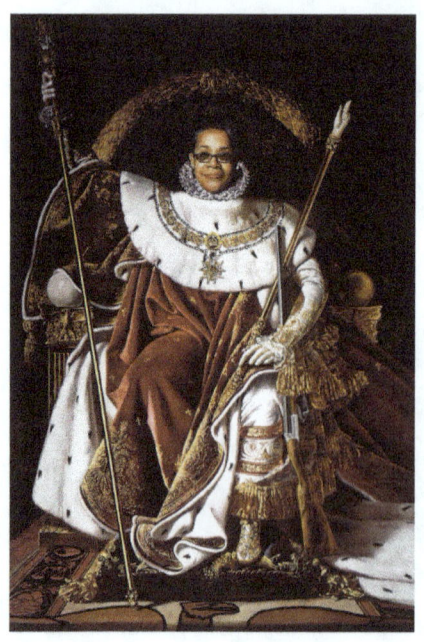

9.10. Kathleen Gilje, *Lowery Sims as Ingres' Napoleon I with a Gun*, 2006, oil on linen, 84 3/4″ x 57 1/2″, Collection of Melva Bucksbaum and Raymond Learsy (After JAD Ingres, *Napoleon I on his Imperial Throne*, 1806, Musée de l'Armée, Paris).

9.11. Kathleen Gilje, *RoseLee Goldberg as Manet's Young Man in a Spanish Costume*, 2006, oil on linen, 72 1/2"x 47 1/2" (After Édouard Manet, *A Young Man in the Costume of a Majo*, 1863, Metropolitan Museum of Art, New York).

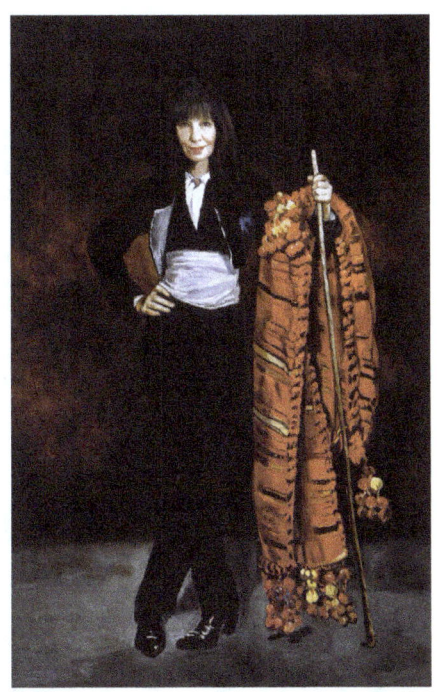

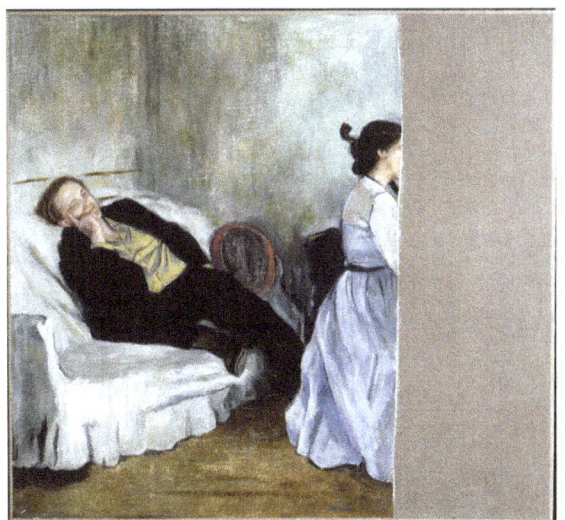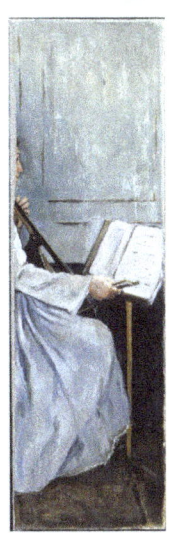

9.12. Kathleen Gilje, *Robert Storr Listening to his Wife (Rosamund Morley) as Degas' Portrait of Manet and his Wife*, 2006, oil on canvas, 26 3/4" x 29 1/2" and fragment *Rosamond Morley Playing the Viola da Gamba*, oil on canvas, 26 3/4" x 8 1/2", collection of Yale Art Museum, New Haven, CT (After Edgar Degas, *Portrait of Monsieur et Madame Édouard Manet*, 1868-69, Municipal Museum, Kitakyushu, Japan).

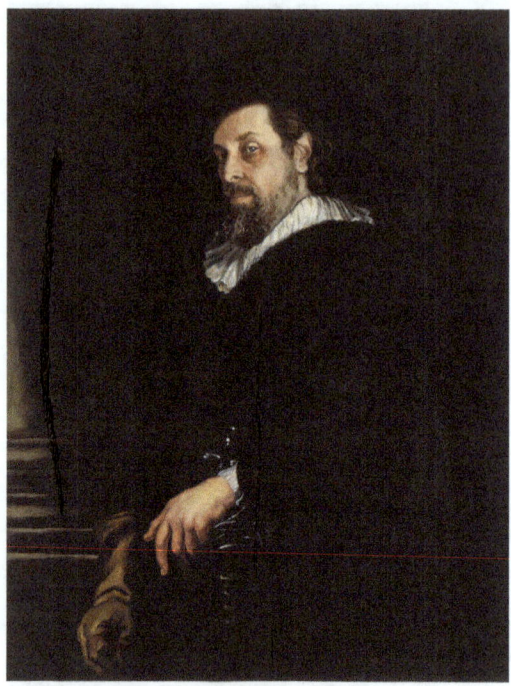

9.13. Kathleen Gilje, *Leo Steinberg as the Self-Portrait of Rubens*, 2005, oil on linen, 44 1/8" x 34 1/8" (After Peter Paul Rubens, *Self-Portrait,* c. 1639, Kunsthistorisches Museum, Vienna).

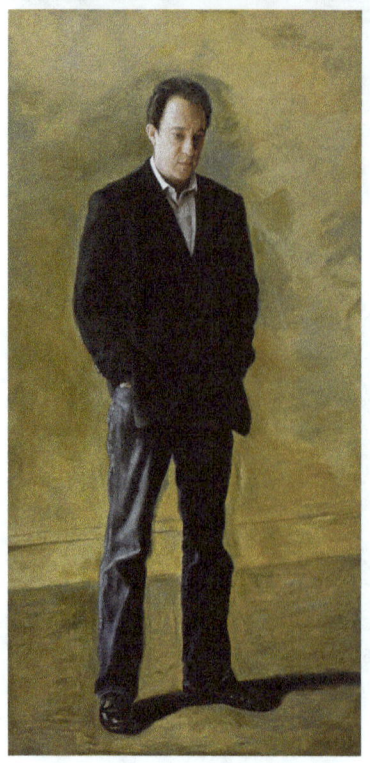

9.14. Kathleen Gilje, *Michael Kimmelman as Eakins' The Thinker*, 2006, oil on linen, 81" x 40 5/8" (After Thomas Eakins, *Portrait of Louis N. Kenton*, 1900, Metropolitan Museum of Art, New York).

9.15. Kathleen Gilje,
*Charlie Finch in the Manner
of Rembrandt*, 2005, oil
on linen, 44 1/2″ x 32″,
Collection of Charlie Finch,
NY (After Rembrandt van
Rijn, *Self Portrait*, 1640,
National Gallery, London).

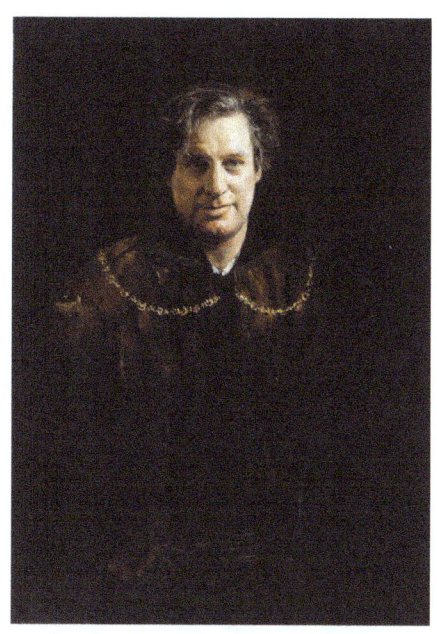

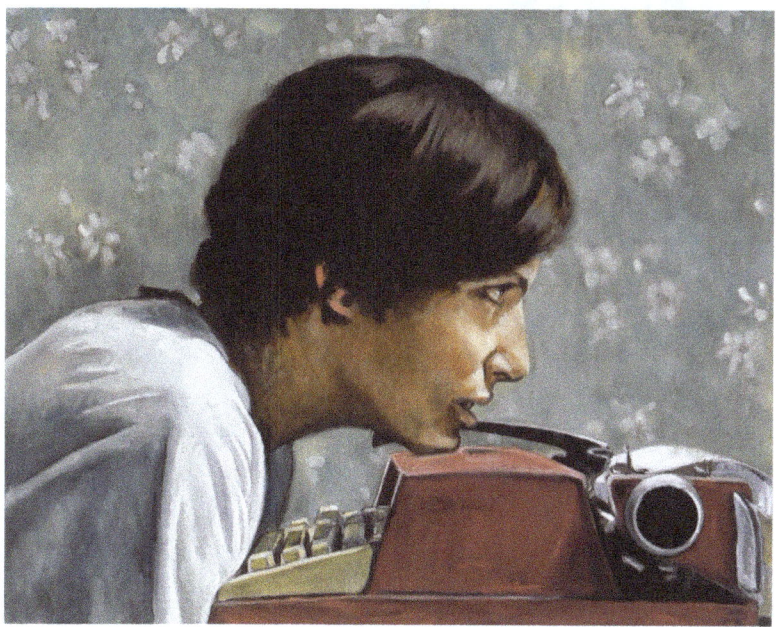

9.16. Kathleen Gilje, *Rosalind Krauss in the Manner of a Painting by Degas*, 2006, oil on linen, 16 3/4″ x 21 1/4″ (After a photograph of Rosalind Krauss working on her dissertation in 1969 by Ann Gabhart), National Portrait Gallery, Washington, DC.

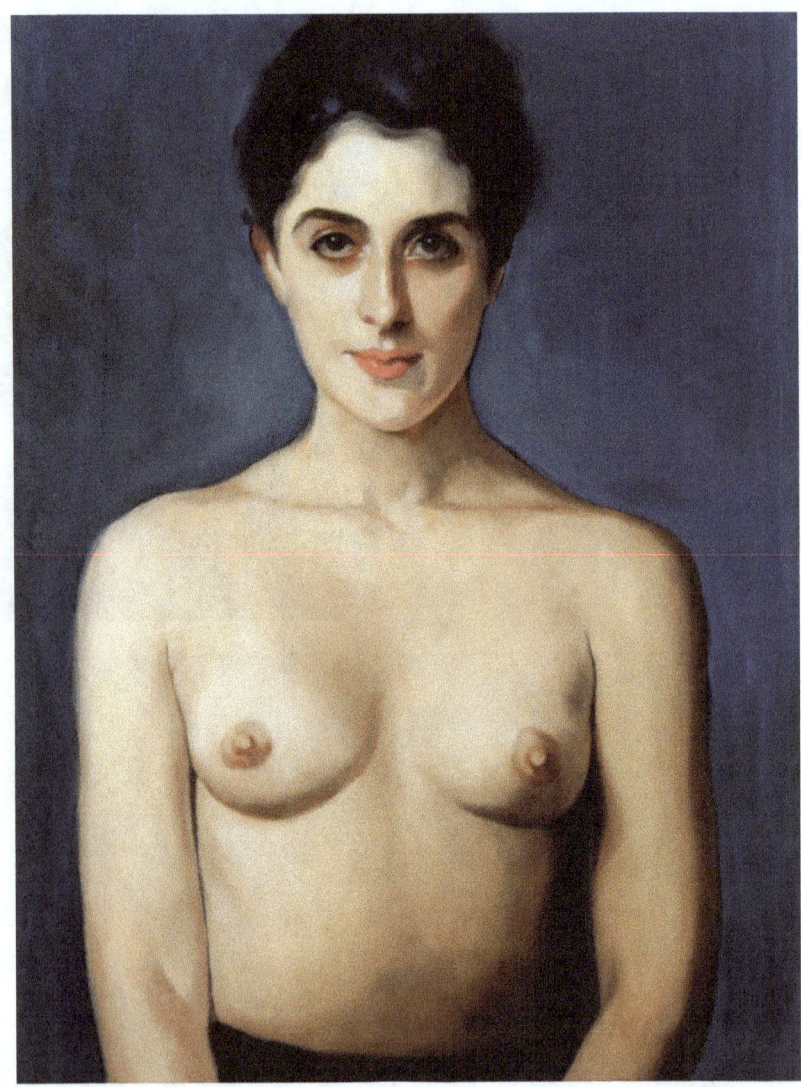

9.17. Kathleen Gilje, *Lady Agnew of Lochnaw, Restored*, 2007, oil on linen, 25″ x 19 1/4″, Collection of Deborah and Michael Troner (After John Singer Sargent, *Lady Agnew of Lochnaw*, 1892-3, National Gallery of Scotland, Edinburgh).

10

Reinventing Silverpoint: An Ancient Technique for the Twenty-First Century

Susan Schwalb

In 1985 the landmark exhibition *The Fine Line: Drawing with Silver in America*, curated by Bruce Weber, opened at the Norton Museum of Art in West Palm Beach, FL. Drawings by forty American artists of the nineteenth- and twentieth centuries were gathered together, and the show toured to three other venues (Pensacola Museum of Art, Pensacola, FL, Arkansas Art Center, Little Rock, AR and Museum of Fine Arts, Springfield, MA). The works were primarily figurative, but there was also a study for an abstract sculpture by John Storrs, along with a few abstract drawings by Michiko Itatani and myself. I would be reluctant to attempt an explanation for the resurgence of interest in an ancient drawing technique at this particular moment in American art history, but there can be no doubt that the Norton show was an essential catalyst. Numerous museum and university gallery shows followed in its wake along with solo and group exhibitions in commercial galleries.[1] In 1985 I knew of less than twenty-five artists working in metalpoint, but that number has now grown to several hundred including artists from other countries. Even on the social networking site, Facebook, there are currently two "groups" of artists devoted to the medium.

It is said that the use of metalpoint as a writing tool for keeping records can be traced back to ancient Egypt, Greece, and Rome. By the Middle Ages (476-1450) scribes and illuminators were using it for spacing guides, note-taking, ruling manuscript pages, marginal sketches, and underdrawings, as well as for ornamentation and illustration. It is even possible that Giotto drew in silverpoint. But it is the Renaissance (1400-1600) that has long been associated with the flowering of drawing as an important art form, and silverpoint reached its zenith with such artists as Da Vinci, Bellini, Botticelli, Dürer, and Cranach. It still remained an important tool for record keeping and note-taking, and merchants continued to use it in the fifteenth century. But in the early part of the sixteenth century many artists began to abandon it, as paper, red chalk, and graphite became more available. Still, there were artists who continued with the technique well into the seventeenth century; Rembrandt, for example, made silverpoint landscape drawings, as well as a famous portrait of his wife Saskia in 1633 shortly after they were married — an exquisite work of art with its warm brown tones and fine lines.

The last revival before the twentieth century took place in nineteenth-century England, as the Pre-Raphaelites experimented with silverpoint as part of their general study of Renaissance techniques. Beginning in the 1890s, one could buy a silverpoint kit from Winsor and Newton in England containing a pad of prepared paper and a stylus, but after the First World War, it was discontinued. It is only in the last several years, with the advent of the Internet, that a few website businesses have begun to sell silverpoint materials, and a kit is now available from NaturalPigments.com based in California.[2]

Undoubtedly sparked by British efforts in the medium, American interest dates from the mid-1890s. Thomas Dewing's (1851-1938) exhibitions inspired many artists, particularly those in Boston such as Joseph DeCamp (1858-1923), Philip Leslie Hale (1865-1931), William McGregor Paxton (1869-1941) and Margaret Foster Richardson (1881-1954). In the New York area, artists like Marsden Hartley (1877-1943), John Graham (1881-1961), Joseph Stella (1877-1946), and Paul Cadmus (1902-1999) also worked in silverpoint. There seems to have been something of a network, and artists tended to inspire each other so that August Mosca began to make silverpoint drawings while he was Stella's assistant between 1938 and 1946. But by and large, interest in the medium developed around artists who taught it in a variety of art schools. Among the leaders, one would have to count Paula Gerard who taught Michiko Itatani and Flora Langlois during her years at the Art Institute of Chicago (1962-1975), and the Layton School of Art (Milwaukee, WI, 1945-1962), James S. Watrous who taught John Wilde and numerous others at the University of Wisconsin (1930-1976), and Roger Anliker at Carnegie Mellon University (in the 1960's) and later at Tyler School of Art. In 1957 Watrous published *The Craft of Old-Master Drawings*, an important book that contains detailed technical information. But in the last ten to twenty years I believe it is primarily museum and gallery shows (along with studio visits) that have led to the current flowering of the medium. Artists have been captivated by the luminosity, the extremely fine and precise lines and the almost iridescent surface, so different from a pencil or ink line. As Margaret Mathews-Berenson puts it in a recent essay,

> At a time when art is being redefined by new and rapidly changing digital tools and technology that often deny the man-made mark, silverpoint offers artists a connection with a potent creative tradition. The fine delicate lines inevitably reveal the artist's hand: an affirmation of human presence. ...... A drawing medium made for quiet meditation, silverpoint remains a venerable instrument of intimate communication for artists today and provides welcome distraction from the dizzying pace of our technocentric world for artists and viewers alike.[3]

In brief, silverpoint requires a piece of silver wire usually placed in a simple stylus (a pin vise or mechanical pencil holder); as it is drawn across a prepared surface, a mark is created by tiny particles of metal that are left behind. Usually a grayish color, it tarnishes to a warm brown over time. In the Renaissance, artists fashioned their tools out of thick rods of metal that were often carved with elaborate and ornate designs. To allow for two different kinds of marks, these tools had points at either end, one sharpened to a fine point and the other somewhat blunt and wider. Nowadays, most artists sharpen their tools on a sandstone or sharpening stone or with a piece of sandpaper. Artists have generally preferred sterling silver but almost any metal can be used, including gold, copper, brass, bronze, aluminum, tin, lead, pewter, steel, iron and platinum. Unfortunately, the words "silverpoint" and "metalpoint" are often interchanged, but to avoid confusion, "metalpoint" should refer to drawings that use a variety of metals while "silverpoint" should be reserved for silver.

In the Renaissance, working in metalpoint was a very labor-intensive process. Although he may not be reliable, Cennino d'Andrea Cennini, in *Il Libro dell' Arte* (*The Craftsman's Handbook*), describes how a ground, made from ground bones (found under the dining room table), combined with animal skin glue, white lead and saliva or oils required at least nine coats before beginning a drawing.[4] Today we have a plentiful supply of commercially prepared gessos and paints; Chinese white watercolor paint, Shiva Casein, polymer or acrylic gesso and even ordinary house paint all work well as grounds and only need a few coats. Golden Artist Colors, Inc. has recently produced a water-based ground especially made for silverpoint, and numerous commercial papers with clay-coated surfaces are also available, most of them printing papers, originally designed for other purposes. But in spite of these conveniences, there are many contemporary artists who continue to prepare their grounds with traditional gesso. Roger Anliker, for example, required his students at Carnegie Mellon University to spend a month sanding the surface between coats in order to make a perfect ground; it is hardly surprising that a limited number of artists in his class continued in the medium. In any case, a minimum of four coats is needed for a traditional ground or an acrylic gesso (the consistency of homogenized milk). Colored grounds can be obtained by adding pigment to gesso or by using paint, but nothing prevents an artist from also experimenting with private techniques, and one thinks of the watercolor drops that Paula Gerard floated onto her wet casein grounds which made abstract patterns that were the basis of her drawings.

The magic of silverpoint and metalpoint drawing lies in the color changes that the initial grayish line undergoes through time. Silver generally turns a warm brown, copper and brass mutate into a yellowish-green. On the other hand, aluminum, gold, platinum and pewter tend to maintain their original color. This tarnishing effect is different on every kind of prepared surface or paper. Since the oxidation is caused by heat and humidity, a winter drawing is different from a summer drawing. In the winter it takes much longer for a line to change color, and identical drawings that make use of identical metals, grounds and papers will have different patinas on the surface if they were made at different times of the

year. Although it is customary to focus on the qualities of the metalpoint line, it must not be thought that a drawing is restricted to
effects of pure linearity. Dark and light tones can be obtained by
slowly building up the lines. And pressing lightly or heavily can
also change the darkness of a line though one has to be careful not
to break the surface of the ground. On the other hand, Joseph Stella
often drew with such vigor on his very free ground that he deliberately broke the surface, thereby creating a forceful effect in some
of his bold self-portraits. But he could also be precise and refined,
especially when he combined silverpoint with colored pencil in his
flower drawings.

Because it is very difficult to erase a metalpoint mark it is generally thought that one must be a master draftsman to use the medium, but in fact, artists have found ways of removing marks by
sanding the surface or by the careful manipulation of an eraser.
However it is generally not possible to draw over a silverpoint line
that has been removed since the ground is damaged and will not
accept the metal. But even this damage can become an artistic opportunity. Morgan O'Hara (born 1941), in recent experiments, uses
eraser marks to create a circle that intersects with lines that radiate outwards from a central point, leaving a ghostly presence that
seems to lurk within the drawing. Joseph Nicoletti (born 1948) has
adapted another highly unusual technique; by repeatedly layering
very thin coats of gesso on top of a drawing as it progresses, he ar-
rives at an interesting multiple image, and the lines under the gesso
never tarnish.

For most of the twentieth century silverpoint art was dominated by figuration. The subject matter consisted primarily of portraits, figures, landscapes and still lives, along with details of plants
and flowers. But many of these artists were aware of the problem
presented by the shadow of the Renaissance masters. They understood that they needed an extraordinary command of the medium
but they also did not wish to be caught emulating the composition
and the techniques of a Renaissance drawing.

With Leo Dee (1931-2004) a single object such as a lemon or
a part of an envelope is transformed into an exquisite meditative
landscape. So refined is his technique that it can be very difficult
to discern the mark-making process even with a magnifying glass.

Dennis James Martin (1956-2001) managed to give his 24-karat gold-point and platinum drawings of reclining nudes a voluptuous and almost pornographic softness. Executed on vellum, these drawings have a blurry quality that resembles an old movie still. Harvey Din-nerstein (born 1928) is certainly one of the most important realists; his work ranges from powerful looking plants to unconventional models (including pregnant women), usually drawn from his com-munity. Several drawings pay special attention to the hair of his models (either facial or head), an unusual focus obviously suggest-ed by the fineness of the silverpoint line.

Marjorie Williams-Smith (born 1953) has restricted her subject matter to flowers, particularly roses. She often draws the flower alone, placed on a pure white ground that has been carefully pol-ished. At times, the exquisite investigation of a part of a flower, as in the work entitled *Close Inspection* (Fig.1), encourages the view-er to marvel at a detail while seemingly caught up in an interior world. The stem appears to disappear into the void, and one be-gins to sense a strong presence far beyond the intimate scale of the drawing.

Some of the most imaginative image-based works are by artists dealing with surrealist or symbolist themes. One of the masters was John Wilde (1919-2005) who favored a style drenched in fantasy and imagination, sometimes described as "magic realism." The process of transformation fascinated Wilde and his human figures frequently morph into birds and other forms (Fig. 2). In 1982-1984 he made an enormous drawing (38x91in.) entitled *The Great Auto-biographical Silverpoint Drawing,* an attempt to recount a part of his life by means of a crowd of symbols and figures, overshadowed by a large tree. Lori Field (born 1955) is another artist who explores personal myths and fantasies. Drawing on a freely painted ground, she is partial to doll-like figures that seem to float in a parallel uni-verse often with animal heads or masks instead of faces. In *Bête Noire,* two figures, one with a cat mask and the other with birds instead of hair, suggest a scene from a strange Victorian drama (Fig. 3). Viewing Field's work is like falling down the rabbit hole in *Alice in Wonderland.*

One of the most unusual developments in contemporary sil-verpoint drawing has been the emergence of artists who are devoted to abstraction as well as conceptual and minimal art. One of the first to develop abstraction in metalpoint was the Chicago artist Paula Gerard (1907-1991), who studied as a young woman in Italy. She first encountered silverpoint while living in Paris, but it wasn't until she returned to the United States in the 1940s that she began to devote herself almost exclusively to the medium. At first her work was figurative but gradually she began to draw silver and goldpoint lines over her watercolor abstractions. In *Currents*, Gerard uses linear patterns and tone to build up a biomorphic world where one might glimpse waves or sea creatures that inhabit the bottom of the ocean. She is one of the few contemporary artists who also worked with metalpoint on parchment and in one of her best known works, *Vortex*, swirls of tone create a sensual vision not unlike how I imagine riptides or whirlpools (Fig. 4).

Cynthia Lin (born 1964) creates small drawings that seem abstract, but are actually (according to the artist) *trompe l'oeil* portraits of dust and hair. Frequently the drawings are placed flat on a specially designed shelf covered by Plexiglas; they play with the confusion between reality and imagination (Fig. 5). Because of the special circumstances, the silverpoint line in these works is delicate, fine and sometimes barely visible. Marietta Hoferer (born 1974) and Michelle Grabner (born 1962) have both been working almost exclusively on black grounds. Hoferer, known for her minimalist, process-oriented, tape and pencil drawings, only began silverpoint quite recently. As if in a meditative state she draws grids of fine lines on black Plike paper (Fig. 6). The works are often quite large (28x28in.) and even though each line is drawn against a straight edge, the hand of the artist is still evident and slight deviations and accidents are an essential part of the process. In the end these subtle drawings seem like a glittering tapestry of lines of varying widths and tones. In Grabner's black drawings on circular canvases or papers, silverpoint lines radiate from the center to give an illusion of deep space. But in a recent show at Minus Space Gallery in New York, there were more than eighteen works on *rectangular* paper and in this instance, Grabner drew vertical lines from left to right, but since she refused to pause to sharpen the tool, they gradually became slightly wider and less precise in each subsequent drawing.

Several artists have pushed metalpoint off the surface of paper onto the wall. Linda Hutchins (born 1957), based in Portland, OR, uses her grandmother's silver spoon to make large wall drawings (9′ x 12′). She tells the story of her frequent lectures on silverpoint over the years, and how, after hearing herself explain how easy it is to make a mark on wall paint, she decided one day to try it herself. In *Lineal Silver (pool)* (Fig. 7) installed at the Tacoma Art Museum, Hutchins draws with her spoon to create a network of lines that swirl and undulate across the wall. Natalie Loveless (born 1971) uses the medium in context-based performances. In an early work entitled *CoOperation*, 2004, she moved in to the gallery space for five days and communicated with friends and strangers through email. She invited her participants to tell her stories of mourning and memory from which she drew a complex map on the wall, marking their location around the world. For a recent installation at the Kentler International Drawing Space in 2009 she invited friends to determine how she should behave with the wall, whether to throw things at it, kiss it, et cetera. After performing these actions, Loveless then used a stylus to draw lines around each one and to connect them. Surprisingly, the final result was a very subtle image, only visible at very close range. When asked why she preferred silverpoint to graphite, for example, Lovelace mentioned many of the same qualities that appeal to other artists in the medium, the "permanence" of a mark that can't be easily erased, the "resonance" of a "precious metal," the fact that it tarnishes over time (although she admits that this is the "softest" reason for her preference since she doesn't work densely or on permanent surfaces) and finally, of course, the link to the Italian Renaissance.

One of the most unusual artists currently working in metalpoint is Carol Prusa (born 1956), based in the Miami area. Prusa became interested in silverpoint after a trip to the Uffizi Gallery in Florence in 2002. Self-taught, she works on three-dimensional plastic domes, some as large as sixty inches in diameter that generally hang on the wall. Using silverpoint, silver leaf, acrylic, and fiber optics, she covers her domes with intricate drawings of cosmic shapes, plant-like forms, and designs (Fig. 8). Many recent domes have also included a small video imbedded in the center of the dome. As Bernadette Ryrnes wrote, "One can recognize Prusa's attraction to science in her microcosmic, domed universes. Her silverpoint lines flower and coil into infinite swirls and eddies on the surface of miniature, spherical planets. Prusa embraces the infinite in the tattooed lacework of her domes."[5]

For more than thirty-five years I have been part of the revival of the technique of silverpoint drawing in America. As I have suggested, most contemporary artists who draw with a metal stylus continue the tradition of Leonardo and Dürer by using the soft, delicate line for figurative imagery. My work, on the other hand, is resolutely abstract, and my handling of the technique has been very varied. In works from the 1970s I tore and burned paper, the smoke provided a free and dramatic contrast to the precise linearity of silverpoint. In works from the 1980s I combined silverpoint with flat expanses of acrylic paint or gold leaf. At times I have used a wide variety of metals to create subtle shifts of tone and color. Finally, in 1996, I began what many think of as my signature works, as I abandoned the stylus altogether in favor of wide metal bands that achieve a shimmering atmosphere reminiscent of the luminous transparency of watercolor as in *Strata #227* (Fig. 9).

Memories of light have been a recurrent source for recent work, and travels to Arizona and New Mexico suggested some of the colors and shapes in my *Afterimage Series*. Other works responded to the light on the Hudson River as I saw it from my studio on the West Side of Manhattan. More recently, the atmosphere has become subtler; no event (such as a horizon line) is allowed to become the focus. Instead, the eye is invited to wander across the surface, comparing and contrasting. It seemed to me that a sense of the passage of time had become central to these works. I work on both paper and on wood panels; many of these panels are carefully beveled so that the imagery seems to float off the wall. In 2010, while on a residency at Virginia Center for the Creative Arts, I returned to the stylus and began using bronze and copper pads. Margaret Mathews Berenson accurately captured my intention when she wrote that:

Schwalb resolutely explores new tools and techniques for greater richness of surface and more varied shifts in light and shadow. She recently discovered soft bronze pads akin to Brillo pads that she now employs in such works as *Madrigal #2 and #3* to create luminous horizontal bands of silver gray, which evoke the whispery mists or atmospheric effects of dawn.[6]

Silverpoint and metalpoint drawing continues to be a medium for quiet, refined, and meditative work, but as my essay has shown, contemporary artists have been radically pushing the boundaries of this time-honored technique. Whether it is combined with other media, used for marking a wall, or for creating large oversized works, silverpoint can no longer be primarily regarded as an ancient technique tied to a conservative sensibility.

End Notes

I want to thank Dorothea Burns for her invaluable advice and my husband, Martin Boykan, for reading and editing the article. My appreciation to all the artists—Carol Prusa, Linda Hutchins, Marietta Hoferer, Cynthia Lin, Lori Field, Marjorie Williams-Smith—and the Arkansas Art Center who graciously agreed to lend their images for the article.

[1] Since *The Fine Line* there have been three other major museum shows of contemporary silverpoint drawing: *Silverpoint Etcetera: Contemporary American Metalpoint Drawings* curated by Charles Schmidt which toured to several museums beginning in 1992, *The Luster of Silver: Contemporary Metalpoint Drawings* curated by Holly Koons McCullough at the Telfair Museum of Art, Savannah, GA in 2006 and *The Luster of Silver: Contemporary Metalpoint Drawings* curated by the artists Koo Schadler and Jeannine Cook at the Evansville Museum of Arts, History & Science, Evansville, Indiana in 2009. Cook and Schadler used the original Telfair show as the source for the Evansville show. In addition there have been numerous solo and group shows of metalpoint and silverpoint drawings in commercial galleries plus two recent shows in non-profit venues: *Reinventing Silverpoint; An Ancient Technique for the 21st Century* at the Kentler International Drawing Space, Brooklyn, NY in 2009 curated by Margaret Mathews-Berenson and Susan Schwalb and *Luminous Line: Contemporary Drawing in Metalpoint* curated by Margaret Mathews-Berenson at Scripps College, Claremont, CA in 2010.

[2] "This Silverpoint Drawing Gift Set has everything needed for silverpoint (and metalpoint) drawing. The kit includes 2 mm and 0.9 mm metal holders (styli), two fine silverpoints (99.9% pure silver), two copper points, two nickel-silver points (a total of six metalpoints), a copper wool

pad, Golden Silverpoint / Drawing Ground, Maped Epure vinyl eraser and step-by-step instructions" all in a wooden case.
http://www.naturalpigments.com/silverpoint-drawing-gift-set.html

[3] Margaret Mathews Berenson, *Reinventing Silverpoint: An Ancient Technique for the 21st Century* (Brooklyn, NY, brochure for the Kentler International Drawing Space, 2009).

[4] The distinguished scholar and conservator Dorothea Burns notes in email correspondence that all of the Italian Renaissance drawings with prepared drawings that she has seen are covered with a dilute material, obviously applied by brush in one layer.

[5] Bernadette Ryrnes, *Silver: Points of Departure* (Nashville, Tennessee, Nashville Arts Magazine, 2011), p. 31.

[6] Margaret Mathews Berenson, *Luminous Line: Contemporary Drawing in Metalpoint*, (Claremont, CA, Ruth Chandler Williamson Gallery, Scripps College, 2010), p. 13.

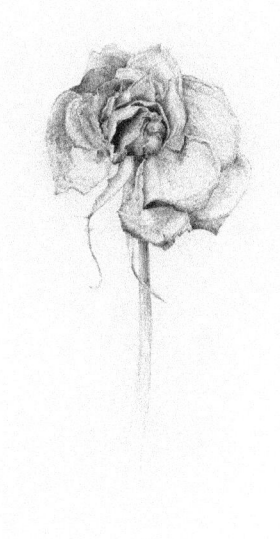

10.1. Marjorie Williams-Smith (American: Washington D.C, 1953), *Close Inspection*, 2002, silverpoint on clay–coated Video Media paper, 10" x 8", collection of Susan Schwalb.

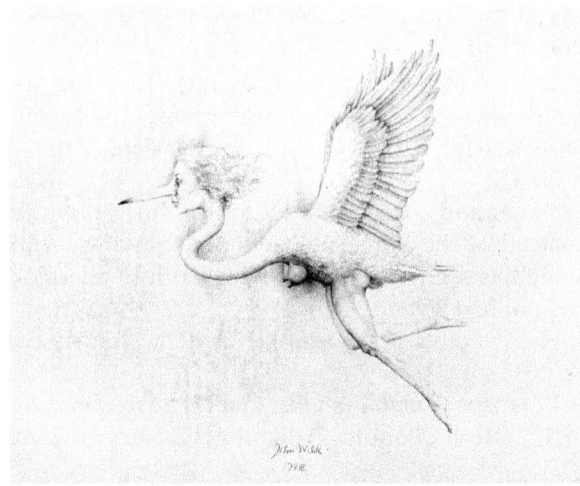

10.2. John Wilde (American: Milwaukee, Wisconsin, 1919 - 2006), *Lady-Bird Series #9* (*Emily Egret*), 1982, silverpoint on paper, 8" x 10 1/4", Arkansas Arts Center Foundation Collection, Tabriz Fund purchase, 1983.024.002.

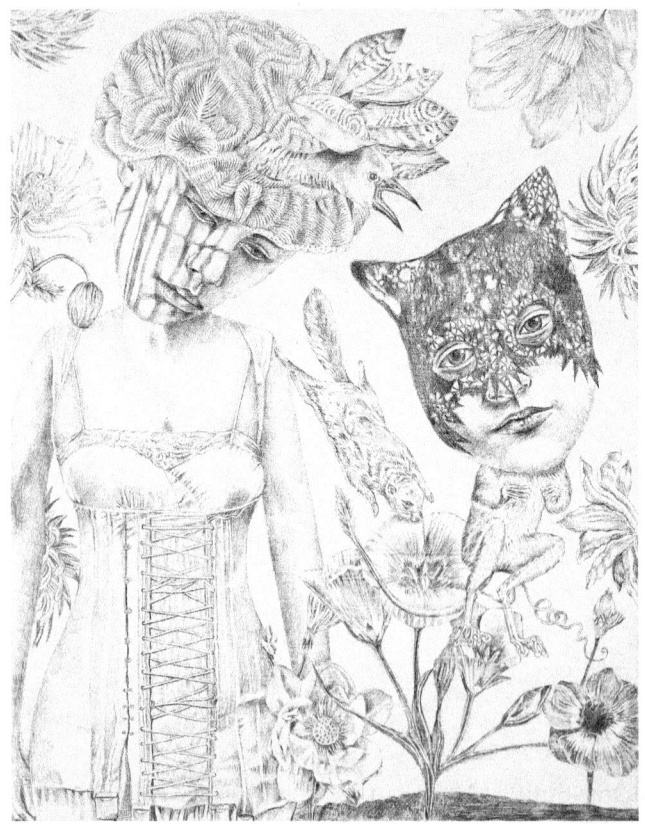

10.3. Lori Field (American: New York, NY, 1955), *Bête Noire*, 2011, silverpoint on panel, 20" x 16", collection of the artist.

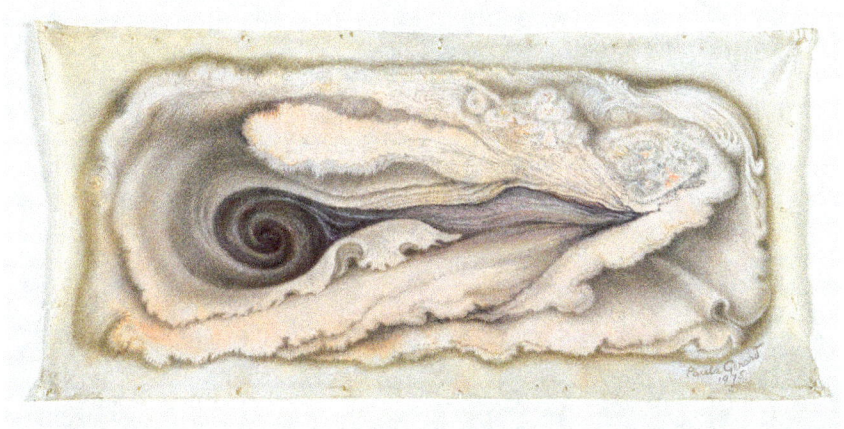

10.4. Paula Gerard (American: Brighton, England, 1907 - 1991), *Vortex*, 1975, silverpoint, goldpoint, watercolor on casein-coated parchment, 4" x 8", Arkansas Arts Center Foundation Collection purchase, 1985.065.

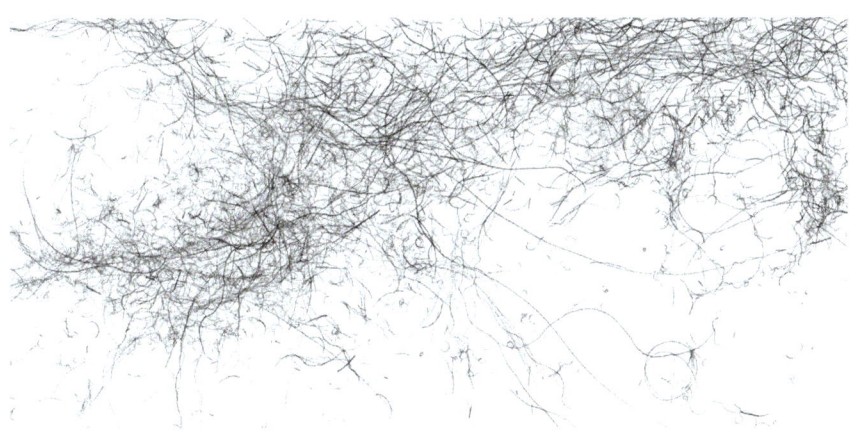

10.5. Cynthia Lin (American: Taiwan, 1964), *Shelf Drawing #3*, 2001 (detail), silver on gesso on paper on wooden shelf, 6" x 21.5", collection of the artist.

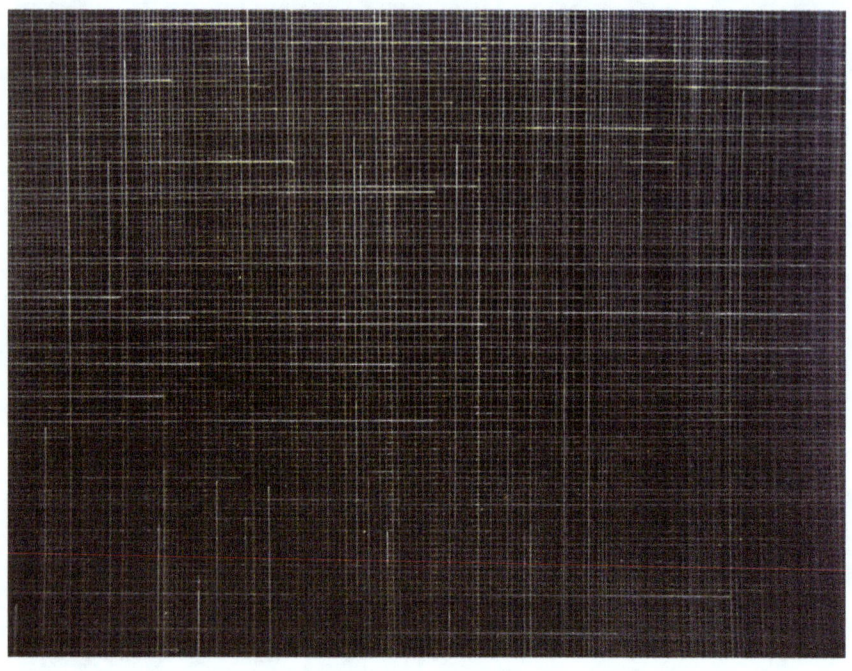

10.6. Marietta Hoferer (American: Hausach, Germany, 1962), *March 3, 2011*, 2011 (detail), metalpoint and graphite on black Pilke paper, 14" x14", collection of the artist.

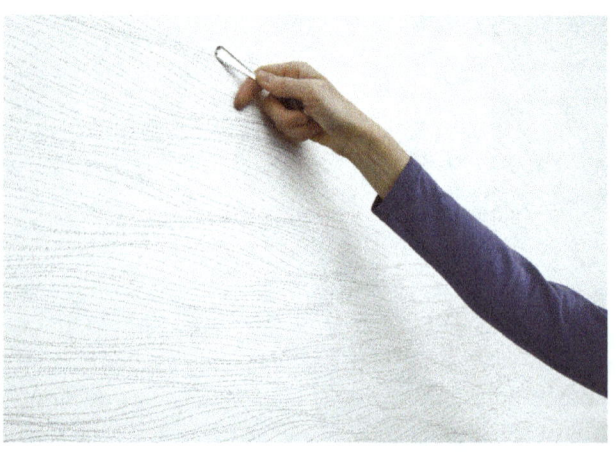

10.7. Linda Hutchins (American), Study for *Lineal Silver (Pool)*, silver spoon on wall, 9' x 12', collection of the artist.

10.8. Carol Prusa,
(American: Chicago,
IL, 1956), *Portal
(Einstein-Rosen),* 2011
(detail), silverpoint,
graphite, titanium
white pigment with
acrylic binder on
acrylic hemisphere
and fiber optics,
50" x 50" x 10".
Collection of
Berenice Steinbaum,
Miami, FL.

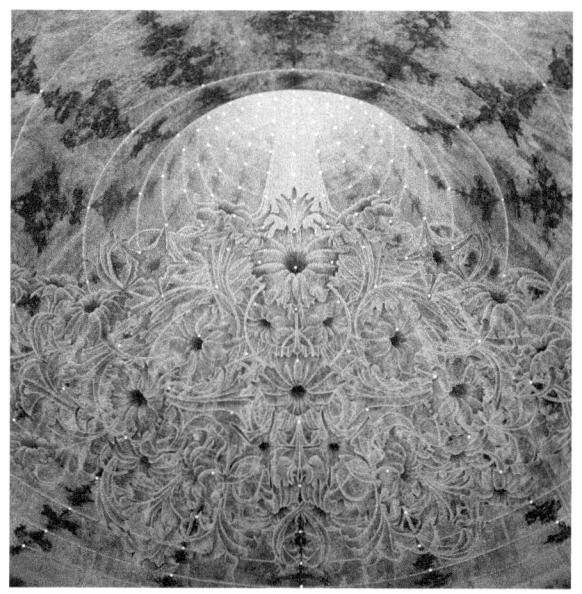

10.9. Susan Schwalb
(American, New
York, NY, 1944),
Strata #227, 1998,
silver/copper/
aluminumpoint on
clay-coated paper,
9" x 9", private
collection.

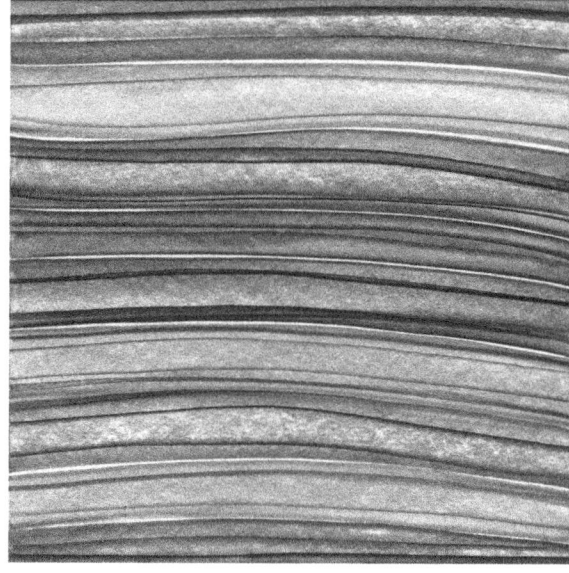

11
New Approaches to Sculpture in The Twenty-First Century

Suzanne Volmer

Influential sculpture of the twenty-first century is about form in relation to audience engagement. Given that occupying the third dimension has inherent worldly physicality it is significant that sculptors today are balancing object identity with viewer connectivity. The purity of iconic sculptural form is being transformed into conceptually driven approaches that are focused on the experiential. Exploration of individual identity and relationship to place propel this new vocabulary.

A psychological dimension that includes the signature of excess does travel forward from the past into present thought, except it is adapted in current context to unconventionally merge materiality with its public component. Today sculpture of a defining nature involves a twist in human dimension. Sculptors are seeing confluence as relevant; they are also asserting new perspectives in three-dimensionality to purposefully enliven public cognition. By integrating the realism of physicality with the abstraction of the ephemeral, contemporary sculptors are intentionally drawing audiences further into the context of situational art.

The use of found materials has evolved as a dominant direction for sculpture in this millennium. This trend stems from an ethos of privation and gleaning as well as stewardship and reinvention. Other contouring influences of today's sculpture sensibility include *Pop Art* perspectives and the manifesto-oriented directions of *Dada*, *Surrealism* and the *Cobra/Fluxus* agenda. It is important to under-

stand that this set of confrontational modern art movements created extraordinary perceptual pivot against convention in their time,
and now are meaningful in terms of understanding the intentions
of materiality most relevant today.

Focusing the present era of change is an intuitive and intentional examination of the idea of relationship. Among factors of influence are the pressures of social compression intensified by such
things as virtual technology and geographic globalization. These
distort individual awareness and dull connection to self and community. Sculptors conceptually re-configuring this social loss find
especially pertinent the processes of physical manifestation. It is
a survival mentality concerned with expanding spatial parameter.

Various influences in our culture have contributed to changing
the terrain of experience so arbitrarily and significantly that relationship has become a compelling and abiding concern. Organically mapping, as a means of visual orientation, has become an important conceptual framework at the present time.

Sculptor Anish Kapoor creates by traditional means but transcends method, making implosively iconic artworks. In contrast,
the explosively intimate is found in sculptures by Louise Bourgeois.
Many working with three-dimensionality today want spontaneity
to inform process. Doug and Mike Starn are among those using
performance-based methods to bring audiences into an experiential dynamic of real-time. Instant gratification is a cultural imperative today, which has led to incorporating interactive multi-dimen-
sional directions within the context of sculpture. This materiality
informs installation sculpture and causes some sculptors seeking
synthesis to combine three-dimensionality with technology. This
direction is known as *New Media*.

Anish Kapoor's polished stainless steel sculptures are emotive
of a surreal force-field of ambiguity, visually securing iconic stature
while reflecting and absorbing the actions of viewers and passers-
by. His use of mirroring illustrates with compelling subtlety how
the interpretation of relational phenomenon has mutated so that
geographic sense of place and personal identity are experienced
with greater fluidity. Viewers recognize themselves in his mirrored
effects and possibly also the reflection of their own social compression (Figs. 1 and 2).

His gleaming biomorphic forms seemingly convey the mercury moment of knowing, concentrating an intellectually magnetic almost hallucinatory feeling of three-dimensionality. Kapoor's combination of western technique and abstract multi-cultural sensibility imbues his sculpture with distortion and lack of equilibrium. The entirety is a fascinating invitation to viewers to experience his elegant and refined aesthetic that creates dissolve between art and audience. Because of the reflective aspect of this artwork the audience becomes a component of figurative imagery that flows through and around Kapoor's abstract vocabulary to enrich content. Such visual trickery is relevant because it distinctively addresses relationship, asserting controlled direction so public consciousness is engaged.

In contrast, the sculptures of Magdalena Abakanowicz are concerned with shape shift in far more literal terms. Her figurative sculpture explores issues of crowd influence and individually. The artist's concept of monumental form suggests imposing mobs, armies, even minions that stretch the experience of materiality to become interactive. By commanding the lockstep of cultural momentum and depicting multitudes she flips the power dynamic of public mass to the potency of individuality (Fig. 3).

The aesthetic of Abakanowicz typically flows like a tide of identification, releasing forms from the limitation of object and directing sculptural emphasis to engagement. The artist's constructed corporality forcefully sweeps viewers from anonymity into identity. It generates thoughts about consciousness, control, freedom, confinement, individuality, integrity, challenge, choice, responsibility, loss and revelation which are all essential aspects of our humanity. Her fields of figuration are declarative and relevant as forms filtering global concern though a close examination of individuality. The sculptural perspectives of Abakanowicz transform spaces, surround form and activate vacuums to become areas of participation. Whereas Kapoor sustains and heightens iconic referencing, Abakanowicz manipulates spatial energy to build then release the power that volume controls. Viewers experience a physical sense of opening, allowing them to consider particular nuances of their individuality.

Abakanowicz often references fabric in her sculptures. In her bronzes the image of fabric is used to shroud human form to accentuate anonymity and create accessibility that targets and facilitates her language of intimacy. Sculptors today are actively transforming the possibilities of their materials, seeking the unexpected.

Shown in spring 2011 at Cheim & Read in New York City were fabric sculptures by Louise Bourgeois exuding hyper-sexualized content. Intimate and confrontationally crude, these sculptures challenge material convention and create provocation. The corporality is revelatory, even shocking with a richness of import that wanders into a dream dimension of the subconscious in which viewers find their own interpretation. Bourgeois exploits familiarity to facilitate an intellectual and emotional engagement. She transfers snippets of conceptual content, as if a three-dimensional mind-meld to imprint her encoded sensibility into the cognitive space of the viewer (Figs. 4 and 5).

Elevating common materials to the sculptural forefront reinforces a sense of reality in the three-dimensional pursuits of many contemporary sculptors. Rope, skeins of yarn and shoelaces are the materials of choice for Sheila Pepe (2011) at Carroll and Sons, Boston, Massachusetts. As a floor-to-ceiling black and blue labyrinth, her entanglement called *Common Sense in Boston* was an environmental sculpture developed to encourage participation. She created an installation that was crocheted, tied, knitted and knotted into a massive room-size snarl. To facilitate public involvement the artist left within the installation chairs and ladders, crochet hooks and needles for viewers to participate in both development and dismantling. The installation was rigged into place and not as spontaneous at the outset as sharing becomes in the end. Viewers were expected to glean and de-construct the artist's installation; therefore their action further defines or gives context to this art. The sensory familiarity of everyday materials is used by the artist to open a dialogue of identification for viewers to include the possibility of their direct involvement (Fig. 6).

Snarls are a much more somber vehicle for sculptor Petah Coyne as she brings soulful extravagance to abstract content imbedded with narrative sub-text. Coyne creates huge lush forms of choreographed debris hung from the ceiling. Typically her signature is to defy the convention of traditional sculptural floor placement. In her retrospective exhibition that traveled to MASS MoCA in western

Massachusetts in 2010 Coyne created a large installation environment that combined ceiling and floor sculptures called *Everything That Rises Must Converge* (Fig. 7).

The installation was a congestion of blackened blobs of innumerable appropriated plastic flowers suspended, snarled, and splattered in a maelstrom of artificiality that ensnared dead, yet vibrant by taxidermy, peacocks and pheasants. The entire assemblage of debris (based on Dante's *Inferno*) references the collateral damage caused by excess. It was a violent diorama concerning hoarding, infallibility and consequence. Coyne's conceptual orientation is informed by her own personal identification points and explodes to become about the larger subject matter of consumerism and destructive aspects of globalization.

Tara Donovan creates ephemeral often ethereal-looking art from appropriated materials. Influenced by the minimalist ideals of pre-fabricated systematized elements developed into larger form she has created sculptures from such things as drinking straws and Styrofoam cups. Typically her materials are plastic stock items from daily life that are disposable in nature and are purchased in bulk. She takes items such as straws and cups then builds them into structures that appear to defy gravity. Donovan obsessively engineers small units into biomorphic, sci-fi influenced room size installations that give the sensory impression of warping space. Her artworks suggest environments of alternate reality built from everyday artifacts of this world. This is perhaps meant as a way to free us from certain aspects of societal compression (Fig. 8).

The Starn Twins have taken the quest for personal identity and relationship to new heights of resourcefulness. They and a team of helpers created *Big Bambú* in 2010 on the rooftop of the Metropolitan Museum of Art in New York as a gutsy massive limited engagement undertaking. To realize its final form it required a system of execution that utilized the skills of trained rock climbers. The result ultimately was a Robinson Crusoe influenced sculptural habitat defining *Adventure Art*. To replicate the dynamic at the 2011 Venice Biennale the Starns gleaned a small number of stem cell inspired core elements from the original then added bamboo from France to organically re-configure a newly exciting site specific *Big Bambú* that was networked above the canals of Venice. Mike and Doug

Starn are engaged in an extremely important trend of materiality known as *Spectacle Art*. It is a dominant and unifying direction in art of the twenty-first century, one that a number of artists included in this article are exploring and defining today (Fig. 9).

Leo Villareal is a technology-based sculptor working elegantly with the glitz of illumination. Creating computer programs he sequences lighting into three-dimensional object identity. In 2011 at Gering Lopez Gallery in New York his show was limited to one artwork. The intimacy of this cameo appearance brilliantly showcased spatial depth and the ephemeral aspect of light to mesmerizing effect. His chandelier-like form *Cylinder* hung in a blackened space. The artist rigged a variety of LED lights to cascade to the floor in linear abstraction. The new-media aspects of the sculpture's lighting effects changed constantly and were programmed by the artist to have alternating light and form patterns. Villareal's approach is influenced by *Pop* and the momentum of 1960s *Mod*. These references contribute to the installation's seductive appeal. Villareal is making a significant conceptual shift in light-based sculpture trending by solidly involving new media with object identity (Fig. 10).

Reviewed in *Art New England* by Alicia Faxon in the May-June 2011 issue, *Clouds Captured:* a sculpture installation experience by Suzanne Volmer combines color and form with helium, electronic circuitry, mechanized kinetics, lighting and a coordinated sound dimension. As an amalgam, *Clouds Captured* has a seductive appeal that draws viewers into interactive space. Large helium-filled color-saturated fabric clouds float in calibrated mechanized breath-like up and down motion enhanced with lighting effects and sounds of rushing wind. The installation maps space while it defines sculptural presence. It also explores Color Field relationships in a three-dimensional context and is a dialogue about environmental issues and belonging. Seemingly weightless, the sensibility is rooted in form. Alicia Faxon wrote,

> With a combination of complementary hues, it approximates the color theory of the impressionists...In a fascinating combination of art and science, *Clouds Captured*, takes on a new dimension of sculpture...It is a project Leonardo da Vinci might have worked on, using hydraulics rather than electricity and helium...The installation is a visual feast,

conceptual triumph, and participatory experience.[1]

Clouds Captured is meant to interrupt time and re-sensitize viewers, creating a situation of identification. Inflatable Art is a contemporary sculpture trend and *Clouds Captured* floats with the lightness and air of life (Fig. 11).

The imperative for sculptors creating in the twenty first century is really to ignite cultural awareness. Overall the dominant direction is to use sculptural form to re-configure viewer relationship bringing new context to sensory participation with materiality. *Dada* and *Surrealism* came about during cultural shift and economic de-stabilization and *Cobra/Fluxus* emerged during a time of cultural hybridization. In different ways a confluence is happening today. In response to the compression endemic of both the information age and globalization many sculptors are focusing their attentions on redefining perceptions of space and placing viewers in a collaborative dynamic of revelation to make and encourage new pathways of thinking.

End Notes

Thank you to Alicia Faxon for her sustained commitment evaluating and championing the work of living artists. In her art criticism she has analyzed their ideas and put their contemporary statements into historical perspective. I would also like to thank the artists and their galleries for granting permission to use the images included in my article.

[1]Alicia Faxon, Review of *Clouds Captured*, *Art New England* vol. 32, no. 3 (May/June 2011), 59.

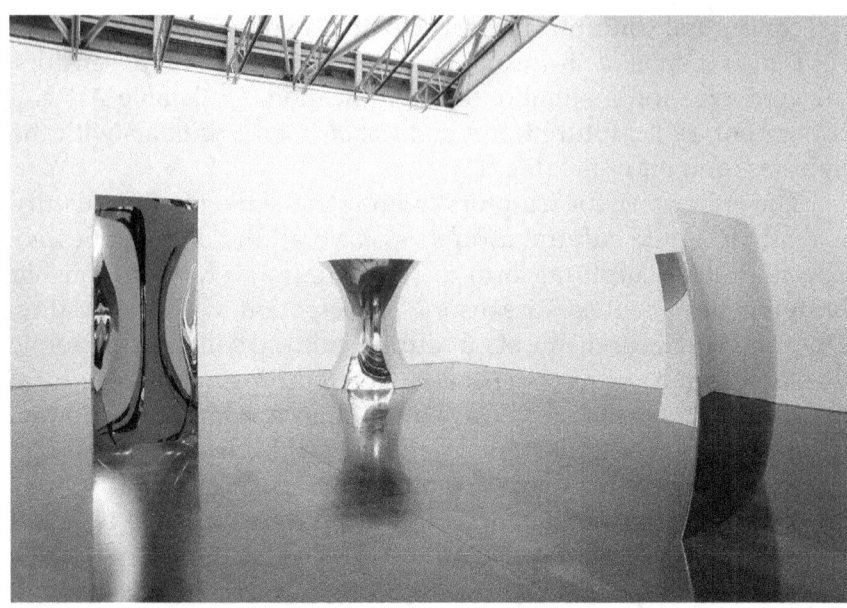

11.1. Anish Kapoor, *Installation View: Gladstone Gallery, New York and Brussels May 12-August 15, 2009*, ©Anish Kapoor, courtesy Gladstone Gallery, New York and Brussels, photo credit: David Regen.

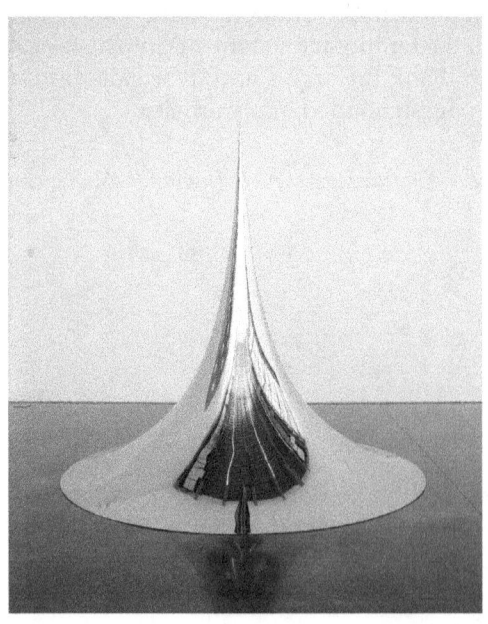

11.2. Anish Kapoor, *Non-Object (Spire)*, 2007, stainless steel, 119" x 118 1/8" x 118 1/8", ©Anish Kapoor, courtesy Gladstone Gallery, New York and Brussels.

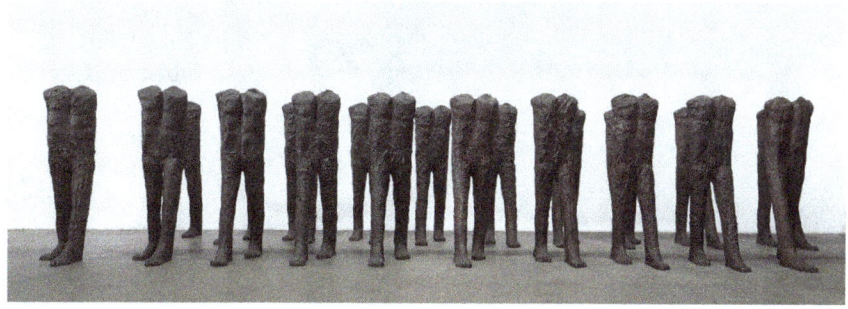

11.3. Magdalena Abakanowicz, *Walking Figures (Right Foot-Nine Figures) (Left Foot-Six Figures)*, 2000, bronze, ©Magdalena Abakanowicz, courtesy of Marlborough Gallery, New York.

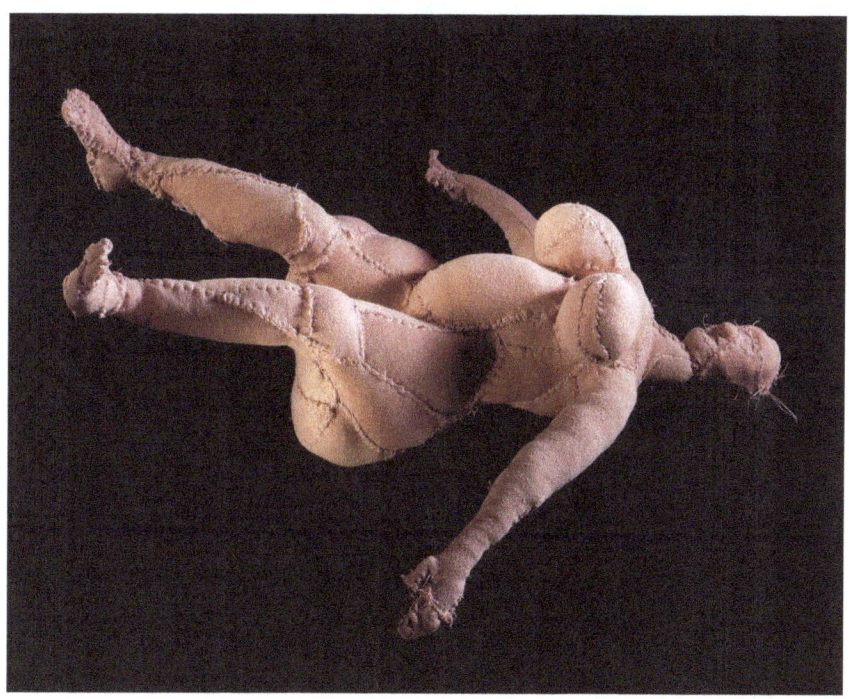

11.4. Louise Bourgeois, *Temper Tantrum*, 2000, pink fabric, 9" x 13" x 20" (22.9 x 33 x 50.8 cm), Private Collection, London, Photo: Christopher Burke, ©The Easton Foundatioin/Licensed by VAGA, NY.

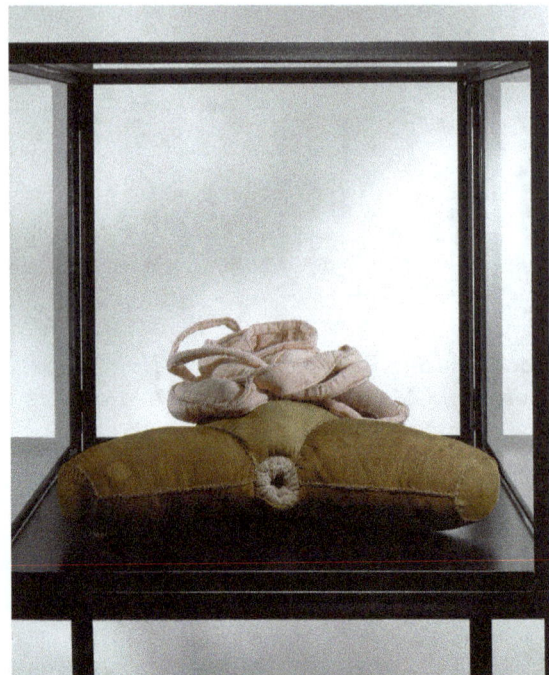

11.5. Louise Bourgeois, *Untitled*, 2001, fabric and steel, 11" x 27" x 21" (27.9 x 68.4 x 53.33cm), Private Collection, Los Angeles, London, Photo: Christopher Burke, ©The Easton Foundation/Licensed by VAGA, NY.

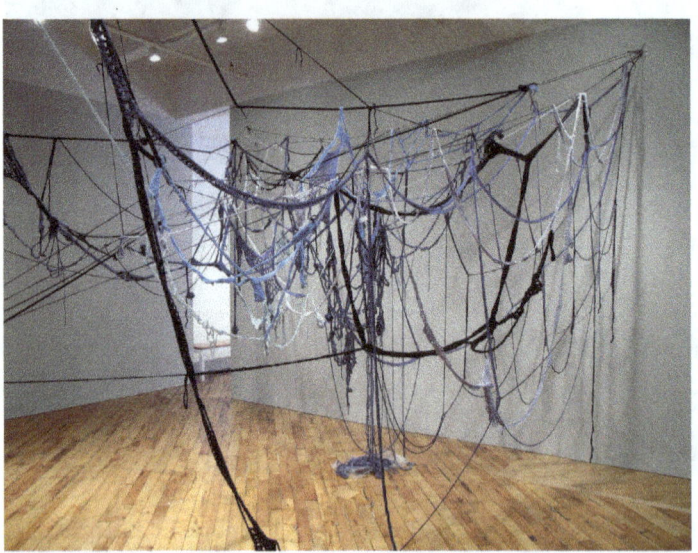

11.6. Sheila Pepe, *Common Sense in Boston*, 2011, rope, shoelaces and crocheted yarn, 11' x 16' 6" x 30', ©Sheila Pepe, courtesy Carroll and Sons, Boston, MA.

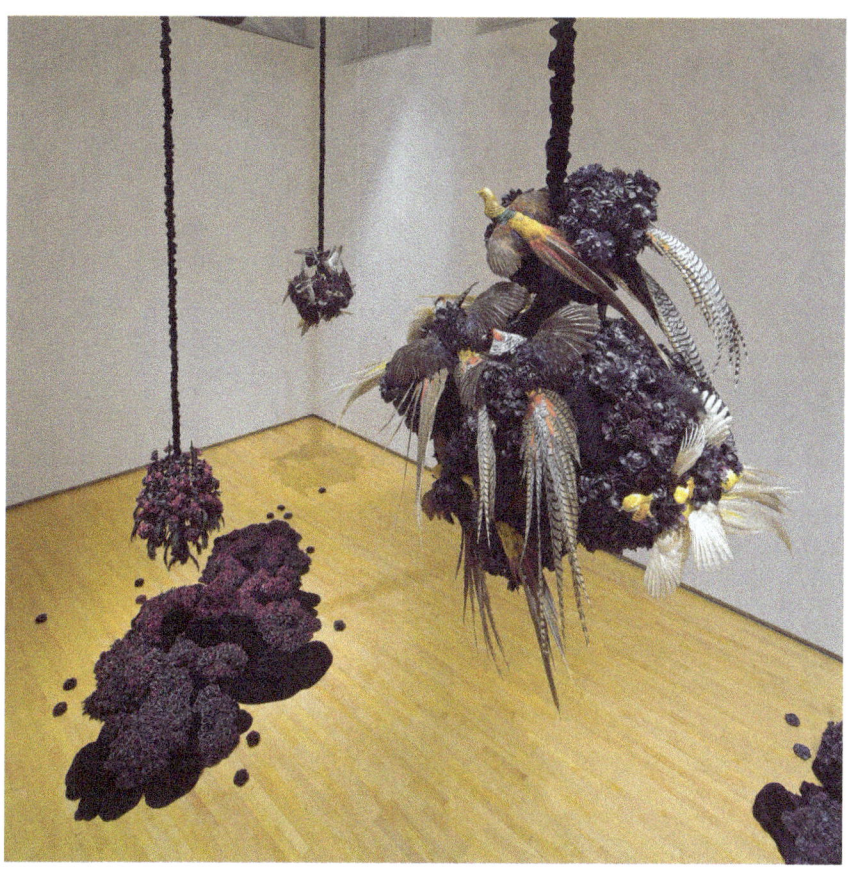

11.7. Petah Coyne, Installation View: *Everything That Rises Must Converge,* MASS MoCA, North Adams, Massachusetts, 2010-2011, pictured front to back: *Untitled # 1176 (Elizabeth-Elizabeth), 2007-2010, Untitled # 1234 (Tom's Twin), 2007-2008, Untitled #1175 (La Notte), 2007-2008,* ©Petah Coyne, courtesy Galerie Lelong, New York, photo credit: Art Evans.

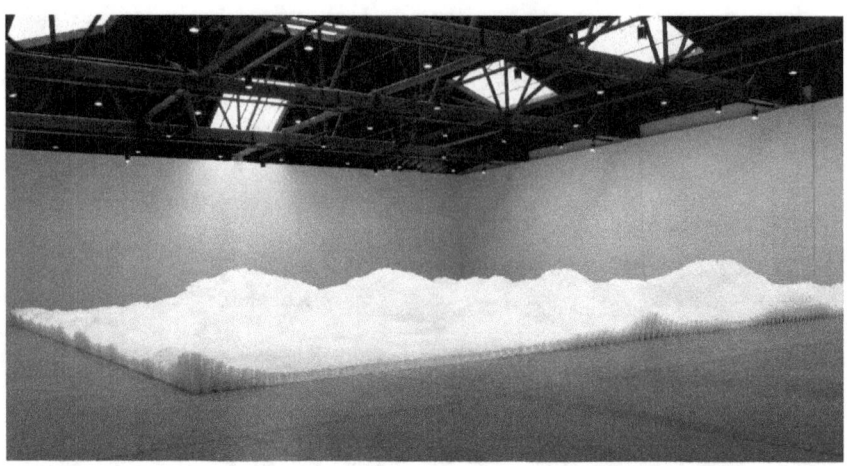

11.8. Tara Donovan, *Untitled (Plastic Cups)*, 2006, plastic cups, dimensions variable, ©Tara Donovan, courtesy Pace Gallery, photography by Ellen Labenski, courtesy Pace Gallery.

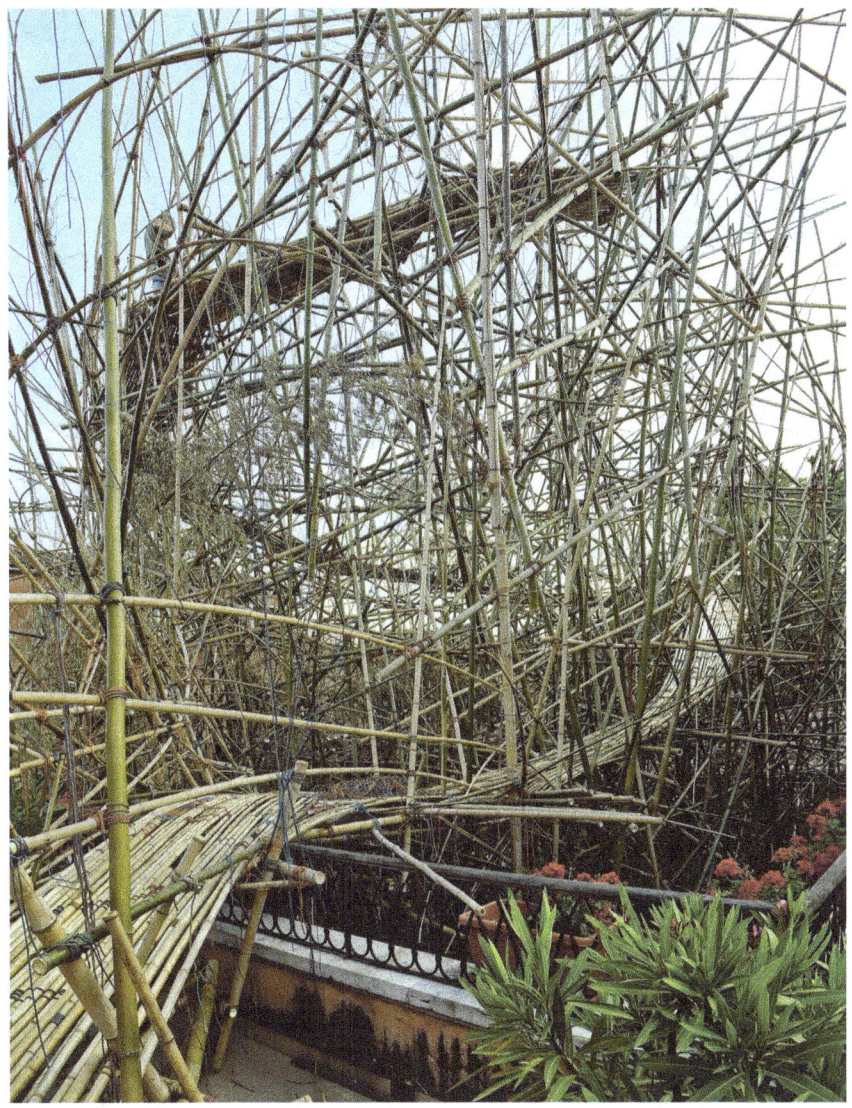

11.9. Mike and Doug Starn, *Big Bambú,* 2011, official collateral exhibition of the 54th Venice Biennale, Venice, Italy, ©Mike and Doug Starn, image courtesy of the artists.

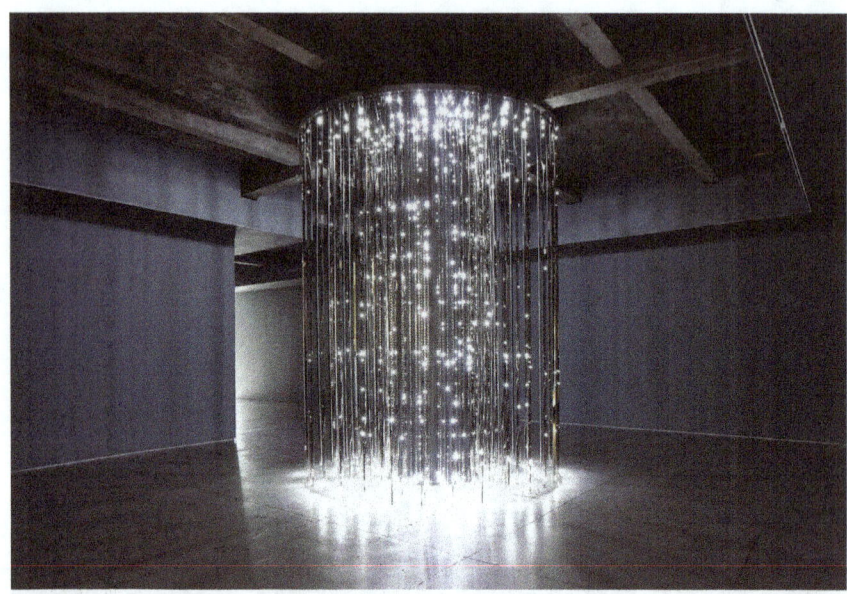

11.10. Leo Villareal, *Cylinder*, 2011, white LED's, mirror finish stainless steel, steel, custom software, electrical hardware, 21' x 9' x 9', Unique, ©Leo Villareal, Photo by James Ewing Photography; Image courtesy Sandra Gering Inc. New York.

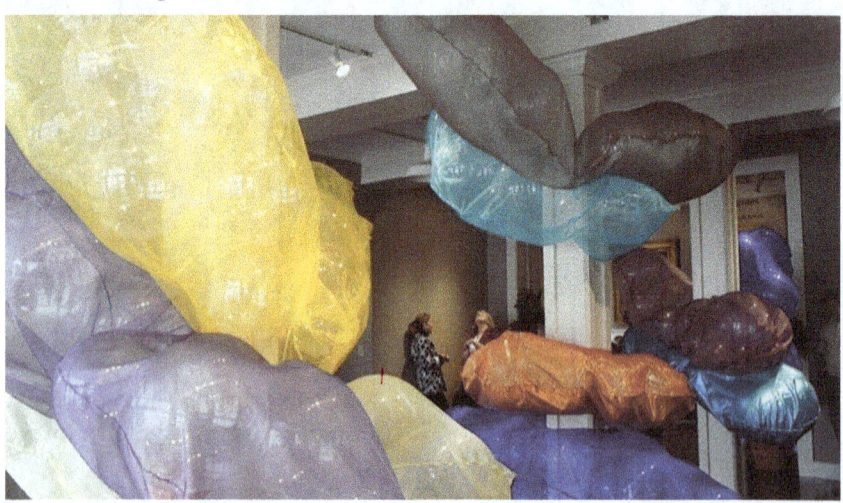

11.11. Suzanne Volmer, Installation View, *Clouds Captured*, 2011, fabric, Mylar, plastic, helium, custom mechanisms and electronics, kinetics, lighting and sound, ©Suzanne Volmer, photo credit: Joann Sherman, image courtesy of Suzanne Volmer.

12
Not Just Jesting: Art and the Fool

Bridget Lynch

"Tutto è follia in questo mondo fuorchè il folleggiare"
(Everything is folly in this world except to play the fool)[1]

Art and the fool have had a torrid affair for a very long time.[2] The fool appears in numerous artistic representations and is popular in theater, performance art, and literature. What is the realm of the fool in art history and contemporary practice? The themes of the fool include humor, the absurd, the grotesque, the folly of life, the sacred and profane, truth-telling to power, and the fool's outsider status.

The artist as fool, or the fool persona, creates works that are humorous, sublime, grotesque in form or content, incorporating low-tech, quirky materials and strategies such as performance and costume. This essay surveys some of the current practitioners of fool work and their historical and cross-cultural antecedents. I argue for the connection between fools, creativity, and social commentary.

Rachel Smith asserts that the power of humor is cross-cultural and insightful. Artists make use of its many idioms, which can be empowering, healing, insulting, or community building—all aspects of the fool. The story of art may undervalue the humorous tradition but artists do not. She notes that, increasingly, contemporary artists use humor to navigate our complex world by employing comedy, mischief, illusion, and trickster antics.[3]

Although the fool's varied roles of clown, trickster, idiot, innocent, and malevolent game-changer can be confusing at first blush, there are some factors in common. As Beatrice Otto points out, fools are transgressive, meaning they overstep the ordinary rules of propriety.[4] These outsider capabilities are what lend fools their powers, whether in the political, religious or creative realm.

"The ridiculous presupposes the sublime, and the sublime in princely graciousness permits the presence of the ridiculous." [5]

Cultural Roles of the Fool

The fool, in his various guises, has significance in many religions. One of the most common types of sacred being is the Trickster deity, who is present in such diverse worldviews as the Native American Coyote, Loki of Norse tradition, West Africa's Eshu-Elegba, the Greek Hermes, China's Monkey King, India's Krishna, and Japan's Fox Spirit. What is a trickster deity? They share a common taste for acting at crossroads, literal and metaphorical; asking questions that turn the discussion on its head; illusions; appetites of all sorts; and they often respond to situations in an ethically-ambiguous way. They may act as go-betweens or as psychopomps. Their conniving actions may stir up trouble. They may act as messengers, or they may turn the tables on the other gods and humans, but in each role Tricksters are expressive of their culture's cosmology. In ways reflective of these beliefs, they perform their inherently destabilizing actions. Whether they tend more to mayhem, sex, mockery, illusions, creativity or silliness depends upon the cultural function of the sacred being. The commonality is that they are constantly pushing the envelope of the expected. Their roles range from the wise to the ridiculous.

Krishna, the Hindu blue-skinned prince deity and an incarnation of Vishnu, presents many of the characteristics of the sacred trickster. As a precocious child, the baby Krishna steals butter from the larder, and his mother, Yasoda, is charmed by his lawyeristic defense: how could he steal when all in the house belongs to the family? A good trickster turns the argument around, re-contextualizing the issue at hand. Later, a sexualized Krishna plays the flute to beguile his milkmaids to join him under the trees, multiplying himself 16,000 times to fully satisfy each of his lovers during a night of song and dance. Krishna's erotic music of the night stirs maidens and married women alike.[6] The trickster often displays a voracious sexual appetite and disregard for standards of behavior.

Krishna, like other trickster deities is a shape-shifter, changing his appearance to facilitate his victories. Joseph Campbell relates how Krishna uses illusion in one of his exploits to best his cruel tyrant of an uncle, Kans. At a wrestling tournament each spectator saw Krishna differently—girls saw a lover, wrestlers saw a mighty athlete, and Kans, who had laid unsuccessful traps for him, saw him as *Mara* or Death. After his wrestling victories, Krishna bounded into the tyrant's box and killed him. He tells Kans's wives that life is a continuous circle of birth and death.[7]

Krishna has a double relationship with fooldom, as the image in Figure 1 suggests. As a prince, he keeps a fool, but as a trickster god, he has fool attributes himself. This bedroom scene shows the intimate connection between the two roles. The lavishly attired Krishna lightheartedly chats with a man on his doorstep who wears a conical jester cap, as does his own sniggering jester to the right of the bed. All three men have a lotus flower, which is associated with the *yoni* (vagina). His lover Radha waits, apparently gesturing for him to come to bed and stop his jesting (Fig. 1).

The Japanese Fox Spirit is capable of assuming human form, both male and female, and can be a malevolent or a helpful being. The Fox Spirit can bewitch or can cast an evil spell or trick an unsuspecting person. A beautiful girl can turn out to be the tricky Fox Spirit.[8] The Norse trickster god, Loki, is also a shape-shifter. He brings up an interesting question: What is the authentic self? Because if, as Lewis Hyde suggests, any form can be assumed, then Loki's mutability of form is like a series of masks, and raises the issue of who is wearing the mask.[9] Loki bridges the gods' world and that of their greatest enemies, the giants. Loki's father was a giant, consequently he is neither entirely god nor giant, and he marries a giantess so his children are also partially giant.[10] He is betwixt and between because of his outsider status in both groups.

Eshu-Elegba,[11] the trickster character of the African Yoruba society, is a gatekeeper of choice and chance. According to tradition, Eshu-Elegba can transform himself into a bird.[12] He can be invisible, can deceive by illusion, and is a magician who with his power can assist or harm both gods and men. John Pemberton tells us of his powers:

> ...Eshu mediates between the demonic and the creative, the powers of evil and the powers of good. He aids in minimizing the presence of death and in maximizing the possibilities of life. He has the knowledge of good and evil, and the wisdom and power to cope with such forces. He is Olodumare's own messenger, and shares in his power.[13]

Another important category of sacred fool is distinctly the opposite of the Trickster deity; this is the Innocent. The Innocent is too good for this world or any world—without guile, forgiving and generous. The Christian Jesus[14] fits into this category, as does the Buddha.

The historical Buddha, Siddhartha, was born a prince but when he became aware of the vast misery in the world, he left his palace and sought to ease the pain of Mankind. Enlightenment came after much meditation and he developed a teachable doctrine called the Eightfold Path. The teaching was predicated on the notion that the sorrows of the world arise from desire. By renouncing desire the human soul could escape the karmic cycle of rebirth necessary to atone for past actions. This code of moral conduct was not joined to reliance on ritual, but to the actions of the person willing to put aside their ego.[15] Later many sects of Buddhist creed and monastic orders developed; including the Zen style of meditative practice. The latter gave rise in the historical world to wise/simpleton Zen monks.

Tension between the sacred and the profane is inherent in the fool concept. It can be termed "the paradox of the fool." How can a fool be the most conniving *and* the most accepting? The Sacred Fool plays many roles: roisterer, trickster, sybarite, wise counselor, shape-shifter, bon vivant, and innocent; the unifying feature is that they share a non-normative worldview. They act as change agents. The fool crosses over the thresholds of order and chaos. This liminal ability is essential to the fool concept. Tricksters, jesters and sacred fools operate at the edges.

The trickster works in both illusion and truth.[16] Dustin Eaton argues that order and chaos are of the same coin.[17] Artists use tricksters as inspiration and emulate their destabilizing activities in their art. Contemporary artist Willie Cole materializes this concept with his mixed media installation *Elegba Principle* (1995).[18] It is a maze of doors for the participant to navigate. It visually embodies the notion of thresholds of chance and choice. This references the West African deity Eshu-Elegba, who traditionally stands at the threshold of decisions. "The Trickster is the eternal outsider, destroyer of boundaries and initiator into a new awareness."[19] Cole, a multidisciplinary artist, playfully examines the African-American experience with a wide variety of homely found and constructed materials. In common with trickster Eshu-Elegba, Cole's works are witty carriers of multiple meanings, obliging us to re-examine our assumptions.[20] The seemingly servile lawn jockey once indicated passage along the Underground Railroad for escaping slaves. Cole's juxtaposition of Africanized and Westernized jockeys visually grapples with the choices for slaves and their future paths.[21] Cole consciously examines power relationships. He sets up the intersection between the ostensibly powerless and the powerful, the subversive nature of the objects often creating an "aha moment" of reversal. This topsy-turvy reordering questions our commonplace perception of reality.

An illustration of trickery as a way to confront force occurs in the Hindu story of King Muchukunda, Krishna, and the attacking barbarian king. Krishna gets the best of the barbarian by illusionary means. Wearing flowers and unarmed, Krishna dashes into a cave just ahead of the barbarian enemy. The enemy follows and is insulted when he sees a relaxed, sleeping figure. He kicks the figure, rousing not Krishna, but the ancient King Muchukunda, who was granted rest by the Gods and as a corollary the means to annihilate anyone who wakened him, with his first glance. The beautiful, youthful Krishna's hoax wins the day and his enemy is reduced to ashes.[22] As in Cole's artwork, assumptions are overturned.

It is clear that many religious deities assume the role of trickster or innocent. On earth, their adherents also make use of the fool guise. Historical examples of the saintly innocent include the memorable Sufi fool, Mullah Nasrudin. In one story, Nasrudin let on that he was a saint, and when asked for a miracle he obliged by calling a tree to come to him. After the third ineffectual command, he walked over to the tree. When queried he said, "The saints and the prophets of God are neither proud nor blind; since the palm won't come to me, I'll go to the palm."[23]

The Japanese poet and Zen master, Taigu Ryokan, called the Great Fool, lived from 1758-1831. Ryokan was a mendicant monk, calligrapher and poet, eschewing monastery life.[24] He enjoyed himself uninhibitedly, as when he cross-dressed, dancing all night during the freewheeling Midsummer Festival.[25] He was deemed a simpleton because he functioned far from the world's concerns. During a tea ceremony, Ryokan drained the tea bowl, leaving none for the next guest, then seeing his mistake, he spat it back into the bowl and offered it to the guest.[26] His purity and lack of desires (positive attributes in the Buddhist religion) were remarkable. He shared his few possessions and food with any in need. There are many stories telling of Ryokan's generosity, to the point of idiocy. One time a thief broke into his hut, and as there was nothing to steal, the thief tugged on the bedding. Ryokan obligingly feigned sleep and allowed him to make off with it.[27] He was highly regarded for his creative gifts, but he made an irresistible target, for some, as a butt of pranks. Ryokan loved to laugh and tell stories despite his marginal existence. Both Nasrudin and Ryokan delighted in using jokes to make their teaching points.

Performance and the Fool

The saintly fool acts in this world, as does another member of the fool troop—that of the jester or professional clown. This type of fool is granted "license," meaning the ability to talk back to power. The jester, whether performing for the Chinese Emperor, the Shah or a European monarch, had the task not only of amusing the king but telling him what he didn't want to hear. It is widely documented that the Chinese court jester had a symbiotic relationship with the ruler and had license to speak freely and reform policy.[28] The fool can also act out a really stupid idea to the logical extension of its stupidity, perhaps hauling us back from the brink.[29] Otto maintains that one of the chief obligations of a fool to his overlord is to produce the *reductio ad absurdum* argument.

One story of *reductio ad absurdum* concerns how the court fool jested his emperor out of an embarrassing or dangerous idea. During the course of hunting, the Emperor Zhuangzong (reign: 923-926 CE) had trampled all over the fields. The local magistrate, protesting on the part of the peasants, was about to be executed for his temerity. The fool, Newly Polished Mirror, jumped in, shouting at the magistrate for his wrong-headedness. What was he thinking? The Son of Heaven loves to hunt; why should the peasants be allowed to plant fields and pay taxes, better that they starve and depopulate the area so hunting would be even better; Death to the magistrate! Leading a chorus of jesters chiming in, he begged the Emperor to grant his wish for the death of the magistrate. This absurdity set the ruler to laughing and the official was pardoned.[30]

The Chinese have an extensive history of fools who speak to power. However, their visual record is much less broad compared to that of the Western tradition.[31] Western art history has a plethora of artists who painted or sculpted the fool character. Some of the best known of an extensive list would be Pieter Bruegel, Hans Holbein, Diego Velasquez, Jacques Callot, Antoine Watteau, Gustave Dore, and Pablo Picasso. More recently, many artists in performative roles have assumed the fool character as part of their art. Some examples are Marcel Duchamp, Cindy Sherman, Eleanor Antin, Adrian Piper, the Yes Men, Paul McCarthy, and William Pope.L. The jester's truth-to-power performative characteristic is one that contemporary artists who work with the fool trope employ all of the time. They assume the role of the fool or clown because it allows for critique, satire, and the possibility of change.

The trickster confounds the usual approach, turning expectations upside down. The Yes Men artists, Andy Bichlbaum, and Mike Bonanno, supported by a number of helpers, are tricksters supreme. Their exploits address environmental, political and corporate crimes and greed. They use the *reductio ad absurdum* argument liberally. Their *modus operandi* is to disrupt board and trade meetings, and to use ridicule to embarrass the objects of their pranks. They have made brilliant use of their internet site, with interviews, video, and background on the companies or political entities they critique.[32] Their costumes and assumed identities are playful, yet their goals are completely serious. Or are they? The Yes Men movies have recorded their antics in action. Yet, we have to ask, "Who was running the camera? Why should we believe they really were at some particular trade meeting? Is the joke on the corporations or on us?" This is high-level trickster work.

Recent writers on aesthetics have engaged with the idea of art as drama. Richard Shusterman *defines* art as dramatization.[33] He contends that drama is a framing and a making of vivid experience.[34] Umberto Eco's concept of "ostentation" is similar.[35] David Osipovich discusses performance as not only separate from text, but also asserts its primacy over text. Each performance is contingent. He says "a live performance *as a whole* is, therefore, unscriptable because it is *as a whole* unrepeatable."[36] The co-experience between audience and performer generates a complicit alternative reality. This framing and audience agreement to this pretense are necessary conditions.[37] Performative fools such as the Yes Men or the Chinese court jesters act as conduits for this alternative reality to become apparent.

Performance artist William Pope.L, styles himself as *America's friendliest black artist*.[38] His art tackles many things: race, gender, class, and consumer society. His propensity for *not* meeting our expectations is part of the fool toolbox. Pope.L dresses-up, making it clear that he is creating a performance, during his "Superman" crawls (Fig. 2). His bespectacled non-hunky body wearing a superman suit is several notches below the non-threatening alter ego of the "real" superman, Clark Kent. Superman has super powers and flies; America's friendliest black artist crawls on his belly. Pope.L's *Great White Way* investigates the fools' progress through the quotidian world. Like armor donned before battle, his "Superman costume" identifies Pope.L as an intentional performer and sets up his "joke" as he scoots around at ground level down Broadway in NYC, or crawls along a train track like a suicidal Pauline in a fractured melodrama (Fig. 2).

Rachel Smith, writing on another work, notes that Pope.L overturns expectations of racial stereotyping in the video documentation of his Harlem performance *Member*, in which he wears a white, very large, phallic appendage, and a ridiculous cock's comb head covering of rubber.[39] Pope.L asks us, via this costume and performance, about our notions of sexual prowess and race.

This propensity of artist/fools and the historical jesters to wear costume is a device to set them apart from the ordinary. John Emigh, writing about traditional and ritual use of masked performance, argues that the mask can be more than just an attribute of an identity worn as a disguise (like Halloween), but can be a transformation.[40] The mask and costume of the performer may reveal meaning that the character is attempting to hide. This duality of knowingness for the audience is part of the pleasure.[41] Fools, in all their varieties, actively set up choices, and instigate, through their often contrary and paradoxical actions, a space for reflecting on what a society values. The fools' costumes, outlandish props and their performative nature, whether in paint or action, emphasize the transgression, fun, or topsy-turvy contradiction of the fool.

Pope.L places himself squarely at the tipping point of the fool's paradox. He is the weakling, foolish scapegoat, opening himself to ridicule, pity and possibly violence. At the same time that he smashes conventions of the stereotypical, physically powerful black male troublemaker, he is sowing doubt and dismay. He pierces the mythology of the black man's position and shows us the reality *vis á vis* white society. He baffles us with his gentle approach—the revolution, if it comes, arises from the viewer. Pope.L's revolution puns on the turning *wheel of fortune*. The king on top becomes the ass (fool) at the bottom—the wheel of fortune is never stable or still. Revolution is also transformative upheaval, but in both senses, it embodies change. This overturning of our received notions of roles opens the possibilities of reversal—the wheel may revolve again and our place in it change.

Fools stand apart, and as such, question business as usual. They may be perceived as scapegoats or troublemakers, wise or idiotic. The fool is *always* on the outside, never part of the inside track; but this outsider stance is the heart of the fool's power.

"Sultorum Plena Sunt Omnia"
(Fools Are Everywhere)[42]

The Political, Literary and Artistic Roles of the Fool

Praise of Folly was written by Erasmus of Rotterdam. It turned into the Humanist bestseller of 1511 among the literati and scholars of Europe, acting as a critique of society in crisis. Its jocular framework was contrived to circumvent the Inquisition. Erasmus, one of the most influential thinkers of his day, wrote *Praise* for his friend Thomas More (it was illustrated by Hans Holbein). Erasmus creates a pseudo Greek goddess, Folly, personifying foolishness. He analyzes human nature through the lens of Folly, and gives biting satirical critique of the Catholic Church, carefully couched in allegory. Goddess Folly avows,

> But, someone may say, the ears of princes are strangers to truth, and for this reason they avoid those wise men, because they fear lest someone more frank than the rest should dare to speak to them things rather true than pleasant; for so the matter is, that they don't much care for truths. And yet this is found by experience among my fools, that not only truths but even open reproaches are heard with pleasure; so that the capital crime, spoken by a fool is received with delight. For truth carries with it a certain peculiar power of pleasing, if no accident fall in to give occasion of offense; which faculty the gods have given only to fools.[43]

Holbein's fool (Fig. 3), is appareled in the traditional ass-eared cap, tipped with bells (he is an ass). The rooster crest coxcomb refers to his sexual appetite and to his inability to keep quiet (he crows). He holds a ball in his left hand, which could be a juggling ball, but is more likely an allusion to the world.

Four hundred and fifty years later, Mikhail Bakhtin, a Russian scholar, wrote critically and influentially on the cultural necessity and functions of fool behavior. He coined the word "carnivalesque," which, roughly speaking, means *of the marketplace*. The internet or the Boston Common function as contemporary examples of the carnivalesque, as they are places of intersection between all sorts of people and their assumptions. This crossroads quality of the marketplace is what Bakhtin finds so compelling. It is place of chance, where order has a hard time asserting itself, is in fact a perfect recipe for fools to prevail.

Bakhtin, writing under the repressive gaze of the Soviet Union, illuminates this concept in his influential book, *Rabelais and His World*.[44] François Rabelais was a sixteenth-century French writer who created the monstrous fool, Gargantua, who had numerous grotesque, sexual, gustatory, and scatological adventures. Rabelais was trying to destroy the official picture of events and Bakhtin permits us to see how this transgressive stance towards power nurtures and educates the societal imagination.[45] Although Bakhtin's topic is ostensibly about Rabelais, and discusses the decline of freedom in the Renaissance with the tightening of mores on speech and body,[46] it functions as its own Rabelaisian poke in the eye to Soviet authority. Bakhtin posits that the gauge of a society's freedom is its capacity to allow the carnivalesque. He asserts that the spirit of carnival is the absurd and the gross, exemplifying a struggle with entrenched power (the Church in the Renaissance, the Soviet state in Bakhtin's time).

Bakhtin delves into the history of medieval feasts, *soties* (fool societies), carnival, and feasts of fools, showing us that performance (action) is certainly not new. These events had a commonality of hierarchy upended. From the late fifteenth until the late sixteenth century the fool societies produced "entertainments" that often combined biting social and political commentary. Their themes turned on the notion that fools are infinite in number. Furthermore, their stock characters were often in "search" of *Roger Bon Temps* (Roger Good Times), a character who never quite shows up. Humor, parody, and satire are an important part of societal self-examination. Bakhtin suggests that Bruegel and Bosch, as painters of the grotesque, ably express the sheer bodily-ness of the cycle of life—decay that begets green growth.[47] Without folk culture's wayward laughter and expressive outlet of carnival, society gets out-of-whack. Laughter, mockery, and low humor (scatological, abusive language) create an "inside out" moment for equality to triumph over hierarchy. Pieter Bruegel the Elder's images of Carnival depict tension and ridiculousness, illustrating what Bakhtin calls the logic of "inside out." The fool embodies the spirit of the carnivalesque. Many artists have dealt with this idea of the world turned upside-down, such as Bruegel's early European example *Land of Cockaigne,* of 1567.

Philosopher Susanne Langer aptly contends in her essay, *The Cultural Importance of Art,* that Art is ubiquitous across cultures and time.[48] Art is a distinctly human activity and it is not a luxury add-on. It is an education in what may be. She argues that art is a non-verbal way to formulate feelings and emotions for understanding. She says art is not religion, or morals, or science or philosophy.[49] Art gives form to imagination. The fool too, works on the imagination, offering possibilities. The folly of life is part of the fool conundrum. Life is a continual death; the clown or jester lives exuberantly, acting as an antidote to death. Playful release is the flipside of the notion of *Vanitas,* and *Mono-no-aware,* a Japanese term for the melancholy awareness of the transience of life.

Figure 4 shows an image by the author of a fool, wearing a cracked-egg cap (an egghead) and reading a book while a bluebird sings bravely into the dark. It is meant to call to mind the fragility of knowledge as well as its pleasure, and mocks our pretension to make progress against the dark. The figure wears a costume that references a flower, the intermediate step between seed and fruit, delicate and innocent.

The clownish fool has an important role politically. Lawrence Mintz connects stand-up comedy with older traditions of jesting. Joke telling is a liminal activity in that it creates communal reflection on what is joke-worthy. [50] A joke-telling, perhaps politically incorrect or low-humored fool might be called the disrupter, and his task is to serve as an escape valve for society, functioning at the edges, making apparent the social and cultural choices of a society and by extension opening the door to change. The context of a joke is part of its impact (who tells it and when). Levity operates at a tipping point of change/no change with regard to society's values, acting as a barometer of what is conventional or shocking. The fool's upending of social roles spans cultures and time.

The historical fool was often an outsider physically or mentally. Many depictions of fools trade on the appeal of the different. Erika

Tietze-Conrat, in *Dwarves and Jesters in Art,* makes the case that this outsider status, whether there is assumed mental feebleness or not, allowed the ruler's other half—the jester—to operate as a strange sort of doppelgänger for the king and allowed a fraternal feeling and freedom of expression not granted to other members of the court.[51] Analogous to the capped- and belled fools or the latter day Harlequins and the Jack Puddings in eighteenth-century England, the fools' role allows license to satirize. Fools are theatrical and mock the foibles of society.[52] Silent film stars like shabby Chaplin or sad-sack Keaton not only entertained but also critiqued as they so ably took up the fool's scepter.[53]

The contemporary artist Paul McCarthy is a trickster and videographer. McCarthy uses masks in his work, playfully allowing them to disarm or repel, creeping up on us with his concerns about the American predilection for excess, inherent in his signature operatic style. His calculated impersonations are grotesque and awkward. The fool often occupies this uncomfortable place. McCarthy's 1995 work, *The Painter,* makes use of masks and gross humor. His 2002 *WGG test* uses buckets of fake blood in an enactment of a chicks-gone-bad flick. The grossness of the over-the-top bloody scenes is leavened by the clearly fake nature of the victim's pain and the blood, as well as by views of the second cameraperson. He tells us:

> In my work there's a kind of theatre…There were pieces that I made in the early '70's…where you don't represent getting shot, you actually get shot. That definition of performance as reality—as concrete—became less interesting to me. I became more interested in *mimicking, appropriation, fiction and representation and questioning meaning* [italics mine].[54]

Fools mimic reality, but by their very representation of it, they distort it. Their mocking sets up questions as to what is normative. McCarthy is more than willing to cloak himself in foolishness. His awkward, grotesque, costumed performances are the "setting apart" that Shusterman defines as art. McCarthy's performances are the fool's invitation to an alternative reality, providing the opportunity to understand what a society values.

To my mind, a little razzle-dazzle is a wonderful tool for commenting on societal mores that many already decry. This would be repetitive unless one can invite the viewer into a construct that frames ideas freshly; satire and allegory are tools to this end. Ellen Leyburn links satire and allegory, saying, "First of all, they are both modes of indirection, of other-speaking."[55] The necessity of aesthetic distance operates within satire. The mirror of satire reflects, but somehow the viewer does not see himself.[56] This sidestep, done aesthetically and with finesse, overcomes the repugnance of the message. Allegory allows for indirectly stating the terms of reality. Further, Leyburn argues that harsh aesthetic realism may not be the only way to understand or feel events.[57] The ironic knowledge of the allegorical fable with its sharp edge is why we like it, however, the best tales do not proselytize but are open-ended for the viewer to resolve or question.[58]

Because of the versatile nature of the fool, his capacity for grabbing chance and acting as a catalyst for change, the fool character shows up frequently in literary sources. These in turn often act as inspiration for films and videos. Familiar stories allow artists to approach social critique sideways, using the literary canon to carry the weight, as Bakhtin did using Rabelais. In Western literature, it is difficult to get more canonical than William Shakespeare.[59] Many artists have been attracted to his themes, using his plays to discuss tyranny, hubris, and the hierarchies of power. Shakespeare's own treatment of power walks a fine line. Within his dramas he explores wise fools and foolish monarchs (*Lear, Henry IV*) along with swift falls from Olympian heights (*Macbeth, Richard III, Julius Caesar*). Both his tragedies and his comedies feature fools of all varieties. Many of his plays sanction the audience to consider good government versus tyranny; this had to be cleverly accomplished amidst the age of the absolute monarch.

Grigori Kozintsev used his film *King Lear* (1971) to discourse on the totalitarianism of the Soviet state. He employed for his translation/screenplay the poet Boris Pasternak, and as the composer, Dmitri Shostakovich. All three artists were enthusiastically acclaimed in the early days of the Soviet Revolution and had set about creating a new language of art. After Stalinization, artists found it extremely unhealthy to continue challenging societal hierarchy. Artists either went underground or conformed. *Lear* is a tightrope journey for these three artists. Using spare poetry and even sparer musical motifs, the setting is a post-apocalypse landscape. The poisoning of the state is not from outside—an enemy hasn't wreaked havoc. It is in fact, the state itself and its people that are responsible.[60] Through this bitter play of blindness, self-delusion and reversals of fortune, Lear's Fool acts as a Greek chorus to the action. He stingingly tells the truth throughout it all, yet is heroically loyal. His capers and witticisms are of the folk marketplace, the carnivalesque that Bakhtin lays bare for us. Kozintsev's film *Lear* is a self-induced horror; all honor lost, and not from an outside defeat but from the enemy within.

Pasternak severely shortened the dialogue into a distilled intensity. Cinematically, Kozinstev utilizes "space as a dramatic gesture."[61] Lear and his Fool traverse vast spaces of a blasted kingdom, indicative, as from a medievalist's viewpoint, that exterior appearance reflects the soul. The state is Lear. The Fool is his reasoning side, the little voice within that can still see clearly.

> Fool: I marvel what kin thou and thy daughters are. They'll have me whipp'd for speaking true; thou'lt have me whipp'd for lying; and sometimes I am whipp'd for holding my peace. I had rather be any kind o' thing than a fool! And yet I would not be thee, nuncle. Thou has pared thy wit o' both sides and left nothing i' the middle.[62]

The fool hasn't an easy task and is everybody's whipping boy. It isn't just in *Lear* that the fool dies because of his loyalty. The fool of Chinese Emperor Liezu of the Southern Tang (reign: 961-76), Gradually Stretching Taller, gave his life for his Emperor and solved a tricky political situation. The Emperor had poisoned wine meant for his minister, Zhou Ben, who, suspicious, took both cups and mixed them, then presented them to the Emperor for a toast to amity and unity. The jester (who was in the know, like many of the horrified court) jokingly grabbed both cups and drained them off, then rushed from the room. Despite the Emperor's medics' best efforts, his brain burst from the poison.[63]

The performative or literary fool entertains and questions. Hu-

mor, grotesquery and surprise are devices to confound expectations. Rene Descartes, in *Passions of the Soul*, enumerates the passions and the "order in which they may thus be found." *Wonder*,
he declares, is the first of the passions. He states that something
different, whether we find it agreeable or no, excites and surprises
us, and has no opposing passion, for the opposite of surprise is not
a passion.[64] As Umberto Eco explains, the idea of the grotesque is
constantly being revised, as each generation's shock-response to
lewdness, body parts or degeneracy becomes passé.[65] Geoffrey
Harpham, in *The Grotesque: First Principles*, clarifies the close connection of the form of the grotesque and response to the grotesque.
To recognize the grotesque, three of four conditions must be met.
He, like Descartes, declares *astonishment* as the essential; of the other
three choices—laughter, disgust, or horror—two must be present.[66]

Jacques de Gheyn's grotesque print features three lewd fools
in a row (Fig. 5). The one on the left is dressed like a woman, and
wears the traditional ass-eared and coxcomb cap of a fool. The
shoes, sleeves and cap have decorative bells. She (?), her left hand
holding a fool's bauble (that perversion of a king's scepter, which
also mirrors her own costume), has her arms around the central figure, who wears an old-man mask and a feathered cap. The middle
figure's large purse slung on his belt draws attention to his crotch
and an ambiguous phallic proturberance. The third figure has a
grip on the central figure's left hand. Apparently facing us, the figure is actually wearing a dog-like animal mask on the back of his
head and has his doublet on backwards. A bird's head and neck (a
cock) juts from his rear, nudging up against the buttocks of the central figure. This third figure neatly captures the waywardness of the
fool. The trio's rambunctious circling dance, outlandish outfits, and
frankly lustful interactions still have the power to astonish.

The movies of Jan Svankmajer, a Czech filmmaker, puppeteer,
and animator, definitely elicit wonder, humor, disgust and horror.
He converges moving image and sculpture. His interest in the absurd and the political unites with his fascination for the grotesque.
Svankmajer's films frequently are based on traditional stories that
utilize these forms. His *Alice* of 1988 is a recounting of Lewis Carroll's stories, and it, like the stories, is rife with inside-out logic.
Faust (1994) is a *tour de force* telling of Faust's pact-with-the-devil

story, a favorite from Marlowe to Goethe to the silent film by F.W. Murnau. Svankmajer's version takes place in our contemporary world, which intersects with a bizarre, theatrical puppet-version of reality. His jesting devils that are life-size puppets dangling from strings are a visual joke on free will. *Faust* is a story of temptation and hubris, the very meat and drink of a trickster deity, who will set up situations for mortals to encounter that they rarely can resist. Trickster deities, such as the Devil in *Faust*, get their jollies from mortals' weaknesses. Trickster Deities are unstable, amoral characters, and may help or intentionally harm the human that crosses their path.

Svankmajer's *Lunacy* (2005) mingles Marquis de Sade and Edgar Allen Poe stories to create an astonishing film of reversals, including our understanding of time. The protagonist is a simpleton, a fool with more compassion than sense. His journey from innocence to experience is filled with inversions of fortune. The film reveals the human condition in all its absurdity. It also alludes to the inside/outside position of the fool. Svankmajer's protagonist voluntarily enters a mental asylum from charitable motives (albeit tinged by lust), but is he really an inmate? He mounts an insurrection against what he perceives to be the power structure, only to find his perception was flawed, and an even more brutal structure takes command. The film revels in depicting the deep cruelty that humans inflict upon each other. Svankmajer is not only an observer of humanity in all its flavors, but is most decidedly a political commentator. *Lunacy,* with its mind-bending traversals between the twenty-first and the eighteenth centuries, manages to comment on both freebooting capitalism and the mother state that infantilizes her citizens.

Svankmajer's performing objects are funny and horrible—in short, grotesque. They also surprise and delight us with their inventive usage. Monroe Beardsley, in *The Instrumentalist Theory of Aesthetic Value,* describes aesthetic objects as "objects *manqués"*[sic]. By this he means that they aren't quite real or present. They call forth reality of experience but it is a make-believe contemplation.[67] Svankmajer's puppets exemplify Beardsley's idea—they are not real people, yet they allow us to contemplate reality. His charmingly magical objects employ all the tools of the performing jester. This power of his objects to imaginatively assert their existence returns us to Susanne Langer's claim of the ability of art to extend, via our imagination, our experience. Svankmajer's use of his puppets and performing objects relies on our ability to accept his conventions within the framework of the film, to "suspend belief." Further, Svankmajer knowingly mines the fool trove for humor, wonder, grotesqueness, and transgression. Whether his protagonist is an innocent (*Lunacy*) or a jaded cynic (*Faust*), their journeys are outside the common experience. They possess the essential condition of the fool, that of being an outsider. This is in fact what allows the fool to operate, to question what is normative, what might be in need of change. Without self-questioning, a society cannot renew or affirm itself.

An excellent literary example of the use of absurdity to explore human nature is Miguel de Cervantes' *Don Quixote,* written in the early years of the seventeenth century. It is synonymous with the ridiculous quest or action. His hyper-honor-conscious gentleman-hero and his earthy servant make us laugh, but their actions were uncomfortably close to the Spanish social issues of the day. Cervantes' book is actually a searing commentary on a society falling into disarray and decline.[68] Herman Melville's novel, *The Confidence Man,* exemplifies the fool's shifting point of view and his revolutionary ability of self-change and re-identification. The book never allows us to get comfortable; our confidence in what the story means and who is telling it is constantly under assault. Melville employs the device of an unreliable narrator, and maintains an amoral, non-judgmental stance concerning the various characters' choices.[69] *The Confidence Man* is a slippery work, Peter Bellis maintains, as its very structure, with its multiple narratives, unreliable viewpoints and a succession of tricksters, quacks and suspect do-gooders "reaches outward toward its readers, challenging those who think self-knowledge—and knowledge in general—too easy or secure."[70]

Fools as Creative Beings

The recognition of fools and artists as extenders of our possibilities is very old. As Enid Welsford informs us, "The Fool is a creator not of beauty but of spiritual freedom."[71] During the seventh to the ninth centuries in Ireland there was an official "Arch-poet and Fool" of all Ireland. The poets were thought to have powers as seers and magicians, and were glorified as "scientists." Artists and musicians also qualified for the post, as did fools, buffoons, and lunatics.[72]

Fool deities and jesters have had a secure place in human cultural history. Rachel Smith notes that, as the world changes, we increasingly need a lens for understanding similarities and differences of all sorts. The very seriousness of this challenge has created a chance for artists to seize a fool moment — to upend expectations. This reversal allows the comic, the illusionist and the trickster an opportunity to connect with their audience.[73]

Fool characters are as malleable as Melville's *Confidence Man*, and travel, *à là* Svankmajer's *Lunacy* protagonist, from innocence to experience. They are wise, profane, sacred, and stupidly funny. The fool is a paradox, illuminating the volatility of identity. The Freudian *id* meets *politesse* as the ritual of comedy allows both a synthesis and a meeting ground.[74] The fool is a force for joining of light and dark, chaos and order, a conduit for a conscious universe.[75] The fool and the artist are change agents. Going past the boundary of the ordinary, they point out the possibilities for renewal or for destruction, and remind us that life is fleeting.

Tilting at windmills is the role of the fool. The fool can be uncool, an outsider, someone we do not really want to be. We can ridicule her or pity her. We can also join in with her wild abandon in the deconstruction of reality. The fool or trickster embodies instability. Many artists play with this volatile dynamic energy. Artists, like fools, do not exist in a vacuum. They reflect, distort, and modify reality by the very practice of their art.

End Notes

[1] Beatrice K. Otto, *Fools are Everywhere* (Chicago: University of Chicago Press. 2001), 31. Quote from Giacomo Leopardi, from *Zibaldone*.

[2] My heartfelt thanks to Jim Stark.

[3] Rachel Smith, *Humor Me — Exhibition Catalogue Essay* (Kansas City, MO: H & R Block Art Space at the KC Art Institute, 2006), 2.

⁴ Beatrice Otto, "Fools are Everywhere," *History Today* vol. 51, no. 6. (2001): 36.

⁵ Wolfgang Zucker, "The Image of the Clown", *The Journal of Aesthetics and Art Criticism* vol. 55, no. 3 (1954): 317. Published by: Blackwell Publishing on behalf of The American Society for Aesthetics Stable.

⁶ Lewis Hyde, *Trickster Makes This World—Mischief, Myth, and Art* (New York: Northpoint Press, 1998), 284-285.

⁷ Joseph Campbell, *Hero with a Thousand Faces* (NY: Meridan Books, 1971), 350-352.

⁸ Ivan Morris, *The World of the Shining Prince—Court Life in Ancient Japan* (Baltimore: Penguin-Peregrine Books, 1969), 143.

⁹ Hyde, 53.

¹⁰ Hyde, 96, 97.

¹¹ John Pemberton, "Eshu-Elegba: The Yoruba Trickster God", *African Arts.* 9, No. 1 (Oct., 1975), Published by: UCLA James S. Coleman African Studies Center. The African deity Eshu is petitioned and offerings are made for successful trade, childbirth, illness, safety from witches and robbers. Flute playing is a common motif with Eshu, 22. "...for like Hermes, Eshu, the magician and trickster, is also the herald of the gods, the divine messenger." His herald status is sacred , 27. (Interestingly the flute motif is also associated with Krishna, but more in the way of sexual blandishment, and much Eshu imagery is distinctly sexual, as many tricksters are also associated with sexual prowess. Additionally they are associated with creativity, as in Hermes' invention of the lyre).

¹² Pemberton, 26.

¹³ Pemberton, 27. Olodumare is the chief god.

¹⁴ Barbara Swain, *Fools and Folly—During the Middle Ages and the Renaissance* (NY: Columbia University Press, 1932), Chapter three, "The Fool Triumphs," is largely an investigation of the type of humble fool that seeks to live in imitation of Jesus. Church fathers such as Paul, Jerome, Augustine, Ambrose and Gregory the Great extol the living of the innocent and pure life. Gregory writes, (originally in Latin): "The wisdom of the world, is to conceal the truth of one's heart by trickery, to veil one's meaning in words to make those things that are false to appear true, to present the truth as falsehood. This prudence is known and practiced by our youth, it is taught to our children as a thing of great value, those who understand it look proudly down upon everyone else...But on the other hand the wisdom of the just is to make no pretences for show, to make one's meaning by one's words, to pursue those things that are true, to shun the false, to do good deeds gladly, to bear evil more willingly than to do it, to seek no revenge for injury, to consider it a gain to sustain scorn for the truth. But this simplicity of the just is laughed to scorn, for worldly wise men believe

the virtue of purity to be foolish…For what seems more foolish to the world than…to pray for those who slander one, to seek poverty, to give up one's possessions, not to resist one who seeks to rob one, to turn the other cheek to him who strikes?" Swain, 36-37.

[15] Benjamin Rowland, *The Art and Architecture of India — Buddhist — Hindu — Jain* (Baltimore: Penguin Book, 1953, revised 1967), 53-55.

[16] Dustin Eaton, "Tools of the Trickster's Trade," *Parabola* vol. 28 No. 4 (Winter 2003), 12.

[17] Eaton, 14.

[18] Youtube video: A maze of revolving doors by artist Willie Cole with an original soundtrack also composed by the artist. http://www.youtube.com/watch?v=zw9CPDwiWcg

[19] Eaton, 12.

[20] Jean Borgatti, "Willie Cole's Africa Remix — Trickster and "Tribe," *African Arts* (Summer 2009), 16.

[21] Borgatti, 17.

[22] Campbell, 193-196.

[23] Otto, 173.

[24] Ryuichi Abé, and Peter Haskel, translators and essayists. *Great Fool — Zen Master Ryokan: Poems Letters and Other Writings* (Honolulu: University of Hawai'i Press, 1996), 203, 208. Ryokan's *waka* style poems written in the *kana* syllabary are distillations of mood or philosophical ideas. Example 1. *Playing ball With the children in this Village Spring day, never let the shadows fall!* Example 2. *Clouds billow upward Skies are clear I go out to beg And receive heaven's gifts.*

[25] *Great Fool — Zen Master Ryokan*, 102.

[26] *Great Fool — Zen Master Ryokan*, 101.

[27] *Great Fool — Zen Master Ryokan*, 104.

[28] Otto, 130.

[29] Otto, 127.

[30] Otto, 129.

[31] Otto, xix.

[32] The Yes Men. http://theyesmen.org/ http://theyesmen.org/hijinks Quoting from their website: http://www.dowethics.com/risk/index.html#ARC concerning their appearance in London at the Dow Chemical board meeting of 2005: [Acceptable Risk™ and the ARC] "were launched on April 28, 2005 at the International Payments 2005 conference, London, in solemn commemoration of the April 30 anniversary of the withdrawal of troops from Vietnam. Dow owes a debt of gratitude to the people of Vietnam for helping Dow define the limits of Acceptable Risk™. Dow's contribution to the War effort was very profitable, and recent appeals for damages by Vietnamese people who received coatings of special Dow

herbicides were rejected by US courts two weeks ago, proving the Dow adage: 'A skeleton in the closet is quite often golden'." See: http://www. dowethics.com/risk/launch.html for more information. This is typical Yes Men prank territory—pretending to be spokesmen for the company or entity they wish to embarrass.

[33] Richard Shusterman, "Art as Dramatization": *Journal of Aesthetics & Art Criticism*, 59 No 4 September 2001, 364.

[34] Shusterman, 368.

[35] Marvin Carlson, *Performance: A Critical Introduction*, 2nd edition (NYC, London: Routledge, 2004), 37.

[36] David Osipovich, "What is a Theatrical Performance?": *Journal of Aesthetics and Art Criticism*. 64, No 4, Fall 2006, 464.

[37] Osipovich, 465.

[38] Patricia C. Phillips, "An Opportunity: The Miss Black Factory Contest" *Art Journal*, 64 no. 1 (Spring 2005): 60.

[39] Smith, 5-6.

[40] John Emigh, *Masked Performance—The Play of Self and Other in Ritual and Theatre* (Philadelphia: UPenn Press, 1996), 22.

[41] Emigh, 28.

[42] Otto, 233.

[43] Desiderius, Erasmus, *In Praise of Folly*, trans. John Wilson of 1668 edition of the 1509 work in Latin called: *Encomium Moriae*. ed. T.N.R.Rogers (Mineola NY: Dover, 2003), 29.

[44] Mikhail Bakhtin, *Rabelais and His World*, trans. Hélène Iswolsky, *Tvprchestvo Fransua Rable* 1965 (Bloomington and Indianapolis: Indiana University Press. 1984).

[45] Bakhtin, 473, 474.

[46] Bakhtin, Michael Holquist, *Prologue: Rabelais*, xxi.

[47] Bakhtin, 27.

[48] Susanne K. Langer, *The Cultural Importance of Art: Philosophical Sketches* (Baltimore: John Hopkins Press, 1962), 89.

[49] Langer, 91.

[50] Lawrence Mintz, "Standup Comedy as Social and Cultural Mediation," *American Quarterly* vol. 37, no. 1 (Spring 1985) Special Issue: "American Humor" (The Johns Hopkins University Press), 73.

[51] Erika Tietze-Conrat, *Dwarves and Jesters in Art* (NY: Phaidon Publishers, 1957).

[52] Sandra Billington, *A Social History of the Fool* (NY: St. Martin's Press, 1984), 62.

[53] Billington, 123.

[54] Timothy Hyman and Roger Malbert, *Carnivalesque*, Touring Exhibition Catalogue (London: Hayward Gallery Publishing, 2000), 94.

[55] Ellen Douglass Leyburn, "Notes on Satire and Allegory," *The Journal of Aesthetics and Art Criticism* vol. 6, no. 4 (June 1948), 323.

[56] Leyburn, 324.

[57] Leyburn, 325.

[58] Leyburn, 327.

[59] Peter Sellars, Interview on Kozintsev and soviet film-making. Sellars is a writer, opera and theatrical producer (Chicago: Produced on DVD by Facets Video www.facets.org 2006). He discusses the use of the literary canon as an essential tool of the artist under an authoritarian regime (Facets video Interview).

[60] Sellars, Interview 2006.

[61] Sellars, Interview 2006.

[62] William Shakespeare, *Sixteen Plays of Shakespeare: The Tragedy of King Lear*, ed. George Lyman Kittredge (Boston: Ginn and Company, the Atheneum Press, 1946), Act 1, Scene 4, lines 198-206.

[63] Otto, 60.

[64] René Descartes, *The Philosophical Works of Descartes — Two Volumes: The Passions of the Soul*, trans. by Elizabeth S. Haldane, Elizabeth S. and G.R.T. Ross (Mineola, NY: Dover Publications, 1955), 358.

[65] Umberto Eco, *On Ugliness,* trans. Alastair McEwen (NY: Rizzoli International Publications, 2007), Chapter 5.

[66] Geoffrey Harpham, "The Grotesque: First Principles," *The Journal of Aesthetics and Art Criticism* vol. 34, no. 4 (Summer, 1976), 264.

[67] Monroe C. Beardsley, "The Instrumentalist Theory of Aesthetic Value," *Introductory Readings in Aethetics,* ed. John Hospers (NYC: The Free Press, 1969), 313.

[68] Miguel de Cervantes Saaverdra, *Don Quiote of La Mancha,* trans, by Walter Starkie (NY: Signet Classic from New American Library, 1964).

[69] Herman Melville, *The Confidence Man*, first edition 1857 (NY: Modern Library, Random House, 2003) intro. John Bryant.

[70] Peter J. Bellis, "Melville's Confidence-Man: An Uncharitable Interpretation," *American Literature* vol. 59, no. 4 (December 1987), 548-569.

[71] Enid Welsford, *The Fool — His Sacred and Literary History* (Gloucester, MA: Peter Smith Publishers, 1966), 336.

[72] Welsford, 101-103.

[73] Smith, 2.

[74] Mintz, 77.

[75] William Willeford, *The Fool and his Scepter* (Evanston, IL: Northwestern University Press, 1969), 103.

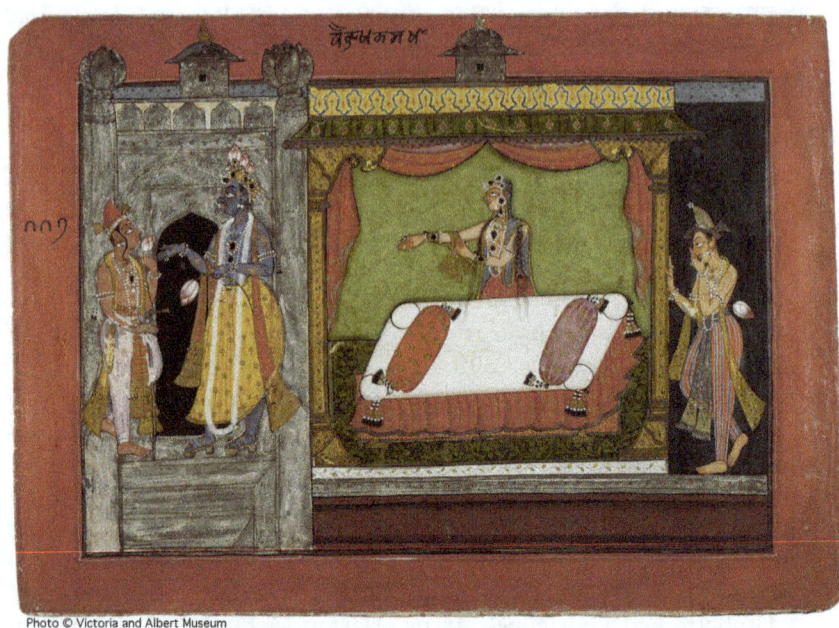

12.1. Unknown artist, India (Basohli), *Krishna and the Jester*, ca. 1660, 230 mm (including border) x 325 mm (including border), photo ©Victoria and Albert Museum, London.

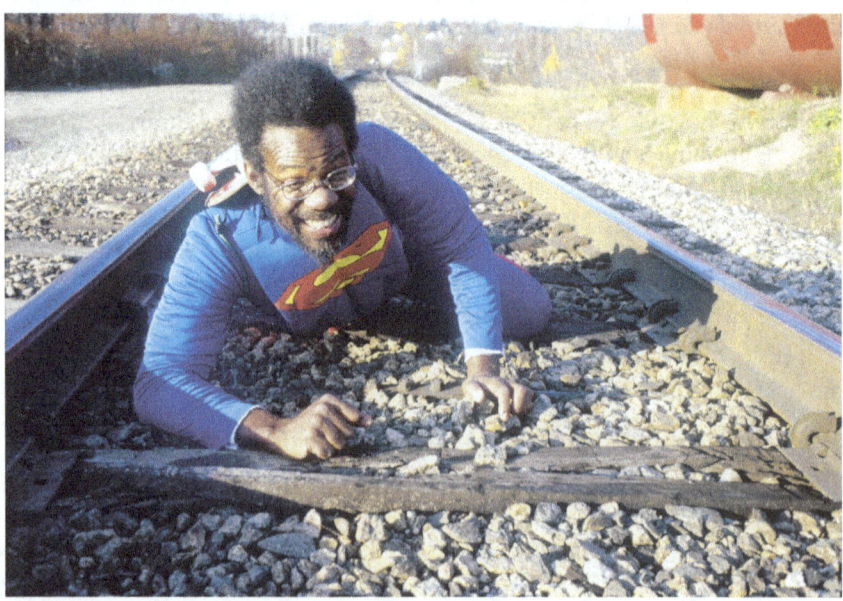

12.2. William Pope.L, *Training Crawl (for The Great White Way, 22 miles, 5 years, 1 street)*, 2001, performance documentation, Lewiston, Maine, © William Pope.L, photo credit: Luc Demers.

12.3. Hans Holbein the Younger *Fool with Coxcomb*, 1515, illustration for *Praise of Folly* by Desiderius Erasmus.

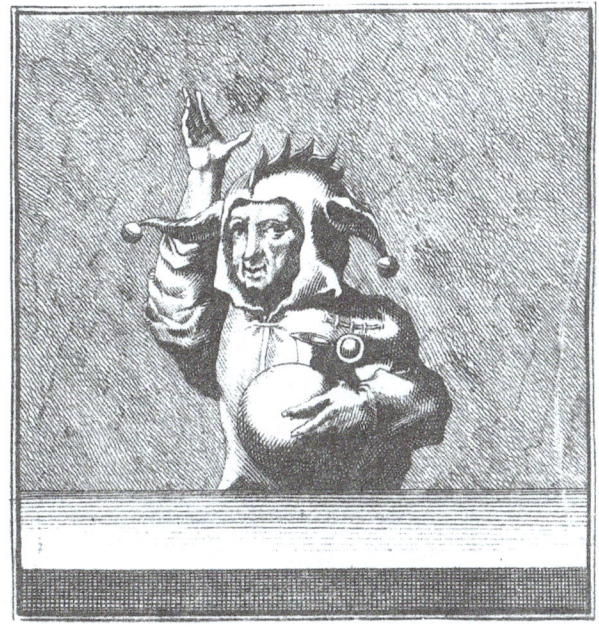

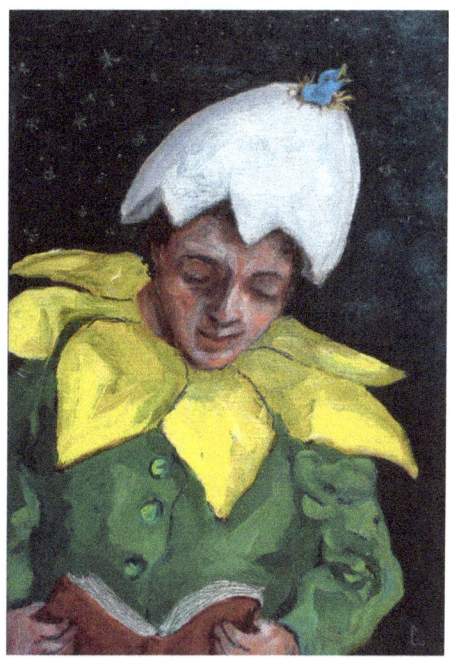

12.4. B. Lynch, *Imagine That*, 2005, oil on panel, 8 1/2" x 5 3/4", © B.Lynch, photo credit: author.

© B. Lynch

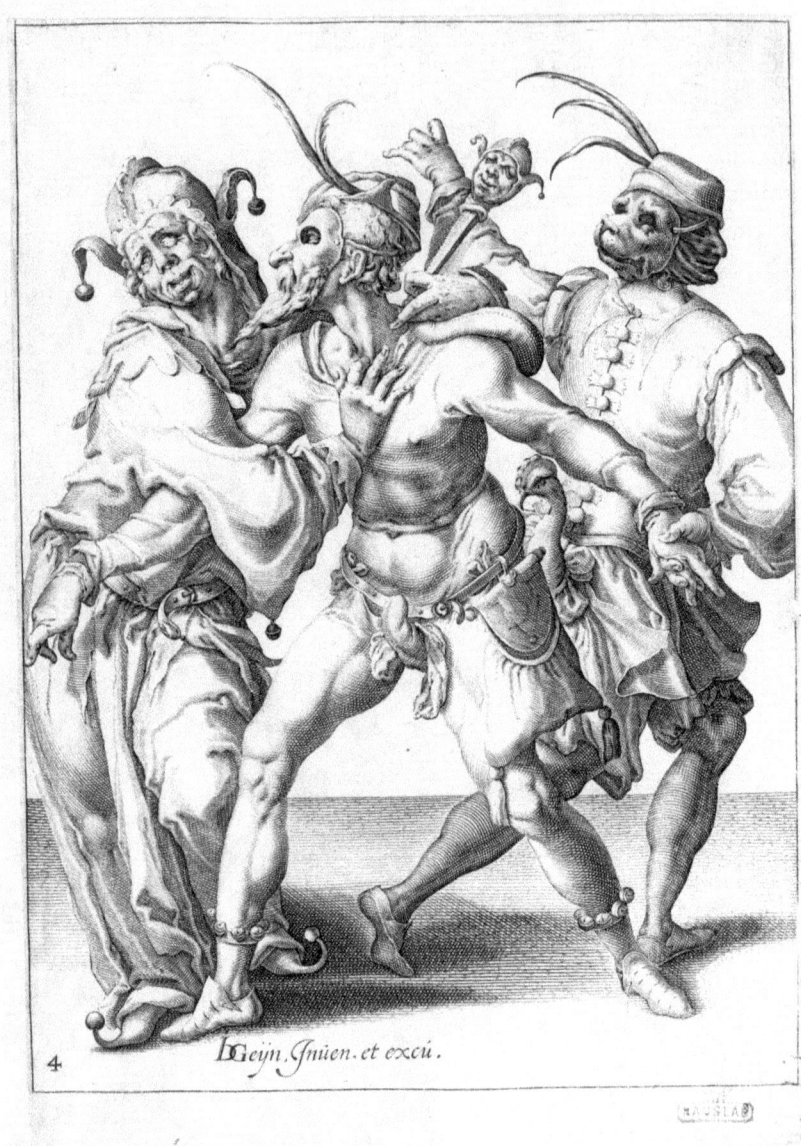

12.5. Jacques de Gheyn (1565-1625) *Untitled (Three Fools Cavorting)*, undated, Height: 28.2 cm Width: 21.1 cm, H. Beard Print Collection—Print Engraving, Photo © Victoria and Albert Museum, London.

Notes on Contributors

Susan P. Casteras
Professor and Chair of Art History, University of Washington
Before moving to Seattle in the late 1990s, Dr. Casteras served for nearly twenty years as Curator of Paintings and Sculpture at the Yale Center for British Art, where she was in charge of Paul Mellon's extraordinary collection. She now serves as Chair and Professor of Art History at the University of Washington in Seattle. The recipient of numerous awards and fellowships, Dr. Casteras graduated Phi Beta Kappa from Vassar College and received her master's and Ph.D. degrees from Yale University, where she also taught in the History of Art Department. She is the author of more than seventy-five books, essays, articles, and reviews focusing primarily on Victorian and nineteenth-century art.

Dr. Casteras curated numerous exhibitions on Victorian art at Yale and elsewhere and has participated in countless academic symposia and conferences. She has lectured extensively throughout America and England, e.g., at the National Gallery of Art in Washington, D.C., the Metropolitan Museum of Art, the Tate Gallery, the Victoria and Albert Museum, the Huntington Art Gallery, the Seattle Art Museum, and many other institutions. A 1997 award from the Fulbright Distinguished American Scholars Programme allowed her to travel, lecture, and do research in New Zealand and Australia. Currently she is working on several projects, from an opus on Victorian religious painting to essays that will be published soon on nineteenth-century racial constructions and another on the commodification of Pre-Raphaelite art.

Liana De Girolami Cheney
Investigadora de Historia de Arte at SIELAE, Universidad de Coruña, Spain.
President of the Association for Textual Scholarship in Art History.
Dr. Cheney received her BS/BA in Psychology and Philosophy from the University of Miami, Florida, her MA in History of Art and Aesthetics from the University of Miami, Florida, and her

Ph.D. in Italian Renaissance and Baroque from Boston University, MA. Dr. Cheney is a Pre-Raphaelite, Renaissance, and Mannerism scholar, author, and coauthor of numerous books and articles, including: *Religious Architecture of Lowell; James Abbott McNeill Whistler Papers; James Abbott McNeill Whistler and His Birthplace; Andrea del Verrocchio's Celebration:1435-1488; Botticelli's Neoplatonic Images; Neoplatonism and the Arts; Neoplatonic Aesthetics in Literature, Music and the Visual Arts; The Paintings of the Casa Vasari; Readings in Italian Mannerism; The Homes of Giorgio Vasari (English and Italian); Self-Portraits of Women Painters; Essays of Women Artists: 'The Most Excellent'; Symbolism in the Arts; Pre-Raphaelite Medievalism; Giorgio Vasari's Teachers: Sacred and Profane Love; Giuseppe Arcimboldo: The Magic Paintings; Giorgio Vasari's Life and Lives: The First Art Historian by Einar Rud; Giorgio Vasari: pennello, pluma e ardore;* and *Giorgio Vasari's Prefaces: Art and Theory.* Her recent books are on Giorgio Vasari's *Artistic and Emblematic Manifestations* and Edward Burne-Jones's *Mythical Paintings.*

Joyce Cohen
Independent scholar

Joyce Cohen taught in the Art and Music Department of Simmons College from 1987 to 2011. Before joining the Simmons faculty, Cohen taught at Clark University, Wheaton College, and the University of New Hampshire. She founded Arts Inter-action, a non-profit community arts organization, and directed a four-year artists-in-residence program in the Massachusetts public schools. From 1983 to 1994 she was a principal in Aptekar and Cohen Art Advisors, implementing independent curatorial projects and consulting to corporate and private collectors.

At Simmons, Cohen taught Arts Administration, Contemporary Art, Women and Art, History of the Art Market, and Objects and Ideas: a Museum-based Art History. In 2002 she founded the Arts Administration Institute, a New York City-based month-long program for students from Simmons and other women's colleges. Cohen has published articles and numerous catalogue essays on the subjects of contemporary art, feminist art, and museums, and cultural change. From 1995 to 2007 she was a frequent art critic for the regional magazine *Art New England.* She has lectured on women artists at the Museum of Fine Arts, Boston, the American Folk Art Museum, and the High Museum in Atlanta, Georgia. She serves on the boards of the Foundation for Self-Taught Artists and Fuller Craft Museum, where she also chairs the collections committee.

Beth Gersh-Nešić
Director, New York Arts Exchange

Beth Susan Gersh-Nešić (Ph.D., CUNY Graduate Center) is the director of the New York Arts Exchange, an arts education service. Dr. Gersh-Nešić teaches art history at Purchase College and Mercy College. She has also taught at New York University, Simmons College, Rhode Island College, and Hartwick College.

Dr. Gersh-Nešić contributes to About.com: Art History and Smarthistory. She writes about modern art, especially Picasso, Cubism, and André Salmon, critic, poet and member of Picasso's Gang. Her most recent book is entitled *André Salmon on French Modern Art* (Cambridge University Press, 2005). Her most recent translation of Salmon's work was published in the Spring 2011 issue of *Source*, an American Translators Association publication of literary works. For this translation and other Salmon projects, Dr. Gersh-Nešić collaborates with Jacqueline Gojard, Professor Emeritus, University of Paris (Sorbonne III) and executor of André Salmon's literary estate. Their website is: www.andresalmon.org

Lucretia Hoover Giese
Professor of Art and Visual Culture, Emerita
Rhode Island School of Design

Lucretia Hoover Giese is professor emerita of the history of art and visual culture, Rhode Island School of Design, Providence, RI. Her teaching focused on North American nineteenth- to early twentieth-century art and Mexican early twentieth-century art. She was assistant curator in the Department of Paintings, Museum of Fine Arts, Boston, until 1978. Her articles on topics of North American and Mexican art have been published by the Center for Advanced Study in the Visual Arts, Washington, D.C.; the Fine Arts Museums of San Francisco, CA; Museum of Fine Arts, Boston, MA; The Albuquerque Museum of Art and History, NM; the Library of Congress, Washington, D.C.; Brown University, Providence, RI; and by journals such as the Smithsonian Institution's *American Art, Visual Resources, Archives of American Art Journal, Winterthur Portfolio, The American Art Journal,* and *Journal of Interdisciplinary History.* In addition to submitting papers at various conferences, Giese contributed to the *Bloomsbury Guide to Art History* (1996), *Drawing the Borderline: Artist-Explorer of the U.S.-Mexican Boundary Survey* (The Albuquerque Museum of Art and History, NM, 1996), *Winslow Homer Paintings of the Civil War* (Fine Arts Museums of San Francisco, 1988), and *Redefining American History Painting* (Cambridge University Press, 1995), which she co-edited with Dr. Patricia Burnham. She has received grants from the Rhode Island School of Design and the Andrew Mellon Foundation.

Sister Ellen Glavin
Professor of Art, Emerita, Emmanuel College

Sister Ellen Glavin is a member of the Sisters of Notre Dame de Namur, and Professor Emerita of Art at Emmanuel College in Boston where she served as Chair of the Art Department. She earned her Ph.D. at Boston University.

The focus of her publications is the American painter, Maurice B. Prendergast (1858-1924). Her revision of the earlier chronologies pertaining to Prendergast, which was published in the 1976 exhibition catalogue of his retrospective at the University of Maryland, clarifies the dating changes in the stylistic development of the artist. Her subsequent discoveries of his family history and culture was published in 1994 in *Newfoundland Studies,* and her documentation of his early art education in Boston was published in 1993 in the *Archives of American Art Journal.* Her studies published in 2002 also in the *Archives of American Art Journal,* examines Prendergast's mature style and explains his life-long ability to understand and elucidate the relationship of American art to European modernism. Glavin has also contributed papers to College Art Association conferences and published in *Arts and Antiques.*

Amy Golahny
Professor of Art History, Art Department
Lycoming College, Williamsport, Pennsylvania

Amy Golahny earned the Ph.D. from Columbia University, the

MA from Williams College-Clark Art Institute, and the BA from Brandeis University. She has worked at the Philadelphia Museum of Art, and recently curated exhibitions, including Stained Glass Windows of Williamsport, at the Taber Museum-Lycoming County Historical Society. Currently she is the President of the international organization promoting Dutch and Flemish art, the Historians of Netherlandish Art.

Internationally recognized as a Rembrandt expert, she has published three books and over fifty articles, not only on Dutch art but also on contemporary and 19th-century artists. She has lectured on Rembrandt, Edgar Allan Poe, Sophia Hawthorne and other topics, most recently in St Petersburg (Russia) and Caceres (Spain). Her scholarly research and publications have been funded by national and international agencies, including the German government (DAAD), Lycoming College, the Prins Bernhard Cultuur Fonds, the National Endowment for the Humanities, Pennsylvania Historical and Museum Commission, The Netherland-America Foundation, and The National Gallery (CASVA).

Margaret A. Hanni, (editor)
Associate Professor of Art History
Chair, Department of Art & Music, Simmons College

Professor Hanni earned her Ph.D. in art history from Boston University, during which time she was the Director of The Lamont Gallery at Philips Exeter Academy. Her research interests include the marriage portrait in eighteenth-century England, the history of collections, and Isabella Stewart Gardner. She has published articles on Mary Cassatt's influence on collectors, Lady Emma Hamilton and has presented papers on Georgian marriage portraits, Hamilton, and the Isabella Stewart Gardner Museum. Since 1996, she has taught at Simmons College, for which she has developed a case study seminar about the Isabella Stewart Garden Museum, a London-based course on the history of collecting in England, and an interdisciplinary course on Informatics for Cultural Heritage Institutions, taught in conjunction with Simmons' Graduate School of Library and Information Science.

Bridget Lynch
Director, Trustman Art Gallery, Simmons College

Bridget Lynch has been a Simmons College, Boston, MA, faculty member for ten years, teaching studio art classes and a unique field trip-based art history class and is Director of the Trustman Art Gallery at the College. Her own artistic work has been intensively engaged with cross-discipline conversations including philosophy, theories of folly, art history, politics, and theatre. She has produced her theatrical and freewheeling installations in multiple university and museum settings nationally. Lynch created the popular participatory *Throne Project 2003* at the Museum of Fine Arts Boston, and was featured this past year in festival and gallery shows of video and sound work at the Carnegie Museum in Pittsburgh, University of CA at Chico State, and the contemporary art space LAL in Lexington KY. Lynch has a BA in Japanese and East Asian Studies from the University of Kansas, and studied traditional theatre in Kyoto, Japan. She trained at the Museum School in Boston with an emphasis in painting, and has a MFA from the Art Institute of Boston at Lesley University.

Diane Radycki
Associate Professor, Moravian College, Director, Payne Gallery

Diane Radycki is the author of *The First Modern Woman Artist: Paula Modersohn-Becker* (Yale University Press, 2013). A recipient of Fulbright and American Association of University Women fellowships, her works have appeared in *Art Journal*, the proceedings of the Zentralinstitut für Kunstgeschichte (American Artists in Munich), *Woman's Art Journal*, *Historically Speaking*, and other publications. She lives in New York City, and is an associate professor at Moravian College, where she directs Payne Gallery. www.dianearthistory.com

Susan Schwalb
Artist

Susan Schwalb is one of the foremost figures in the revival of the ancient technique of silverpoint drawing in America. Most of the contemporary artists who draw with a metal stylus continue the tradition of Leonardo and Durer by using the soft, delicate line for figurative imagery. By contrast, Schwalb's work is resolutely abstract, and her handling of the technique is extremely innovative. In recent works, Schwalb creates a counterpoint between fine lines drawn with a stylus and broad swatches of bronze or copper tones.

Schwalb's oeuvre ranges from drawings on paper to artist books and paintings on canvas or wood panels. Her work is represented in most of the major public collections, including the Museum of Modern Art, New York, the National Gallery, Washington DC, The British Museum, London, The Brooklyn Museum, NY, The Fogg Art Museum, Harvard University, Kupferstichkabinett - Staatliche Museen zu Berlin, Germany, Victoria and Albert Museum, London, The Ashmolean Museum, Oxford, England, Museum of Fine Arts, Houston, TX, The Achenbach Foundation of Graphic Arts, The Fine Arts Museums of San Francisco, The Library of Congress, Washington, DC, The Rose Art Museum, Brandeis University, Waltham, MA, Yale University Art Gallery, New Haven, CT, Rhode Island School of Design Museum of Art, The National September 11 Memorial and Museum, New York, NY, The Columbus Museum, Columbus, GA, Evansville Museum of Art and Science, the Arkansas Arts Center, Little Rock, AK and The Israel Museum, Jerusalem.

Susan Schwalb has been in residence at the Virginia Center for the Creative Arts, the MacDowell Colony, Yaddo, and has had two residencies in Israel in 1994 at Mishkenot Sha'ananim, Jerusalem and the Tel Aviv Artists' Studios. She has had over thirty-five solo exhibitions and has exhibited nationally and internationally.

Suzanne Volmer
Artist

Suzanne Volmer is an artist working across mediums. *Clouds Captured* and *Aquatic* are recent multi-media dimensional sculptural installations of hers which combine a process-oriented approach toward form with color saturation, kinetics, mechanical features, electronics, lighting effects and sound. She is critically recognized for her expertise with heat-based technology and praised as an innovator with porcelain and steel. Her artworks are included in a number of collections and she has shown in galleries and museums throughout the United States and abroad including exhibitions in Paris, France, and Mannheim Museum, Mannheim, Germany. She has exhibited her porcelain sculptures alongside artworks by Peter Voulkos, and other innovators at Twining Gallery, New York, New York.

Suzanne Volmer graduated with Honors from Pratt Institute in Brooklyn, New York. She has worked as an assistant to various artists including Mary Frank and was a preparator at Leo Castelli Gallery in New York City. She also wrote features and reviews for *Arts Magazine*, New York. Suzanne Volmer has taught at Rhode Island School of Design and was a guest artist at Massachusetts College of Art, Boston, MA. She is a regular contributor to *Artscope Magazine*, Boston Publishing House LLC, and she is a contributor to *Sculpture Magazine* of the International Sculpture Center, Washington, DC, and a member of the International Association of Art Critics.

Index

www.ingramcontent.com/pod-product-compliance
Lightning Source LLC
Chambersburg PA
CBHW060824170526
45158CB00001B/73